Guide to Chamber Music

Guide to Chamber Music

MELVIN BERGER

DODD, MEAD & COMPANY
NEW YORK

Published by Dodd, Mead & Company, Inc.
79 Madison Avenue, New York, N.Y. 10016

Distributed in Canada by
McClelland and Stewart Limited, Toronto

Manufactured in the United States of America

Designed by Berta E. Lewis

First Edition

Library of Congress Cataloging in Publication Data

Berger, Melvin.
    Guide to chamber music.

    Discography: p.
    1. Chamber music—History and criticism.   2. Chamber
music—Analysis, appreciation.   I. Title.
ML1100.B45   1985   785.7'009   85-1469
ISBN 0-396-08385-4

For Gilda,
with all my love

Contents

—*Contents*—

—Contents—

—Contents—

—Contents—

—Contents—

Preface

I WROTE this book to help music lovers—neophytes as well as experienced concert-goers—deepen their understanding and enhance their enjoyment of chamber music. At the same time, I hope to provide a unique, practical sourcebook for chamber music players, performers, and teachers.

The book presents 231 of the best-known and most frequently performed pieces of chamber music by fifty-five outstanding composers, arranged alphabetically by composer. For each composer there is a brief biography, followed by discussions of the individual compositions, which are presented, with some few exceptions, in chronological order. In instances where composers conceived works in a group, such as Beethoven's String Quartets, Op. 59, Nos. 1, 2, and 3, I offer a short description of the common features before considering the separate pieces more fully. Generally speaking, each composition is first set in a historical and musical context, and then the salient features of the music are discussed, including its formal organization, musical content, and any extra-musical associations. For the most part, I avoid technical terms; the few unfamiliar words I use for reasons of clarity or efficiency are defined in the Glossary.

Obviously, an attempt to provide a comprehensive guide to chamber music within a book of manageable length presents many problems of selection. I exchanged ideas and opinions with many leading chamber players, read through stacks of concert programs and repertoire lists, consulted bibliographies of published chamber music, and researched record catalogs of the last several years. When the time came to formulate the final contents, I incorporated this information into my own thoughts, derived from many years of chamber music playing, teaching, and writing, to compile what I believe is a complete, balanced list.

In the process I followed a few specific guidelines: to cover all types of instrumental chamber music, for modern string, woodwind and brass instruments and piano; to confine my selections to works for three to eight players; and to include as many significant contemporary composers as possible. I present the results knowing that, despite my best efforts, I may have omitted certain composers or compositions that others consider essential. If so, I can only offer my assurance that the decisions were not made lightly or without due consideration.

Over the years, it has been my privilege to be intimately involved with chamber music and to experience the exceptional pleasure and happiness that derives from this very special form of music. I will be specially gratified if this book succeeds in bringing to others the same joy, inspiration, and deep satisfaction that perceptive listening can generate.

Acknowledgments

IT IS virtually impossible to thank all those who have contributed to the writing of this book. I would like, however, to express my sincere appreciation and gratitude to: Elliott Carter, Aaron Copland, George Crumb, Leo Kraft, Ezra Laderman, George Rochberg, Gunther Schuller, and Elie Siegmeister, who were kind enough to check the entries dealing with their lives and music for factual accuracy; to Mark Shuman (Composers String Quartet), William Stone (formerly Kroll Quartet), Jack Rosenberg (Cremona String Quartet), Karl Kraber (Dorian Wind Quintet), and Robert Biddlecome (American Brass Quintet), who provided me with especially valued ideas and insights; to my colleagues in the Metropolitan String Quartet and Connoisseur Chamber Ensemble (Carol Feuer, Joyce Liebman, Susan Rubner, Albert Stwertka, and Louise Stone), who offered much help and support; to William Rorick and the staff of the Music Library of Queens College, City University of New York, and the staffs of the Research Division, Music Library at Lincoln Center, the Great Neck Library, and the C. W. Post College Library, for their skillful assistance; and to Barbara Sand and Benjamin Dunham of Chamber Music America for their advice and encouragement.

Anton Arensky

Born July 12, 1861, at Novgorod, Russia
Died February 25, 1906, at Terioki, Finland

ANTON ARENSKY was a composer, a professor at the Moscow Conservatory and music director of the Imperial Chapel in Saint Petersburg (now Leningrad). His music is particularly interesting for the traces one hears in it of the two opposing streams that flowed so vigorously in late nineteenth-century Russian music. One influence was Rimsky-Korsakov, Arensky's teacher at the Saint Petersburg Conservatory, and a member of The Five, the group of nationalistic Russian composers who strongly advocated the use of native folk melodies and rhythms in concert music and rejected the view that folk music is not a fit subject for serious musical composition. The other was Tchaikovsky, who was far less concerned with expressing the Russian national character and declared that his music was modeled on the style of Mozart and the Italian opera composers.

In addition to his highly successful Piano Trio No. 1, Arensky's other chamber compositions include String Quartet No. 1, Op. 11 (1888); String Quartet No. 2, Op. 35 (1894), originally for violin, viola, and two cellos, but later transcribed for the more traditional combination; Piano Quintet, Op. 51 (1900); and Piano Trio No. 2, Op. 73 (1905).

Piano Trio in D Minor, Op. 32

I. Allegro moderato.   II. Scherzo: Allegro
molto.   III. Elegia: Adagio.   IV. Finale: Allegro non
troppo.

Arensky is not generally considered an important figure in the history of music. Yet his First Piano Trio is among the more popular and

1

appealing works in the chamber music repertoire. Little is known about the circumstances of its composition beyond the fact that he wrote it in 1894 and dedicated it to the memory of Karl Davidoff (1838–1889), first cellist of the Saint Petersburg Opera and later director of the Saint Petersburg Conservatory.

Over a murmuring triplet figure in the piano, the violin sings a flowing first theme that seems to have drawn its inspiration from Tchaikovsky. After an agitated transition, the cello is entrusted with the somewhat more vocal second theme. The tempo picks up for the forceful, vigorous concluding theme of the exposition. The following, richly Romantic development section is mostly concerned with the opening theme. The recapitulation brings back all three themes, little changed from the exposition. A slow, quiet coda, really an augmentation of the principal theme, fades out at the end.

The Scherzo pits a florid, virtuosic piano part against extremely spare writing for the strings. A folk influence can be heard in the slightly slower middle section, a lilting waltz with a Slavonic cast. Here the piano is relegated to the role of accompanist as the strings weave their strands of sound into the appealing waltz melody. The movement is rounded off with a slightly expanded return of the Scherzo.

The center of gravity of the entire trio is the Elegia, the movement in which Arensky specifically pays homage to Davidoff. Both strings are muted, giving them an attractive, veiled dark tone color. The tempo increases, and the mood brightens for the middle part of the movement. For the reprise of the opening, the original tempo resumes.

Lively and rhythmic, the Finale explodes in a burst of sound. The quieter second theme seems to be a transformation of the Elegia's main theme. Toward the end, the tempo slows for a reminder of the first movement theme, before concluding with a fast, brilliant coda.

Samuel Barber

*Born March 9, 1910, in West Chester, Pennsylvania
Died January 23, 1981, in New York City*

SAMUEL BARBER displayed his very considerable musical talents early, starting piano lessons at age six, composing at seven, holding a position as church organist at twelve and entering the Curtis Institute of Music at fourteen. Success in his career came equally fast. Two of his student works, *Dover Beach* (1931) for voice and string quartet, and overture to *The School for Scandal* (1931) for orchestra, were premiered by major orchestras while the composer was still in his twenties. This acclaim and recognition continued throughout his long career, winning for Barber two Pulitzer Prizes, the Prix de Rome, two Pulitzer Traveling Scholarships, the New York Critics' Circle Award and two Bearns Prizes.

Contibuting to Barber's popularity was his outstanding ability to write long, flowing melodies, with particularly attractive vocal qualities. This talent, plus his instinctive sense of form and rigorous musical logic, allowed him to develop his extended melodic subjects into well-structured and skillfully organized compositions with the greatest economy of means.

Barber's expressivity, highly developed lyricism, and emotionality usually lead him to be classified among the Post Romantics; his essentially diatonic style, an extension of eighteenth- and nineteenth-century tonality, has given much of his music a conservative tag. Unlike many other twentieth-century composers, Barber was unaffected by such modern trends as atonality, serialism, electronic or aleatoric composition, or minimalism. While his independent course explains his lack of favor among the avant-garde in contemporary music, it does not detract in the slightest from his wide acceptance by concert audiences everywhere.

Dover Beach for Voice and String Quartet, Op. 3

In 1931, when he was twenty-one years old and still a student at the Curtis Institute in Philadelphia, Samuel Barber composed *Dover Beach,* a setting of Matthew Arnold's poem for voice (either mezzo soprano or baritone) and string quartet. Shortly after, Barber played the work to Ralph Vaughan Williams, singing the voice part and performing the instrumental parts on the piano. Vaughan Williams, already recognized as one of England's leading composers, was obviously very impressed and congratulated the shy young man. "I myself once set *Dover Beach,*" he said, "but you really got it!" Barber later commented on the occasion: "Enthusiasm for my music was rather uncommon at the time. Coming from a composer of the stature of Vaughan Williams, I found it especially gratifying."

From the very opening, the gentle rocking motion of the string parts captures the melancholic and elegiac mood of the poem. The ebb and flow of the music very sensitively represents the endless shifting of the sea which, in Arnold's poem, is a metaphor for the flow of human existence. In creating this extended vocal form, Barber alternates between quite literal settings of the words and vague suggestions of their meanings as he builds to the impassioned ending.

> The sea is calm to-night,
> The tide is full, the moon lies fair
> Upon the straits;—on the French coast the light
> Gleams and is gone; the cliffs of England stand,
> Glimmering and vast, out in the tranquil bay.
> Come to the window, sweet is the night-air!
> Only, from the long line of spray
> Where the sea meets the moon-blanch'd land,
> Listen! you hear the grating roar
> Of pebbles which the waves draw back, and fling,
> At their return, up the high strand,
> Begin, and cease, and then again begin,
> With tremulous cadence slow, and bring
> The eternal note of sadness in.
>
> Sophocles long ago
> Heard it on the Aegean, and it brought
> Into his mind the turbid ebb and flow
> Of human misery; we
> Find also in the sound a thought,
> Hearing it by this distant northern sea.

4

The sea of faith
Was once, too, at the full, and round earth's shore
Lay like the folds of a bright girdle furl'd.
But now I only hear
Its melancholy, long, withdrawing roar,
Retreating, to the breath
Of the night-wind, down the vast edges drear
And naked shingles of the world.

Ah, love, let us be true
To one another! for the world, which seems
To lie before us like a land of dreams,
So various, so beautiful, so new,
Hath really neither joy, nor love, nor light,
Nor certitude, nor peace, nor help for pain;
And we are here as on a darkling plain
Swept with confused alarms of struggle and flight,
Where ignorant armies clash by night.

Dover Beach was first performed in New York City on March 5, 1933, by Rose Bampton and the New York String Quartet.

String Quartet, Op. 11

I. Molto allegro e appassionato.   II. Molto adagio; Molto allegro.

A few popular favorites of the orchestral repertoire originated as individual movements, usually the slow movement, of string quartets. Haydn's Serenade from his String Quartet, Op. 3, No. 5, the Andante Cantabile of Tchaikovsky's String Quartet, Op. 11 and the Notturno of Borodin's Second Quartet come immediately to mind. The most recent addition to this list is Samuel Barber's Adagio for Strings, the composer's transcription of the second movement of his String Quartet, Op. 11. The string orchestra arrangement, which Barber prepared at the request of Arturo Toscanini, conductor of the NBC Symphony Orchestra, has become one of the most widely performed works of contemporary American music.

The first movement of Barber's two-movement string quartet bursts forth with a bold unison statement of the main theme, made even more striking by its slightly awkward rhythmic pattern. In time this gives way to the subsidiary subject, a quiet choralelike section in

5

flexible tempo that is soon interrupted by a brief, skittish transformation of the opening melody. A wide-ranging, spun-out legato melody follows. After a succinct working-out of the three subjects, they are all returned for a pithy recapitulation.

The Adagio is constructed around one long, sinuous theme that moves slowly and deliberately in step-wise motion. Starting with the utmost calmness and tranquility, Barber carries the theme to an intense, exciting climax, with each instrument straining at the uppermost limit of its range. A subdued, sober coda concludes the Adagio. After a short pause, Barber then recapitulates the themes of the first movement, creating a kind of brief third movement that brings the entire quartet full circle, back to its original character.

Barber wrote his Opus 11 in 1936, while on a Pulitzer Traveling Scholarship; the Pro Arte String Quartet gave the premiere in Rome in December of that year.

Summer Music for Woodwind Quintet, Op. 31

Slow and indolent. With motion. Faster. Lively, still faster. Faster.

Most composers receive commissions either from wealthy patrons, highly successful performers, or established performing organizations. Barber's commission for a woodwind quintet from the Chamber Music Society of Detroit, though, was unique. The society underwrote the project with contributions that it solicited from its members in amounts as small as one dollar. The premiere was given on March 20, 1956, at the Detroit Institute of Arts by the principal wind players of the Detroit Symphony.

Although some of the composer's marking on the score, such as a tempo direction of "slow and indolent" and instructions for the clarinet to play a passage "with arrogance," might indicate that Barber had specific images in mind, there are no other indications of extramusical meaning. Instead, the music seems to be shaped entirely by Barber's highly developed musical thinking and expert craftsmanship.

The piece starts with a brief phrase played twice by the bassoon and French horn and answered in turn by flourishes in the flute and clarinet. This proves to be the germ cell from which the entire one-movement work grows. The phrase ends with the French horn playing several repeated descending half steps in short-long rhythm,

6

which gives rise to the extended cantabile line that the oboe sings in the following With Motion section. An abrupt change of tempo and style signals the Faster episode with its perky rhythmic pattern. After bringing back quotations from earlier sections, the tempo picks up again, and the oboe introduces a jaunty, seemingly new tune. Careful listening, however, reveals that it starts with the same repeated notes as the opening phrase and then moves in a rather free mirror image of that melody. The quintet ends with brilliant virtuosic writing for the various instruments, including several references to melodic material previously introduced.

Béla Bartók

Born March 25, 1881, in Nagyszentmiklós, Hungary (now Rumania)
Died September 26, 1945, in New York City

BARTÓK'S MOTHER, a piano teacher, reported that as an infant he already could pick out tunes on the piano; at age five he started music lessons and in a few years was composing little pieces. When he was eleven he gave his first piano recital. On the program was an original composition, "The Danube River," which traces the river's path by using melodies from each of the countries through which it passes. Where the river enters Hungary he wrote a gay, happy polka, commenting, "It is jubilant, for it has come to Hungary." When the river departs the country, the music turns sad. Bartók's intense love for Hungary was even then apparent.

While a student at the Royal Academy of Music in Budapest, Bartók became involved in the Hungarian nationalistic movement, and the struggle to free the land from Austrian domination. He extended the effort to his own music, saying that the times "called for something specifically Hungarian to be created in music." Inspired by these patriotic feelings, he composed his first major work, *Kossuth* (1903), an orchestral tone poem that uses folk melodies to describe the 1848 Hungarian revolt led by Lajos Kossuth.

Then, in the summer of 1904, a significant new dimension was added to his involvement with Hungarian national music. While on holiday in the remote Hungarian countryside, he heard an eighteen-year-old peasant girl singing a hauntingly beautiful melody—different from anything he had ever heard before. He discovered it was a local folk song, completely unknown outside the area. With great difficulty, Bartók copied down the strange melody and irregular rhythms as the girl sang it for him again. For the first time the thought of collecting truly authentic Hungarian peasant songs occurred to him, and with fellow composer, Zoltán Kodaly, he began combing the countryside, recording and transcribing the many outstanding examples they were able to unearth.

The two composers envisioned composing music that would draw on this source as its inspiration: "In our case it was not a question of merely taking unique melodies and then incorporating them in our works. What we had to do was divine the spirit of this unknown music, and to make this spirit the basis of our works. According to the way I feel, a genuine peasant melody of our land is a musical example of a perfected art. I consider it as much a masterpiece, for instance, as a Bach fugue or a Mozart sonata."

Bartók's study of folk music became an important part of his life, as he collected, recorded, transcribed, studied, codified, and prepared for publication literally thousands of heretofore unknown examples of this music. He became a leading pioneer in the field of ethnomusicology. But, perhaps of even greater significance, the essence of this wealth of little-known music seeped into his being. The directness of expression, the musical honesty, along with the characteristic turns of melody and rhythmic patterns, became an integral part of his original compositions. He did not have to quote peasant tunes; he had completely assimilated their qualities into his every musical thought. He created, in effect, a perfect fusion between folk and art music.

Although Bartók's music was largely rejected by performers and audiences during his lifetime—an attitude that made him bitter and angry—he refused to turn away from the musical direction he was following. Only his utter conviction that he was on the right path, and the respect and admiration of a small number of disciples, kept him from giving way to despair. The worldwide realization of his amazing musical accomplishments, both as a composer and as an ethnomusicologist, had to wait until after his death. By now Bartók is considered, along with Stravinsky and Schoenberg, a central figure of twentieth-century music. And in the area of chamber music, many rank his six string quartets as the greatest contribution to that genre since Beethoven's works in the form.

String Quartet No. 1, Op. 7

I. Lento.　II. Allegretto.　III. Allegro vivace.

When Béla Bartók was in his mid-twenties he was struggling to resolve a number of musical, social, and personal conflicts. Largely under the musical influence of Richard Strauss, but also attracted by such disparate composers as Wagner, Brahms, Debussy, and Liszt, he was seeking to evolve his own personal style, one that was to be considerably enriched by recently undertaken studies of the folk music of his native Hungary. Then, torn between the prevailing Austro-German cultural outlook of his native land and the rising spirit of Hungarian nationalism, he was publicly expressing sympathy with the latter group by wearing a peasant outfit instead of the more traditional business suit. And, perhaps most painful of all, he was coming to the unhappy end of his first serious love affair.

It was during this period of turmoil that Bartók began preparing sketches for his first string quartet. (He had written a quartet in 1899, which he suppressed.) It was finished on January 27, 1909, and the premiere was given in Budapest on March 19, 1910, by the Waldbauer Quartet.

In its composition, the first quartet shows great economy of means and remarkable integration, with almost every melodic fragment appearing in various guises. The first movement opens with a double canon of noble dignity based on two motifs: a melodic phrase characterized by the descending intervals of a sixth and a second, and later a rising syncopated rhythmic figure. Bartók weaves these elements into expressive lines of great tensile strength with increasing intensity, until the viola, playing in its lowest register, interrupts with an impassioned outcry. Seemingly unaware of all the fiery agitation in the viola, the first violin enters with its own sedate, high-pitched melody, which is then answered by the cello. Following a passage of stunning tonal effects, Bartók brings back the opening section for a free, highly compressed reprise.

The second movement follows without pause, accelerating gradually from the previous slow tempo to the faster Allegretto, using thematic material derived from the rising syncopation figure heard earlier. Once up to speed, Bartók creates a new four-note motif by reversing the intervals of the first movement theme into a descending second followed by a sixth. This is treated as an ostinato while other melodic fragments are introduced. After a largely unison transition, the second theme, a waltzlike melody based on the first fragment, is played by the two middle voices. The cello interrupts with a striking, pizzicato rhythmic motto. Rustic in character and playful in mood, the rest of the movement works out and returns varied versions of the melodies that have already been presented.

The finale is the only movement in which Hungarian folk elements appear. The slow introduction alternates forceful declamatory passages with short cello cadenzas that have an improvised folk quality about them. The faster main theme, heard against rapid repeated notes in the violins, is a derivative of the second movement's four-note motif and the syncopated pattern from the first movement; it captures perfectly the spirit of a vigorous folk dance. In one of the episodes that follow, a new theme that combines several familiar elements is introduced. All of this material is developed until a markedly slow section interrupts; it is heard against sustained trills and is based on the Hungarian folk song melody, "The Peacock Flies." Bartók rebuilds the energy and intensity leading to an abrupt conclusion. Perhaps Zoltán Kodaly was most accurate when he described this movement as a *"retour à la vie"* ("return to life").

String Quartet, No. 2, Op. 17

I. Moderato. II. Allegro molto capriccioso. III. Lento.

The turmoil and devastation of World War I made it very difficult for Bartók to compose, although he was able to devote great amounts of time and energy to the study of folk music of his native Hungary, the surrounding countries, and North Africa. The few pieces that he did write were seldom performed, and when they were heard, the reactions ranged from apathy to antagonism. Nevertheless, he managed to start work on his second quartet in 1915, finishing it just before the end of the war, in October 1917. It is dedicated to the Waldbauer Quartet, which introduced the work in Budapest on March 3, 1918; it has since become one of the most frequently performed of Bartók's six quartets.

Zoltán Kodaly, Bartók's friend and fellow composer, characterized the three movements of the second quartet as "1. A quiet life. 2. Joy. 3. Sorrow." Just after the opening of the first movement, the first violin plays the leading motif, a rising three-note motto that quickly and smoothly moves upward by comparatively large steps. Other motifs follow—some are outgrowths of the initial phrase, others are made up of new material. After presenting the various motifs, Bartók transforms and reworks them in the development section, which the viola starts with the three-note figure after a short silence. The recapitulation reinforces the importance of the opening motto and the related themes, downplaying the other subjects. The coda starts quietly with plucked cello chords accompanying one of the themes heard before, builds up to a climax and then fades away.

The fierce, barbaric middle movement shows some of the early results of Bartók's folk music studies. There are long stretches of repeated notes that sound like primitive drums or a continuous drone. For example, the second violin plays the exact same four notes for forty measures, stops for one measure, and resumes, this time with the first violin, for twenty more. Then there are bits of jagged melody in wild peasant rhythms. And finally, all the musical material is organized into mosaiclike patterns, resembling the folk dance forms that Bartók knew so well. The principal subject, a vigorous, rocking back-and-forth melody, is heard several times in various forms throughout the movement. Between its appearances are various interludes, giving the movement a structure similar to a rondo. Perhaps the most striking presentation of the main theme is the last one, when the tempo accelerates to a breakneck speed so that the notes speed by like a murmuring buzz. The movement ends with four loud, deliberate notes that reaffirm the all-important rocking motion.

The reflective last movement is somber in mood and slow in tempo. After some sustained introductory notes, the first violin plays a theme that is closely related to the initial motif of the first movement. Three more themes follow in chainlike progression. Bartók then briefly recalls three of the four melodies, before allowing the music to end with two desolate pizzicato notes in the viola and cello.

String Quartet No. 3

Prima parte.   Seconda parte.   Ricapitulazione della prima parte.   Coda.

In the third string quartet, Bartók integrates two major tendencies of his music: the pervasive influence of folk music and some compositional devices of the pre-Bach period.

"The melodic world of my string quartets," Bartók wrote, "does not essentially differ from that of folk song, only the framework is stricter." His music, though, seldom quotes or imitates folk melodies. Rather, he has completely absorbed and assimilated the folk tradition into his own musical thinking, giving his compositions the sureness of expression, the directness and honesty one associates with the finest examples of such music. For instance, he once wrote, "It must have been observed . . . that I do not like to repeat a musical idea without change, and I do not bring back one single part in exactly the same way." This practice is based on the improvisations and embellishments folk musicians use and is directly linked to Bartók's concept of continuous thematic variation and transformation.

Bartók described how early Baroque music now affected his development in a letter to Edwin van der Nüll: "In my youth my ideal of beauty was not so much the art of Bach or Mozart as that of Beethoven. Recently the situation has somewhat changed, for in the last few years I have concerned myself a good deal with pre-Bach music." The fact is that Bartók employs many of the techniques associated with that period: canons and fugatos, in which one melody is played sequentially by different instruments; inversions, in which the melody is turned upside down; augmentation, in which each note of the melody is extended in length; diminution, in which the notes are shortened, and so on.

Another concept from the past that Bartók adopts is *affektenlehre*, the idea that each piece or movement should portray a single emotional state. Often he achieves this goal by having essentially one thematic gesture predominate over an entire section. In the third quartet, the *affektenlehre*, combined with Bartók's predilection for short, pithy motto themes, leads to the whole opening section being derived from a three-note motif.

Although the quartet is in one continuous movement, it is divided into four distinct sections, marked Prima parte, Seconda parte, Ricapitulazione della prima parte, and Coda. The first segment, moderate in tempo, grows from a three-note cell made up of a rising interval (a fourth) and a smaller descending interval (a third), which is heard after a few measures of introduction. Bartók subjects this brief motto to continuous development, so that in one form or another it is heard virtually throughout this whole part, including a section of "night music" that evokes the mysterious rustling sounds of a desolate forest.

The principal theme of the fast Seconda parte—a simple rising and falling scale line—is first played pizzicato by the cello. In expanding this subject, Bartók employs many of the compositional techniques he learned from the music of the past, along with a dazzling number of instrumental effects, including *col legno* (hitting the string with the wood of the bow) and *ponticello* (bowing near the bridge).

The Ricapitulazione della prima parte is indeed a condensed recapitulation of the first part, but so freely varied that the connections may be hard to hear. A few reminders of the three-note motif, however, serve as landmarks. The Coda might aptly be called Ricapitulazione della seconda parte, since it is mostly concerned with a telescoped recollection of materials first heard in that section. The treatment of the scalelike motif grows extremely complex and intricate before the quartet's harsh ending.

Bartók completed the quartet in Budapest in September 1927, and the premiere was given by the Waldbauer Quartet in London on February 19, 1929.

String Quartet No. 4

I. Allegro.   II. Prestissimo, con sordino.   III. Non troppo lento.   IV. Allegretto pizzicato.   V. Allegro molto.

"The fourth quartet comes close to being, if it does not actually represent, Bartók's greatest and most profound achievement." So wrote Halsey Stevens, the eminent composer and Bartók scholar. Audacious in concept and brilliant in execution, the work surely occupies a most notable place in twentieth-century chamber music.

Bartók conceived the five movements of the quartet as a perfectly symmetrical arch or bridge form, with the central movement serving as the keystone to the entire structure. According to his plan, two pairs of movements—one and five, two and four—share the same themes, mood, and character. And then, to assure the perfection of the symmetry, Bartók organized the third movement into three-part A-B-A form, making the B section the crux of the entire piece.

After a few highly dissonant measures of introduction, the cello states the germinal cell that informs both the first and fifth movements, a motif that is simply made up of three rising and three falling notes. The process of expansion and development of this basic motif starts right away. Each instrument plays it; it is inverted; the intervals between the notes are widened; the rhythm is altered; it is treated canonically; it is overlapped with other statements; and new melodies are derived from the original—in short, the melody is explored in every conceivable way. While the movement follows the general scheme of sonata form, all of the thematic content is drawn from the same motivic source.

The four strings, muted throughout, race through the next movement. Replete with *glissando* (sliding the left hand finger), *ponti-*

cello (bowing near the bridge to produce a glassy tone), and even *pizzicato glissando* (plucking the string while sliding a finger), Bartók creates an amazing display of tonal effects. The principal subject is an undulant line that moves up and down by the smallest possible intervals. There are contrasting episodes, but they maintain the same fast tempo and do not disturb the motoric forward rush of the music.

The cello solo that opens the third movement is known as a *tarogato* melody, named after an ancient Hungarian folk instrument related to the oboe. Traditionally, its music consists of elaborate improvised embellishments around a slow-moving, almost static, melody. The middle section, the focus of the entire quartet, is what Bartók referred to as "night music," full of distant bird songs and other sounds of the forest and nature. The bird songs continue as the *tarogato* melody returns to end the movement.

Bartók wrote of the fourth movement, "Its theme is the same as the main theme of the second movement: there it moves in the narrow intervals of the chromatic scale, but here it broadens in accordance with the diatonic scale." The viola presents the theme, with the same fluctuating line as the melody heard two movements earlier but with slightly wider intervals between the notes. All four instruments play pizzicato throughout. Bartók, however, achieves some remarkable sounds by having the players—in addition to plucking in the normal manner—strum the strings or pull on them so hard that they actually snap back against the fingerboard.

The last movement opens with grating dissonances from which the two violins emerge with a melody derived from the first movement motif. By the end of the movement, though, the motif has moved closer to its original shape, and the final two measures are almost identical to the ending of the first movement.

Bartók wrote the quartet in Budapest from July to September 1928. Although the work is dedicated to the Pro Arte Quartet, the Waldbauer Quartet gave the first performance in that city on March 20, 1929.

String Quartet No. 5

I. Allegro. II. Adagio molto. III. Scherzo: Alla bulgarese. IV. Andante. V. Finale: Allegro vivace.

Having devoted much of his life to the collection and study of the folk music of his native Hungary and other lands, Bartók believed that composers could use this material in any one of three ways. They could incorporate folk melodies in their music, compose original melodies in folk style, or absorb the essence of the folk idiom and integrate it into their own compositions.

For the three years before writing the Fifth Quartet, Bartók was actively involved with the first approach, spending a good deal of time collecting, transcribing, and arranging folk songs and dances. The Fifth Quartet, though, belongs solidly in the third category. No peasant melodies, original or imitation, are to be heard. Instead Bartók uses the vitality and expressiveness of folk music as the inspiration for a highly sophisticated, completely original composition.

The quartet consists of five movements arranged in an arch or bridge form; that is, the first and fifth sections are fast and share thematic material, the second and fourth are slow and similar in mood, and the third forms the central keystone of the entire work. The opening theme is a series of repeated hammered notes that reminds Bartók's biographer, Lajos Lesznai, of the laments sung by the Szekely people from the southern part of what is now Rumania. After being so firmly rooted on one note, the angry, dissonant second theme is distinguished by gigantic upward leaps in all the instruments. The tempo gradually slows for the second violin's presentation of the third theme, a lyrical line that gently rises and falls in contour. The three themes are developed before Bartók brings them back for the recapitulation. But in keeping with the overall mirror image of the quartet, they are heard in reverse order. Also, they are inverted, so that the third theme falls and rises, and the second theme dives downward.

The Adagio molto is a wonderful example of Bartók's so-called night music, his unique evocation of the distant sounds of nature on a still dark evening. Out of the bird-call trills and half-heard murmurings, little wisps of melody call to mind dimly remembered folk songs. As the air clears, a pained, anguished melody emerges, but it too soon disappears into the shadows.

Bartók's familiarity with Bulgarian folk songs probably inspired the Scherzo's rhythmic asymmetry, which he achieves by dividing the nine notes of each measure into groups of four, two, and three. The fluid melody, however, flows easily over the irregular accents of the accompaniment. A slightly faster trio functions as the fulcrum of the movement and of the entire quartet. The viola states its slightly out-of-balance, folklike melody over the first violin's muted rustling. The movement ends with a much modified repeat of the Scherzo.

The fourth movement recreates the night-music mood of the second movement, perhaps now with an added edge of coldness and aloofness. An agitated and passionate middle section is heard before the opening mood returns.

In the Finale, Bartók brings back the peasantlike vitality of the first movement. Certain thematic connections appear, but they are more obvious to the eye than to the ear. Near the end of the movement, Bartók interrupts the breakneck forward motion with a puzzling brief section that he marked *Allegretto, con indifferenza*, a banal little tune that grows increasingly out of tune as it progresses. The original vigor then resumes to end the movement.

Bartók composed the quartet in the uncharacteristically short time of one month, from August 6 to September 6, 1934, on commission from the Elizabeth Sprague Coolidge Foundation. The dedication is to Mrs. Coolidge, who was such a remarkable and perceptive patron of chamber music. Its first performance was given in Washington, D.C., by the Kolisch Quarter on April 8, 1935.

Contrasts

I. Verbunkos. II. Pihenö. III. Sebes.

While on holiday in Switzerland in August 1938, Bartók received a letter from Joseph Szigeti, a Hungarian violinist who had emigrated to the United States. It was written on behalf of clarinetist Benny Goodman, the "King of Swing," who wanted a classical piece that he could perform with Szigeti. The composer set to work at once on a clarinet/violin duet with piano accompaniment, and by September 24, *Rhapsody,* consisting of two dance movements, was completed. On January 9, 1939, Joseph Szigeti, Benny Goodman, and pianist Endre Petri played it in New York. When Bartók was in New York in April of the next year to record the work with Szigeti and Goodman, however, he decided to add a third, middle movement, and to change the name to *Contrasts.*

The opening movement, Verbunkos, is named after a wild eighteenth-century Hungarian recruiting dance in which an army officer in full uniform proudly prances about in order to entice young men into the service. A short introduction in the violin precedes the clarinet's statement of the marchlike principal melody. After a slightly varied repeat by the violin, that instrument presents the subdued second subject, with the short-long repeated rhythmic pattern so characteristic of Hungarian folk music. Brilliantly exploiting the full technical resources of all three instruments, Bartók works out these two ideas, ending the movement with a clarinet cadenza.

Pihenö, or relaxation, combines the tonal qualities of a Balinese gamelan orchestra with the sounds of Bartók's night music—the whispered nocturnal flutterings and trills heard in country fields, forests, and along mountain streams.

For the opening of the Sebes, or fast dance, the violinist is instructed to use a mistuned violin, with the bottom string raised a half step and the top string lowered the same interval. The initial effect is that of a *danse macabre*, but a robust, gay mood quickly asserts its primacy. A middle, slower section, in the odd meter of thirteen beats to a measure, is based on the irregular rhythm of Bulgarian folk music. The ending of the movement is similar in character to the opening and features a violin cadenza and some fascinating chirping sounds on all three instruments.

String Quartet No. 6

I. Mesto; Vivace. II. Mesto; Marcia. III. Mesto; Burletta. IV. Mesto.

Seriously troubled by the rise of Nazism and the threat of World War II, Bartók nevertheless forced himself to continue composing through the late 1930s. On August 18, 1939, he wrote to his son from Saanen, Switzerland, where he was staying, that he was starting his Sixth String Quartet for the New Hungarian Quartet. But several days later, after receiving word of the German-Russian nonaggression pact, Bartók stopped composing and headed home to Budapest. For nearly three months Bartók only worked haltingly, deeply disturbed by the outbreak of war. He did not actually complete the quartet until near the end of November. It proved to be the last composition that Bartók wrote in Europe; less than one year later he and his wife emigrated to the United States.

It is not difficult to hear in the Sixth Quartet some of the anguish Bartók must have been suffering as the civilized world tottered on the brink of destruction, and as it became clear that he would have to flee his beloved Hungary. Perhaps one bit of musical evidence of his despair is the linear progression of the four movements in this work—each one is slower than its predecessor—that finally ends in a mood of bleak resignation. One theme, marked Mesto (''mournful or sad''), serves to introduce each movement and binds the entire work together.

In the first movement, the viola leads the way with the Mesto theme, the others then joining in for a forceful unison passage that Bartók transforms into the fleeting, ascending first theme of the section. A second theme follows, with the characteristic Hungarian folk music rhythm of trochees and iambs (long-short followed by short-long). The character is light, lively, and playful, as Bartók works out the two themes and brings them back for a varied recapitulation.

The cello ushers in the second movement with the Mesto theme, this time with a counter melody in the first violin and a hushed tremolo accompaniment in the second violin and viola. The body of the movement is a march, but laden with anger, irony and savage satire. Even when it is repeated quietly and with some tenderness, one gets a feeling of hollow mockery. The middle section, introduced by the solitary cello, features a highly intense melody for that instrument. When the march returns, now with ghostly overtones, it can aptly be called a *marche macabre*.

The third movement is introduced by the Mesto melody in the first violin, with counter melodies in the second violin and cello. As in the previous Marcia, the Burletta (''burlesque, jest'') is bitter and cutting. True, it has elements of humor, but the underlying spirit is cynical and sardonic. To intensify the satire, near the opening Bartók directs one violin to play the same notes as the other but a quarter-tone flat, creating grating dissonances. A nostalgic, wistful middle section provides a welcome change of mood before the final part brings back the feeling of the opening; included here is considerable use of pizzicato and *jeté* (thrown bow), along with a recollection of the second theme from the first movement.

All four instruments join in the fourth presentation of the Mesto theme; this time, though, it is not just introductory, it continues as the principal theme of the movement. Bartók also recalls the two themes from the first movement, now in somber tones bereft of their earlier vitality. Lovely in tone and highly emotional, the movement communicates a sense of beatific acceptance, until the viola provides a final glimpse of the Mesto theme and the quartet ends.

The premiere was given in New York by the Kolisch Quartet on January 20, 1941.

Ludwig van Beethoven

Born December 16, 1770, in Bonn
Died March 26, 1827, in Vienna

BEETHOVEN IS widely accepted as the most influential and revolutionary composer of all time, an emancipator who freed composition from the constraints and restrictions of eighteenth-century Classicism.

He was born in what was then the small, provincial German town of Bonn. His father was a dissolute, untalented court musician who could scarcely feed his family; his mother died of tuberculosis when Ludwig was only seventeen. For a while the young Beethoven supported his brothers by giving music lessons and playing viola in a theater orchestra. In 1792 he settled in Vienna, where he completed his studies with Franz Joseph Haydn and others, quickly winning success as a pianist and composer. At age twenty-eight, though, he realized that he was losing his hearing. Nevertheless, for the rest of his life, even while struggling against deafness, ill health, and a never-ending round of personal, familial, and financial crises, Beethoven was able to produce some of the greatest works of music our world knows.

As a young man, Beethoven was well aware of the winds of social, political, and economic change that were blowing through Europe, climaxing in the French Revolution of 1789. Although poorly educated in subjects outside music, Beethoven read widely and believed passionately in the principle of the revolution—the right of all people to live in freedom and dignity, protected from the egregious greed and power of the nobles. During his lifetime the focus of music was shifting away from the church and the drawing rooms of kings and aristocrats, to the concert halls of the bourgeoisie. In giving shape and substance to this new music, Beethoven helped change the role of the composer from craftsman, who provided music to satisfy his patron's needs, to creative artist, who composed in response to his own inner needs and urges.

Beethoven's great musical gifts, coupled with the force of his personality, allowed him to break free of the musician's usual menial station and attain a position of equality, at least in the sphere of music, with the most powerful people of his time. "It is easy to get on with the nobility," Beethoven explained, "if you have something to impress them with." Short, with a pockmarked, swarthy face, wild hair, protruding teeth, usually ill-kempt and poorly dressed, Beethoven did not cut a very impressive figure. Yet he was highly respected by the nobles, many of whom were very knowledgeable in music, appreciated his genius, and were willing to contribute to his support—in part because he convinced them it was his due and their duty!

Through his orchestral works, chamber music, and solo compositions, Beethoven extended and expanded compositional practices that he inherited from such giants as Haydn and Mozart by infusing them with new force and flexibility, providing a vastly increased scope, more powerful emotional content, and an imposing monumentality. He pushed Classicism to its very limits, preparing the soil on which the seeds of nineteenth-century Romanticism were to take root and flourish.

Beethoven's music, with the chamber works occupying a very central position, is often considered in three major creative periods. The first period, lasting until the early 1800s, is characterized by a continuation of late eighteenth-century compositional techniques, and embraces the chamber works of Opp. 1, 8, 9, 11, 16, 18, 20, 25 and 29. Although traditional in form and style, these works are already pressing against the established boundaries. In addition to being uniquely personal, emotional, and highly expressive, they are also embellished with wonderful touches of Beethoven's rough humor.

During the second period, the decade starting around 1804, Beethoven battled the fate that was robbing him of his hearing and depriving him of love, marriage, and family, and that saw his aristocratic patrons slowly losing their wealth and power. His output during those years included the chamber works Opp. 59, 70, 74, 95 and 97. These compositions are even further removed from the classical models in terms of length, intensity, and originality of musical invention.

In the third and final period, Beethoven is at the greatest distance from his classical forebears. The struggle is largely over; he has proved to himself and to others that he can compose despite his awful affliction. These last works, all quartets, Opp. 127, 130, 131, 132, 133, and 135, introduce a completely new spirituality into chamber music. The formal scheme is now determined exclusively by the musical content; it is not a preset structure into which appropriate musical thoughts are placed. These late quartets achieve a heightened expressivity in which Beethoven transcends earthly concerns and soars to the loftiest planes the human imagination can reach.

When Beethoven died in 1827, he left as a legacy to the world a body of string quartets and other chamber works that are the mainstay of the chamber music repertoire and provide fascinating insights into Beethoven the man and the rapidly changing world in which he lived.

Piano Trios, Op. 1, Nos. 1, 2, and 3

For all composers, Op. 1 represents a signal point in their development. It marks the transition from juvenile and student works to music that the composer considers mature and worthy of publication. Beethoven, whose Op. 1 consists of three piano trios, was surely aware of this significance when he so designated these works after having already completed nearly twenty chamber music pieces.

The composer probably did most of the work on the trios during 1791 and 1792 while still living and studying in Bonn, the city of his birth. It is even possible that he performed individual movements at private concerts there. In 1792, though, Beethoven became eager to move to a city more musically active than Bonn, both to advance his career and to escape the hordes of refugees who were flooding the city because of the war with France. When Maximilian Franz, elector of Bonn, offered to pay for the twenty-two-year-old's trip to Vienna and to contribute toward his expenses while there, Beethoven was only too happy to accept.

Beethoven arrived in Vienna in November 1792 and soon started studies with Franz Joseph Haydn. He also continued work on the Op. 1 trios. About one year later, Beethoven, joined by Ignaz Schuppanzigh, violin, and Anton Kraft, cello, gave the first performance of the three trios at the Viennese house of Prince Carl Lichnowsky, to whom they are dedicated.

Most of the musical elite of Vienna, including Haydn, were present at the performance. The older composer expressed his approval of trios one and two, but suggested that Beethoven withhold number three from publication. Ferdinand Ries, Beethoven's student, later wrote that the remark "astounded" his teacher, especially since he believed the third was the best and most effective of the trios. Beethoven began to think, according to Ries, that Haydn was "envious, jealous and ill-disposed" toward him. But the fact that Beethoven continued reworking the third trio after the performance and later said, "When I was a beginner I should have perpetrated the most flagrant follies in composition but for Papa Haydn's advice," would seem to indicate that Beethoven did not really distrust Haydn's opinion.

In any case, Beethoven waited nearly two years before submitting all three trios for publication. Most scholars believe that Beethoven did this largely for commercial reasons, waiting for word of mouth about the pieces to spread among the many amateur piano trios in Vienna who, Beethoven calculated from the start, would provide a ready market for the printed music.

Piano Trio in E Flat Major, Op. 1, No. 1

I. Allegro.   II. Adagio cantabile.   III. Scherzo: Allegro assai.   IV. Finale: Presto.

The trio opens with a melodic figure characterized by upward-rushing broken chords known as "Mannheim Rockets." This musical gesture is so named because it was frequently used by composers connected with the Mannheim court in the mid-eighteenth century to add a special virtuosic brilliance to their music. A second subject, starting with three quiet, repeated notes, follows. It is gentle and sober in character and moves step-wise within a narrow range, in contrast to the wide-flung energy of the opening. A concluding theme alternates staccato ascending scales with short legato snatches. Traditional development and recapitulation sections lead to an extended coda, almost a second development section, which concludes the movement.

Beethoven does not break any new ground in the Adagio cantabile. Well-crafted and in close conformity with the stylistic tenor of the time, it is, however, enlivened with a few typically Beethovenesque rhythmic and harmonic surprises. Structurally, it is a rondo, with the three slightly varied appearances of the theme separated by contrasting interludes.

The Scherzo is a gay, spirited romp. In the sharply contrasted trio,

the strings play long sustained lines as the piano speeds through figures reminiscent of gentle Mannheim Rockets. The movement ends
with a literal repeat of the opening section and a brief coda.

Beethoven immediately sets the insouciant, carefree mood of the
Finale with the extra-large leap of a tenth in the piano that introduces
the jaunty first subject. A second theme, with its measured descending pattern, comes next. Exhibiting elements of both sonata and
rondo form, the movement dances on in irresistible good humor. A
coda, with some fleeting reminders of the Rocket theme, brings the
entire trio to a brilliant conclusion.

Piano Trio in G Major, Op. 1, No. 2

I. Adagio; Allegro vivace.   II. Largo con expressione.   III. Scherzo: Allegro.   IV. Finale: Presto.

In some ways, the G major is the most elusive and hardest to cate-
gorize of the Opus 1 trios. At times it adheres closely to eighteenth-
century compositional strictures, including the emotional restraint,
while at other times it anticipates the freer and more obviously expressive nineteenth-century style. There are also tentative and inse-
cure sections, as well as extended passages that clearly exhibit the
hand of a confident, mature master. These disparities, however per-
plexing, provide valuable insights into this period of Beethoven's extraordinary growth and development.

After a slow introduction that includes a preview of the movement's main theme played by the violin, the central body of the
movement arrives with the statement of the subject in the piano,
though seemingly in the wrong key and strangely subdued. The
strings, however, soon join in the presentation of the melody, setting
everything right; it is clearly in the key of G, and has all the expected
verve and vitality. The dancelike second subject is brought in by the
violin and immediately expanded by the others. A rhythmically
quirky, mock-mysterious concluding theme rounds off the exposition. The start of the development includes some highly advanced
harmonies, but Beethoven, as though aware of a trespass, quickly
returns to a traditional development, recapitulation, and coda.

The gravitational center of the trio is the Largo. The expressivity
and perfection of line of the two main melodies, the richness of the
textures, the harmonic freedom—all combine to produce a profoundly moving movement.

The atypically subdued character of the Scherzo, which after all means "joke" in Italian, is established by the cello opening at the very bottom of its range. Even the misplaced accents, which usually add their own special bit of spice to the music, do little to lift the cloud that seems to hover over the movement.

The sparkling brilliance of the Finale, though, quickly dispels the serious mood. From the rapidly repeated notes of the bright first theme to the piano statement of the warm lyrical second theme, the music bubbles forth in delightful vivacity.

Piano Trio in C Minor, Op. 1, No. 3

I. Allegro con brio.   II. Andante cantabile con variazione.   III. Menuetto: Quasi allegro.   IV. Finale: Prestissimo.

The key of C minor always had a special meaning for Beethoven; his "Pathétique" Sonata, Fifth Symphony, Third Piano Concerto and Fourth String Quartet can be cited as evidence. His Third Piano Trio in C Minor also belongs in this group, since it is widely considered the most advanced of the Op. 1 trios and the first composition to bear the unmistakable stamp of his unique musical personality.

A compact, highly dramatic theme opens the work. After coming to a halt, it continues with a piano melody, a considerably lighter, tripping tune, which moves downward in direction. Beethoven expands both themes before introducing the second subject, a lyrical, singing melody that all three instruments share. The exposition ends with a reminder, starting in the cello, of the descending figure of the first subject. In a brilliant example of musical alchemy, the development starts with a transformation of the opening theme into a charming little waltz, but it soon gives way to an intense and stormy exploration of the theme. After a short working out of the second part of the first subject, Beethoven freely reviews the melodic material from the exposition and ends the movement with a short coda.

The utter simplicity of the second movement theme serves two purposes: it is easy to hold in memory, and it provides space for the increased complexity of the following five variations. Beethoven, though, goes beyond merely elaborating and ornamenting the original melody. By subjecting it to a series of expressive transformations, he exposes the wide range of moods and emotions inherent in the theme itself.

The third movement is an unexpected return to traditional minuet form after the highly expressive first movement and the advanced theme and variations. The descending scale that starts the trio calls to mind the striking scales Beethoven introduced in the development section of the opening movement.

The brusque, commanding opening of the Finale closely resembles the contour of the E flat trio, with the Mannheim Rocket detonating between repeated chords. After being brought to an abrupt close, a subsidiary melody of beguiling charm emerges, simply stated first by the violin and then the piano. A calm second subject follows the extension of these two ideas and leads to the development. The recapitulation comes after an extended chromatic scale for the piano, but it starts with the lighter second part of the first theme, excluding the imperious outburst. In another departure from convention, instead of providing the more usual strong ending, Beethoven allows the music to disappear in a whisper.

String Trio in D Major, Op. 8, "Serenade"

I. Marcia: Allegro. II. Adagio. III. Menuetto: Allegretto. IV. Adagio; Scherzo: Allegro molto. V. Allegretto alla Polacca. VI. Andante quasi Allegretto; Allegro. VII. Marcia: Allegro.

By using the subtitle "Serenade," Beethoven lets the listener know that his String Trio, Op. 8 is a kind of night, or outdoor, music, written in a style to be sung by a lover under the window of his lady. The Op. 8 is made up of a series of short tuneful movements, many dancelike in character. It does not have the seriousness or profundity of many other Beethoven works, but once we accept the idea that here pleasure and entertainment are his main goals, we see that Beethoven succeeds admirably. Written between 1795 and 1796, while the composer was working on many other projects, it was published in 1797.

True to the serenade tradition, the work opens with a march, from the common conceit that the players are heard approaching and then departing the performance. Like the other movements in the trio, this one is lighthearted with pleasant, easily remembered melodies organized into a simple formal construction. Lilting and energetic in in character, it has a number of abrupt and exciting changes in dynamics and accents.

The gentle, melodious second movement is warm and intimate

without ever becoming maudlin or sentimental. It builds to one climax, but quickly backs away. At the end the violin and viola, over a rolling cello figure, alternately climb up the notes of a broken chord to reach the subdued conclusion.

In the Menuetto Beethoven follows rough, gruff chords with dainty, pointed responses. The middle section, or Trio, features a wonderful singing melody in the violin, an equally attractive counter melody in the cello, and an accompanying figure that bounces along in the viola. After the minuet is repeated, there is a brief coda, which sounds much like a mechanical dancing doll with its spring winding down.

After three rather conventional movements, Beethoven's unique musical personality comes to the fore in the Adagio, which starts somberly, with the melody played in octaves by the violin and viola over a simple cello accompaniment. After rising to a climax, the music quiets and seems to stop when the first violin, unexpectedly, takes flight with the viola in hot pursuit and the cello loudly barking its displeasure at such unseemly behavior. The abrupt outburst is brought to a halt for the return of the lugubrious Adagio. The violin briefly spurts forward again, but all too soon the mock seriousness of the Adagio returns to establish its primacy.

The delightful and stately Polacca (Italian for "polanaise"), is a Polish national dance characteristically in moderately fast triple meter with a strong rhythmic impulse, which is frequently adapted for virtuosic display. Most of the melodic burden falls on the violin, with the notable exception of a striking high passage for cello.

The Andante movement is made up of a theme and five variations that are little more than ornaments and decorations on the original melody. Beethoven later arranged the charming little theme into a song, *"Sanft wie die Frühlingssonne"* ("Soft as the Spring Sun").

The concluding Marcia that follows without pause is a literal repeat of the opening movement. The performance is over, and the imaginary band of musicians is marching away.

String Trios, Op. 9, Nos. 1 and 3

Beethoven arrived in Vienna in 1792 from his home city of Bonn and spent the following years studying with such leading musicians as Haydn, Salieri, and Johann Albrechtsberger, as well as establishing

himself as a composer and performer. This first phase of his stay in
Vienna ended triumphantly in 1795. In that year he concluded his
formal studies, made his highly successful debut as a pianist, had his
Op. 1 piano trios published, was invited to compose dances for the
prestigious Artists' Ball, and in December played his own piano concerto at the concert welcoming Haydn back from London!

Fresh from these peak experiences, Beethoven composed the three
string trios of Op. 9—No. 1 in G major, No. 2 in D major, and No.
3 in C minor—over the following two years. These proved to be his
final works in the form. Scholars speculate that in 1798, when he
composed his first string quartets, he found them more satisfying and
therefore felt no need to return to the string trio combination.

While numbers 1 and 3 of Op. 9 are solidly established in today's
repertoire, number 2 has found less favor and is rather infrequently
performed.

String Trio in G Major, Op. 9, No. 1

**I. Adagio; Allegro con brio.   II. Adagio, ma non tanto
e cantabile.   III. Scherzo: Allegro.   IV. Presto.**

The three notes of a descending G major chord, stately, rich, and
sonorous, open the slow introduction, followed at once by a simple
little figure of sixteenth notes for the violin. The figure, which passes
from instrument to instrument, leads directly into the Allegro. In
fact, the last four notes of the figure serve as the opening of the first
subject. A lyrical melody, also built on the descending G chord and
first sung out by the cello, becomes the second part of the same subject. The second theme is made up of soft, staccato notes, a kind of
condensed, skeletal melodic outline. After developing the themes,
Beethoven brings back the sixteenth note melodic figure from the
introduction and uses it as a transition to a restatement of the themes.

The second movement is a magnificent song for all three instruments, almost like an operatic aria with the violin as soprano. A number of different melodic strains are presented, often highly
ornamented and frequently accompanied with pulsating figures that
lend them a special intensity.

The carefree Scherzo is a marked contrast to the fervent preceding
movement. The opening theme recalls the rhythm of the first movement's Allegro. The solid, robust middle section further emphasizes

the deft lightness of the opening, which is repeated to close this graceful, energetic movement.

The brilliant, virtuosic finale has elements of a *perpetuum mobile* as the violin wings its way through the opening theme. After a slightly more lyrical passage, the music resumes its headlong flight. A rich soaring melody, stated in octaves by the violin and viola, functions as the second subject. Exploiting the technical resources of the three instruments, the movement progresses in classical sonata form, developing the themes and bringing them back before a speedy coda concludes the work.

String Trio in C Minor, Op. 9, No. 3

I. Allegro con spirito.   II. Adagio con
espressione.   III. Scherzo: Allegro molto e vivace.
IV. Finale: Presto.

The dark, portentous unison sound of the opening, including the striking interval of the augmented second between the second and third notes, puts the listener on notice that this is a serious, important movement. And indeed it is. After expanding the initial motto into a proper theme, Beethoven maintains the high, concentrated energy level through a series of violent, accented chords that lead to the second theme, an insistent, repeated-note figure that passes down through the three instruments. The intensity is somewhat relieved with the third group of themes, but repeated sets of hammered chords prevent complete relaxation. The development, which follows, is rich in texture, with many heavily accented notes. It is brought to a close by the cello, which plays the four-note opening motto beneath busy violin and viola parts—except that it is in the "wrong" key. Then, while the violin continues its figuration, the viola and cello sneak in with the opening notes, this time in the "right" key. After a brilliant, though shortened, recapitulation, Beethoven supplies a rather lengthy coda, which is almost another development section.

While some aficionados may debate whether this trio's first or second movement is the more outstanding, most listeners respond strongly to the rich expressivity of *both* movements. In the Adagio con espressione, Beethoven frequently uses double stops, in which one or the other instrument plays two notes simultaneously in order to enrich the harmonies. Beethoven explores a wide emotional range in the music, moving adroitly from calm repose to ennobling or dramatic sentiments with perfect ease.

The Scherzo is fast and sprightly and is propelled forward by a nervous energy, but it is not especially gladsome. The middle trio section alternates rapidly rising, arpeggiated passages with repeated-note figures before presenting a shortened reprise of the Scherzo.

Flashing triplets separated by tutti punctuations make up the first theme of the Finale, a pattern almost identical to the last movement of Beethoven's String Quartet, Op. 18, No. 1. A more lyrical second theme serves as a contrast to the brilliance of the opening subject. After working out the various themes, all forward motion stops as the viola and cello repeatedly sound their clashing, dissonant notes and the violin sidles in with the start of the recapitulation. The coda builds up to a climax, which then quietly fades away to end the movement.

Trio for Clarinet, Cello, and Piano in B Flat Major, Op. 11

I. Allegro con brio. II. Adagio. III. Tema: *Pria ch'io l'impegno.*

Historical facts concerning this trio are hard to come by, although it is generally believed that Beethoven wrote it for the Bohemian clarinet virtuoso, Joseph Beer, probably in 1796, and had it published two years later. In any case, it is a fresh, spontaneous, and charming work, with no illusions about being a serious or profound musical utterance.

A bold, unison statement of the first of several themes that together make up the primary subject group is heard at the outset. After two powerful chords bring this section to a close, a transition passage leads to the second theme, first given out by the clarinet. A robust syncopated melody concludes the exposition, followed by a compressed development and recapitulation. Beethoven toys with the listener at the end, tossing in a couple of false endings before reaching the final conclusion.

The cello introduces the expressive, cantabile melody of the Adagio. The second theme of the succinct sonata form starts with the cello's ascending scale, which is answered by the clarinet. A short, dramatic development section is followed by an ornamented reprise of the first theme, again stated by the cello, a more traditional return of the second theme, and a short coda.

The theme on which Beethoven based the variations of the last movement is the aria *"Pria ch'io l'impegno"* ("Before what I intended"), from Joseph Weigl's opera *L'Amor Marinaro* (*The Corsair*). According to some accounts, Beethoven later expressed displeasure with the finale because he had not been told the source at the time it was suggested to him by his publisher, Artaria. Others say that Beer suggested the theme, and Beethoven subsequently felt it was not a suitable subject for variations. Beethoven subjects Weigl's gay, captivating melody to nine variations that are essentially playful improvisations, meant mainly to delight and amuse the listener.

To broaden its appeal—as well as to improve the sales—Beethoven transcribed the trio for violin, cello, and piano; the violin part is almost identical to the original clarinet part.

Piano Quintet (Quartet) in E Flat Major, Op. 16

I. Grave; Allegro, ma non troppo.   II. Andante cantabile.   III. Rondo: Allegro, ma non troppo.

The program at the first performance in Vienna on April 6, 1797, of Beethoven's just completed Op. 16 read, "A Quintet for the Fortepiano and Four Wind Instruments." Yet, when the work was actually published in 1801, it appeared both as a quintet for piano and winds (oboe, clarinet, French horn, and bassoon) and as a quartet for piano and strings (violin, viola, and cello). Both versions had the same opus number and were nearly identical, given the different number and capabilities of the instruments. Having been inspired by Mozart's highly successful and delightful Quintet in E flat (K.452), written little more than a decade before, it is not surprising that Beethoven chose the quintet form. The string transcription, it is believed, was probably a way to make the music more available to a wider public, including the many amateur piano and string groups that were active in Vienna at that time.

The quintet/quartet opens with a slow, dignified, and rather long introduction in the pompous style and dotted (long-short) rhythm of late seventeenth-century French overtures. The following Allegro strips away any hints of pretentiousness as the three main themes, all characterized by a simple, relaxed charm, are introduced one after another. Beethoven underscores the lightness of mood by playfully inserting a false recapitulation in the wrong key, before returning the themes in the proper and expected way. Then, in the same frisky manner, he omits the second part of the first subject until after a short, written-out piano cadenza is played near the end of the recapitulation.

The principal theme of the Andante cantabile is a long phrased melody, introduced by the piano and then taken up by the others. After a contrasting episode in minor the melody returns, somewhat embellished and with additional countermelodies. This is followed by another minor-key interlude, after which the main melody returns, further ornamented, and with an even richer contrapuntal texture. A coda, with scale fragments in contrary motion between the piano and other instruments, brings the movement to a quiet close.

Beethoven calls the last movement a Rondo, which is usually described as three repetitions of a theme separated by contrasting episodes; it can be diagrammed as A-B-A-C-A, where A is the theme, and B and C are the contrasts. In this movement, though, the C section is really a development of A, and with the B section brought back at the end, the organization comes closer to the sonata form, with its A-B-development-A-B form. The writing throughout is witty and high spirited. At one performance, Beethoven jestingly extended to considerable length the very short piano cadenza that comes just before the first return of A—to his great delight and to the other performers' considerable discomfort. But it must be added that, when he heard his pupil Carl Czerny make a few minor alterations in the part, such as doubling some of the piano notes, Beethoven scolded him for taking such liberties!

String Quartets, Op. 18, Nos. 1, 2, 3, 4, 5, and 6

On June 29, 1801, Beethoven wrote to his friend, Franz Gerhard Wegeler: "For the past three years my hearing has been growing constantly weaker . . . . For two years now I have ceased to attend any social function for I cannot bring myself to tell people, 'I am deaf.'" The realization that he was, at age twenty-seven, gradually being drawn into a world of impenetrable silence can scarcely have left unaffected the six Op. 18 quartets, composed between mid-1798 and 1800. The impact of the steady deterioration of what Beethoven called his "noblest faculty" can only be imagined. In these quartets one can hear the conflicting emotions, the deep despondency, and the defiant anger that his affliction aroused. Here we can also find the natural optimism and joie de vivre of robust youthfulness clashing with the preternatural maturity and seriousness forced on the fearful and burdened composer.

At this time, Beethoven was undergoing another kind of turmoil as well. While carrying on the musical traditions of Haydn and Mozart before him, Beethoven was also absorbed with a search for new and unique forms of expression. Just the fact that the Op. 18—Beethoven's first essays in the quartet form—contains six works is evidence of his homage to Haydn, who published most of his quartets in groups of six, and to Mozart, whose six quartets dedicated to Haydn were outstanding contributions to the form. By departing from his previous practice of publishing a single work or a group of three in each opus, as in Opp. 1, 2, 9, 10, and 12, Beethoven not only follows the tradition of the older masters but acknowledges them as his sources of inspiration. Yet, while in the Op. 18 quartets "the clarity and freshness of Haydn are found linked with the grace of Mozart," as Joseph de Marliave wrote, Beethoven's distinctive musical personality and forward-looking musical vision undeniably shape every note.

Based on Beethoven's music sketchbooks, scholars now believe that the quartets of Op. 18 were not written in the order in which they were published. The sequence of composition was probably No. 3 (D major), No. 1 (F major), No. 2 (G major), No. 5 (A major), No. 6 (B major), and No. 4 (C minor). Considered the high point of Beethoven's first period, the Op. 18 quartets were dedicated to Prince Karl Lobkowitz, an Austrian nobleman, and are therefore sometimes referred to as the "Lobkowitz" quartets. Their premieres were given at Friday morning musicals held at the Viennese home of the prince around the turn of the century, and they were published in 1801.

String Quartet in F Major, Op. 18, No. 1

I. Allegro con brio. II. Adagio affettuoso et appassionato. III. Scherzo: Allegro molto. IV. Allegro.

Beethoven most likely chose the F major as the first quartet, even though it was composed second, because it is the biggest and most impressive work of the group. The particularly brilliant opening and closing movements, as well as its unequalled dramatic sweep and emotional tension, distinguish the F major from the other quartets of Op. 18.

Five pages in one Beethoven notebook and eleven pages in another bear witness to the composer's titanic struggle to bring the all-important motif, which starts and dominates the first movement, to its final form. The process was largely one of simplifying and concentrating his original musical idea into the most terse and pithy statement that one writer, Joseph Kerman, describes as "a coiled spring, ready to shoot off in all directions." Although he introduces a subsidiary subject, a charming, light, syncopated melody, and casts the two themes in sonata form, the opening motto clearly maintains its ascendancy throughout the movement, even as it changes its character from laconic to prolix, from tender to aggressive, from somber to joyful. In the summary coda, Beethoven surprises the listener with a completely *new* theme, an ascending scale passage that he then combines with the main motif, which reasserts its dominance in the closing measures.

About the deeply passionate and tragic Adagio, Beethoven wrote at the end of one sketch, "*les derniers soupirs*" ("the last breath"). It is reported that when Beethoven played the movement for Karl Amenda, his friend said, "It pictured for me the parting of two lovers." "Good!" Beethoven replied, "I thought of the scene in the burial vault in *Romeo and Juliet*." The first violin sings the first theme, a poised arching melody that floats lightly over the gently pulsating accompaniment. The second violin introduces the subsidiary subject, a one-measure descending phrase, and the viola is entrusted with the concluding subject, also one measure in length and downward in direction. Although the three themes are quiet in character, Beethoven in the ensuing development invests them with an energy and agitation that far exceeds the range of eighteenth-century quartet writing.

After the emotional heights reached in the Adagio, the listeners, though not the performers, are allowed to relax with the modest and very charming Scherzo. Adding a touch of wit and humor in the middle Trio section, Beethoven sends the first violin on rapid flows of notes between rhythmically limping unison passages. The trio is followed by a literal repeat of the Scherzo.

The first subject of the final movement, a flashy run of notes ending with three concluding chords, bears a striking resemblance to the Finale of the C minor string trio. With virtuosic parts for all four instruments, the movement is cast partly in rondo form, with a repeated theme and contrasting episodes, and partly in sonata form, with two contrasting themes that are developed and returned.

String Quartet in G Major, Op. 18, No. 2, "Compliments"

I. Allegro. II. Adagio cantabile. III. Scherzo: Allegro. IV. Allegro molto quasi presto.

The G major, the briefest and seemingly least ambitious quartet of Op. 18, emerges as a charming and witty work, very close in style and temperament to the best examples of eighteenth-century Rococo chamber music. Despite its apparent light, happy character, though, Michael Tree of the Guarneri Quartet, among many other musicians, considers it the most difficult of all Beethoven quartets to perform. And Beethoven's notebooks reveal that the lightness was achieved only after a lengthy and arduous struggle, covering thirty-two notebook pages, to blend many disparate elements into a smooth, artistic creation.

The subtitle, "Compliments," comes from the opening of the quartet in which a series of short, balanced phrases of supple elegance conjure up, as described in Theodor Helm's 1885 book on the Beethoven quartets, an "eighteenth-century salon, with all the ceremonious display and flourish of courtesy typical of the period . . . with bows and gracious words of greeting." A gruff bridge passage, starting with a repeated note, leads to a second subject and a closing theme that are attractive, but not particularly distinctive. The development is devoted exclusively to the melodies of the first subject and the bridge. The original themes are brought back in the recapitulation, but this time they are treated with greater vehemence and more freedom.

The Adagio cantabile features the solo violin at first, with the other instruments playing secondary roles. Before long, though, Beethoven takes the closing, cadential figure of this section, quadruples its tempo, and sends the music scurrying off in a parodylike Allegro interruption to the serious business at hand. Ending on a climactic note, the slow, gentle strains of the Adagio cantabile return, now in variation and shared by all players.

The two violins gleefully toss back and forth the melodic flourish of the Scherzo tune until the other instruments join in to introduce a more sober note. But the cheerful idea is not to be repressed, and in the trio that follows the two contrasting moods, playful and serious, are expanded. In the transition back to the repeat of the Scherzo, the cello plays a descending scale line, and the violins, unable to contain their enthusiasm, anticipate the repeat of the first section.

Beethoven referred to the last movement, which continues the high spirits and good humor of the Scherzo, as *"Aufgeknopft"* ("unbuttoned"), connoting a free, informal character. Starting with perfectly symmetrical, four-square phrases, it goes on to an impish second theme with a syncopated start and a delightful counter melody. Rollicking along lightheartedly, it builds to a brilliant conclusion.

String Quartet in D Major, Op. 18, No. 3

I. Allegro.   II. Andante con moto.   III. Allegro.   IV. Presto.

Although a Beethoven notebook dated 1798 is filled with fifty-eight pages of sketches for the D major quartet, scholars conjecture that a missing notebook contained even more preliminary studies for this composition, which is believed to be his very first mature string quartet. Overall, it is exceedingly quiet and pensive and is clearly indebted to the Classical masters for its concept and formal organization.

Calmly and tenderly, the first violin floats the main subject, with its striking opening interval of a minor seventh, over the soft sustained chords of the other instruments. The broad cantilena line of this subject is different from the melodies constructed of pithy motifs that characterize so many other pieces by Beethoven. The second subject, also stated by the first violin, is slightly more agitated than the first; the staccato bass line adds to the feeling of unease and disquiet. Following the exposition and development, Beethoven brings back most of the material from the exposition and ends with a short coda.

The warm, simple theme of the Andante cantabile is presented, uncharacteristically, by the second violin. Poetically conceived and richly textured, the movement is in neither rondo nor sonata form, but falls somewhere in between. Its serious nature, great length, and especially careful realization seem to suggest that Beethoven attached a central importance to this movement. Although it has been faulted by some for lacking a depth of feeling, no one denies its obvious sincerity.

In keeping with the generally contemplative mood of the quartet, the third movement has neither the rhythmic verve of a minuet nor the sparkling vivacity of a scherzo, the typical quartet third movements. Instead, Beethoven supplies what might be called a gentle and graceful intermezzo. Especially attractive is the minor-key trio, a marked contrast to the opening in major and distinguished by flowing passages in the violins over descending scale fragments in the other instruments. The major opening section returns after the trio.

The energetic Presto combines in equal measure the unceasing flow of a perpetual motion, the rhythmic drive of a tarantella, and the melodic turns of a Mexican hat dance. The movement's surging motion is liberally seasoned with sharp and abrupt changes in dynamics until the bombast plays itself out, and the movement ends with a whispered farewell.

String Quartet in C Minor, Op. 18, No. 4

I. Allegro ma non tanto.   II. Scherzo: Andante scherzoso quasi allegretto.   III. Menuetto: Allegretto.   IV. Allegro.

Curiously, no notebook sketches have ever been uncovered for Beethoven's fourth quartet, probably the last one composed in Op. 18. This has led to speculation that the composer did not go through his usual throes in working out the problems or that he based it on a previous composition in which he had already resolved any problems. The only minor-key quartet in Op. 18, the C minor is probably the most popular work in the group, and like all of Beethoven's works in this key, it is a musical statement with an especially heightened dramatic tension throughout.

The first theme, dark-hued and throbbing with an inner passion, traces an irregular path up from the violin's lowest note to the top of its range. Beethoven caps off the climb with a series of powerful chords and a final outcry, before a sudden hush falls and the bridge passage leads to the second subject. This melody, first stated by the second violin, is very obviously derived from the second part of the first theme, but in a different key. After some concluding episodes in the exposition, Beethoven works through the material in the development section. During the transition to the recapitulation, the rapidly repeated notes in the second violin and viola give the effect of a tremolo, creating an almost orchestral sound. The first subject, even more agitated than before due to the syncopated figure in the two middle voices; the second subject, now stated by the first violin; the little changed concluding themes; and a climactic coda fill out the remainder of the movement.

Instead of following the powerful first movement with a conventionally slow and emotional second movement, Beethoven treats us to a moderately paced, witty Scherzo. Although there are three distinct themes—the first heard at the opening, the second a turning-on-itself line shared by the two violins, and the third a descending and ascending scale introduced by the second violin—they all include a figure of three repeated notes either in the theme or the accompaniment. The texture is mostly polyphonic, with the tunes being blithely tossed from instrument to instrument in a profusion of canons and fugati.

The somber and serious Menuetto recaptures to some extent the mood of the first movement. Beethoven's recurrent use of third-beat accents distances it from typically dancelike minuets. The middle section, or trio, is essentially a dialogue between second violin and viola, to which the cello supplies a bass line and the first violin contributes a running triplet commentary. The Minuetto is repeated after the trio, but Beethoven directs that this time it be played at a faster tempo.

Ferdinand Ries, a pupil of Beethoven, recounted an anecdote connected with the last movement of the C minor quartet that gives an insight into his teacher's independent and unorthodox spirit of composition. In response to Ries's discovery of an instance of parallel perfect fifths in the last movement, a practice forbidden by all teachers of composition, Beethoven replied, "Ah! Well!, who is it who says perfect fifths are wrong?" After Ries named several leading music theorists of the day who forbade them, Beethoven said simply, "Very well, *I* allow the use of them!"

There are few other surprises in the final movement, a clearly defined rondo, very much in the style of Haydn. The sparkling main theme melody, played by the first violin, has elements of the Turkish style so favored by eighteenth-century composers, including Haydn and Mozart. The second violin has almost exclusive rights to the richly lyrical episode that follows. A varied return of the main theme leads to another contrast in which the instruments enter one after the other in a gruff, pyramidlike sequence. After a third reprise of the opening melody, there is a lengthy coda, ending with a rapid-fire finish.

String Quartet in A Major, Op. 18, No. 5

I. Allegro. II. Menuetto. III. Andante
cantabile. IV. Allegro.

There seems to be little question that certain resemblances between this work and Mozart's quartet in the same key are not entirely co-incidental. As Carl Czerny wrote in 1852, "Beethoven once saw at my house the score of six quartets by Mozart dedicated to Haydn. He opened the Fifth in A and said: 'That's what I call a work! In it Mozart was telling the world: Look what I could create if the time were right!'" Also, we know that Beethoven became familiar with the Mozart work when he copied over the last two movements as a way of studying Mozart's compositional technique.

The first movement of Beethoven's A major quartet is more direct and simpler than those found in the earlier quartets in Op. 18. The opening group of themes is made up of a number of individual phrases of varied character that go directly to the minor-key unison of the second subject without a bridge. The development, instead of focusing on the most important melodic material, is based on subsidiary and transitional motifs. The recapitulation almost literally repeats the exposition, except for the necessary adjustments in key. And the short coda is merely a fragmented A scale, with the first violin out of synchronization with the others.

As with Mozart, Beethoven places the Menuetto next, instead of the more usual slow movement. The gently rocking, almost waltzlike theme sets the mood for this sweet, sedate movement. The use of third beat accents in the more thickly textured trio gives the impression of a poorly played accordion. The Menuetto is repeated after the trio.

Over the theme and variations third movement, Beethoven wrote the word "pastoral," a clue to his conception of the music's character. The rather plain melody consists of a descending and ascending scale, with only minor deviations. But the five variations leave behind the eighteenth-century variation concept, which tends to keep the theme's harmonic outline while varying the details of figuration, rhythm, and tonality. In his variations, Beethoven reveals different aspects of the theme's expressive concept. Particularly striking is the contrast between the fourth and fifth variations; the fourth is hushed and almost mystical, while the fifth is rude, robust, and full-voiced. In the lengthy coda Beethoven effectively introduces the theme in its original form, pitting it against a double-time scale figure that essentially moves in contrary motion. At the very end the tempo slows down, leading to a subdued conclusion.

The nervous, agitated first theme of the final movement is in sharp contrast to the organlike sonority of the second theme, which sounds much slower but is actually in the same tempo. The quick four-note motto that opens the movement pervades the following development section, and after a full stop, the recapitulation brings back the previously heard material. The coda, with the four-note phrase still dominant, summarizes the movement.

String Quartet in B Flat Major, Op. 18, No. 6, "La Malinconia"

I. Allegro con brio.   II. Adagio, ma non troppo.   III. Scherzo: Allegro.   IV. La Malinconia: Adagio; Allegretto quasi allegro.

Although written fifth, Beethoven probably placed the B flat major quartet last because of the lengthy, slow introduction to the last movement, La Malinconia ("melancholy"), which gave the work its subtitle. From the viewpoint of musical development, this introduction is decades ahead of the rest of Op. 18. In some ways it presages the late quartets of the 1820s, with its moving evocation of grief and despair; it provides, as well, an insight into the depths of Beethoven's emotional state.

The first movement opens with a vigorous, upward-leaping theme in the first violin that eventually becomes a duet with the cello. The far less agile subsidiary theme stays rooted on one note and then another, all within a rather narrow range. The development section ends with a held note, anticipating the return of the melodies, little changed from their original appearance.

A refined, dignified melody is the main theme of the Adagio, which is organized into three-part, ternary form. The theme is introduced by the first violin over a bare-bones type of accompaniment. For the second violin repeat, the importance of the accompanying voices is considerably higher. The entire quartet joins for a brief episode together before the violin states the theme for the third time, now in a highly ornamental style. The contrasting section arrives with a thin, tenuous line played in octaves by first violin and cello. A short bridge passage and a rising chromatic scale in the first violin lead to the return of the opening theme, this time even more highly decorated than in its first hearing.

The Adagio's stately mood is unceremoniously shattered by the eccentric and very original Scherzo that follows. Full of rhythmic verve, it is constantly being tripped up and sabotaged by misplaced accents and cross rhythms. One can only marvel at Beethoven's ability to squeeze such intricate and complex rhythmic patterns into straightforward triple meter. The slight trio, a flowing violin solo with a short transition, leads back to a literal repeat of the Scherzo.

The finale, the climax of the entire composition, begins with the astounding La Malinconia, which Beethoven directs ''must be played with the greatest delicacy.'' The introduction falls into two parts, the first characterized by repeated tones and the second by a fugal, imitative texture. Woven throughout is a three-note turn, or *gruppetto*, which is inserted as a decoration before a longer note. Several times, loud and soft chords alternate, each one preceded by a *gruppetto*, which adds even more gloom to the phrase. The main body of the movement is fast, in the style of a *danza alla tedesca*, or German dance, which was very popular at the time. Although the *tedesca* never succeeds in raising the somber pall cast by La Malinconia, as if to underscore the point, Beethoven twice interrupts the gay dance with short reminders of the slow introduction, before letting the *tedesca* dash furiously to the powerful last chords.

Septet in E Flat Major, Op. 20

I. Adagio: Allegro con brio.   II. Adagio
cantabile.   III. Tempo di Menuetto.   IV. Tema con
variazioni: Andante.   V. Scherzo: Allegro molto e
vivace.   VI. Andante con moto alla Marcia; Presto.

Beethoven began preparing sketches for the septet (violin, viola, clarinet, French horn, bassoon, cello, double bass) in 1799 and completed the work early the next year. After a private performance at the home of Prince Schwarzenberg, the septet was introduced to the public at Vienna's Burgtheater on April 2, 1800. This concert, known as an *Akademie*, became the first in a series of programs Beethoven gave throughout his life both for his own financial benefit and to introduce new compositions.

Written during a period of great personal anguish over his hearing loss, the septet is nevertheless resolutely cheerful and optimistic. At first Beethoven felt extremely satisfied with the piece. "This Septet has pleased me greatly," he wrote his publisher; and after the very successful premiere, on the same program as Haydn's *Creation*, he remarked to composer Johann Dolezalek, "This is my *Creation*!" Yet, as the years went on and the septet became his most popular work by far and was put out in numerous arrangements and transcriptions (including the composer's own Op. 38 for piano trio), Beethoven denounced it for lacking seriousness, especially when compared with his later compositions. Following its sensational London reception in 1815, Beethoven remonstrated to Charles Neate, "That damn work; I wish it could be burned!" And to an enthusiastic admirer Beethoven insisted, "The septet was written by Mozart!"

The eighteenth-century Rococo *style galant* of Mozart and Haydn does indeed pervade the pages of the septet. It follows the light, entertaining divertimento form, so favored by the two masters, with its many short, tuneful movements. The first movement, the most symphonic in scope, has a slow introduction that starts with a motto of three iterated notes; it is followed by a fast section in regular sonata form. The first theme, initially stated by the strings, is repeated by the winds. The bridge to the second subject utilizes the three-note motif from the introduction. A slow-moving melody made up of slightly separated long notes, again heard first in the strings and then in the winds, opens the second group. A concise development of these themes leads to a free recapitulation and a full-length coda.

The Adagio cantabile is endowed with a plenitude of attractive lyrical melodies. After introducing the various themes, Beethoven freely varies and develops them, and brings them back for the concluding section.

Beethoven borrowed the theme for the third movement from his own Piano Sonata, Op. 42, No. 2, which he composed in 1796. It is an effervescent little gem with an especially humorous trio in which each of the gentle comments by the strings calls forth an agitated horn or clarinet response. The first part returns at the end.

Some claim that the theme of the fourth movement is a folk song from Germany's lower Rhine valley, but a specific source has never been cited. The attractive melody passes through a series of five original and imaginative variations, each one full of brilliant tonal colors and rich sonorous phrases, ending with a coda.

The French horn introduces the rough, rude theme of the lusty Scherzo. The sharply contrasted middle section, or trio, gives a soaring cantilena melody to the cello, before the literal repeat of the Scherzo.

The minor-key introduction to the sixth movement injects the first note of solemnity into the septet. But the cloudiness is soon dispeled by the skittish, major-key theme of the Presto. A bright, ebullient melody played by violin and cello serves as the second subject. The development section of the sonata form movement bubbles along until a substantial cadenza in the violin signals the return of all the melodies in the recapitulation and a climactic conclusion.

Serenade in D Major for Flute, Violin, and Viola, Op. 25

I. Entrata: Allegro. II. Tempo ordinario d'un Minuetto. III. Allegro molto. IV. Andante con variazioni. V. Allegro scherzando e vivace. VI. Adagio; Allegro vivace disinvolto.

The serenade emerged as a popular, tuneful, and melodious instrumental form around the year 1770. It favored light, catchy tunes, used straightforward harmonies and rhythms, and was made up of a number of short, simple dances, marches, and symphonic sections. Based on the Italian *serenata,* from *sera* ("evening"), a serenade evolved from music played beneath a beloved's window to music written in a clear style suitable for outdoor performance. Among the composers who wrote serenades of major interest—Haydn, Mozart, Brahms, Dvorak, and Elgar—Beethoven's essays in this form rank very high indeed.

The jaunty, marchlike rhythms of the Entrata, literally meaning entrance, set the spirited tone of the entire piece. A contrasting middle section, played by the violin and viola on their lower strings, with little witty comments by the flute, is heard before a repeat of the first section.

A fluid, smoothly flowing minuet follows. Although the flute's blithe melody is interrupted a few times by loud, harsh chords in the strings, the flute carries on, unperturbed by the rude outbursts. Of the two trios in this movement, the first is characterized by rapid passages in the strings, the second by similar figures for flute. The minuet reappears three times altogether—before, between, and after the trios.

The offbeat accents superimposed on the speeding musical line of the Allegro molto conjure up the image of a lame runner bravely competing in a race. A middle section that includes several fanfare-like calls comes before a literal repeat of the opening section.

The fourth movement is a theme and variations of ingenuous beauty. The calm, dignified theme is played by all three instruments before each one is given the opportunity to shine in an individual variation. All come together in the coda to round out this egalitarian movement.

A tiny wisp of a movement, the Allegro scherzando gallops in, prances around a bit, grows briefly quiet for an intricate contrapuntal section, and then with equal verve bounds away again.

While the slow introduction to the last movement is somewhat pensive, the tempo soon quickens and the cheerfulness returns. Cast as a rondo, with repetitions of the main theme separated by contrasting episodes, the music certainly lives up to Beethoven's designation, Allegro vivace disinvolto, "fast and lively, with easygoing assurance."

Viola Quintet in C Major, Op. 29, "Storm Quintet"

**I. Allegro moderato. II. Adagio molto
espressivo. III. Scherzo: Allegro. IV. Presto.**

Beethoven's viola quintet is a transitional work; it draws inspiration for its first two movements from the Classical style of the late eighteenth-century Viennese masters, while it anticipates the independence and freedom of the next century's Romantic style in its third and fourth movements. The addition of a viola to the string quartet to enrich the harmonies and to reinforce the bass line is believed to have been initiated by Franz Joseph Haydn's brother, Michael, around 1770. Only a comparatively limited number of composers, notably Mozart, Brahms, Mendelssohn, Dvořák, and Bruckner, along with Beethoven, have written significant works in quintet form.

Beethoven composed his quintet in 1801 and had it published the following year. The first performance was given in Beethoven's apartment in Vienna on November 14, 1802. Because Beethoven was already well established in musical circles, another publisher saw fit to put out a pirate edition, embroiling the composer in public claims, counterclaims, and legal actions that occupied his attention for nearly a decade.

The opening movement projects a sense of repose and gently flowing grace. The first theme, moving within a narrow melodic range, is simply presented; the first violin plays the melody over the cello's mirror image of the same melody, while the first viola murmurs an accompaniment figure. The continuation of the first theme, an interlocking chain of triplets, later becomes a major component of the development section. The second subject, which is similar to the first in character, achieves its contrast by being in the unexpected key of A major, instead of the more traditional G major or perhaps A minor. After the development of the movement's main themes, the recapitulation begins with a repeat of the first theme, this time garnished with some flavorsome chirping in the second violin.

The formal structure of the slow movement is elementary in that the varied strains of melodic material are presented and then simply reprised. But within this basic form Beethoven spins out a number of lovely, warm cantilena phrases. The part writing is rich in contrapuntal detail, and each instrument's tone colors are most effectively used to create the opulent sonorities.

The entire first part of the Scherzo grows from a three-note motto that is heard in eighty of its eighty-eight measures! In later years, this idea of using a brief motif to generate an entire movement became increasingly important to Beethoven. The trio's long, arching melody presents a counterpoise to the cellular Scherzo, which is repeated to end the movement.

Over rapid repeated notes in the other instruments, the first violin gives out the surging, fragmented first theme of the finale. This theme, with its blustery character and occasional flashes of lightning, gave the work its subtitle, "Storm Quintet." A transition leads to a more cantabile second theme. In the development section Beethoven superimposes a new meter (2/4, with four eighth notes to a bar), on the established meter (6/8, with six eighth notes to the same bar). This enables him to introduce a marchlike counter melody into the second viola part, against the continuing development of the first theme. Then, just before the recapitulation, Beethoven departs even further from tradition by completely changing the tempo (to *Andante con moto e scherzoso*) and the meter (to 3/4) and introducing a completely new, charming little song tune. To confound us even more, he then starts the recapitulation with the right theme but in the "wrong" key (F instead of C). The music, though, quickly grows louder for a proper, full-voiced recapitulation in C major—including one more glimpse of the song tune before the coda ends the movement.

String Quartets, Op. 59, Nos. 1, 2, and 3, "Rasoumowsky" Quartets

Count Andreas Rasoumowsky, Russian ambassador to the Imperial Court at Vienna at the turn of the nineteenth century, although a well-known figure in his time, would rank as little more than a footnote in the history books were it not for a group of three quartets he had the good sense to commission from Beethoven late in 1805. The count wanted to have the quartets performed at concerts in the lavish palace being built for him in Vienna. Since they are universally known as the "Rasoumowsky" quartets, his name is perpetuated in the world of music, if not in the annals of world events.

Having decided "to devote myself almost wholly to this work," Beethoven completed the first quartet by July 5, 1806, and on September 3 wrote his publisher that all three were done. The premieres were given in February 1807, probably by Ignaz Schuppanzigh's quartet, at an unknown site in Vienna, since the Rasoumowsky palace was not yet ready.

The reactions to the Op. 59 were among the harshest Beethoven had ever received, especially when compared to the high acclaim given his Op. 18 quartets. Carl Czerny wrote, "When Schuppanzigh first played the 'Rasoumowsky' Quartet in F, they laughed and were convinced Beethoven was playing a joke and that it was not the quartet that had been promised." But when violinist Felix Radicati said to Beethoven, "Surely you do not consider this music," the composer was ready with a prophetic reply: "Not for you, but for a later age." And of Schuppanzigh, who complained of the difficult parts, written for skilled professionals instead of amateurs as in the earlier chamber works, Beethoven reportedly said, "Does he really suppose I think of his puling little fiddle when the spirit speaks to me and I compose something?"

Much had happened to Beethoven in the six years since he wrote Op. 18, changing both the man and his music. At first his growing deafness had aroused in him feelings of fear, anger, and defiance.

Now he was convinced that this affliction, like other tragedies in life, could be overcome and his creative genius would flourish. In a sketchbook containing the Op. 59 quartets, he asked himself the rhetorical question: "Can anything in the world prevent you from expressing your soul in music?" The strongly affirmative answer can be found in the "Rasoumowsky" Quartets, the *Eroica* Symphony, the opera *Fidelio*, the "Appassionata" Sonata, and the other major works of his second period, which were characterized by a newfound assurance of truly heroic conception and proportion.

String Quartet in F Major, Op. 59, No. 1

I. Allegro. II. Allegretto vivace e sempre scherzando. III. Adagio molto e mesto. IV. Thème Russe: Allegro.

The first "Rasoumowsky" Quartet seems more like the consummation of a style than the beginning, in chamber music, of Beethoven's middle period. The spacious conception, the high expressivity, the sweep of formal structure, the beautiful melodies, the rich harmonies, the surging rhythms, and the brilliant string writing—all attest to surety, confidence, and maturity.

The monumental Allegro opens with a serene and noble first theme, starting low in the cello and soaring up to the first violin's highest register. Several other distinctive melodic phrases round out the first group of themes before the first violin introduces the upward-stretching second subject. Again, further themes fill out this second group. A codetta, based on a melody obviously derived from the first theme, concludes the exposition. The development, which starts like a repeat of the exposition, is vast in size and imaginatively varied, with a brilliant fugal center section. The cello sneaks in to start the recapitulation under a descending scale in the first violin. The building and enriching process continues through the recapitulation and concluding coda.

Musicians in Beethoven's day considered the opening rhythmic drumming on one note in the second movement strange and oddly amusing. Although the movement is lighter in mood than the Allegro, it still is somewhat restless and ill at ease. As in the previous movement, Beethoven uses many themes, some dancing and gaily abandoned, others more lyrical and songlike. The structure can be interpreted either as a scherzo with two trios or as sonata form; in

48

any case it is a thoroughly satisfying movement that grows organically and inevitably from the melodic material.

Scholars suspect that the enigmatic words, "A weeping willow or acacia tree upon my brother's grave," penned by Beethoven on the sketches for this movement, give an insight into the intent of this great and profoundly moving slow movement. Some say that the brooding intensity has to do with the composer's distress over his brother Casper Carl's marriage to Johanna Reiss, six months pregnant, and his belief that Casper's life had effectively ended. Others hold that the sorrow was evoked by the memory of another brother, born one year before Ludwig, who died in infancy. In any event, the lament, written in sonata form, has two cantilena themes, both characterized by wide intervals between the notes. The first is stated at the outset by the first violin; the second is sung by the cello while the violin weaves a filigree accompaniment above. The rest of the movement grows from these two melodies, as Beethoven continuously reexamines, reworks, and recasts them until a series of brilliant runs in the first violin brings the movement to an end.

The Thème Russe ("Russian theme") of the finale follows without pause. No one is sure whether Count Rasoumowsky asked Beethoven to include a Russian melody in the quartet, or whether the composer did it to honor his patron. Nevertheless, it has been determined that Beethoven derived the melody from a collection of Russian folk songs published by Ivan Pratsch. While the song was originally in minor and in a slow tempo, it appears here in major and at double the speed. In this sonata form movement, the dance-like rhythm of the first theme is followed by a contrasting legato subsidiary subject played by the second violin. At the very end Beethoven slows down the last statement of the Thème Russe by a factor of four before a brilliant flourish concludes the quartet.

String Quartet in E Minor, Op. 59, No. 2

I. Allegro. II. Adagio molto. III. Allegretto. IV. Finale: Presto.

Of the three "Rasoumowsky" Quartets, the E minor is probably programmed least often. Perhaps this is because it offers less overall bravura display than the other quartets. But for interest, appeal, and musical worth, this predominately lyrical work surely ranks as high as either of the others.

The quartet opens dramatically with two sharp, imperious chords, followed by a tense measure of silence. The subsequent tender, melodic phrase also ends abruptly. The melody, repeated one note higher, is again cut off. Then the mystery and foreboding end as phrase after energetic phrase pour forth, each one little more than a fragment, yet all seamlessly interwoven into an extended musical line that continually pulls the listener forward. While the form is somewhat obscured by the plethora of themes, Beethoven organizes them according to the standard principles of sonata form. The concluding coda, which almost seems to be another development, climaxes in an affirmative unison statement of the opening motif, after which the movement very quickly fades away to a quiet ending.

Like the Adagio molto in Op. 59, No. 1, this movement is sublimely eloquent, exhibiting a majestic calm that rises serenely above human concerns and interests. About its genesis, Beethoven's friend Carl Czerny wrote, "The Adagio . . . occurred to him when contemplating the starry sky and thinking of the music of the spheres." Another possible extramusical association comes from the fact that the main theme's first four notes are derived from a transposition of the musical spelling of Bach's name. (In German, B,A,C,H are the notes B flat, A,C,B.) At one point in the development section, the cello actually plays these exact notes. The individual sections of the sonata form are molded so unobtrusively that they flow one into the other to create the impression of one extended, glorious song.

The Allegretto, falling between a scherzo and an intermezzo in character, starts quietly, as though not to disturb the lofty sentiment of the Adagio molto. Despite its surface grace, however, it is immediately apparent that this movement is based on a quirky and highly eccentric rhythmic pattern. The middle section melody, in major, is a Thème Russe, the patriotic hymn "Slava," taken from Ivan Pratsch's collection of Russian folk songs and included either to pay homage to Count Rasoumowsky or at his request. The anthem was also used by Moussorgsky in his opera, *Boris Godunov,* and by Rimsky-Korsakov in *The Tsar's Bride*. Instead of varying or developing this theme, Beethoven repeats it a number of times, scored differently and with an assortment of countermelodies. Following the traditional scherzo form, the opening section reappears, but then, in a departure from the ordinary, Beethoven brings back both the Thème Russe and the beginning part one more time.

The brilliant Finale sets off at once on a high-speed, high-spirited rhythmic gallop. The organization combines elements of rondo and sonata form. The first violin plays the lyrical second theme, while the other instruments echo the turns of melody. A return of the opening leads to another section, which can be considered a third theme or a development of the first. After bringing back the various themes in a spirit of playful liveliness, Beethoven picks up the tempo for a spectacular dash to the final chords.

String Quartet in C Major, Op. 59, No. 3, "Hero"

I. Introduzione: Andante con moto; Allegro vivace. II. Andante con moto quasi Allegretto. III. Menuetto: Grazioso. IV. Allegro molto.

The subtitle "Hero" (or "Eroica") refers to the last movement of the quartet and acknowledges its truly mighty conception. Just as Beethoven's *Eroica* Symphony vastly expanded the scope of symphonic writing, so the grandiose finale of the third "Rasoumowsky" Quartet made all previous string quartets seem modest by comparison.

The eerie introduction that opens the quartet, without any forward motion and seemingly suspended in time, seems to contradict Beethoven's tempo direction, Andante con moto ("moderate speed with motion"). The jaunty first theme is, in effect, "kicked off" by a short upbeat and long arrival note—a rhythmic figure that remains important throughout the movement. Several other first group themes gradually lead to the start of the exuberant second subject— the first violin playing an ascending passage that ends with a long sustained note, which is imitated in order by the viola, cello, and second violin. The development section provides flashy virtuosic passage work for all the instruments with frequent reappearances of the short-upbeat/long-resolution motto. The exposition skips the first theme and deals entirely with the triumphant second melody before the arrival of a brief sparkling coda.

The second movement has variously been described as a "lament" by Vincent D'Indy, the "mystery of the primitive" by Joseph Kerman, and "some forgotten and alien despair," in the words of J.W.N. Sullivan. These reactions are mostly evoked by the first theme, a heavy, despondent violin line over repeated cello pizzicato notes. The melodic interval of the augmented second, with its Middle Eastern overtones, adds to the poignancy of the effect. The dispirited opening serves as the perfect foil to the warm, frothy second theme that follows. Both themes are developed and returned according to traditional sonata form, but in a surprise move, the composer brings them back in reverse order.

Beethoven probably returned to the traditional eighteenth-century minuet style for the third movement because a brilliant scherzo would have been inappropriate before the monumental finale he had in mind. The first part is gentle and languorous, despite a great deal of inner rhythmic drive. The sharper and more penetrating trio precedes a repeat of the Menuetto and the brief coda that leads, without pause, to the finale.

The last movement starts softly, but at a very fast tempo, with the viola playing the theme alone. The second violin enters with the same melody while the viola continues with a countermelody—a fugal treatment in which one theme is successively imitated by the individual players. The cello and then the first violin join in with the original melody to bring the section to a powerful climax. As the movement proceeds, Beethoven audaciously juxtaposes homophony (accompanied melody), on the richly textured polyphony (independent voices) of the opening fugal section, with absolutely thrilling results. Beethoven endows every note, from first to last, with a force and energy that propels the musical line irresistibly forward. He also calls on the players to stretch their tonal resources to the very limit, to produce the maximum sound possible. The result is a movement of stunning impact—a triumphant conclusion to this most impressive work.

Piano Trios, Op. 70, Nos. 1 and 2

Beethoven composed the Op. 70 piano trios in the fall of 1808, after being given rooms in the capacious Vienna apartment of the Hungarian noblewoman and excellent amateur pianist, Countess Maria von Erdödy. He dedicated the trios to her and gave their first performance in her salon during Christmas of the same year. Scholars dispute whether or not Beethoven was in love with the countess, but the fact that he often called her his *Beichvater,* or "father confessor," might seem to contravene such a claim.

From Beethoven's letters and other writings of that time come an explanation of the alternating optimism and despair that characterize these and other works from his middle period. Having arrived at an uneasy peace with his steadily worsening deafness, Beethoven now rejoiced in the knowledge that, despite his tragic malady, he was still able to compose and find fulfillment through his music. Certainly the trios express despondency over the burden he had to bear, as well as intimations of the purification and joy he felt because of his triumph over what he considered the worst of all possible physical failings.

Piano Trio in D Major, Op. 70, No. 1, "Geistertrio" ("Ghost Trio")

I. Allegro vivace con brio. II. Largo assai et espressivo. III. Presto.

The overall structure of the D major piano trio follows an arch shape. The two outside movements are lucid and direct in style; the high point of the trio is the middle movement, the foreboding Largo, from which the piece takes its subtitle.

The first movement opens with a highly rhythmic assertive figure that is forcefully played in unison by all three instruments. This immediately gives way to a two-measure cantabile phrase in the cello, but soon imitated by the others. After elaborating on this latter motif, the piano introduces the second subject played over rolling scale-like figures in the strings. The concentrated development section is followed by a recapitulation that includes further expansion of the melodic material.

The opening piano figure of the Largo, the ghost movement, is associated with Beethoven's sketches for the witches' scene from an opera based on *Macbeth* that he was planning at the time. Set off by solemn progressions of notes in the strings, the theme very effectively casts its mood of tension and suspense. The melancholy motif dominates the movement, each appearance slightly altered in pitch, but little changed in character. In a rare departure from his typical chamber music practices, Beethoven gives the piano some passages mostly for coloristic tonal effects, rather than for melodic or accompaniment purposes.

Following the dark despair of the Largo, the last movement projects a most welcome warmth and brightness. The music evokes the same sense of relief and recovered self-composure that one feels after having survived a trying experience or near disaster. Although modeled on Classical sonata form, the movement flows along effortlessly and seamlessly, without any sharp contrasts to disturb the newfound calmness and serenity.

Piano Trio in E Flat Major, Op. 70, No. 2

I. Poco sostenuto; Allegro ma non troppo. II. Allegretto. III. Allegretto, ma non troppo. IV. Finale: Allegro.

The E flat trio finds Beethoven in an amiable, almost placid mood; it is a work of great freshness and high appeal. Few moments are pervaded by morbid gloom or infused with ecstatic joy; instead there is an overall *gemütlichkeit*, a kind of cozy comfortableness expressed in muted colors and subdued emotion.

The slow introduction starts with a sedate melody, moving downward and upward by step, which passes sequentially from instrument to instrument. In the faster body of the movement, the first theme, although marked forte, or loud, tends to be more lyrical than forceful; the subsidiary subject, despite no change in tempo, seems much slower as each instrument deliberately spins out the melody, an obvious reworking of the introduction. The emotional temperature rises a bit in the ensuing development, which leads to a rather freely altered recapitulation and a coda that is interrupted by a final remembrance of the introduction.

In place of a true slow movement, which Beethoven so often invests with great emotional feeling, there follows a graceful, gavotte-like Allegretto. There are two main musical ideas, the first elegant and delicate, the second loud and blustery with strong offbeat accents. Beethoven varies the themes in alternation until the coda, where he combines the two melodies.

The third movement, a sort of idealized scherzo, shows little of the brilliance that characterizes more typical examples of this form. The cantabile main theme, borrowed with little change from Beethoven's earlier Piano Sonata, Op. 26, has a folklike purity, with perfectly symmetrical phrases and a simple setting. The following section, a tit-for-tat dialogue between the strings and piano, maintains absolute equality of phrase length. Toward the end of this section there is a hint of pain or suffering as we hear repeated musical sighs. Both parts of this movement are then repeated to achieve an overall five-part—A-B-A-B-A—form.

The violent piano runs at the opening of the Finale are interrupted by string interjections that appear to be derived from the first movement introduction. The remainder of the first subject is devoted to a lyrical melody initially stated by the piano. The ascending second theme, forceful and incisive, follows after a brief bridge passage. A rhythmically vivacious third theme concludes the exposition. The remainder of the movement is devoted to developing the three thematic groups, bringing them back in the recapitulation, and then capping everything off with a spacious, summarizing coda.

String Quartet in E Flat Major, Op. 74, "Harp"

I. Poco Adagio; Allegro.   II. Adagio, ma non troppo.   III. Presto.   IV. Allegretto con variazioni.

Several important events occurred during 1809, while Beethoven was composing his E flat major quartet. Early in the year he was granted an annual stipend from three noblemen. With this financial security, Beethoven proposed marriage to Therese Malfatti, his teenaged pupil—and was devastated by her family's rejection of his suit. The French army attacked Vienna in May, bombarding and laying siege to the city (the account of Beethoven cowering in a cellar during the shelling, pillow clamped over his ears to save his little remaining hearing, dates from this time), followed by an occupation that lasted until October. During the military seizure, Louis de Vienny, a French music lover, called on Beethoven and left this description of the composer's living quarters:

> His lodging, I believe, consisted of only two rooms, the first one having an alcove containing the bed, but small and dark, for which reason he made his toilet in the second room, or salon. Picture to yourself the dirtiest, most disorderly place imaginable—blotches of moisture covered the ceiling; an oldish grand piano, on which the dust disputed the place with various pieces of engraved and manuscript music; under the piano (I do not exaggerate) an unemptied *pot de nuit*; beside it, a small walnut table accustomed to the frequent overturning of the secretary placed upon it; a quantity of pens encrusted with ink, compared wherewith the proverbial tavern pens would shine; then more music. The chairs, mostly cane seated, were covered with plates bearing the remains of last night's supper, and with wearing apparel . . .

No one can say exactly how the personal and political turmoil and the squalor of his surroundings affected the composition of the Op.

74 quartet, but it is known from his letters that Beethoven found it difficult to compose under wartime conditions; the thirty notebook pages devoted to working out the quartet attest to his struggles. Also, the quartet does not push forward into new and unexplored regions, but rather demonstrates a consolidation of previous growth, with some backward glances over well-traveled Classical pathways.

Although widely accepted, the subtitle, "Harp," was not devised by Beethoven but was added later. It is an unfortunate choice of name, since it calls undue attention to some pizzicato accompaniment figures in the first movement that are of minor musical importance, even though they probably shocked listeners in the early 1800s.

The slow introduction to the first movement centers around a four-note motif heard immediately from the first violin and repeated a number of times. Twice Beethoven interrupts the placid flow with a powerful chord before continuing in unruffled tranquility. The top notes of the three sharp chords that open the main body of the movement follow the same general contour as the introductory motif. Two other melodic fragments—a flowing line in the second violin and a cantabile melody in the first—fill out the first group. The transition to the second group includes the first appearance of the pizzicato figure that gives the quartet its nickname and of forceful chords reminiscent of the introduction. The viola introduces the second theme, a long note followed by a flurry of descending and ascending notes, but is soon joined in imitation by all the instruments. A closing theme, with jarring offbeat accents, brings the exposition to a close. After ordinary and rather predictable development and recapitulation sections, the coda is particularly striking with brilliant passage work in the first violin and expansion by the others of pizzicato arpeggios and melodic fragments heard earlier.

The Adagio, a movement of profound spirituality, foreshadows Beethoven's sublime late quartets. The superb, though simple, melodies convey a great richness of emotional content. The movement revolves almost entirely around the tender, almost sentimental main theme initially stated by the first violin, which is heard three times in varied repetitions separated by contrasting episodes—the first repeat in minor, conveying a weighty despondency, the second, loftier and more spiritual.

The concentrated energy and drive of the third movement, really a scherzo, make this the climax of the entire quartet. Still obsessed with the dot-dot-dot-dash rhythm of his Fifth Symphony from one year earlier, Beethoven gives this movement a power and force that is rare in chamber music. Nor is there any relaxation in the following section, introduced by the cello. Beethoven marks it *Più presto* ("faster"), but contradicts himself by giving it the same metronome setting as the opening, in what some say is a parody on academic counterpoint exercises. Both parts are repeated before a third hearing of the opening, hushed in tone, acts as a transition to the last movement, which follows without pause.

The disarming finale, with its simple drooping tune, seems almost anticlimactic after the furious third movement. Its form is a theme and six variations, in which variations 1, 3, and 5 are strong and active, while numbers 2, 4, and 6 are gentle and lyrical. The coda accelerates in tempo, leading to a high-speed, brilliant conclusion based on the melodic line of the third variation.

The "Harp" Quartet received its premiere at the Vienna home of Prince von Lobkowitz in the fall of 1809 and was published the following year.

String Quartet in F Minor, Op. 95, "Serioso"

I. Allegro con brio. II. Allegretto ma non troppo. III. Allegro assai vivace ma serioso. IV. Larghetto; Allegretto agitato.

Beethoven's Op. 95 quartet is the only one he supplied with a subtitle, "Serioso," an obvious reference to the prevailingly somber mood of the piece. The composer's growing deafness, precarious health, frustration in love, financial insecurity, and unhappy family life had combined to make him angry, bitter, and deeply despondent. In a letter to his old friend Dr. Franz Wegeler on May 2, 1810, he wrote, "If I had not read somewhere that no one should quit life voluntarily while he could still do something worthwhile, I would have been dead long ago and certainly by my own hand. Oh, life is so beautiful, but for me it is poisoned forever."

Although extremely short, the "Serioso," which Felix Mendelssohn called Beethoven's most characteristic work, is not a miniature. It is a compressed, concentrated composition, highly integrated movement to movement, with an emotional range that far exceeds its limited size. Usually classified as one of the final works of Beethoven's middle period, many of its pages anticipate the exalted third period quartets that were to follow some fourteen years later.

Beethoven began the quartet late in the summer of 1810, and finished it in October of that year. His dedication to Nikolaus von Zmeskall is significant, because it is the first quartet inscribed to a friend from the middle class rather than a noble patron. The work received its premiere in Vienna in May 1814, played by the Schuppanzigh Quartet.

The first movement, the shortest Beethoven ever wrote, lashes out with an angry, laconic phrase, played in unison by the entire quartet. Two features stand out: the five-note opening turn and the general descending and ascending contour. A suspenseful silence follows, after which the first violin whips up and down in forceful octave jumps. After briefly expanding the opening fragment, the quieter, rolling second theme is introduced by the viola and then picked up by the others. The violins state the tender third theme to complete the very concise, and not repeated, exposition. The short development, which opens in a fury based on the first theme, leads to a truncated recapitulation. The coda reaches a climax as the viola insistently repeats the opening five-note turn until, as though exhausted by the effort, it finally fades away.

Beethoven relates the second movement to the first by starting at the same soft level as the other ended and by giving the introductory cello phrase the same falling-rising shape as the quartet opening, although minus its decorative turns. The first subject then enters, a warm cantabile melody over a sinuous, weaving accompaniment. After a full stop, the viola announces the second theme, which Beethoven treats as a fugato, passing it from part to part in imitation. The fugato section is interrupted for a reminder of the cello opening before continuing with even more complex fugal treatment of the viola melody, including the addition of a countermelody, shortening the gap between entrances and inverting the theme. An abbreviated restatement of the beginning section precedes the coda ending.

The third movement continues without pause, starting with a figure drawn from both the rhythm of the octaves and the sudden, dramatic silences of the first movement. The roughness and strong propulsive energy provide a sharp contrast to the contemplative mood that Beethoven has established. The middle section, resembling at once a solemn chorale and a grim march, is probably the source of the *serioso* in the movement and quartet titles. The lower instruments move along in grave block chords as the first violin weaves a decorative filigree around the measured tread. Beethoven then returns to the opening and finally provides brief glimpses of both parts before concluding the movement.

The finale is related to the third movement by a slow introduction based on that movement's opening rhythmic figure. To continue the chain of interconnections, the introduction's repeated last pair of notes is transformed into the head of the first subject of the ensuing Allegretto agitato. The first part of the theme is restless and anxious; the second part, weak and listless. In contrast, the following subject is blustery and violent, an evocation of a thunderstorm with flashing bolts of lightning. Unremitting restlessness and nervous anxiety pervade the movement until nearly the very end. Then, in an abrupt change of mood, Beethoven speeds up the tempo, changes mode from minor to major, and ends with a gay conclusion that attests to the indomitability of the human spirit, no matter how sorely tried by bad fortune.

Piano Trio in B Flat Major, Op. 97, "Archduke"

I. Allegro moderato. II. Scherzo: Allegro. III. Andante cantabile, ma pero con moto. IV. Allegro moderato.

When Beethoven composed the "Archduke" Trio in March 1811, Napoleon, the most heroic figure of the age, was rapidly approaching his downfall. At the same time the aristocrats of Vienna, who supported Beethoven and for whom he composed most of his music, were losing their wealth and power; the age of heroes and nobles was drawing to an end. They were being replaced by the middle class, the bourgeoisie, who were coming to the fore with their growing wealth and influence.

In view of these revolutionary social changes Beethoven found it difficult to continue his so-called heroic style of composition. Yet he objected to what he called "the frivolous and sensuous spirit of the times" and strenuously sought to resist the mounting current of conservatism. In the "Archduke," his single major composition from this time, Beethoven found an approach that substituted a new *gemüchtlichkeit*, a warm, emotional style with broadly sung, moderately paced melodies and appealing dance rhythms, for the grandiose gestures of the past.

Along with the diminishing affluence of the aristocrats came a corresponding drop in the amount of time they were able to devote to mastering difficult musical instruments and performing the compositions of Beethoven and other composers. Eventually professional musicians from the middle class replaced the aristocratic amateurs, and public concert halls instead of palace salons became the site of most chamber music-making. The "Archduke" was in the first wave of music composed expressly for professional players, to be presented in a public hall for a middle-class audience.

The nickname, "Archduke," came from Beethoven's dedication of the work to Archduke Rudolph, younger brother of Emperor Leopold II, and a longtime student and patron of Beethoven. The work was composed in three weeks, from March 3 to 26, 1811, and the premiere was given at a charity concert held at Vienna's Hotel Zum Romischen Kaiser on April 11, 1814, with Beethoven playing the piano, Ignaz Schuppanzigh, violin, and Joseph Linke, cello. The performance was also notable because, due to his worsening deafness, it was the last time Beethoven played in public. Composer Ludwig Spohr described the performance: "In *forte* passages the poor deaf man pounded on the keys until the strings jangled, and in *piano* he played so softly that whole groups of notes were omitted."

The spacious opening theme of the first movement emerges quiet, warm, and smooth-flowing. It is followed by some subsidiary material that Beethoven introduces in a leisurely fashion before moving on to the second theme, which is staccato in articulation and made up of pairs of descending phrases. Although the thematic material is comparatively simple and straightforward, and the subsequent working out is in traditional sonata form, Beethoven is able to achieve a movement of great nobility of spirit and moving expressivity.

Instead of a conventional slow second movement, the lively and disarmingly naive Scherzo comes next. Bearing an unmistakable resemblance to the Scherzo of Beethoven's String Quartet, Op. 59, No. 1, the movement starts with a rhythmic figure played by the cello alone that bounces along in its light humorous way until the cello introduces the sinuous mysterious chromatic line of the trio. Before too long, though, Beethoven brings in the second theme of the trio, a gay, dancing melody that falls somewhere between a sturdy peasant Ländler and a classical ballet melody. Both sections are repeated, creating an overall form of A (scherzo)-B (trio)-A-B-A-coda.

Beethoven bases the Andante cantabile on a simple but exquisite, hymnlike theme that he states at the beginning and then subjects to five interconnected variations. The variations follow the eighteenth-century model, essentially transforming the original melody by elaborating on the rhythmic patterns while maintaining the fundamental melodic and harmonic features, to create a movement of ineffable beauty.

The last movement, following the lofty Andante cantabile without pause, provides the same rude shock that observers frequently reported after hearing Beethoven improvise at the keyboard. Apparently it was Beethoven's habit, after catching everyone up in the magic of his music, to slam his fist down on the keys and burst into raucous laughter, as though embarrassed by the spiritual experience they had just shared. Likewise, the energetic, dancelike last movement impudently intrudes on the serene, otherworldly atmosphere Beethoven had created in the previous movement. But, once having broken the spell, the movement fairly bubbles along with great wit and humor, to reach a brilliant conclusion.

String Quartets, Opp. 127, 130, 131, 132, 133, and 135, "Late Quartets"

During the period from the completion of the "Archduke" Trio in 1811 until the early 1820s, Beethoven produced few major works. In addition to suffering poor health and, starting in 1816, complete deafness, his unrequited love affairs, a succession of draining experiences as guardian of his nephew Carl, the death or desertion of his patrons, and difficulties with his publishers left him bereft of all personal happiness and financial security.

Yet, despite his obvious distress, Beethoven was able to write his publisher in 1822: "I sit pondering and pondering. I have long known what I want to do, but I can't get it down on paper. I feel I am on the threshold of great things." Soon after there began a period of incredible artistic creation in which Beethoven composed his *Missa Solemnis,* the Ninth Symphony, and the crowning achievement of his life's work—the "Late Quartets," which include the *Grosse Fuge* (Op. 133), a single movement, plus five complete quartets.

The first three were commissioned by Prince Nikolai Galitzin, a Russian nobleman and amateur cellist, who wrote from Saint Petersburg asking Beethoven "to compose one, two, or three quartets, for which labor I will be glad to pay you what you think proper." From May 1824 to November 1826, a scant four months before his

61

death, Beethoven devoted all of his energy and genius to the execution of the three quartets for Galitzin, Opp. 127, 130, and 132, and the two others, Opp. 131 and 135, he wrote without commission.

In these last works Beethoven leaves the realm of personal self-expression and enters the domain of the universal—plumbing the full depth of the human soul and psyche. Within these quartets are moments of joy and wonder, of complete abandon and ecstasy, of shattering pain and anguish, of glowing warmth and tenderness, and of the most sublime emotions that people can experience. Beethoven here moves beyond many of the accepted musical norms, creating new formal structures and organizing principles, vastly increasing the music's length and scope, demanding more from the players than was ever dreamt possible, and subverting everything to the most perfect realization of his musical vision. In a sense, it is music that transcends music, that even transcends human feelings and thoughts, to achieve a spiritual level above all worldly concerns. In Beethoven's words, "He who divines the secret of my music is delivered from the misery that haunts the world."

String Quartet in E Flat Major, Op. 127

I. Maestoso; Allegro.   II. Adagio, ma non troppo e
molto cantabile.   III. Scherzando vivace.   IV. Finale.

In response to Prince Galitzin's commission, Beethoven began composing his Op. 127 quartet in May 1824, completing it in February of the following year. The premiere was given by the Schuppanzigh Quartet in Vienna on March 6, 1825, but because the group had only two weeks to rehearse, it was very poorly played and just as poorly received. Beethoven then invited a quartet led by Joseph Böhm to prepare the music under his guidance. Since he was already completely deaf, he coached them by watching their bow and finger movements. The highly successful performance on March 26 delighted Beethoven and led to a total of nine more performances over the next several weeks.

The short, slow introduction that opens the quartet is broad, strong, heavily accented, and thickly written. It is followed by the faster first group of themes, starting with a lyrical melody that Beethoven marked *teneramente,* or tenderly. Over sharp repeated notes in the second violin and viola, the first violin introduces another, more forceful theme to conclude the first group. The second group returns to the cantabile character of the opening, minimizing the contrast that customarily occurs between the groups of themes in sonata form. The development starts with a return of the introduction, one level louder, and then, back in the faster tempo, the music builds to a powerful emotional climax. Before the development is finished, though, the introduction returns for a third time, louder even than before. Beethoven goes back to the faster tempo once more, which leads to the sneaky start of the recapitulation and proceeds to a coda and soft ending. The result is a stunning movement that follows the law, if not the spirit, of standard sonata form.

The Adagio is a set of five free variations based on two themes of sublime, serene simplicity. Left behind are previous variation movements in which Beethoven maintains the underlying melody, harmony, and rhythm and merely embellishes and elaborates the original theme. In Op. 127, he expresses the loftiest, most profound sentiments through his emotionally complex transformations and transfigurations of the two themes. As Robert Schumann said of this movement, ''One seems to have lingered not fifteen short minutes, but an eternity.''

The Scherzando vivace, with its energy, its *élan vital,* brings the listener down to earth from the exalted spiritual plane to the Adagio. After four pizzicato chords of introduction, the cello states the rhythmically incisive main theme, which is then expanded and developed to enormous proportions. In a whirling, virtuosic middle section, the first violin takes whispered melodic flights over repeated notes in the other instruments. This is followed by a literal repeat of the opening section.

In a curious lapse, Beethoven marks the last movement Finale, but without any tempo indication; the musical content, though, seems to call for a bright, fast tempo. After a brief unison phrase of introduction, the first violin sings out the lighthearted first theme. A second theme, starting with sharp, repeated notes and continuing with heavy accents, follows. After developing and returning the thematic material, Beethoven appends a coda in a strikingly different key, meter, and tempo, creating a completely new tonal aura and rhythmic pattern (although based on the movement's opening theme), which ends the quartet on a strongly positive note.

String Quartet in B Flat Major, Op. 130, "Liebquartett" ("Dear Quartet")

I. Adagio ma non troppo;
Allegro. II. Presto. III. Andante con moto, ma non
troppo. IV. Alla danza tedesca: Allegro
assai. V. Cavatina: Adagio molto
espressivo. VI. Finale: Allegro.

The B flat is the third and last of the quartets Beethoven composed for Prince Galitzin, but it was published second, between Op. 127 and Op. 132. In some ways, Op. 130 is the most appealing of the late quartets. It follows the Classical order of movements, fast, scherzo, slow, and finale, except that Beethoven adds an extra scherzo and slow movement just before the finale. The treatment also makes obeisance to Classical concepts, even though the melodies, harmonies, rhythms, and internal formal structures are handled quite freely.

Beethoven began the composition in March 1825 and was finished eight months later. The subtitle comes from the conversation books Beethoven used for daily communication in face of his total deafness, in which he affectionately referred to Op. 130 as "Liebquartett" ("Dear Quartet"). For some unknown reason Beethoven did not attend the premiere, given in Vienna by the Schuppanzigh Quartet on March 21, 1826, but waited in a nearby tavern. When Karl Holz, second violinist and Beethoven's close companion, rushed over to tell him of the excellent reception, including the audience's insistence on repeats of movements two and four, Beethoven reportedly replied: "Yes, these delicacies! Why not the Fugue [the original finale, which he later replaced]?" Then, after a moment's thought, Beethoven contemptuously exclaimed, "Cattle! Asses!"

Despite the positive reaction, the final movement, an exceedingly long and elaborate fugue, confounded most listeners and invited much criticism from players and audience alike. Beethoven's publisher, Matthias Artaria, and many others felt it should be replaced with a finale more in keeping with the rest of the quartet. Well aware of Beethoven's strong and principled nature, Artaria designed a roundabout way to get him to write a new last movement. Claiming that the public was demanding the fugue as a separate piece, Artaria first offered to pay Beethoven for a transcription for piano for four hands, and then convinced him to compose a substitute last movement—for an additional fee. Although the extra money probably played some part in Beethoven's acquiescence, he most likely would have refused unless he agreed that the fugue was indeed too massive and powerful for the rest of the quartet. The published version of Op. 130, therefore, includes Beethoven's new Finale, while the original, the *Grosse Fuge* ("Great Fugue"), appears separately as Op. 133.

The serene opening Adagio is not a prelude to what follows, but is an integral part of the thematic material; it reappears several times and binds the movement together. The high-spirited Allegro simultaneously flings out two striking phrases—a running sixteenth-note pattern in the first violin, and repeated notes followed by a jump up to a held note in the second. The third motif of the first group, a figure made up of cascading three-note turns introduced in the second Allegro by the first violin, is an outgrowth of the cello melody from the opening Adagio. At one point in this Allegro, the music quiets for two measures of cello alone that lead to the subsidiary theme, which proves to be a transformation of notes 4 through 7 of the introduction. The short, relaxed development includes three brief fragments of the Adagio. The Adagio does not appear again in the recapitulation, but is heard between statements of the opening theme in the coda. In his novel, *Point Counter Point,* Aldous Huxley describes the slow and fast parts of this movement as "majesty alternating with a joke."

The very short, engaging second movement presents the outgoing, jocular side of Beethoven's nature and offers a startling change from the complex first movement. With humor and charm, the simple opening section merely repeats one melodic cell in symmetrical four-measure phrases. The contrasting middle part is similarly built on a single measure that is heard again and again until, suddenly, the four players join in an ominous ascending scale that ends with the first violin slithering down a chromatic scale. Twice more the violin goes sliding down in a devilish bit of fun, before leading a shortened reprise of the opening section.

The third movement projects a contrary air of mingled gaiety and melancholy. After two bars of introduction the viola states the somber principal theme in its darkest, lowest register, against which the other instruments contribute fresh, charming countermelodies and accompaniment figures at the same time. The first contrasting melody is unabashedly sprightly and joyful; it is followed by a shortened, revoiced statement of the opening theme. For the second interlude, the first violin plays a sighing, drooping melody; the second violin's jaunty comments, however, prevent it from getting too sentimental or maudlin. The rest of the movement, essentially a freely varied repeat of what has come before, ends effectively with a loud, exclamatory chord.

Functioning as a second scherzo, the Alla danza tedesca (like a dance in the German style) is innocent and whimsical in mood. It is organized in ternary form. The first part captures the swaying rhythmic robustness of the Ländler, a three-beat German peasant dance. The middle section is also in a rustic dance style, with three repeated staccato notes serving as its most prominent melodic feature. The expanded and elaborated return of the opening includes a particularly intriguing passage near the end in which the melody is fragmented, measure by measure.

The poetic and predominantly soft Cavatina (Italian for "short aria") exemplifies Beethoven's "interior music," spiritual and emotionally intense utterances of the utmost eloquence. His friend, violinist Karl Holz, wrote that Beethoven "composed the Cavatina of the quartet in B flat amid sorrow and tears; never did his music breathe so heartfelt an inspiration, and even the memory of this movement brought tears to his eyes." The passionately sad movement is essentially one continuous outpouring of melody loosely organized into a three-part form. The climax comes just before the return of the opening melodic gesture, in a brief seven-bar passage marked *beklemmt* ("oppressed"), when the first violin whispers its disconnected cries of pain and anguish over pulsing repeated notes in the other instruments.

The Finale, which Beethoven substituted for the original monumental fugue, was written at his brother's house in Gneixendorff, in November 1826, between bouts of serious abdominal illness that were to lead to his death four months later. Delightful and cheery on the surface, the new finale reflects several connections with earlier movements: the opening rhythm derives from the Presto; the subsequent active subject comes from the Allegro theme of the first movement; and the closing rhythm recalls the quartet introduction.

The Schuppanzigh Quartet introduced the new Finale in December 1826 and gave the premiere of the entire reconstituted quartet on April 22, 1827, nearly one month after the composer's death.

String Quartet in C Sharp Minor, Op. 131

I. Adagio, ma non troppo e molto
espressivo.   II. Allegro molto vivace.   III. Allegro
moderato.   IV. Andante, ma non troppo e molto
cantabile.   V. Presto.   VI. Adagio quasi un poco
andante.   VII. Allegro.

Beethoven once confided to friend Karl Holz that, while each of his sixteen quartets was unique, "each in its way," his favorite was the C sharp minor, Op. 131. When Schubert heard the piece, Holz reported that "He fell into such a state of excitement and enthusiasm that we were all frightened for him." Down to our own day many people, musicians as well as listeners, consider it the greatest quartet even written.

Lasting close to forty minutes, the quartet is divided into seven sections that are played without pause, creating a completely organic, well-integrated whole. The burden for projecting this underlying unity rests with the performers, who must maintain the proper relationships of tempo and mood for the work to flow smoothly from beginning to end.

Beethoven began to work on Op. 131 late in 1825, after he had completed the three-quartet commission (Opp. 127, 130, 132) for Prince Galitzin, and presented it to the publisher on July 12 of the next year. Beethoven's flippant note on the score—"Put together from pilferings from this and that"—caused the publisher great concern, and the composer had to assure the publisher that the music was completely original, and his remark was only a joke. In retrospect it now seems that his comment may have referred to the seven separate movements making up a unified work. The quartet was dedicated to Baron Joseph von Stutterheim, Field Marshal, in gratitude for accepting Beethoven's nephew Karl into the baron's regiment. Scholars believe that the first hearing was at a private concert in Vienna in December 1826, but that the initial public performance did not take place until 1835, long after Beethoven's death.

The very slow introductory Adagio, which Richard Wagner said "reveals the most melancholy sentiment in music," is basically a fugue, followed by four episodes and a coda, all based on the sober melody originally stated by the first violin. More than sorrowful or pitying, the music is contemplative and serene, surmounting personal despair and sadness. The section ends with a quiet rising C sharp octave leap, which finds an echo in the ascending D octave leap that opens the second section.

The fast second movement sails forth, cheery and open-faced, with none of the profundity or expressivity of the first movement. Even the thematic material contributes no striking contrasts to create dramatic tension; the same kind of warm, good spirits prevail throughout. Performers traditionally use the two soft isolated chords at the end of the movement to set the tempo for the two loud answering chords that start the Allegro moderato.

The short movement that follows, only eleven measures long, is in effect a recitative, a rhythmically free introduction to the Andante that follows without pause.

The fourth movement is an expansive theme and variations that provides the pivotal central focus of the entire quartet. The syncopated theme, which Wagner called the "incarnation of innocence," is shared by the two violins. Beethoven then puts the melody through a series of six variations in which it is completely shaped and fashioned to reveal fully all of its expressive potential. The two notes heard at the very end determine the speed of the next movement; they are usually made equal to a full measure of the Presto.

The Presto corresponds to the Classical scherzo movement, playful and humorous in spirit. The lightness of character, though, disguises a score that is treacherously difficult for the musicians. It requires great delicacy of touch and split-second reaction times to interweave the four parts and achieve the smooth flow that is necessary. After the abrupt four-note growl by the cello that opens the movement, the first violin picks up the dancelike tune. Passages of smooth legato articulation interrupt statements of the bright, bouncy main theme. Beethoven directs that the final return of the opening tune be played *ponticello* (bowed near the bridge), producing a glassy, whistlelike sound. The whirlwind motion continues until two sets of chords effectively end the movement.

The short, introspective Adagio, only twenty-eight measures long, provides a transition between the gay flight of the preceding Presto and the rhythmic excitement of the finale. Based on a mournful, meditative melody, which is first played by the viola, the Adagio moves directly to the last section.

Two bold, angry unison phrases precede the martial main theme with its dotted (long-short) rhythm, which recalls the last movement of Beethoven's E minor quartet, Op. 59, No. 2. Forcefully, and with great thrust, the melody builds up momentum until a quiet contrasting melody, obviously derived from the melody of the opening fugue, intercedes. The second theme, a long descending line that slows down as it jumps to three high notes at the end, is heard before a shortened development, recapitulation, and full-length coda. In summarizing this movement, Richard Wagner wrote:

> This is the fury of the world's dance—fierce pleasure, agony, ecstasy of love, joy, anger, passion, and suffering; lightning flashes and thunder rolls; and above the tumult the indomitable fiddler whirls us on to the abyss. Amid the clamour he smiles, for to him it is nothing but a mocking fantasy; at the end, the darkness beckons him away, and his task is done.

String Quartet in A Minor, Op. 132

I. Assai sostenuto; Allegro. II. Allegro ma non tanto. III. Heiliger Dankgesang eines Genesenen an die Gottheit, in der lydischen tonart: Molto adagio; Neue Kraft fühlend: Andante. IV. Alla marcia, assai vivace. V. Allegro appassionato.

While working on his Op. 132 quartet during the winter of 1824–1825, Beethoven fell gravely ill with liver disease, bowel inflammation, and other painful and debilitating abdominal maladies. The condition left him seriously weakened, but he was still able to finish the work by July 1825. Although it has the highest opus number of the three quartets (Opp. 127, 130, and 132) that he composed at the behest of Russian nobleman and amateur cellist, Prince Galitzin, it was actually second in order of composition. Study of his sketchbooks shows that he originally planned the quartet in the traditional four movements, but on recovering from his sickness decided to replace the two middle sections with three movements, including the central Heiliger Danksgesang.

The quartet starts with a short, slow introductory motif that bears a similarity to the ones heard at the opening of the quartet Op. 131 and the *Grosse Fuge,* Op. 133. Some think Beethoven used this motif—a slow, rising half-step followed by a large leap—as a way of unifying these three works; others believe that the motifs resemble each other because they were all composed around the same time, and the inadvertent repetition of certain favorite melodic turns is almost inevitable. Emerging from the introductory measures is a brilliant violin flourish that leads to the main theme, played high in its register by the cello. Following some expansion, a new idea, starting with three repeated notes, is heard and quickly passes through the quartet, leading to still another distinctive idea—a flowing melody in the second violin over a nervous, agitated triplet accompaniment. Although one can conceive these themes as the subjects of traditional sonata form, such analysis violates the free spirit in which Beethoven created this amazing movement.

Wistful and nostalgic in tone, the second movement has two motifs that run throughout the entire opening section. The first is a pair of rising three-note figures; the other, and more important, is a long note that drops down with a little flurry of faster notes. After many repetitions of the two melodic cells, Beethoven moves on to the middle section, a sort of *musette,* with the first violin sustaining a bagpipelike drone under its high-pitched melody. The movement ends with a literal repeat of the opening section.

Over the third movement Beethoven inscribed the words, *Heiliger Dankgesang eines Genesenen an die Gottheit, in der lydischen Tonart* ("Holy Song of Thanksgiving to the Divinity by a Convalescent, in the Lydian mode"). The sublime hymn expresses his gratitude for the return of good health; use of the Lydian mode, an ancient ecclesiastical scale (corresponding to the modern F scale, but without a B flat) gives the music a spiritual tone. The music consists of five lines of a slow, solemn chordal hymn, with each line preceded by a faster moving contrapuntal prelude. The vital and vigorous contrasting second section, *Neue Kraft fühlend* ("Feeling of new strength"), evokes a sense of strength through alternating loud and soft measures that surge with a powerful, propulsive force. After varied returns of both sections, the movement ends with a free restatement of the *Heiliger Dankgesang,* marked on the score by Beethoven to be played *Mit innigster Empfindung* ("with the most intimate emotions").

The raucous Alla marcia provides the sudden change in mood, from heavenly to earthy, which Beethoven seems to need, following moments of deeply emotional expression. After a brief aggressive march, the music completely changes character and takes on the style of a recitative, a rhythmically free section, in which the first violin plays an improvisatory speechlike melodic line over a minimal accompaniment in the other parts.

70

The finale follows the recitative without pause. Structurally, it combines rondo and sonata form. The basic songful and lyrical character is modified by an underlying turbulent rocking motion that throws an uneasy cast over the proceedings.

The first private performance of the A minor quartet was before an audience of fourteen persons at the Tavern Zum Wilden Mann in Vienna by the Schuppanzigh Quartet on September 9, 1825. The same players gave the public premiere two months later, on November 6, 1825.

Grosse Fuge ("Great Fugue"), Op. 133

Beethoven composed the *Grosse Fuge* in 1825 as the final movement of his String Quartet, Op. 130 (see page 64). His publisher later asked Beethoven to substitute another last movement, to which he agreed, and the *Grosse Fuge* was issued posthumously, in May 1827, as a separate piece, Op. 133. Performance practices today differ. Most quartets perform Op. 130 with the substitute last movement and play the *Grosse Fuge* independently: a few, though, play the *Grosse Fuge* as Beethoven originally intended.

The intense and often frenzied *Grosse Fuge* baffles many listeners with its giant leaps, clashing dissonances, and overwhelming rhythmic drive. Harold Bauer, who often performed Beethoven's four-hand piano transcription of the *Grosse Fuge,* believed that the work was misinterpreted. "The *Grosse Fuge* is more like a glorified polka-scherzo," he said. "People play it as if it were profoundly mystical which it is not. They put philosophy into it instead of music." Most other interpreters and analysts disagree. They are stirred by its rage and vehemence and are awestruck by its grand proportions and symphonic elements. It is a brilliant paradigm of various fugal techniques, some harking back to the polyphony of Bach, others looking ahead to the advanced musical thinking of Liszt and Wagner.

The brief opening section, marked *Overtura* by Beethoven, resembles the introduction to an opera, but instead of presenting tunes from the opera it sets out four different statements of the main fugal subject. It is first presented in broad, loud, accented tones: the next statement is much faster and rhythmically altered. The tempo then slows for a quiet, smooth, legato statement of the same theme. A final presentation, first violin alone, reveals the melody in note-by-note fragmentation.

The *Overtura* is followed by the *Fuga,* the fugue proper, which starts with the violin flinging out a subsidiary subject, an angular, leaping melody against which the viola pounds out the fragmented main subject. For over 125 measures of the fugue Beethoven does not drop below a relentless *fortissimo* ("very loud") dynamic level, with accents to add even more power to the wild music. Then suddenly the music quiets, the key changes, and another fugal episode, based on the subsidiary theme and the main subject ensues, all *pianissimo* ("very soft"). The third episode, faster in tempo, is based on a rhythmic transformation of the main theme. Varied sections follow, all growing from the same material though reworked and refashioned into an amazing variety of shapes and forms. The coda offers fleeting glimpses of the different subjects in a similar manner to the *Overtura* and then builds to still another climax and an abrupt ending.

String Quartet in F Major, Op. 135

I. Allegretto. II. Vivace. III. Lento assai, cantante e tranquillo. IV. Der schwer gefasste Entschluss: Muss es sein? Es muss sein! Es muss sein! Grave, ma non troppo tratto; Allegro.

Op. 135, the sixteenth and last complete string quartet that Beethoven wrote, represents a sharp departure from the other late quartets. For one thing, the work is quite short, vying with Op. 18, No. 2 as the briefest of them all. One possible explanation of its brevity is supplied by the composer's friend, Karl Holz, who reported that Beethoven, believing that his publisher had not paid him enough for the work, had said: "If [he] sends circumcised ducats he shall have a circumcised quartet. That's why it is so short."

In addition to the modest length of the quartet, the work has less emotional intensity and spirituality than the other late quartets, and a deeper sense of calmness and peaceful resignation. Those who hear in it a serene acceptance of the inevitablity of death refer to a letter Beethoven sent with the quartet to his publisher, Moritz Schlesinger: "Here, my dear friend, is my last quartet. It will be the last; and indeed it has given me much trouble. For I could not bring myself to compose the last movement. But as your letters were reminding me of it, in the end I decided to compose it. And that is the reason why I have written the motto: 'The difficult decision— Must it be?—It must be, it must be!' "

For some listeners, Op. 135 represents a return to middle-class taste, "a touch of Biedermier," the conservative movement in the decorative arts of the early 1800s. Brevity, accessibility, and the use of more traditional compositional techniques were some of the particular qualities that Beethoven associated with music written for the bourgeoisie. The fact that Beethoven dedicated the quartet to Johann Wolfmayer, a cloth merchant, and not an aristocrat, lends some credence to this belief.

And finally, the light and humorous Op. 135 following the profundity of Op. 131 (in order of composition) seems to fit Beethoven's penchant for turning to a more buoyant work after creating music of great depth and personal involvement. The relaxed geniality of Op. 135 probably also provided Beethoven with a much-needed release from the intensity and emotional involvement with the works that preceded it.

Beethoven composed his final quartet during August and September 1826, finishing it on October 30 at his brother's country estate in Gneixendorf, Austria. It was published in September 1827, and the Schuppanzigh Quartet gave the premiere in Vienna on March 23, 1828, almost one year to the day after the composer's death.

The opening movement's warm, conversational tone derives in part from its first subject group of five separate motifs, each with its own inflection and character, and tossed from instrument to instrument as though engaged in informal discourse. An ascending staccato arpeggio and a frolicsome descending run are pitted against each other in the second subject. With supreme confidence and assuredness, Beethoven develops the material he has introduced, brilliantly expanding the various motifs and presenting them in intriguing new guises and combinations, before bringing them back for the recapitulation. A coda based on motifs from the first subject ends the movement.

The swift and scintillating Vivace functions as the scherzo movement; it is propelled forward by its pointed syncopations and cross accents. A rising scale in the viola and cello and a repeated-note accompaniment introduce the contrasting middle section, which continues the breakneck tempo and sends the first violin out into death-defying acrobatic leaps while the others doggedly repeat an *ostinato* measure a full forty-seven times! The movement closes with a shortened reprise of the opening section.

The Lento assai is a sublime example of Beethoven's most inspired "interior music." It was added as an afterthought to the originally conceived three-movement quartet. Over sketches for the simple main melody, in the key of D flat major, which Beethoven associated with the expression of sentiment, he wrote: *Susser Ruhegesang, Friedengesang* ("sweet restful, peaceful song"). Simply and lovingly, Beethoven puts this eight-measure, stepwise-moving melody through four variations played without pause that never rise above a *piano* ("soft") dynamic level to create a section of rich, satisfying beauty and repose.

The final movement, *Der Schwer gefasste Entschluss* ("the difficult resolution"), asks the question *Muss es sein?* ("Must it be?"). The answer is the ringing affirmation, *Es muss sein! Es muss sein!* ("It must be! It must be!"). Although in his letter to Moritz Schlesinger, Beethoven assigns a profound meaning to the exchange, its origins were simple, even humorous. Presumably, Beethoven refused to give Ignaz Dembscher, a government official and friend, a copy of his quartet, Op. 130, because Dembscher had not attended the premiere performance. Wanting to set matters right, Dembscher asked Karl Holz to intervene. Holz suggested that Dembscher send Schuppanzigh, whose quartet gave the first performance, the cost of a subscription, 50 florins. Dembscher asked, *"Muss es sein?"* and Holz replied *"Es muss sein!"* When Holz recounted the story to the composer, Beethoven burst into laughter and immediately sat down to compose a canon on the dialogue. Later Beethoven expanded the musical material of the canon into the quartet's last movement. In slow, solemn tones the two lower strings pose the question, a setting of the words, *Muss es sein?* and in forceful, joyful musical phrases, the two violins deliver the exultant response with which Beethoven may indeed avow his triumph over death.

Alban Berg

Born February 9, 1885, in Vienna
Died December 24, 1935, in Vienna

JUST AS Alban Berg's life bridged the nineteenth and twentieth centuries, so his music combines the fervid expressivity of Post-Romanticism with new, advanced compositional techniques. Although Berg's music is limited to a scant fifteen mature compositions, his ability to integrate the older style with the modern musical concepts in a profound and sensitive way assures him a place among the great composers of our time.

Born into a well-to-do merchant family, young Alban showed a keen interest in music and embarked on the traditional piano lessons at an early age. Despite rather meager musical preparation, he started composing when he was fifteen, producing about eighty songs and a number of piano duets over the next four years. They were intense and unashamedly emotional, showing a strong affinity for such Austro-German composers as Mahler, Wagner, Brahms, and Richard Strauss.

At age nineteen, Berg began six years of study with Arnold Schoenberg, his only composition teacher, and by far the most important musical influence. Schoenberg, a major twentieth-century composer and pioneer in new musical techniques, gave the young Berg a solid grounding in basic compositional skills. He also introduced Berg to atonality, an advanced approach to composing that strove to transcend the traditional concepts of melody and harmony that had pervaded music for about 400 years. In his atonal works, Berg organized the music to minimize any feeling of key or of tonal center.

Somewhat later, Berg adapted another compositional approach, known as the twelve-tone method, which Schoenberg had devised in the early 1920s. Simply stated, it requires that all twelve notes of the chromatic scale be used before any may be repeated. The generating cell for each twelve-tone composition is a tone row in which the twelve notes are arranged in a particular order. The notes of the row may be heard sequentially, as in a melody, or simultaneously, as in a chord. Often it is presented as a combination of both. Twelve-tone music is a logical extension of atonality. By avoiding any repetition of particular tones or chords, the listener loses all sense of key and tonal center.

Although Berg's atonal approach in the early works, and his later use of the twelve-tone system, were of great significance to the composer, they are of less concern to the listeners. Berg often spoke of his *Kunststück,* his "cunning trick," which hides the method of composition, leaving the listener free to focus on the musical content.

According to his pupil, Willi Reich, Berg believed that there was a close connection between his music and the ideas of Sigmund Freud. Although the composer did not accept many of the specific tenets of psychoanalysis, he believed that the function of music is to explore the unconscious part of the mind. In his compositions, he attempted to bring to the surface feelings and thoughts that normally lie buried.

During Berg's lifetime, the Austro-Hungarian Empire and the ruling Hapsburgs entered a period of decline. Their collapse in World War I brought about the destruction of the established political, social, and economic orders. Like other artists of the time, Berg strove to understand the emerging new world order and searched for ways to illuminate the changed reality. It is said that he was guided by the motto of the Vienna Secessionists led by his good friend, painter Gustav Klimt: "To the Age its Art, to Art its Freedom."

While Berg's music is often characterized by sharp dissonance and jagged melody lines, it is suffused with a human warmth and passion that speak with great immediacy to listeners today.

String Quartet, Op. 3

I. Langsam.   II. Mässiger viertel.

Berg's musical talent grew and flourished under the tutelage of Arnold Schoenberg. The String Quartet, his last apprentice work, Berg later wrote, was "received directly from Schoenberg." Most experts, though, also consider the quartet Berg's first mature composition. Written during the spring and early summer of 1910, it exhibits freshness, assurance, and mastery of technique.

The work approaches the boundary between tonality and atonality. Certain devices recall the musical vocabulary of Wagner, Mahler, and other late-nineteenth-century composers, who had already stretched the limits of tonal relationships. But in other respects it looks ahead to the twentieth century's rejection of traditional tonality.

The quartet contains just two movements: the first, introspective and lyrical; the second, intense and agitated. There are the usual two subjects in the first movement. The opening theme includes all twelve notes of the chromatic scale, although it is not treated as a tone row. After a short silence and some portentous sounds, played *ponticello* (on the bridge), by the cello, the tender second subject is introduced by the violin. In the unusually brief development section that follows, Berg is mostly concerned with working out the second theme. A new marchlike figure is introduced in the recapitulation, characterized by a glassy *ponticello* sound. An extended slow coda, based on the march melody and the other material heard before, ends with a reminder of the opening theme.

The second movement is in rondo form, with five repeats of one theme separated by four contrasting episodes. Each appearance of the melody, though, is not an exact restatement, but a free transformation of the original. Toward the end of the movement Berg brings back the first movement's opening subject, effectively unifying the entire quartet.

The String Quartet, Op. 3 was first presented on April 24, 1911, in Vienna by an ad hoc quartet made up of Brunner, Holzer, Buchbinder, and Hasa. It was, however, the performance by the Havemann Quartet at the First International Festival for Chamber Music in Salzburg on August 2, 1923, that attracted wide attention and established Berg's worldwide reputation in musical circles.

Lyric Suite

I. Allegretto giovale. II. Andante
amoros. III. Allegro misterioso. IV. Adagio
appassionato. V. Presto delirando. VI. Largo
desolato.

The Lyric Suite is highly dramatic, deeply introspective, and intensely emotional. Berg's student and friend, Theodor Adorno, aptly described it as a "latent opera." The composer's description of each of

the six movements—jovial, amorous, mysterious, passionate, deliri-
ous, desolate—gives some indication of the shifting emotional range
and character of the work. To heighten the effect, in a process Berg
called "mood intensification," the movements alternate in tempi,
with each fast movement faster than the one before and each slow
movement slower than its predecessor.

In the Lyric Suite, composed sixteen years after the String Quartet, Op. 3, Berg first applies Schoenberg's twelve-tone method of
composition. He uses a tone row, a specific arrangement of the twelve
notes of the chromatic scale, devised by his pupil Fritz Klein, as the
organizing principle for the first and sixth movements and parts of
the third and fifth.

Berg's use of twelve-tone technique in the Lyric Suite has long
been recognized. But the 1977 discovery of a printed score, with many
of Berg's handwritten annotations, by Berg scholar George Perle gave
a completely new interpretation to the work. The score, which Berg
gave to his friend Hanna Fuchs-Robettin, reveals a clandestine love
affair between the couple that lasted the final ten years of Berg's life,
despite the fact that both were married and living with their spouses.

On an opening page Berg wrote, "I have secretly inserted our
initials H.F. and A.B. into the music." In German, H is the note
B, and B is B flat. With one slight change in Klein's tone row—
which is, as Berg said, "not important to the line, but is important
to the character-suffering destiny"—he produces the notes A, B flat,
B, and F in the proper order. Any doubt of the composer's intent is
resolved by the short sentence that Berg also inscribed into the score,
"May it be a small monument to a great love."

The joyful opening movement, "whose almost inconsequential
mood," Berg wrote, "gives no hint of the tragedy to follow," resembles the traditional sonata form. The three abrupt chords that
open the movement include all the notes of the tone row. The row
is then clearly heard as the first violin states the opening subject.
After a short transition, the slightly slower second theme is given out
by the second violin. The rising scales that follow present the concluding theme of the exposition. Then Berg skips the development
and brings the subjects back in altered shape for the recapitulation.

The notation to Hanna Fuchs-Robettin at the start of the tender
second movement reads, "To you and your children I have dedicated
this rondo—a musical form in which the themes (specifically your
theme), closing the charming circle, continually recur." Hanna's
lovely melody, played by the first violin, begins with a descending

figure that is interrupted twice—by a slightly faster rhythmic interlude (Munzo, her son) and a slower, syncopated section (daughter
Dorothea, nicknamed Dodo), who is represented by the viola's repeated Cs, or *dos,* according to Italian *solfeggio,* the singing method
using *do, re, mi,* etc.

Over the third movement, Berg inserted "May 20, 1925," the
date the lovers began their relationship. Berg explained the *misterioso* character and repressed emotion of the section by writing,
"everything was still a mystery—a mystery to us." The agitated outbursts in the middle section, *trio estatico,* relieve the ghostly mur-
merings, but the original character returns, completing the movement's three-part form.

The fourth movement, the climax of the entire work, starts with
a sinuous figure that works its way up through the quartet. The music
builds in intensity to an impassioned peak of excitement. Following
this, where the music quiets, Berg carefully penned these words
widely spaced apart, "and fading — into — the wholly, ethereal,
spiritual, transcendental . . ."

Berg's commentary on the fifth movement, Presto delirando, with
its dark, *Tenebroso* ("gloomy") middle section, is particularly revealing:

> This *presto delirando* can be understood only by one who has the fore-
> boding of the horrors and pains which are to come. Of the horrors of
> the days, with their racing pulses . . . of the painful *tenebroso* of the
> nights, with their darkening decline into what can hardly be called
> sleep—and again the day with its insane, rapid heartbeat. . . . As though
> the heart would rest itself—*di nuovo tenebroso* with its heavy breathing
> that can barely conceal the painful unrest.

The Largo desolato includes the words of Baudelaire's sonnet, "De
Profundis Clamavi," from his *Fleurs du Mal.*

> *I beg your mercy, You, the one I love,*
> *Deep in the dark gulf where my heart now lies.*
> *It is a gloomy world with leaden skies;*
> *Where horror and blasphemy at night fly above.*
>
> *For half a year a cold sun can be seen,*
> *And for the rest there is darkness over all;*
> *It is a land bleaker than the Northern Pole;*

—No animals, nor brooks, nor forests green!
No horror in the wide world can surpass
The vast cruelty of this sun of ice
Of this long night of ancient Chaos;

I envy the dumbest beasts
Who in brutish sleep oblivion can find,
Time creeps as the skeins of time unwind!

Berg's placement of the words on the score reveals that the music is an actual setting of Stefan George's German translation of the poem. Of added interest is the brief quotation by Berg, about half-way through the movement, of the well-known motif from the Prelude to Wagner's *Tristan und Isolde*.

A slow and painstaking worker, Berg took a year, from September 18, 1925, to September 30, 1926, to complete the Lyric Suite. The premiere was given by the Kolisch Quartet in Vienna on January 8, 1927. In its original version, as well as in the composer's arrangement of movements two, three, and four for string orchestra, the Lyric Suite has become one of Berg's most loved and enduring instrumental works.

Alexander Borodin

Born November 12, 1833, in St. Petersburg (now Leningrad)
Died February 27, 1887, in St. Petersburg

ALEXANDER PORFIREVICH BORODIN was the illegitimate son of Prince Luka Seminovich Gedeanov but, according to the custom of the time, was registered as the child of Porfiry Borodin, one of the Prince's serfs. He was raised by his mother, Avdotia Konstantinovna Kleinecke, the wife of an army doctor. By age eight, he already showed the two major talents that were to inform his whole life—music and chemistry. His musical talent was first noticed when he was able to reproduce perfectly on the piano the marches he heard a military band play; as a result, his mother arranged for instruction on the flute and later provided lessons on various other instruments. As for his scientific bent, it took the form of making his own fireworks and performing experiments on the effects of electricity on the body.

Borodin's formal education was in both areas, chemistry *and* music. While his principal occupation was teaching and doing research at the Medico-Surgical Academy in Saint Petersburg, he was not musically inactive. On the contrary, he composed whenever he could, turning out a small number of works that won him great respect and high regard.

Borodin became part of The Five, nickname for *Moguchaya Kuchka,* or "The Mighty Handful," a group that also included composers Mily Balakirev (the only full-time composer), Nikolai Rimsky-Korsakov (also a naval cadet), Modest Mussorgsky (government official), and Cesar Cui (army officer). Inspired by the 1861 decree freeing the serfs, The Five used their music and writings to replace the "old" Russian music and its foreign influences with a new style based on national folksongs, dances, legends, and heroes. The effect of The Five on Borodin's opera *Prince Igor,* his tone poem "In the Steppes of Central Asia," and his three symphonies was very strong.

81

It is far less noticeable in his chamber music, which includes string quartets in A and D major, and a piano quintet in A minor, because it is much more difficult to introduce programmatic elements into chamber music than into orchestral or dramatic works. Nevertheless one can detect the same folk elements and reaction against musical conservatism in Borodin's chamber works as in his other music.

String Quartet No. 2 in D Major

I. **Allegro moderato.** II. **Scherzo:**
Allegro. III. **Notturno: Andante.** IV. **Finale:**
Andante; Vivace.

Always a slow worker because of the demands of his full-time career as a research chemist, Borodin usually took a long time to complete a major composition: *Prince Igor,* eight years, and still left unfinished; First Symphony, five years; and Second Symphony, seven years. Yet Borodin composed his Second String Quartet in just two months, July and August 1881, during a summer holiday at a country estate in Zhitovo, near Moscow. (While some sources suggest that it was not completed until 1885, Serge Dianin's biography of Borodin reproduces the program of the premiere, dated January 26, 1882, in Saint Petersburg.) The quartet's lyrical, almost amorous tone, coupled with the dedication to his wife and the fact that it was composed exactly twenty years after they met, suggest that Borodin presented the composition to her as a special anniversary present.

The cello sings out the first theme of the Allegro moderato, a flowing, songlike line that is immediately taken up by the first violin. After some expansion of this melody, the first violin introduces the equally lyrical second theme in the minor, over a flowing pizzicato accompaniment. The tempo picks up slightly for the descending chromatic concluding theme played by the viola. Without ever disturbing the cantilena character, Borodin develops the various themes and brings them back for a concluding recapitulation and coda.

The light, fleeting Scherzo melody is played by the two violins over a sustained countermelody in the viola. For the second theme, Borodin slows the tempo and gives an inversion of the viola melody to the violins. According to biographer E. M. Brando, Borodin said that this tune "attempted to conjure up an impression of a light-hearted evening spent in one of the suburban pleasure gardens of Saint Petersburg." Instead of the usual trio as the central part of the scherzo, Borodin develops the two themes, and ends with a modified return of the first part.

The tender Notturno is one of the best known movements in the entire string quartet repertoire. In fact, there are seven recorded string orchestra transcriptions of the Notturno, compared to only five string quartet recordings of the entire work! It has also been made into a popular song, "And This is My Beloved" from the Broadway musical *Kismet,* which was all based on melodies borrowed, or rather stolen, from Borodin. Essentially, there is only one theme in this movement, the passionately romantic melody first played by the cello. For contrast there is a fast, nervous rising scale that then descends with repeats of the first two measures of the original theme.

The Finale starts with a slow preview of the two phrases that make up the first theme. The fast body of the movement starts with the cello and viola, respectively, playing the two motifs in the quicker tempo. A more lyrical second theme is presented by the first violin. Following the general outlines of sonata form, Borodin builds this movement up to a brilliant climax.

Johannes Brahms

Born May 7, 1833, in Hamburg
Died April 3, 1897, in Vienna

BRAHMS'S MUSICAL talent was recognized early by his father, a double bass player, and at age ten he gave his first public performance as a pianist. To add to the family income, he started playing piano in the brothels and taverns of Hamburg, while continuing his musical studies. Later, Brahms commented that these early experiences with the ladies of the night (''those who turned me against marriage'') were responsible for his lifelong inability to sustain normal relationships with women.

The year 1853 was a significant one for the twenty-year-old Brahms. While on tour with the Hungarian violinist, Eduard Reményi, the handsome young pianist, with his long fair hair and blue eyes, became acquainted with Joseph Joachim, a leading violinist, who became a close friend and musical confidante. He also met Robert and Clara Schumann. Robert, already established as a composer, was willing to further Brahms's beginning career in composition. In a widely circulated article, Schumann extolled the young Brahms (''Here is one of the elect.'') and recommended him to a publisher.

Brahms's acceptance as one of the leading composers of the time was swift and largely untroubled. His works were performed widely, and he often traveled around the continent (though never to England or America because of his fear of ships) to introduce his new compositions and to appear as pianist or conductor. As his fame grew, however, so did his penchant for making biting, sarcastic remarks. When a quartet player asked Brahms if he approved of a particular tempo, the composer reputedly replied, ''Yes—especially yours.'' After spending several minutes carefully studying a new piece brought to him by a young composer, Brahms asked, ''Tell me, where did

85

you get this splendid music paper?" And, on leaving a party one time, Brahms turned to the guests and said, "If there is anybody here I have not insulted, I apologize."

But, under this sometimes gruff exterior, Brahms had an equally strong bent for kindness and good deeds. He befriended a number of younger composers, including Dvořák and Grieg, and championed their music. In the pockets of his slightly short, usually stained trousers, he carried candies which he distributed to any children he met on the street.

Brahms himself furnished a few clues to the influences that shaped his music. He often said, for example, that the two most important events in his lifetime were the publication of the collected works of Bach, begun in 1850, and the unification of Germany by Bismarck in 1871. We can guess that from his studies of Bach's music he acquired his taste for polyphony; and that from his nationalistic fervor came the frequent use of folk songs and folklike melodies in his compositions.

Further, early in his career as a composer, Brahms adopted the notes F-A-F as his musical motto. One can hear it in his A minor string quartet; it is even more prominent as the first three notes of his third symphony, even though here the note A is lowered to A flat. The three letters also stand for the words *Frei, aber froh* ("Free, but glad").

Commentators have long speculated on the significance of the word "but" in this quotation. Wouldn't *Frei, darum froh* ("Free, therefore glad") be more appropriate? Not if Brahms means the F-A-F to express his conviction that true freedom is the willing subjection of the creative urge to certain fixed rules and limitations, rather than complete indulgence, unfettered by any bonds or constraints. Willing to abide by these strictures, Brahms was able to realize his full potential as a composer. His outlook, it is worth noting, was also held by Goethe, who wrote, "The law can only bring us freedom."

Generally speaking, the outlook conveyed by Brahms's motto is much closer to the esthetic of Haydn, Mozart, and other late eighteenth-century Classical composers, than it is to that of his contemporaries, Wagner, Berlioz, and Liszt, the leading voices of nineteenth-century Romanticism. Yet, in his music Brahms succeeded in reconciling Classicism and Romanticism, these two seemingly irreconcilable musical styles. The use of traditional forms and avoidance of extramusical associations indicate his kinship with the music of the past. At the same time, his soaring melodies, fluid rhythms, and rich harmonies show that he was spiritually and musically in tune with his own era. While subject to the same developments that were shaping the "new music" of the time, Brahms's contribution lay not in pushing forward into new realms, but in exploring and expanding the rich musical and national heritage of the past.

During his lifetime, Brahms was labeled a conservative by some musicians who looked on Wagner as the composer who was doing the most to advance the course of music. Later, there were times when his music fell from favor, as during the construction of Boston's Symphony Hall when some wag suggested that the signs should read, "Exit—in case of Brahms!" But despite the views of his severest critics, Brahms has earned a permanent place among the immortals of music.

Piano Trio in B Major, Op. 8

I. Allegro con brio. II. Scherzo: Allegro molto. III. Adagio. IV. Allegro.

In 1854, at the age of twenty-one, Brahms allowed his first chamber work, the Piano Trio, Op. 8, to be published. Although he had already written dozens of chamber music compositions, none had met his very exacting standards, and all had been consigned to the furnace. Over the years, however, Brahms grew dissatisfied with the trio, and thirty-six years after publication, he decided to alter the work. He wrote one friend that the revision "did not provide it with a wig, but just combed and arranged its hair a little." To Clara Schumann he commented, "I have written my B major trio once more. . . . It will not be so muddled up as it was—but will it be better?"

It is the 1890 version, shorter by one-third than the original, that is widely performed today. The earlier edition, however, is published, and a comparison of the two renderings provides valuable insights into the way a mature composer goes about improving a youthful work.

The main theme of the first movement, which survives intact from the earlier manuscript, is broad and stately. It grows gradually from a quiet statement in the piano, through the addition of the cello, to reach a sonorous, full-voiced peroration by all three instruments. The second subject is likewise introduced by the piano, but soon expands to include the strings and builds to a massive climax. After the development of the thematic material, a concise recapitulation is heard, introduced by the strings playing the first subject in unison.

The light, fleeting Scherzo, virtually unchanged from the 1854 version, scurries along, dramatic outbursts alternating with hushed whisperings, until a waltzlike tune presages the somewhat slower trio. The trio, warm and sentimental at first, becomes increasingly exuberant toward the end. An almost literal repetition of the Scherzo, and a brief coda, conclude the movement.

The Adagio is cast in a simple three-part form, but with an intensely rich texture throughout. The opening melody is a dialogue, with piano statements and string responses. After the piano and strings combine forces, an ardent cello melody appears, one that is eventually carried on by the violin. The first section then returns, somewhat elaborated, to bring the movement to a quiet close.

The cello introduces the first theme of the finale, creating an aura of disquiet and agitation. All the restlessness is dispelled, however, by the four-square (though in triple meter) second theme, given out forcefully by the piano, with off-beats in the cello. Both themes are treated quite freely, leading to the coda, in which the opening theme is strongly affirmed.

The original trio received its premiere in New York on November 27, 1855, played by William Mason, piano, Theodore Thomas, violin, and Carl Bergmann, cello. The revised version was given its first performance, with the composer as pianist, at a concert in Vienna offered by Arnold Rosé on February 22, 1890.

String Sextet in B Flat Major, Op. 18

I. Allegro ma non troppo. II. Andante, ma moderato. III. Scherzo: Allegro molto. IV. Rondo: Poco Allegretto e grazioso.

In September 1857, Brahms accepted a three-month-a-year position at the Court of Detmold, a castle set deep in the Teutoburger forest. His light duties consisted of piano lessons for the Princess, conducting the chorus, and performing at court concerts. The rest of the time was available for composing and for long solitary walks in the woods.

The anguish of the past years—the despair over the death of his dear friend and staunchest advocate Robert Schumann and the unfulfilled love for Clara Schumann—had been left behind, and the young composer was more cheerful than he had ever been. ''Passions are not natural to mankind,'' he wrote to Clara from Detmold. ''They are always exceptions or excrescences. The ideal, genuine man is calm in joy and calm in pain and sorrow.''

In the relaxed, pastoral setting of Detmold, suffused with a new-found contentment, Brahms began his sextet for two violins, two violas, and two cellos. Sunny and pleasant in outlook, with an almost naive directness of expression, it hearkens back to the music of Mozart and Beethoven.

There are three distinctive melodies in the opening group: the first, a warm, rich line sung by the first cello; the second, a fleeting, descending figure in the first violin; and the third, a languorous waltz given out by the entire ensemble. The first cello is also entrusted with the principal theme of the second group, a more energetic statement that reaches higher and higher in pitch. The concluding theme of the exposition is played by the two violins and the first viola. The subjects are then fully developed before being brought back for a recapitulation and brief coda.

In the following slow theme-and-variations movement, the first viola states the straightforward, rugged Hungarian Gypsy melody at the outset, with the first violin echoing each statement one octave higher. During the first three variations Brahms gives the impression of increasing speed by using figurations of, respectively, four, six, and eight notes to a beat, even though the underlying tempo remains the same. The quickening subdivisions of the beat are interrupted by the hymnlike Variation IV in the major mode. A very charming imitation of a mechanical music box serves as Variation V. The first cello's soulful recollection of the original theme in Variation VI gently ends the movement.

Bright and bouncy, the Scherzo sets all toes tapping at first, until false accents begin to throw the rhythm off. The middle Trio section fairly gallops along, loudly and at a breakneck pace, before the Scherzo proper is repeated and a lively coda wraps it all up.

The opening of the finale, with its charming melody and delicate accompaniment, could easily have been written by Mozart nearly a century earlier. A more dramatic second theme played by the violins and violas adds a bit of spice to the musical discourse. Falling between rondo and sonata form, the movement gracefully unfolds until the accelerating coda brings the proceedings to a rousing conclusion.

As was his wont, Brahms continued to work on the sextet after he left Detmold, spending the period from March to September 1860 completing the composition. The sextet received its first performance

October 20, 1860, in Hanover, played by the augmented Joachim Quartet.

Piano Quartet in G Minor, Op. 25

I. Allegro. II. Intermezzo: Allegro ma non troppo. III. Andante con moto. IV. Rondo alla Zingarese: Presto.

Of the three Brahms quartets for piano and strings, the energetic G minor is probably the most popular of all. Begun in 1856 or 1857, it received its first run-through performance in 1861 with Clara Schumann as pianist; the official premiere was in Vienna on November 16, 1862, played by Brahms and members of the Hellmesberger Quartet. It marked Brahms's first appearance in Vienna, and the great enthusiasm aroused at the concert led Joseph Hellmesberger, leader of the quartet, to hail him with the ringing words: "This is Beethoven's heir!" The Viennese public, too, quickly accepted the handsome young Brahms as one of the outstanding composers of the time.

The bold and expansive first movement overflows with musical inventiveness. The principal subject is divided into two contrasting parts: the first, a serene and poised melodic line; the second growing from a repeated, descending melodic step that comes after a brief silence. While the three string instruments sing out a repetition of the first motif, the piano tosses off a rapid four-note figure that appears to lead to the second theme played by the cello. Actually, it is just an anticipation of the real second theme, which is soon played in all its glory by the violin and viola in unison. After an agitated, intense closing theme and a brief development that mingles the two parts of the first theme, Brahms starts the recapitulation, which includes some further expansion of the opening motif and the four-note rhythmic figure.

Brahms first called the gentle, wistful second movement Scherzo, but changed the title to Intermezzo, probably because it bore so little resemblance to the fast, rough scherzos of Haydn and Beethoven. A particularly attractive veiled tone color pervades the movement, produced in part by having the violin playing with a mute to muffle the sound. The opening section is followed by a slightly faster trio in which Brahms achieves a certain piquancy by his use of cross rhythms. He then returns the opening part, capping everything off with a short, fast coda based on the trio.

The third movement is dominated by a melody that is, at once, broadly expressive *and* bold. In the midst of this highly romantic outpouring, Brahms draws us up short with a sharp contrast—a marchlike interlude that sounds like nothing so much as a parade of toy soldiers. The viola and cello, however, soon set things right with a transition back to the initial melody for a varied reprise of the opening.

Despite the beauty and charm of the preceding movements, it is the boisterous Rondo alla Zingarese (Rondo in Gypsy Style) that captivates most audiences. This movement clearly shows the folk music element—albeit not German—that was so important in Brahms's music. The first of four distinct themes bursts forth at the opening of the movement. The second theme borrows the last two notes of the principal theme and uses them as the springboard for a series of ferocious scales. After a reminder of the opening theme, a lightly scampering piano melody appears, accompanied pizzicato by the strings. Again the opening theme returns, followed now by the final theme with its stentorian start and soulful conclusion. The various tunes are called back; there are some cadenzalike passages for the piano; and the movement ends with a brilliant *molto presto* glimpse of the principal theme.

Piano Quartet in A Major, Op. 26

I. Allegro non troppo. II. Poco Adagio. III. Scherzo: Poco Allegro. IV. Finale: Allegro.

Brahms began composing his Piano Quartet in A major in Detmold in 1857, just after he had started his G minor piano quartet. The simultaneous creation of these two compositions illustrates Brahms's penchant for creating pairs of works in the same genre. His first two symphonies, first two string quartets, the two clarinet sonatas, and the *Academic Festival* and *Tragic* overtures are other examples of this striking synchronism. Often, as in the piano quartets, the two works are complementary rather than similar; they are in the same form, but different in scope and character.

Both piano quartets were completed in the fall of 1861. Brahms dedicated the A major quartet to Frau Dr. Rösing, at whose home in Hamm, a suburb of Hamburg, he boarded while completing the piece. The first performance was given in Vienna on November 29, 1862, just thirteen days after the successful premiere of the first quartet. The performers were members of the Hellmesberger Quartet, with Brahms at the piano. The following day Brahms wrote to his parents: "I had much joy yesterday. My concert came off very well. The quartet was well reviewed, and I had extraordinary success as a pianist."

The opening theme is simple, staid, and perfectly symmetrical, made up of four measures of detached notes followed by an equal number of measures of smoothly connected notes. There is a tension in the line, though, that comes from the silence on the expected accented beat in the first four measures and the interplay of two and three notes to a beat throughout. The second theme adds to the rhythmic conflict, as the soaring piano melody pits pairs of notes against triplets in the strings. The development swells with intensity and emotion before the piano serenely begins the recapitulation. The concluding coda treats the opening melody as a canon, with the strings imitating the piano melody one beat later.

The hauntingly beautiful second movement is suffused with a wealth of melodic material and musical detail. The principal sustained melody, heard in the piano, is lovingly embellished and colored by the muted strings with their weaving patterns of notes that are actually drawn from the piano line. Perhaps the most striking part of the movement is heard at the end of the first theme and again later, as the piano ripples up and down an arpeggio, at first answered quietly by the cello, then more strongly by the cello and viola, and finally with forceful intensity by all three strings. In 1889, Brahms contemplated shortening this movement but decided against it, because the work was already so firmly established in the chamber music repertoire.

The subdued Scherzo has little of the boisterous good humor usually associated with this form. The opening section has two ideas—the first, a flowing melody played in unison by the three strings; the second, a lilting little tune introduced by the piano. The trio starts with a brash canon in which the strings trail the piano's lead by one measure. This is contrasted with a lyrical second melody, which is also treated polyphonically. After the trio, there is a literal repeat of the Scherzo.

The folk-dance vigor of the Finale is immediately established by the syncopation of the principal subject. Contrasting sections have the effect of putting the brake on the headlong flight, but the propulsive energy of the four instruments triumphs as the movement races to its climactic conclusion.

Piano Quintet in F Minor, Op. 34

**I. Allegro non troppo.   II. Andante, un poco
Adagio.   III. Scherzo: Allegro.   IV. Finale: Poco
sostenuto.**

One evening Brahms was asked how he had spent the day. "I was working on my symphony," the composer replied. "In the morning I added an eighth note. In the afternoon I took it out."

Spurious as this anecdote may be, it does furnish some insight into the slow, careful way Brahms fashioned his music and the difficulty he had in bringing certain works up to his incredibly high standards. The piano quintet is a particularly good illustration of a composition that underwent several major revisions before publication.

The original version was a string quintet for two violins, viola, and two cellos, which Brahms composed in 1862. Joseph Joachim, the composer's close friend and trusted musical advisor, liked the piece at first, but after rehearsing it, told Brahms that he thought it lacked charm and that the composer should "mitigate the harshness of some passages." A slightly altered work was played at another rehearsal, but it too proved unsatisfactory.

The following year, Brahms entirely transformed the piece into a sonata for two pianos, which he performed with Karl Tausig in Vienna early in 1864. (Although Brahms burned the original cello quintet version, he preserved the two-piano realization, which is published as Op. 34b.) Critics gave it a generally poor reception saying it lacked the necessary warmth and beauty that only string instruments could provide.

Finally, during the summer of 1864, Brahms reworked the same musical material once more, this time shaping it into its final piano quintet form. Brahms, at long last, was satisfied. He allowed it to be published in 1865. It is now considered the composer's most epic piece of chamber music.

The massive and complex first movement is replete with a superabundance of melodic strains and rhythms. Yet, despite this rich diversity, Brahms achieves a musical synthesis through the use of various unifying techniques that are skillfully woven into the music. To take but one example, the movement opens with piano, first violin, and cello singing the noble, sonorous first theme. After a pause, the piano begins a passage of running notes that seems unrelated to the opening statement. Careful listening, though, reveals that the passage is nothing more than a free, speeded-up transposition of the melody we have just heard! Brahms's delight in counterpoising twos against threes is evident in the subdued second subject, with its *ostinato* triplets underpinning the equal pairs of notes in the melody. A closing theme that contrasts sustained, legato measures with staccato, rhythmic measures leads to a comparatively brief development, a recapitulation, and a coda that starts slowly and quietly but builds to a brilliant climax.

The slow movement is serene, tender, and simple—especially in comparison with the majestic sweep of what has come before. The opening subject, a warm, gently swaying melody, is played by the piano to a restrained, rhythmical string accompaniment. The intensity increases as the second violin and viola, in unison, introduce the subsidiary subject. Calm returns as the main theme returns to close the movement.

The Scherzo has great rhythmic verve and a plenitude of melodic material. There are three basic musical ideas: an eerie, slightly offbeat melody over an insistent cello pizzicato; a crisply rhythmic figure in the strings; and an exultant, full-voiced exclamatory statement from all five players. After expanding and developing these themes, the music builds powerfully to a sudden cut-off, which is followed by the contrasting cantabile melody of the Trio. Brahms then directs the players to repeat the Scherzo section.

The Finale opens with a slow introduction that casts a mood of dark foreboding. In a while the shadows disperse as the cello saunters forth with a fast, jolly tune. After a dramatic outburst, a second melody appears, slightly faster in tempo, but drooping with feigned sorrow. A vigorous, syncopated theme brings the exposition to an end. The freely realized development and recapitulation lead to the coda, a summing up of the entire movement in an unrestrained whirlwind of orchestral sonority.

The first public performance of the quintet was given in Paris on March 24, 1868, by pianist Louise Langhans-Japha and four unidentified string players.

String Sextet in G Major, Op. 36, "Agathe"

I. Allegro non troppo. II. Scherzo: Allegro non troppo. III. Poco Adagio. IV. Poco Allegro.

Brahms met and fell in love with Agathe von Seibold in 1858 and one year later exchanged rings with her. When a friend told him that they were becoming a subject of gossip and that for the sake of propriety he should propose marriage, Brahms wrote Agathe: "I love you! I must see you again, but I cannot wear fetters! Write me whether I may come back to fold you in my arms, to kiss you, to tell you that I love you!" Agathe refused to see Brahms, and thus their relationship ended.

Although Brahms fell in love many times over the following years, he continued to suffer feelings of guilt over his handling of this early love affair. "I have played the scoundrel toward Agathe," he said. And he chose his second string sextet as the means to clear his conscience. Even though his initial work on the sextet antedated his involvement with Agathe (he quoted the third movement theme in a February 1855 letter), by the time he finished the piece during the summer of 1864, he had woven her name into the music. By leaving out the T, which is not a musical note, he made A-G-A-H (the note B in German) -E part of the second theme of the first movement. As he explained in a letter to his friend Joseph Gänsbacher, "Here I have freed myself from my last love."

Although the sextet tends to be romantic and highly expressive, it displays a certain air of restraint, and the emotional content is somewhat veiled. Over a wavering two-note accompaniment figure played by the first viola, the first violin sings the soaring, widely spaced notes of the opening theme. After some further episodes and transitional material, the first cello emerges with the warmly expressive second theme. The music gains in intensity, and at the climax the first violin and first viola forcefully give out the five-note "Agathe" motto, repeated three times. Throughout the following development section the wavering runs almost without stop as Brahms varies, transforms, and juxtaposes the various motives already heard, including an inversion of the ascending opening theme that leaps downward. The themes are then returned, and Brahms adds a reflective coda to conclude the movement.

A wistful, slightly mysterious character pervades the Scherzo. The upper instruments play the deliberate melody over a pizzicato figure in the lower strings. The mood changes as the first violin and first viola start a whispered triplet passage, but it proves not to be a complete departure as Brahms uses the continuing triplets in the first cello to accompany the original melody, which is now inverted and syncopated. In the middle of the movement the tempo picks up for a heavily accented, rough-hewn peasant dance. When the energy is spent, a shortened version of the opening Scherzo comes back.

Eduard Hanslick, a contemporary critic, described the third

movement as "variations on no theme." It is indeed a set of five variations, in which the original melody undergoes wide-ranging changes and transformations. But the theme itself, which bears some resemblance to the up-reaching opening theme of the sextet, does not have a distinctive enough musical profile to make it particularly memorable as the basis for the imaginative variations. Perhaps most striking are the third and fourth variations, in which fragments of melody are energetically tossed back and forth from instrument to instrument.

The first theme of the last movement is divided into two contrasting parts, a nervous chattering followed by a broadly sung melody. The skittering opening returns to introduce the second subject, an undulating line played by the first cello. After some fugal development of the fast tune the two spacious melodies are brought back, minus their lively introductions. A brilliant coda brings the sextet to a hearty, full-voiced conclusion.

Horn Trio in E Flat Major, Op. 40

I. Andante. II. Scherzo: Allegro. III. Adagio mesto. IV. Finale: Allegro con brio.

Brahms began the composition of his horn trio in the spring of 1865, just months after the death of his mother. Several of Brahms's biographers, including Max Kalbeck and Richard Specht, hear evidence in the music of this tragic event's effect on the composer. They cite Brahms's choice of the French horn, rather than the more traditional cello, as a sentimental remembrance of his studies on that instrument as a child in Hamburg. The melancholy Adagio mesto they interpret as an elegy to his recently departed mother, particularly a theme heard in that movement and again in the Finale that is derived from the German folk song "In der Weiden steht ein Haus" ("In the Meadow Stands a House"), another reference to his childhood.

The richly romantic trio has a noble simplicity that is dictated, at least in part, by the character of the French horn, with its somewhat limited facility. Despite the fact that the more fluent valve horn was already in widespread use, Brahms specified the older *waldhorn*, or natural horn, probably because of its clearer tone. Today's performers, though, almost always play on the modern valve horn.

The first movement is cast in an unique form, not found in any other work by Brahms. There are two themes: the first, graceful and flowing; the second, slightly faster and more restless. Instead of developing these themes, as in traditional first movements, though, Brahms merely alternates them—first, second, first, second, first, ending with a coda that includes some striking plaintive sighs in the French horn.

The Scherzo rings with echoes of ancient hunting horn calls. With its defiant melody rapped out, now softly, now more loudly, the Scherzo speeds along with bracing vigor and great rhythmic energy. The trio section, a slower, broadly sung folklike melody, functions as a contrast before the repeat of the Scherzo.

The brooding, introspective slow movement starts with an introductory phrase in the piano before the violin and horn enter with the first theme proper. The unaccompanied horn announces a new strain, which is treated canonically, with the other instruments imitating the melodic line. In a clever bit of musical magic, Brahms gives the violin the last statement of the second theme, while the piano starts the return of the first theme. During this return, the horn slips in a new melody, the old German folk song. But it is soon interrupted by the opening theme, at this time sonorous and resplendent in the major mode.

The folk melody that Brahms just introduced now bursts forth as the opening of the Finale. Much faster in tempo, considerably changed in rhythm, and completely different in articulation, it becomes the principal theme of the Finale. Full of exultant joy, the movement speeds along to a climactic conclusion.

Brahms himself played the premiere of the trio at Karlsruhe, Germany, on December 5, 1865, with two musicians identified only as Strauss (violin) and Segisser (horn).

String Quartet in C Minor, Op. 51, No. 1

**I. Allegro. II. Romanze: Poco
Adagio. III. Allegretto molto moderato e
comodo. IV. Allegro.**

To the listening public of the day, Brahms was the musical heir of Beethoven—a burden he did not bear easily. "You do not know what it is like," Brahms wrote, "hearing his [Beethoven's] footsteps constantly behind me." It is, therefore, not surprising that the two forms in which Beethoven produced such enduring masterworks, the string quartet and the symphony, were precisely those in which Brahms felt the greatest pressure to measure up to his model. Consequently, he wrote and destroyed some twenty string quartets and then spent about two decades revising and polishing his first quartet before he allowed it to be published in 1873, when he was 40. His first symphony appeared only after an equally long period of gestation.

Brahms began work on his C minor quartet in the early 1850s. Several times over the following years, he asked various musicians to read through the work. Following each rehearsal, however, he withdrew the music. It was not until the summer of 1873, which he spent at Tutzing on Starnberg Lake, that the quartet finally measured up to his expectations. In September he submitted it for publication, and on December 11, 1873, the Hellmesberger Quartet gave the premiere performance in Vienna.

The quartet opens with an heroic ascending theme. After two sustained notes in the viola, the first violin presents a languid descending counterpart to the vigor of the previous phrase. The second theme proper, played by the two violins, enters over a rapid leaping figure in the viola. The poised concluding theme is given to the first violin, over a rhythmically complex texture. All of the thematic material is worked over in the brief development section and then recapitulated, leading to an exciting, agitated coda.

Intimate and pensive, the second movement has been described as a song without words, a favorite romantic nineteenth-century character piece. It is ternary in form: the gently expressive opening section; a wistful contrast; and the return of the opening melody, ending with a coda that includes both themes, although in reverse order.

The third movement, really a charmingly simple intermezzo, is removed in mood from the somewhat severe and reserved character of the rest of the quartet. The delightful melody of connected pairs of notes is played by the first violin, while the viola strives for attention with its attractive countermelody. Various episodes follow, until the tempo picks up for a contrasting middle section. To accompany the graceful, naive melody, the second violin employs an effect known as *bariolage,* in which the same note is played on two different strings, producing a tonal effect not unlike a jazz trumpet player using a wah-wah mute. The movement ends with an exact repeat of the opening section.

Spiritually akin to the first movement, the finale starts with a terse, forceful motto theme derived from the opening of the first movement. An excited, passionate melody ensues but with no diminution of energy or drive. The second violin introduces the more relaxed subsidiary subject. There is barely any development before Brahms brings back all three themes to end the movement, and the quartet, with an extended coda.

String Quartet in A Minor, Op. 51, No. 2

I. Allegro non troppo. II. Andante moderato. III. Quasi Minuetto, moderato. IV. Finale: Allegro non assai.

The Brahms second string quartet has a history similar to that of his first essay in this form. Begun in the 1850s, it was subjected to countless revisions over the following decades before he finally submitted it for publication in 1873. It was given its premiere in Berlin by the Joachim Quartet on October 18, 1873, some two months before the C minor.

If it can be said that the first quartet was written under the specter of Beethoven, the spirit that informs the second belongs to Bach. The music abounds in polyphonic devices that were favored by the older composer. Brahms made particular use of canons, in which one instrument imitates a line first played by another, starting a little after the first. (A round, such as ''Frère Jacques,'' is an example of a canon.) Although polyphony requires a keen intellectual grasp, Brahms, like his forebear, puts the craft to expressive purpose, successfully concealing the technical concerns behind the musical effect.

The quartet also pays homage to Brahms's good friend, Joseph Joachim, the outstanding violinist, composer, and organizer of the Joachim Quartet. Joachim's personal motto was the notes F-A-E, standing for *Frei, aber einsam* (''Free, but lonely''). Brahms made these notes the second, third, and fourth notes of the first movement's main theme. Inspired by Joachim, Brahms chose as his motto, F-A-F, *Frei, aber froh* (''Free, but glad''), and also wove these notes into the musical texture. Brahms probably would have dedicated the two Op. 51 quartets to Joachim, but a petty dispute at the time of publication led him to inscribe them instead to Dr. Theodor Billroth, a well-known physician and avid chamber music player.

The quartet opens with the gracefully arching F-A-E theme, followed by a three-note upbeat, which also appears later in the theme of the last movement. The development section is an outstanding demonstration of polyphonic writing, replete with canons, inversions, and retrograde motion, in which the melody is, respectively, imitated, turned upside down and played backward. At the start of the recapitulation, the viola plays the Brahms three-note F-A-F motto; just before the coda, the second violin plays F-A-F overlapped with Joachim's F-A-E.

Over a sinuous, implacable line in the viola and cello, the first violin sings the warmly lyrical theme of the second movement. As this melody is extended, the first violin and cello, in canon, interrupt with an outburst that is almost operatic in character. When the first violin comes back with the opening melody, however, it is a false return in the wrong key. Finally, the cello sets things right by bringing the melody back in the expected key of A major.

The Quasi Minuetto is marked by a charmingly archaic quality. Two sparkling interludes, though, come along to disturb the calm flow. Following each of the interludes are passages that display the telling effect of Brahms's canonic skills. In an amazing double canon, the first violin and viola play a slowed-down augmentation of the interlude theme in imitation, while the second violin and cello have a variant of the minuetto theme, also in imitation.

The Finale sparkles with the musical and rhythmic energy of a *czardas,* a fast, wild Hungarian dance. Alternating with the varied statements of the *czardas* tune is a relaxed, waltzlike melodic strain. The coda starts with the cello and first violin giving out the opening melody slowly and quietly in canon; then the entire quartet plays it even more softly, with notes of longer duration. Eventually, the four instruments pick up speed and volume, bringing the music to a brilliant conclusion.

Piano Quartet in C Minor, Op. 60, "Werther"

**I. Allegro non troppo. II. Scherzo:
Allegro. III. Andante. IV. Finale: Allegro comodo.**

Brahms first worked on the C minor piano quartet from 1854 to 1856, a period of great strain and anxiety for the young composer. With his benefactor and dear friend Robert Schumann suffering with severe mental illness, Brahms found himself torn between fidelity to Robert and deep affection for Clara, Schumann's wife. When Robert was hospitalized, Brahms rushed to Düsseldorf to help Clara and her seven children through those difficult days. During that period Brahms wrote to her, "Would to God that I were allowed this day . . . to repeat to you with my own lips that I am dying for love of you." He remained with her only until Schumann died in July 1856.

Many of the complex and turbulent emotions Brahms was suffering seem to have flowed into the piano quartet. When Brahms played through the piece, though, he was not pleased and set it aside for further work. Seventeen years later, in 1873, Brahms finally returned to the quartet. He transposed the key to C minor, from the original C sharp minor, thus making the parts easier for the string players. Of the original work, he kept the third movement intact, revised the first, and composed entirely new second and fourth movements.

The recast version was completed during a summer holiday near Heidelberg in 1875, some twenty years after its original conception, but the feeling tone remained the same. "You may place a picture on the title page," he wrote to the publisher when submitting the manuscript, "namely a head—with a pistol in front of it. This will give you some idea of the music. I shall send you a photograph of myself for the purpose. Blue coat, yellow breeches, and top-boots would do well, as you seem to like color printing." Because the description fits Werther, the morbidly sentimental hero of Goethe's novel *The Sorrows of Werther,* who kills himself for the unrequited love of his friend's wife, the quartet acquired the subtitle, "Werther."

The tragic character of the C minor piano quartet is most strongly felt in the first movement. The opening subject grows from a descending minor second, a musical sigh of pain. The gloom is relieved somewhat by the lyrical second theme in the major mode, but its descending melodic line casts a slight pall. Brahms immediately varies this theme before developing both themes and bringing them back for the recapitulation.

The theme of the nervous and intense Scherzo is heard in the piano; occasional misplaced accents trip up the forward-rushing notes. After a brief pause, the strings state the second theme, which starts sedately enough, but immediately develops a sort of musical twitch. A calmer interlude in major serves as the contrasting trio before the return of the Scherzo proper.

The emotional center of the entire quartet, and the putative favorite of Brahms, is the Andante. To many listeners, it is a lovely, deeply sentimental love song. Biographer Richard Specht considers the opening cello melody to be Brahms's reluctant farewell to Clara, a pained acknowledgment of their doomed relationship. The tender syncopated second theme adds a beguiling beauty to this exquisite movement.

The essential texture of the Finale is fabricated from the strings spinning out expansive, cantabile melodies, while the piano skitters along in a rushing, perpetual motion of rapid figurations. Charm and warmth prevail, but never without a tinge of sadness. Of especial interest are the two choralelike sections that seem to recall a religious hymn.

Brahms and members of the Hellmesberger Quartet gave the first performance in Vienna on November 18, 1875.

String Quartet in B Flat Major, Op. 67

I. Vivace. II. Andante. III. Agitato (Allegretto non troppo). IV. Poco Allegretto con Variazioni.

Brahms did most of the work on his third and last string quartet at Ziegelhausen near Heidelberg, during the summer of 1875, a particularly pleasant, relaxed time for the composer. "My rooms and my daily life are most agreeable," he wrote. "In short, life is only too gay." To some extent, though, his work on the quartet was a surcease from the strain of working on his monumental first symphony, which he was composing at the same time. In a letter he once described Op. 67 and some smaller pieces from that time as "useless trifles, to avoid facing the serious countenance of a symphony." About fifteen years later, however, he viewed Op. 67 in a different light, confiding that it was the favorite of his three quartets.

Perhaps Brahms favored this quartet over the others because it is the most joyous and lighthearted and is filled with many delightful details. Take the cheerful hunting horn call that opens the first movement. By tossing in accents on the "wrong" notes, that is, on the third and sixth notes of the six-note groups, Brahms gives it a wonderfully piquant, jesting touch. Then, a few measures later, when the horn call is heard again, the violins fixate on the third and sixth notes before launching the rapid descending scales that introduce the second theme, which maintains the same frivolous mood with its own misplaced accents. A hushed transitional passage (which becomes important in the last movement) leads to the concluding theme, a rollicking, rhythmic melody firmly in 2/4 meter (two eight notes to a beat) that playfully competes with the already established 6/8 meter (three eight notes to the same beat). Brahms savors the uncomfortable fit between the two meters by juxtaposing one on top of the other. The rest of the movement works out this material to wonderfully gladsome effect.

The second movement is a bit more serious. After a brief introduction, the first violin states the serene, reverential theme. An angry
interruption breaks the mood, but the rage soon subsides, leading
back to the opening melody, more richly accompanied now than in
its original form.

Despite the designation, Agitato (''agitated''), Brahms refers to
the third movement as ''the tenderest and most impassioned movement I have ever written.'' Although somewhat elusive in character,
there is no mistaking the extraordinary tonal effects he achieves as
the muted violins and cello are pitted against the viola playing without a mute. The middle section brings forth a melody in the three
muted instruments that sounds like a new subject. Soon, though,
the viola enters with a variant of the first melody, showing that the
music has not strayed far from its roots. A literal repeat of the first
part and a brief coda close out the movement.

Some critics consider the finale the musical focus of the quartet.
It is cast as a theme and eight variations. The theme itself has a simple, naive beauty. In the first two variations the viola, seemingly eager to maintain its newfound prominence, elaborates on the basic
melody. The first violin reasserts its hegemony in the following two
variations. Variation V finds the two-note groupings of the melody
played off against a persistent three-note figuration in the cello, and
in the sixth variation the leading line is shared by the cello and viola,
which are played pizzicato (''plucked'') to the bowed syncopated accompaniment of the others. The big surprise comes in the seventh
variation, when the horn call that opened the quartet returns. It is
all the more amazing to realize that the first, third, and sixth notes
of the horn figure make up the outline of the original last movement
theme! Variation VIII, then, is based on the transition passage from
the first movement. And the coda combines the themes from the
two outside movements for a brilliant ending.

The Joachim Quartet gave the first performance in Berlin on June
4, 1876.

Piano Trio in C Major, Op. 87

I. Allegro. II. Andante con moto. III. Scherzo:
Presto. IV. Finale: Allegro giocoso.

The C major, the second of Brahms' three trios for piano, violin, and
cello, was begun in 1880; he completed the first movement in March

of that year and the remainder a little over two years later. A run-through performance was held at a private home on August 29, 1882, with Ignaz Brull, a friend as well as a composer and pianist, at the piano. Despite the stern visage shown in most of his photographs, Brahms was not above playing practical jokes. He had his fun on this occasion by introducing Brull as the composer of the trio! The official premiere came on December 29, 1882, when Brahms and two leading musicians of Frankfurt—Heermann, violin, and Müller, cello—performed it in that city.

The C major trio finds the forty-nine-year-old composer at the peak of his creative power. The music explores a wide emotional range—from surging passions to ghostly whispers, from stirring pronunciamentos to tender sentiments. The instrumental writing is idiomatic throughout, with Brahms quite often doubling the two string instruments to match the tonal weight of the piano. Brahms bestows an abundance of melodic material on each movement, which he then proceeds to expand, vary, and transform.

The two strings, playing in unison, state the stirring principal theme. Throughout this movement this tune remains the exclusive domain of the violin and cello. Only at the very end is the piano allowed to join in—but what a glorious moment that is! Other thematic fragments are introduced to complete the first group of themes. After the wide-spaced leaps of the principal theme, the piano brings in the sedate, step-wise rise and fall of the second theme. But there are more melodic pleasures in store, including a charming falling phrase that is shared by the strings and piano. To conclude the exposition, a highly rhythmic theme is given out by the piano, with an accompaniment of plucked chords in the strings. Brahms then develops and expands the thematic material. A particularly inspired point comes as the strings present the opening theme in augmentation, lengthening the duration of each note. The traditional return of all the themes and an extended coda end the movement.

At the outset of the second movement the strings play a melody that sounds most like a lusty Hungarian folk song with a characteristic rhythmic device—a rapid short-long pair of notes, called a Scotch snap. The piano accompanies with solid, offbeat chords. Five variations follow: the first, third, and fifth based on the string melody; the second and fourth derived from the piano accompaniment.

The ghostly and eerie sounds of the Scherzo immediately cast a mysterious aura over the activities. Demanding the utmost delicacy and control from all three players, particularly the pianist, the mood is sustained throughout, with but a few flashes of lightning to illuminate the arcane proceedings. Suddenly, though, minor gives way to major, and the sunny, confident, almost naive trio is heard. All too soon, however, the bleakness returns with the reprise of the Scherzo.

The final movement, which Brahms labeled *giocoso,* or "playful," is indeed spirited and good-humored, but with an intensity that largely precludes any truly humorous effect. The movement grows from two contrasting themes: the first, fervid and expressive, with the strings mostly playing together; the second, lighter in character and capitalizing on the juxtaposition of groups of two in the strings against threes in the piano.

Viola Quintet in F Major, Op. 88, "Spring"

I. Allegro non troppo, ma con brio. II. Grave et appassionato; Allegretto vivace. III. Allegro energico.

For most of his life, Brahms followed the same basic yearly schedule: winter, he traveled around Europe on leisurely concert tours; spring and summer, he took accommodations in a resort area and worked on his compositions. And thus it was during the spring of 1882, at the Austrian resort of Bad Ischl, near Salzburg, that he completed his first string quintet for two violins, two violas, and cello. Because Brahms dated each movement "in the Spring of 1882," and due to its sunny spirit and bright cheerfulness, the work has been dubbed the "Spring" Quintet.

The first subject starts radiant and lyrical, but then becomes gay and frolicsome. The flowing second theme, given out by the first viola, moves along in groups of threes, at the same time as most of the other instruments are playing in twos or fours. This rhythmic clash is continued in the following development. About halfway through this section, the cello plunks down on its lowest note, the open C string, and sits there with but few interruptions until the first violin starts the recapitulation with a forceful statement of the opening theme. The first viola is again entrusted with the second theme. The music then quiets to the slightly slower coda, which ends, though, with a brilliant flourish.

The main theme of the second movement is a saraband (a slow, dignified, triple-meter dance dating from the seventeenth century) that Brahms originally composed for piano in 1855. Over a quarter of a century later he adapted the melody for use in this quintet. The movement is organized in rondo form, with the three appearances of the deeply expressive saraband theme separated by two faster interludes. With both slow *and* fast sections combined in this single movement, Brahms skips the traditional scherzo and proceeds directly to the last movement.

"The crown of this work is its finale," writes Walter Niemann, the eminent Brahms scholar, calling it, "a magnificent masterpiece." The concept is audacious: Brahms combines a fugue (in which a single melody is imitated by different instruments at different times) with sonata form (where two contrasting melodies are stated, developed, and recapitulated). Two powerful chords launch the fugue melody in the first viola. After two more explosive chords by the second violin, the first violin and cello in turn play the same melody. While the first viola persists with the fugue theme, the first violin sings out the poetic rising and falling second theme. In the development, the running, energetic fugue theme is played against this melody. A much compressed recapitulation follows, giving way to a fast coda based exclusively on the fugue theme.

Although there were some private performances of the quintet toward the end of the summer of 1882, the official premiere was given in Frankfurt on December 29, 1882, by five local musicians.

Piano Trio in C Minor, Op. 101

I. Allegro energico. II. Presto non assai. III. Andante grazioso. IV. Allegro molto.

Daniel Gregory Mason, in his book on the chamber music of Brahms, likens the C minor trio, the last of three that the composer wrote, to a Greek tragedy. Just as most classical dramas have a single overriding theme—jealousy, revenge, love, or some other powerful human emotion—so the trio is dominated by one pithy musical motive. And, just as the universal themes of ancient Greek literature can be simply stated, so Brahms derives a huge richness of musical meaning from the stark, ascending motto of the trio.

The all-important three-note figure is heard in the left hand of the piano at the very outset of the first movement. The defiant, forceful opening leads to some rhythmic episodes before the subordinate theme, first stated by the strings, smooths out and extends the three-note motto into a wonderfully broad and moving melody. For the rest of the movement, Brahms eloquently explores the full depth and musical implications of the melodic material he has introduced.

Phantomlike, the same pattern of three notes, although rhythmically altered, starts the second movement. Tiny wisps of melody flit through all the instruments, until some solid block chords in the piano and a plucked accompaniment in the strings signal a contrasting interlude. The opening section comes back after the interlude, and the brief coda, a sort of afterthought, follows with the notes of the tune lengthened, which completely changes its character. A final peek at the tune in its previous form ends the movement.

Three rising notes open the Andante, not in stepwise movement as before, but this time encompassing larger intervals. The basic melodic unit extends for seven beats, which is very rarely heard in contrast to the ubiquitous two, three, four, or six-beat meters. Brahms presents the melody as a tender dialogue between the strings, which pose the question, and the piano, which responds. An air of unease in introduced with the slightly more animated interruption. Here the three-note motto is inverted, heading downward. The meter now is basically in five: the three beats of the motto and a two-beat tail at the end. The seven-beat pattern returns briefly to bring the movement to a close.

The last movement theme maintains the rising three notes, which now consist of two repeated notes and an upward jump. A second theme, starting with the three notes in a descending pattern, exposes still another aspect of the original motto. Varied manipulations of these two themes follow until, gently and quietly, the detached notes of the first theme become smooth and connected, and the key changes from minor to major for the radiant warmth of the coda and a ringing, affirmative concluding statement.

The trio was written in Thun, Switzerland, during the summer of 1886. Brahms gave informal performances of the work in this charming town that same summer and in Budapest in December of that year. The accepted premiere date, however, is February 26, 1887, when it was played by Brahms and members of the Heckmann Quartet in Vienna.

Viola Quintet in G Major, Op. 111

I. Allegro non troppo, ma con brio. II. Adagio. III. Un poco Allegretto. IV. Vivace ma non troppo presto.

When Brahms submitted the manuscript of his G major string quintet to publisher Fritz Simrock in December 1890, he enclosed a note:

"With this letter you can bid farewell to my music—because it is certainly time to leave off . . ." Around the same time, the fifty-seven-year-old composer, though still in good health and at the height of his popularity, was heard saying, "I have worked enough; now let the young folks take over."

Despite all that Brahms said, however, there is no clue in the quintet that it was composed by a man in the twilight of his career. For the most part the music is strong and zestful, as fresh and vital as anything in the chamber music repertoire. True, the middle movements tend to be reflective and perhaps a bit nostalgic, but the unequivocal force of the outer movements bespeaks a positive, affirmative outlook. Even Brahms must have recognized the joyful buoyancy of the work. When a friend commented that the first movement reminded him of the Prater, the beautiful park in Vienna, the composer replied, "You've guessed it! And the delightful girls there."

In the inspired opening of the quintet, the four upper instruments create a shimmering backdrop against which the cello sends forth the proud, resounding first subject, with its athletic leaps and rich sonorities. After this bold assertion, the violas enunciate the second theme, its passion and fervor tempered slightly with hesitancy and shyness, creating a perfect foil to what has come before. A final theme, gentle and lovely, is then introduced by the second violin. The development section, mostly concerned with the first and third themes, alternates passages of quiet introspection with moments of climactic intensity and even includes a false recapitulation, until the cello cuts through a veritable wall of sound to announce the true return of the first theme. The second and third themes follow, and the movement concludes with a coda that starts softly but builds rapidly to an impetuous and impassioned ending.

The moving and poignant principal theme of the slow movement is introduced by the first viola. Three more times Brahms states the subject, though each time varied and scored differently, giving each appearance a new feeling and character. A brief cadenza in the first viola leads to a final hearing of the same theme in still another guise.

Pensive, wistful, and dreamy, the third movement has some of the qualities of a slow waltz, but without any strong rhythmic underpinning. A feature of the opening section is the use of imitative writing, with one instrument stating a melody that is copied by another. The middle section features a conversation between the violas and the violins, with the flowing cello line moving the dialogue along at a comfortable pace. After returning the opening part, Brahms modulates to the major and inverts the start of the conversation theme for a brief coda.

The first viola quietly introduces the saucy, perky principal theme of the finale, with everyone joining in for the forceful, accented continuation. After the presentation of some other melodic material, the second theme, a rolling arpeggio figure, is played by the first violin. In a spirit of jolly good humor, Brahms works out the various themes, ending the movement with a vigorous, dashing Hungarian-style dance.

The Rosé Quartet with an added violist gave the premiere in Vienna on November 11, 1890.

Clarinet Trio in A Minor, Op. 114
I. Allegro. II. Adagio. III. Andante grazioso. IV. Allegro.

By the end of 1890, the fifty-seven-year-old Brahms let it be known that he did not plan to write any new compositions. He proposed only to complete a few unfinished works, and to destroy the rest. "He rejected the idea that he . . . would ever compose anything," according to his friend, Dr. Theodor Billroth.

Then, in March 1891, on a visit to Meiningen, Brahms heard a performance by Richard Mühlfeld, principal clarinetist of the Ducal Orchestra. So captivated was the composer by Mühlfeld, whom he called the greatest wind player alive, that he took up the pen that he had recently set aside and, over the next few years, created for Mühlfeld the Clarinet Trio, Op. 114, the Clarinet Quintet, Op. 115, and two clarinet sonatas of Op. 120. Brahms composed the trio during June and July 1891 at Bad Ischl, Austria. The first private performance was given in Meiningen on November 24, 1891, with Brahms (piano), Mühlfeld (clarinet), and Robert Hausmann (cello). The public premiere was held in Berlin on December 12 of that same year.

The cello introduces both themes of the somber Allegro: the first, sedately arching up and down; the second, shaped in reverse, descending before starting up. After some strikingly brilliant writing for all three instruments in the development section, the recapitulation of both melodies, somewhat altered, is given to the clarinet. The movement ends as the clarinet and cello fleetingly dash through whispered, high-speed runs.

In the intimate second movement, the three instruments shape their inmost thoughts in a free-flowing musical give-and-take. Particularly beautiful is the way Brahms takes advantage of the full pitch and tonal range of both the clarinet and cello.

A number of critics consider the Andantino grazioso the most appealing movement of the trio. At times, it swings along like a true Viennese waltz; at other times, though, Brahms complicates the rhythm to such an extent that it becomes difficult to sense the underlying triple meter.

The melodies in the final movement are vintage Brahms. The oscillating effect, moving up and down in pitch around a fixed note, can be likened to a swinging pendulum—sometimes arching widely, other times more limited in range—but always focused on a single point. Throughout, the highly rhythmic activity of the opening subject is contrasted with the sustained subsidiary theme that serves as a brake to the more exuberant first theme. Eventually, though, it is the vigorous first theme that triumphs in a shower of musical fireworks.

Clarinet Quintet in B Minor, Op. 115

I. Allegro. II. Adagio. III. Andantino; Presto non assai, ma con sentimento. IV. Con moto.

Early in the spring of 1891, Brahms heard clarinetist Richard Mühlfeld play, and it called forth what scholar Karl Geiringer calls a "surge of fresh creative power." That summer Brahms wrote his clarinet trio for Mühlfeld and sent a copy to his friend Eusebius Mandyczeweski with a note that enigmatically referred to another work in progress, "a far greater piece of foolishness," that he was trying to "nurse along." The piece that he spoke of so lightly proved to be the monumental Clarinet Quintet, Op. 115.

While the general tone of the clarinet quintet tends toward autumnal melancholy, there are long stretches of great joy and rapture. Perhaps these buoyant passages reflect the aging composer's delight in finding his inspiration and skill undiminished. Or they may have to do with his enchantment with the tonal potentialities of the clarinet, especially as played by Herr Mühlfeld. Whatever the reasons, the quintet is unsurpassed in displaying the clarinet's most telling effects—its clear high soprano voice in the *clarino* register, the hollow, breathy mystery of its middle tones, and the dark, romantic cast of its low, *chalumeau* range.

The quintet opens with a fetchingly lovely theme played by the two violins. The theme, typical of the melodies Brahms crafted in his later years, was termed by him to be *Unscheinbarket,* or "unobtrusive." Rather than amazing the listener with its startling originality, the theme insinuates itself into one's consciousness with its tender beauty. A close analysis shows that set within the few measures of the melody are the seeds, as it were, that inform and shape the rest of the composition and provide it with a satisfying unity of conception and mood. After the opening theme, the excitement mounts, and there follows a transition built around forceful, staccato notes. This leads to the second theme, played by the clarinet, which is directly derived from the opening theme's rapid-note figure. These two themes provide the raw material out of which Brahms, using traditional sonata form, creates the entire eloquent movement.

The slow movement theme, in the clarinet, is a love song, serene and dreamlike in character. The viola countermelody, though, has tendrils reaching back to the previous movement. It comes from a figure played by the first violin just after the last statement of the first movement theme, which is derived, in turn, from the quartet's opening rapid-note figure. The middle section that follows is a wild, Hungarian-style improvisation for the clarinet, in which the muted strings are relegated to supplying a cimbalomlike accompaniment and sadly echoing the clarinet's impassioned flights of fancy. This section, too, is related both rhythmically and melodically to the opening phrase. After a return of the earliest part of the movement, the clarinet recalls once more the germinal initial motif.

The principal theme of the Andantino is an augmentation made up of fragments found within the now-familiar opening phrase, the group of notes 3, 4, 5, and the group of 10, 11, 12. After the clarinet spins out the broad melody, and the others join in for its expansion, the lighter, faster Presto begins—a high-spirited elaboration of the beginning notes of the Andantino theme. The clarinet ends this charming movement with a fleeting glimpse of the Andantino theme in its original form.

The finale is made up of a theme and five variations. The theme, similar in nature to the principal Andantino melody, is seamlessly woven between the first violin and clarinet and derives from the second, rocking motif of the opening melody. Each variation explores a different aspect of the theme, until in the fifth variation we become aware that we have come full circle—the last variation is also a modification of the opening subject of the first movement. Lest there be any doubt of what has happened, Brahms underscores the point by presenting the opening melody nearly in its original form in the coda. The journey is over—and we're back home!

The first performance of the quintet was given in Berlin by Mühlfeld and the Joachim Quartet on December 12, 1891. The work made such a deep impression on the audience that the musicians were recalled many times by enthusiastic applause and were finally compelled to repeat the Adagio movement before being allowed to leave the stage.

Benjamin Britten

Born November 22, 1913, at Lowestoft, Suffolk, England
Died December 4, 1976, at Aldeburgh, Suffolk, England

BENJAMIN BRITTEN'S early musical development was fostered by both his mother, who played piano and sang in the local choral society, and his father, who refused to buy a radio or phonograph for fear it might interfere with family music-making. Early on, young Ben determined to become a composer. By age five he was already "composing," that is, placing random dots on music paper and joining them together with long curved lines. Not long after, he started piano lessons and learned to associate the notes with their sounds. Now he began composing in earnest, writing, as he said, "elaborate tone poems, usually lasting about twenty seconds, inspired by terrific events in my home life." His facility and dedication were so great that by age fourteen he had already finished a symphony, six string quartets, and ten piano sonatas!

On graduation from London's Royal College of Music in 1933, Britten was offered a position writing music for the documentary films being produced by the British Post Office. It proved to be an excellent post-graduate course in how to achieve musical results with the greatest economy of means. "The film company I was working for," Britten wrote, "had very little money. I had to write scores, not for large orchestras, but for six or seven players, and to make these instruments make all the effects that each film demanded."

Britten's admiration for the outstanding seventeenth-century English composer Henry Purcell also influenced his musical development. Purcell's qualities, which Britten described as "clarity, brilliance, tenderness, and strangeness," were among the traits that he wanted to incorporate into his own writing.

Through most of his life, Britten passionately upheld the conviction that music should communicate directly with people, speak to them in ways that they could understand, and evoke their deepest feelings and emotions. He summed up his credo: "As an artist I want to serve the community." Further, he also said: "I believe in the artist serving society. It is better to be a bad composer writing for society than to be a bad composer writing against it. At least your work can be of *some* use."

Britten's command of compositional technique is faultless; he never miscalculates in his writing, nor does he ever set down musical thoughts that are ill-conceived or badly realized. His compositions are characterized by a natural flow and an ease of creation and are distinguished by what he calls "clear and clean" writing. Because of his warmth and concern for others and his sincere desire to communicate, Britten's music is always direct and honest in its appeal, intellectually stimulating and engaging.

In addition to the two string quartets and the Phantasy Quartet discussed below, Britten composed a third string quartet, Op. 94, in the fall of 1975, a little more than a year before his death.

Phantasy Quartet, Op. 2

The title "Phantasy," or its more common variants, "Fantasy" or "Fantasia," usually connotes a piece of imaginative, fanciful music, spontaneous and free of formal restraints. However, every composer knows that, to achieve an open, improvisational air without descending into meaningless chaos, there must be an impressive mastery of technique. In the Phantasy Quartet for oboe, violin, viola, and cello, Benjamin Britten exhibits the skillful control of the musical elements necessary to attain the requisite freedom of spirit.

The quartet, which is in one movement, opens with the cello and then the other strings establishing a cryptic, eccentric, marchlike backdrop, over which the oboe sings a cantabile line, the antithesis of the string character. A series of trills brings this section to a close. Two more themes follow, introduced respectively by the violin and cello. Although they are very different in character from the opening string motif, they are really offshoots of the first idea.

After Britten varies and expands the various themes, the viola starts a contrasting section for strings only, with a new theme that is derived from the oboe's first melody. The violin immediately continues the viola line with a charming little syncopated tune. The rest of the quartet is involved with bringing back, in modified form, the several themes that have already been heard. The work ends, much as it began, with the cello playing the somewhat mysterious march rhythm.

The Phantasy Quartet was composed in September and October 1932, while Britten was still a student at the Royal College of Music in London. It was introduced in London on December 12, 1932, played by Leon Goossens, oboe, and members of the International String Quartet.

String Quartet No. 1 in D Major, Op. 25

I. Andante sostenuto; Allegro vivo. II. Allegretto con slancio. III. Andante calmo. IV. Molto vivace.

In Benjamin Britten's childhood home, music was considered an essential part of daily life. The earliest sounds that he could remember, though, were not of singing or piano playing, but of World War I bombs exploding near his home on the North Sea coast of England. Perhaps this terrifying memory helped turn Britten into a committed pacifist, leading him to flee his much beloved England for America just before the outbreak of World War II. It was in July 1941, while living in the small seashore town of Amityville, Long Island, that he composed his first string quartet under a commission from Elizabeth Sprague Coolidge. The work received its premiere in Los Angeles in September 1941, played by the Coolidge String Quartet. It was later awarded the Library of Congress medal.

The overall witty character of the quartet is belied by the introduction's unmoving, dissonant cluster of tones played in an extremely high register by the violins and viola. Before long, though, an exuberant, rhythmic tune is flung out forcibly and with crackling energy. Maintaining the same rhythmic vitality, but softer and lighter, another theme, hardly more than an ornamented ascending and descending scale, is heard. The rest of the movement is then essentially devoted to alternating the slow introductory material and the highly charged contrasts.

The second movement, a sort of scherzo, tiptoes in lightly and delicately. All goes well until the viola rudely intrudes with a loud three-note turn. Sensing the impropriety, though, the viola gets in step with the others. As the movement progresses, however, the tread grows heavier, and there are more and more interruptions, until the triplet figure begins to dominate, in various guises, the remainder of this impish, joyful movement.

The slightly asymmetric five-beat meter gives the Andante calmo a sedate lilt. Its repeated opening notes, a consonant echo of the first movement's dissonant introduction, become the background for the simple, conjunct melody. A slightly faster middle section, with bold, disjunct declamatory statements from individual instruments, along with snatches of the opening interposed, is heard next, before the first section returns for a quiet close.

Britten starts the finale with a flip, quirky phrase that he whips into an intricate fugal passage. A rush of descending sixteenth notes transforms the phrase into the cello accompaniment for a sustained melody in the violins and viola. A second theme, quiet and static, follows. Britten works over these various thematic threads, weaving them together to create a boisterous climax.

String Quartet No. 2 in C Major, Op. 36

I. Allegro calmo senza
rigore. II. Vivace. III. Chacony.

Most music historians agree that the two leading English composers were Henry Purcell in the seventeenth-century and Benjamin Britten in the twentieth. It is very fitting, therefore, that Britten's second string quartet, probably his best-known chamber piece, was composed to commemorate the two hundred and fiftieth anniversary of Purcell's death. He finished the work on October 14, 1945, and it was first played in London on November 21, 1945 by the Zorian String Quartet.

The quartet starts with the ascending wide-spaced interval of a tenth—an octave *plus* a third. The first violin and cello play it as the beginning of the first theme, joined by the second violin for the phrases that continue the melody. The viola accompanies with a drone made up of two notes at the same interval of the tenth. Two more times in quick succession the same opening is heard, starting on different notes, played by various combinations of instruments, and featuring varied melodic extensions. With very simple means, Britten then proceeds to build the movement on this material. After the themes are developed and varied, the cello begins a loud rolling arpeggio figure, on which the others superimpose the all-important interval of the tenth, and then finally present the several melodic ideas simultaneously.

An explosion of sound signals the opening of the following move-

116

ment, a rather somber scherzo. A quiet arpeggio figure in the second violin and viola emerges, against which the other two players give out the well-marked, heavily accented theme. Sharp dynamic contrasts abound, as Britten expands this melody and introduces other melodic material. A change of character in the three lower instruments ushers in the trio section, in which the first violin states the powerful new subject—really an augmentation of the scherzo melody. A transition of arpeggios in the cello leads to a very freely realized return of the scherzo.

The last movement pays homage to Purcell, even to the extent of using the old English spelling of the title, Chacony. A chaconne, using the more familiar spelling, is a Baroque form in which a brief melody, usually in moderately slow triple meter, is subject to continuous variation. Britten's nine-measure melody passes through twenty-one variations. They are separated, though, into four groups or sections. As Britten wrote, "The sections may be said to review the theme from (a) harmonic, (b) rhythmic, (c) melodic, and (d) formal aspects." The first group contains six variations based on an evolving harmonic scheme. A cello cadenza leads to the second group of six, in which the rhythm is varied. This time a viola cadenza marks the break, to be followed by six more variations based on a countermelody that Britten introduces in the second violin. The first violin has the final cadenza, setting the stage for the last three variations, which act as a coda to the movement.

Anton Bruckner

Born September 4, 1824, in Ansfelden, Upper Austria
Died October 11, 1896, in Vienna

DURING HIS lifetime, Anton Bruckner was eclipsed by such contemporaries as Wagner, Brahms, and Richard Strauss. Aside from a small, enthusiastic group of pupils and disciples, his compositions attracted little interest from most performers or audiences. And over the decades following his death, even less of his music was heard. In fact, it is only since around 1960 that Bruckner has been recognized as one of the outstanding Post-Romantic composers, and his works have begun to appear regularly on concert programs.

The very qualities that are lauded today were long disparaged. The expansive dimensions of his music were thought to be dull prolixity; his grandiose conceptions were called pompous; his nobility, dignity, and serenity earned him the nickname "Adagio Composer"; and the highly charged intensity of his style was attributed to neuroticism. Critics castigated him for being "the Wagnerian symphonist," while Wagner said, "I know of only one who may be compared to Beethoven, and he is Bruckner."

Born to a village schoolmaster in rural Austria, Bruckner's life was as uneventful as his personality was unassuming. He was given his first music instruction by Augustine monks, as part of the training to follow his father's career as a school teacher. Nevertheless, his special talent led him to the more serious study of the organ and composition and the decision to pursue a life in music. After some years as a church organist, he devoted himself to teaching music (at the Vienna Conservatory from 1868 to 1891) and to composing.

In the highly sophisticated musical world of late-nineteenth-century Vienna, Bruckner was considered a naive, country bumpkin. He was not exceptionally well-read or educated; his personal library contained mostly books on religion and music. Attired as he usually was in ill-fitting clothes—shirts and jackets that were overly large, trousers that were too short, and sporting a very close, peasant-style hairdo—Bruckner was hardly an imposing figure.

Two incidents with Hans Richter, a leading conductor and magisterial personality, illustrate Bruckner's naivete. After the final rehearsal of his Fourth Symphony, the appreciative Bruckner pressed a *thaler* into the dumbfounded conductor's hand, saying, "Take this and drink a mug of beer to my health." And following a performance of his Eighth Symphony, Bruckner met Richter at the stage door with a bag of forty-eight *Krapfen,* large doughnuts, which he suggested that they should eat together.

Throughout his entire life, Bruckner maintained an unswerving belief in Catholicism and a profound devotion to God. He regarded musical composition as an act of worship, a spiritual manifestation of his religiosity. His faith was so deep that every day he kept a list of the prayers he recited, and if the Angelus sounded while he was lecturing, he would stop, kneel, and pray before continuing.

Bruckner is best known today for his large scale works, in particular his nine symphonies, the *Te Deum,* and the several masses. He only wrote one chamber work, the Viola Quintet, but it too is part of today's repertoire. It took nearly a century, but Bruckner has finally earned the recognition he so surely deserves.

Viola Quintet in F Major

I. Gemässig; Moderato. II. Scherzo: Schnell. III. Adagio. IV. Finale: Lebhaft bewegt.

In 1861 Joseph Hellmesberger, violinist, conductor, director of the Vienna Conservatory, and organizer of the string quartet that bore his name, asked Bruckner to write a piece for his group. Never one to be rushed, Bruckner started the composition in December 1878 and completed it in the middle of the following year. Instead of a string quartet, though, he composed a quintet, adding a second viola to the usual complement of instruments.

Upon receiving the score, nearly twenty years after he had given the commission, Hellmesberger pronounced the Scherzo movement too difficult. Bruckner, in his eagerness to have his piece performed, quickly wrote an Intermezzo to replace the Scherzo. Still, Hellmesberger hesitated. Another group, assembled by Bruckner's pupil, Franz Shalk, finally gave the premiere performance (less the Finale) in Vienna on November 27, 1881. After the concert, Bruckner withdrew the Intermezzo and reinserted the Scherzo, and it was in this form that Hellmesberger's quartet, with an extra violist, finally performed it on May 18, 1885.

A warm, lyrical, almost sentimental first theme with a characteristic descending interval starts the sedate and stately opening movement. The second theme, announced in a powerful unison, is stronger and more energetic, reversing the usual order of the character of the themes in a sonata form first movement. A quiet melody sweeping upward in direction brings the exposition to a conclusion. Bruckner then develops this thematic material in leisurely fashion with the first theme predominating. A brief cadenzalike passage for the first violin leads to a return of the three themes of the exposition.

Light and playful in character, the Scherzo that had bedeviled Hellmesberger does not seem to pose any particular technical problems for today's performers. The tunes have some of the quality of the Austrian folk songs and dances that Bruckner knew so well. After a complete halt, the somewhat grotesque, mocking melody of the slightly slower trio section follows. Good spirits come back, though, with the repeat of the Scherzo.

The Adagio, it is generally agreed, is the crowning movement of the quintet. Essentially one theme prevails, a glowing, rich, soulful melody. What might be considered another theme is, in fact, an inversion of the first melody; it starts with the same rhythms, but rises in pitch instead of descending as in the original. After reaching an exciting, impassioned climax, the reversed theme and fragments of the original are heard again, and the movement ends quietly.

The Finale does not have the same melodic abundance as the earlier movements. Bruckner provides wisps of themes and motifs rather than fully developed, memorable melodies. The movement does, however, have an inner vitality and an orchestral ending that most fittingly and positively concludes the entire quintet.

Elliott Carter

Born December 11, 1908 in New York City

AT THE conclusion of the first performance of Carter's String Quartet No. 1, just before the applause began, a listener in the rear of the auditorium at Columbia University stood up, slammed his seat back loudly, and proclaimed, "My God!" as he stomped out of the exit doors. At a small gathering after the concert, Carter and the performers expressed delight that they had aroused so vehement a reaction from an "indignant subscriber!"

Indeed, Carter's music is not always easily grasped by mass audiences at first hearing. Perhaps that is because he is writing for "ideal listeners," people who are willing to give his highly complex, dense scores the kind of attention and concentration they require for full enjoyment and understanding. He approaches every new piece as a problem, a challenge that he must solve and conquer. This has led him to rethink many of the traditions of musical composition and in particular the treatment of the various aspects of rhythm. Just as Schoenberg and others in the early years of the twentieth century created new concepts of melody and harmony, so Carter suggested more advanced ways to manipulate beat, meter, and tempo. Through a technique he calls "metric modulation," Carter devised ways to write independent, simultaneous rhythms, sometimes accelerating or decelerating at the same time, which create new dimensions of musical discourse and are able to express a wide range of musical and emotional effects.

Despite the intricacy of his compositional style, a good percentage of the listening audience finds that Carter's music provides them with intense, heightened musical experiences and that his strong, uniquely personal style of communication transcends the technical details that are, ultimately, of much greater interest to the composer and performer than to the listener. In Carter's compositions we find sections of great beauty, loveliness, and tenderness, with many examples of warmth, wit, and whimsy, along with challenging, intellectually stimulating passages that convey a sense of profound depth and seriousness.

Carter was educated at Harvard University, where, despite his overriding interest in music and desire to become a composer, he first earned a degree in English literature before starting his graduate studies in music. He completed his formal training in Paris with Nadia Boulanger, the outstanding pedagogue who taught so many of the leading American composers in the early decades of this century. Over the following years, in addition to his composing, Carter served as music director of Ballet Caravan and held various teaching positions at Columbia, Yale, and Cornell universities and at the Juilliard School of Music.

Since 1953, when he attracted international attention with his String Quartet No. 1, Carter has come to occupy a very special, most distinguished position as perhaps the leading intellectual composer of our time. A slow, careful worker, Carter has not produced a large body of music. But the imposing list of honors he has received testifies both to the quality of his compositions and to the high esteem in which he, as a musician, is held: two Guggenheim Fellowships; two Pulitzer Prizes; the Prix de Rome; the New York Critics' Circle Award; honorary degrees from Princeton, Yale, Harvard, and Cambridge universities; membership in the Academy of Arts and Sciences and the Academy of Arts and Letters, from which he received a Gold Medal for Music—to mention but a few!

Eight Etudes and a Fantasy

I. Maestoso. II. Quietly. III. Adagio possible. IV. Vivace. V. Andante. VI. Allegretto leggero. VII. Intensely. VIII. Presto. IX. Fantasy: Tempo giusto.

Carter once asked a class of music students to prepare short compositions that would demonstrate the special characteristics of each woodwind instrument. Disappointed with the results, Carter quickly wrote out some original brief passages of his own. He later expanded these spur-of-the-moment creations to become *Eight Etudes and a Fantasy,* for flute, oboe, clarinet, and bassoon, a piece of great charm and wit that has become a concert favorite.

The individual etudes are brief, epigrammatic studies, each one displaying a distinct musical or instrumental effect. The stately, bold first etude is an introduction to what follows. The parts are written in very tight imitation, giving the impression that one or the other instrument is slightly out of synchronization.

The theme of number two is a florid figure that starts out in a single instrument and is handed to another with increasing overlap, until at the end all four instruments are playing together.

Carter instructs the players to make "sneak entrances" in the following slow etude. The effect is a smooth sustained stream of sound with only minor perturbations as notes change or as instruments start and stop.

The recipe for the Vivace is simple. Take two notes that rise a half step and toss them around in dizzying patterns among the four instruments. The result? A bright, sparkling example of musical legerdemain.

In the next, slow etude, the composer creates a unique tonal ambiance by having the oboe and bassoon play near the top of their range, while the flute and clarinet hover around their lowest notes.

The listener's attention in the Allegretto leggero is drawn to the tonal effects—the flutter tonguing and the changes of color on a single tone.

Number seven is a compositional tour de force—an entire movement made up of only one note!

The last etude is reminiscent of the second, with a complex *perpetuum mobile* melody dominating throughout.

The Fantasy starts out with a fugato based on a marchlike tune. Highly contrapuntal in its treatment, it wraps up the work very neatly by bringing back the subjects of each etude.

Composed in 1950, *Eight Etudes* was first played in New York on October 28, 1952, by members of the New York Woodwind Quintet.

String Quartet No. 1

I. Fantasia; Allegro scorrevole. II. Allegro scorrevole; Adagio. III. Variations.

In 1951, a Guggenheim Fellowship allowed Elliott Carter to spend a year in Tucson, Arizona, realizing several new musical concepts in an extended composition, his First String Quartet. He described his effort as creating "a musical pattern that had to be invented at every step of the way."

Carter drew his inspiration for the quartet from Jean Cocteau's film, *Le Sang d'un poete.* The movie opens with a slow-motion shot of a tall chimney being dynamited. Just as it starts to fall, the scene shifts, and the dreamlike sequences of the movie itself begin. At the end, the shot of the chimney is resumed, showing its complete collapse. The composer described how he adapted this concept to his quartet:

> A similar interrupted continuity is employed in this quartet's starting with a cadenza for cello alone that is continued by the first violin alone at the very end. On one level, I interpret Cocteau's idea (and my own) as establishing the difference between external time (measured by the falling chimney, or the cadenza) and internal dream time (the main body of the work)—the dream time lasting but a moment of external time but from the dreamer's point of view, a long stretch. In the First Quartet, the opening cadenza also acts as an introduction to the rest, and when it reappears at the end, it forms the last variation in a set of variations. Not only is this plan like that of many "circular" works of modern literature, but the interlocked presentation of ideas parallels many characteristic devices found in Joyce and others—the controlled "stream of consciousness," the "epiphany," the many uses of punctuation, of grammatical ambiguities, including the use of quotation.

Mr. Carter has supplied the following analysis of the quartet.

> The first movement, a contrapuntal fantasy, is built on four main and several subsidiary themes, each in a different speed and character. Various polyrhythmic combinations of these are made and this resolves into a rapidly flowing scherzo, "allegro scorrevole," with a dramatic trio section. The scherzo is interrupted, before it is concluded, with a pause of the kind that usually comes between movements. It is resumed briefly after the pause and leads into an Adagio that features a vigorous recitative between viola and cello, answered by a quiet duet between the muted violins. Later the duet and the recitative are heard together leading to a shadowy, fast coda that prefigures the variations of the last movement. These variations are made up of a number of ideas which become slightly faster at each repetition. The one heard in the cello at first reappears frequently from beginning to end of the movement where it finally becomes so fast that it turns into a tremolo; other themes reach the vanishing point sooner and give place to new ones. The work ends with a variation in the form of a cadenza for the first violin that is also

a continuation of the one heard in the cello at the very opening of the work.

The quartet, which received its premiere at New York's Columbia University on February 26, 1953, by the Walden Quartet, was awarded first prize at the Concours Internationale de Quatour in Liege, Belgium.

String Quartet No. 2

Introduction. Allegro fantastico. Cadenza for
Viola. Presto scherzando. Cadenza for
Cello. Andante espressivo. Cadenza for First
Violin. Allegro. Conclusion.

Elliott Carter's Second String Quartet is one of the most honored of modern chamber music works, having been awarded the Pulitzer Prize for Music (1960), the New York Music Critics' Circle Award (1960), and the International Rostrum of Composers Award (UNESCO) (1961).

In this work, which Carter composed in 1959, each instrument has its own musical personality and style, "like a character in an opera," the composer wrote. The first violin, for example, might be said to play in a bravura manner; the second violin is anti-lyrical in temperament; the viola is highly expressive; and the cello tends toward the lyrical. Further, each instrument maintains "its own repertory of musical speeds and intervals." And melodically, there is almost no repetition, but instead "an ever-changing series of motives and figures having certain internal relationships with each other."

Because of the independence of the individual parts, Carter first thought to have the players seated at the four corners of the stage; he later realized that this would be impractical. He does suggest, though, "a special stereophonic placement which helps to sort them out, although this is not absolutely necessary, since the total effect at any given moment is the primary consideration, the contribution of each instrument secondary." The composer has written the following analysis:

> The form of the quartet itself helps to make the elements of this four-way conversation clear. The individuals of this group are related to each other in what might be metaphorically termed three forms of respon-

siveness: discipleship, companionship, and confrontation. The Introduction and Conclusion present in aphoristic form and in "companionate" manner the repertory of each instrument. The Allegro fantastico is led by the first violin, whose whimsical, ornate part is "imitated" by the other three, each according to his own individuality; the same occurs in the Presto scherzando led by the second violin and the Andante espressivo led by the viola. The final Allegro, although partially led by the cello—which eventually draws the others into one of its characteristic accelerations—tends to stress the "companionship" rather than the "discipleship" pattern.

In between these movements are cadenzas of instrumental "confrontation" or opposition: after the Allegro fantastico, the viola plays its expressive, almost lamenting cadenza to be confronted with explosions of what may be anger or ridicule by the other three; after the Presto scherzando, the cello playing in its romantically free way is confronted by the others' insistence on strict time; finally, after the Andante espressivo, the first violin carries on like a virtuoso, to be confronted by the silence of the others, who, before this cadenza is over, commence the final Allegro. Throughout the entire quartet, the second violin acts as a moderating influence, using its pizzicato and arco notes to mark regular time, its half or double—always at the same speed.

The Second String Quartet was first performed in New York on March 25, 1960, by the Juilliard String Quartet.

String Quartet No. 3

DUO I	DUO II
(Violin and cello)	*(Violin and viola)*
Furioso	*Maestoso*
Leggerissimo	*Grazioso*
Andante espressivo	*Pizzicato giusto, meccanico*
Pizzicato giocoso	*Scorrevole*
	Largo tranquillo
	Appassionato

In his Third String Quartet, Elliott Carter establishes a unique relationship among the four instruments. He divides the players into two independent duos: Duo I, violin and cello; Duo II, violin and viola. Duo I is instructed to play freely. *Quasi rubato* is the term Carter uses, which he further defines as requiring an "expressively intense, impulsive style." Duo II, though, is restricted to playing strictly in time.

The movements of the quartet are broken into substantial fragments, which are first heard in listed order and later in different sequences. Further, the changes between sections do not occur simultaneously, so that one duo is carrying on its movement while the other duo is proceeding from one to another.

Carter has written the following analysis:

The work begins with Duo I playing Furioso (associated with the major seventh) against Duo II's Maestoso (perfect fifth). Later, I's Furioso reappears during II's Pizzicato giusto, meccanico (augmented fourth) and continues when II changes to Grazioso (minor seventh). Later I's Furioso is expanded for a longer stretch, coming in while II plays its Largo tranquillo (major third) and continuing through II's pause and part of II's Scorrevole (minor second). The Maestoso of Duo II can be traced in a similar way; at the beginning it is combined with I's Furioso and continued through I's short pauses, stopping after I has taken up Leggerissimo (perfect fourth). Later II's Maestoso returns during I's Pizzicato giocoso (minor third), continuing during part of I's Andante espressivo (minor sixth).

The sections are not, of course, of the same length nor their components of the same salience, since each whole movement, although fragmented, has its own overall shape, with some sections more emphatic than others.

Dramatically and technically one of the principal interests of this formal play was the possibility of contrasts between the "unmotivated," abrupt changes from one movement fragment to another with the "motivated" continuities within the movements in which one thing clearly grows out of another.

Elliott Carter composed his Third String Quartet in 1971 for the Juilliard Quartet, which gave the first performance in New York on January 23, 1973, the same year it was awarded his second Pulitzer Prize for Music.

Quintet for Brass

Elliott Carter's Quintet for Brass is a highly dramatic work, in which the individual instruments function as the *dramatis personae*. He achieves this by giving each instrument its own particular character and certain favorite musical intervals. Since the parts have such independence, the result is a multilayered work, able to portray a broad range of contrasting attitudes and emotional states.

The quintet is organized into nineteen short sections. Every third movement throughout is a *quodlibet,* from the Latin, "what you please," a potpourrilike succession of melodies for the entire ensemble in which, to quote Carter, "the instruments oppose each other with contrasting parts of their individual repertories." Surrounding the six different appearances of the *quodlibet* are various duos and trios, each with its own combination of instruments and its own character. Near the midpoint there is one solo, for French horn.

Below is a detailed description of the quintet's formal plan, with the instruments involved and the specific temperament of each section:

1. *Quodlibet:* "calm." 2. *Trio:* two trumpets and trombone, "lightly." 3. *Duo:* trombone two and horn, "vigorous." 4. *Quodlibet:* "angry." 5. *Duo:* trumpet 2 and horn, "humorous." 6. *Trio:* trumpet 1, horn, trombone 2, "majestic." 7. *Quodlibet:* combines "humorous," "majestic" and "calm." 8. *Trio:* two trumpets and horn, "smoothly flowing." 9. *Duo:* two trombones, "extravagant." 10. *Quodlibet:* combines "extravagant," "majestic" and "humorous." 11. *Trio:* trumpet 1 and two trombones, "lyric." 12. *Horn solo:* "menacing." 13. *Quodlibet:* interjections while horn continues. 14. *Duo:* two trumpets, "furious." 15. *Trio:* horn and two trombones, "angry." 16. *Quodlibet:* different fragments. 17. *Slow movement:* "calm." 18. *Duo:* trombone 1 and trumpet 2, "dramatic." 19. *Coda:* previous movements recalled.

Carter wrote the Brass Quintet during the summer of 1974 for the American Brass Quintet, which gave the premiere on October 20, 1974, in a broadcast on the BBC from London. The American premiere was at the Library of Congress on November 15, 1974.

Aaron Copland

Born November 14, 1900, in Brooklyn, New York

AARON COPLAND is often called the "Dean of American music," both for the outstanding corpus of his own compositions, and because he has so actively promoted the cause of modern American composers and music. This devotion to music was unexpected and unanticipated by his immigrant Russian-Jewish parents, who did little to encourage or develop his talent. "No one ever talked music to me or took me to a concert," he has written. "The idea was entirely original with me." Yet, at age fifteen, he decided to become a composer.

Copland's first teachers discouraged him from pursuing the new directions in composition that he wanted to explore. In 1921 he went to France, where he became the first American to study composition with Nadia Boulanger, an extraordinary teacher who provided a firm grounding in basics but also encouraged him to follow his own musical instincts. After three years in Paris, Copland returned to New York, eager to develop a personal style, one that would "exteriorize [his] inner feelings" and yet do it in an uniquely American way.

For the first few years, Copland absorbed elements of jazz in his music, infusing his works with the characteristic melodies, harmonies, rhythms, and tone colors of ragtime and the blues. In the late 1920s, Copland started to compose works that were abstract, austere, and highly concentrated; he described them as "more spare in sonority, more lean in texture." Over the following decades, however, the Great Depression and his desire to reach more people caused Copland to modify his style. "I began to feel an increasing dissatisfaction with the relations of the music-loving public and the living composer." He tried to express what he wanted to say in a simple way that spoke directly to the people. Drawing on American folklore, Copland incorporated gospel hymns, cowboy songs, and folk tunes into original works. His most popular compositions, *El Salon Mexico* (1936), *Rodeo* (1942), *Lincoln Portrait* (1942), and *Appalachian Spring* (1944), all date from this period.

In 1950, with his piano quartet, Copland returned to a "difficult" style, as he adapted Schoenberg's twelve-tone method of composition to his own musical needs. By then, all of the different tendencies had been fused and integrated to form Copland's very distinctive musical vocabulary. Having achieved the unity he sought between musical technique and national identity, Copland no longer felt self-conscious about his need to write American music. "Because we live here and work here," he has said, "we can be certain that when our music is mature it will also be American in quality."

Vitebsk, for Piano Trio

While attending a New York performance of S. Ansky's *The Dybbuk*, by the Moscow Art Theatre during the 1926–1927 season, Aaron Copland was struck by the hauntingly beautiful melody that served as the play's background music. After he learned that the melody was a Jewish folk song from Vitebsk, the Russian village of Ansky's birth, Copland decided to write a piece of music based on this theme. Begun in 1927, *Vitebsk,* subtitled "Study on a Jewish Theme," was finished early in 1929 and premiered in New York on February 16 of that year.

Copland described *Vitebsk,* the only piece that he wrote with a Jewish theme, as "a dramatic character study." The one-movement trio opens with several stark, declamatory chords on the piano. The piano chords are simultaneously in major and minor, creating harsh, jarring dissonances that suggest quarter tones, notes in between the traditional half steps, to Copland. He therefore has the strings respond with quarter-tone, out-of-tune-sounding wails. From the fervid ardor of the introduction emerges the Vitebsk folk melody, expressively sung by the solo cello, with sharp, chordal piano interjections.

A sudden change in tempo and meter, marked by a flourish in the piano, introduces an agitated Eastern European saltatory section; Copland calls it "a Chagall-like grotesquerie." Over the persistent rhythm and offbeat accents, the three notes of the folk tune are heard as a recurring motto.

An abrupt pause interrupts the forward motion and the Vitebsk melody suddenly appears, now played with great intensity by the violin and cello. An evocation of the introduction and a final glimpse of the folk song conclude the work on a solemn, doleful note.

Sextet

I. Allegro vivace.   II. Lento.   III. Finale: Precise and rhythmic.

The Sextet had its origins as an orchestral work, titled *Short Symphony* (1933), which was premiered by Carlos Chavez and the Orquestra Sinfonica de Mexico on November 23, 1934. Subsequently scheduled performances of the *Short Symphony* by the Philadelphia and Boston Symphonies, though, were canceled because the work was considered too difficult to prepare in the available time. Not wanting this substantial composition to languish because of its complexities, Copland rewrote sections and transcribed it for string quartet, clarinet and piano. The somewhat easier Sextet, first performed in New York on February 26, 1936, has become one of Copland's most beloved chamber works. The three movements—fast, slow, fast—are played without pause.

The first movement, Allegro vivace, starts with a bold five-note flourish in the strings, capped off by a sweeping piano figure. Copland then develops this motif with a dazzling display of changing meters and cross accents. A second theme, jazzy and syncopated, is announced by the piano and strings, with saucy fillips at the end of each phrase tossed off by the clarinet. After a short development of this theme, both subjects are brought back, albeit much altered.

A melancholic melody of simple, unadorned descending scale fragments played by the clarinet opens the Lento. The middle section, slightly more rhythmical, faster, and lighter in mood, follows. The movement ends with a climactic return of the lamenting opening part, which then acts as a bridge to the Finale.

A succession of sparkling and lilting figures serve as the basis for the last movement, which Copland marked "precise and rhythmic." One tune, played by the violins in unison, is based on a melody from the German film *Der Kongress Tanzt,* which attracted Copland, although he attached no extra-musical importance to it. Copland works out the melodic material in highly complex rhythmic formulations, including snatches of the Charleston and of popular Mexican dance figures, as well as brief quotes from the first movement. The work ends with a slow, pensive recollection of the opening five-note flourish and a driving, energetic cadence.

Piano Quartet

I. Adagio serio.   II. Allegro giusto.   III. Non troppo lento.

"A barn in Richmond, Massachusetts, with a beautiful view of open meadow and distant mountains," Copland wrote, "housed me during the summer of 1950, and it was there that I first consciously tried my hand, in my Piano Quartet, at twelve-tone composition. I found this approach to be liberating in two respects: it forces the tonal composer to have less conventional thoughts in respect to chord structure, and it tends to be a refreshing influence so far as melody and figuration are concerned."

The twelve-tone method Copland used was devised by Arnold Schoenberg in the 1920s. It requires that all twelve tones of the chromatic scale, as arranged in a specific order called a tone row, be heard before any can be repeated. In adapting this method to his purpose, however, Copland does not abandon the more traditional tonality; his tone row contains eleven instead of twelve notes and very strongly suggests a whole-tone scale. Thus, in a highly original way, Copland combines Schoenberg's twelve-tone method with twentieth-century diatonicism, as exemplified by Stravinsky, to create a work that is unmistakably Copland.

The entire Adagio serio movement grows from the eleven-note tone row, first stated by the violin and given a fugal presentation, with the other instruments imitating the original statement. Copland creates the rest of the movement by his manipulations of the row. One device, first heard in the piano, is inversion, in which he reverses the melodic contour; instead of starting with five descending notes and then leaping up, the inversion rises for five notes and then jumps down. He also uses retrograde motion, introduced by the cello, where the row is actually played backward.

The principal theme of the Allegro giusto is the jazzy little phrase tossed off by the violin and cello at the start of the movement. Subsidiary subjects include a busy, driving melody with all sorts of "wrong-beat" accents and a section built around ringing clangorous chords in the piano, which Copland directed to be played *con umore,* "with humor." After presenting expanded versions of all three subjects, he reviews them again to complete the movement.

The final, slow movement is divided into five sections. The first, for strings alone, is introductory in nature. The piano's entrance marks the second section. Its notes, resembling the opening of "Three

Blind Mice,'' are really the first three notes of the tone row. They become the accompaniment to a cantabile string melody that nonetheless is characterized by immense leaps. The third part is a forceful, hymnlike climax to the movement, with the piano providing bell-like accompanying chords. Copland then brings back the first two sections and ends with sustained notes in the strings, as the piano plays fragments of the tone row.

Completed on October 20, 1950, the Piano Quartet was introduced in Washington, D.C., by the New York Quartet on October 29 of that year.

George Crumb

Born October 24, 1929, in Charleston, West Virginia

DURING THE late 1960s, when the internecine warfare that raged between the various factions and schools of contemporary composition was particularly fierce, George Crumb came to prominence with music that sought to synthesize the conservative trends, the use of a chromatic vocabulary, and the most avant-garde experimental approaches. Although Crumb's music is integrative, the exact mix is, of course, determined by his personal style and the particular requirements of the work.

Crumb has said that his principal influences are Debussy, Mahler, and Bartók. Moreover, he is much attracted by the ritualistic and exotic, producing scores that are distinguished by the delicate perfection of their tonal effects, as well as by their new sonorities. In seeking to achieve his strong musical images, Crumb employs such unconventional means as masks for the performers, electronically amplified instruments, and tuned water glasses, which are played during *Black Angels for Electric String Quartet.*

George Crumb was born into a musical family; his father was a band leader, his mother, a cellist, and his brother played flute. He received his training at the Mason College of Music (Charleston) and the University of Illinois and received a Doctor of Musical Arts degree from the University of Michigan. His most important composition teachers were Eugene Weigel and Ross Lee Finney. Crumb's teaching career began at the University of Colorado (1959–1965); since then he has been at the University of Pennsylvania, where he was named Composer in Residence. He has received honors and awards from the Rockefeller, Koussevitsky, Guggenheim, and Coolidge foundations, and the National Institute of Arts and Letters. In 1968 he received the Pulitzer Prize for Music.

137

Black Angels for Electric String Quartet

Black Angels, subtitled "Thirteen Images from the Dark Land," is, as the composer has written, a "parable on our troubled contemporary world" based on "the essential polarity God versus Devil," or Black Angel. The thirteen separate sections, which portray "a voyage of the soul," are organized into a huge archlike design in three stages: Departure (fall from grace), Absence and Black Angels! (spiritual annihilation), and Return (redemption).

Crumb has identified the thirteen short movements as:

I. *Departure.*   1. (Tutti) THRENODY I: Night of the Electric Insects.   2. (Trio) Sounds of Bones and Flutes.   3. (Duo) Lost Bells.   4. (Solo: Cadenza accompagnata) Devil-music.   5. (Duo) Danse macabre (Duo alternativo: Dies Irae).

II. *Absence.*   6. (Trio) Pavana Lachrymae (Der Tod und das Mädchen) (Solo obbligato: Insect Sounds).   7. (Tutti) THRENODY

II. *Black Angels!*   8. (Trio) Sarabanda de la muerta Oscura (Solo obbligato: Insect Sounds).   9. (Duo) Lost Bells (Echo) (Duo alternativo: Sounds of Bones and Flutes).

III. *Return.*   10. (Solo: Aria: Aria accompagnata) God-music.   11. (Duo) Ancient Voices.   12. (Trio) Ancient Voices (Echo).   13. (Tutti) THRENODY III: Night of the Electric Insects.

The composer has written the following comments on the music:

> The numerological symbolism of *Black Angels,* while perhaps not immediately perceptible to the ear, is nonetheless quite faithfully reflected in the musical structure. These "magical" relationships are variously expressed; *e.g.,* in terms of phrase-length, groupings of single tones, durations, patterns of repetition, etc. An important pitch element in the work—ascending D-sharp, A and E—also symbolizes the fateful numbers 7–13. At certain points in the score there occurs a kind of ritualistic counting in various languages, including German, French, Russian, Hungarian, Japanese and Swahili.

> There are several allusions to tonal music in *Black Angels*: a quotation from Schubert's "Death and the Maiden" quartet (in the Pavana Lachrymae and also faintly echoed on the last page of the work); an original Sarabanda, which is stylistically synthetic; the sustained B-major tonality of God-music; and several references to the Latin sequence Dies Irae ("Day of Wrath"). The work abounds in conventional musical sym-

138

bolisms such as the *Diabolus in Musica* (the interval of the tritone) and the *Trillo di Diavolo* (the "Devil's Trill" after Tartini).

The amplification of the stringed instruments in *Black Angels* is intended to produce a highly surrealistic effect. This surrealism is heightened by the use of certain musical string effects: *e.g.*, pedal tones (the intensely obscene sounds of the Devil-music); bowing on the "wrong" side of the strings (to produce the viol-consort effect); trilling on the strings with thimble-capped fingers. The performers also play maracas, tam-tams and water-tuned crystal glasses, the latter played with the bow for the "glass-harmonica" effect in God-music.

Black Angels was commissioned by the University of Michigan and first performed by the Stanley Quartet. The score is inscribed: "finished on Friday the Thirteenth, March 1970 (*in tempore belli*)."

Voice of the Whale

Late in the 1960s, George Crumb heard a tape recording prepared by a marine scientist of the sounds emitted by the humpbacked whale. He was struck both by the quality of the sounds themselves and by the amazing natural phenomenon of these behemoths of the sea singing as they course through the waters. In 1971 Mr. Crumb drew on these sounds as the inspiration for a chamber work, *Voice of the Whale,* composed for the New York Camerata and scored for flute, cello, and piano.

Crumb made several specific suggestions for performances of *Voice of the Whale.* The sounds of all three instruments are electronically amplified. The performers wear either black half-masks or visor masks. "The masks," Mr. Crumb explains, "by effacing the sense of human projection, are intended to represent symbolically the powerful, impersonal forces of nature, that is to say, nature dehumanized." And he has asked that, whenever possible, the music be performed under deep blue stage lighting.

Crumb has described the music in the following words:

The form of *Voice of the Whale* is a simple three-part design, consisting of a Prologue, a set of variations named after the geological eras, and an epilogue.

The opening vocalise, marked in the score, "Wildly fantastic, grotesque," is a kind of cadenza for the flutist, who simultaneously plays his or her instrument and sings into it. This combination of instrumental and vocal sound produces an eerie, surreal timbre, not unlike the sounds

139

of the humpbacked whale. The conclusion of the cadenza is announced by a parody of the opening measures of Strauss's *Also Sprach Zarathustra*. The sea theme, marked in the score, "Solemn, with calm majesty," is presented by the cello in harmonics, accompanied by dark fateful chords of strummed piano strings.

The following sequence of variations begins with the haunting sea gull cries of the Archeozoic, marked, "Timeless, inchoate," and gradually increasing in intensity, reaches a strident climax in the Cenozoic, marked, "Dramatic, with a feeling of destiny." The emergence of man in the Cenozoic era is symbolized by a restatement of the *Zarathustra* reference.

The concluding *Sea Nocturne,* marked, "Serene, pure, transfigured," is an elaboration of the sea theme. The piece is couched in the luminous tonality of B major, and there are shimmering sounds of antique cymbals played alternately by the cellist and flutist. In composing the *Sea Nocturne* I wanted to suggest a larger rhythm of nature and a sense of suspension in time. The concluding gesture of the work is a gradually dying series of repetitions of a ten-note figure. In concert performance the last figure is to be played in pantomime, to suggest a diminuendo beyond the threshold of hearing.

Ingolf Dahl

Born June 9, 1912, in Hamburg, Germany
Died August 6, 1970, in Bern, Switzerland

BORN IN Germany to Swedish parents, Ingolf Dahl received his first compositional training at the Cologne Conservatory, with Philipp Jarnach and Hermann Abendroth, and did advanced work at the Zurich Conservatory and the University of Zurich, with an additional period of study under Nadia Boulanger. In 1938, on the eve of World War II, he emigrated to the United States, settled in Los Angeles, and started his career in America as an arranger for film and radio. In Hollywood he also became closely associated with Igor Stravinsky and deeply involved in fostering performances of contemporary music on the West Coast.

Under Stravinsky's influence Dahl moved away from the highly dissonant and polyphonically complex expressionistic composition style he had favored in Europe and adopted an approach that was clear, direct, and in general, more traditional. Dahl began to use standard harmonies and became interested in exploring the different tonal colors, timbres, and virtuosic potential of the various instruments.

Chamber music was an important component of the small body of music he produced. In addition to his well-known Music for Brass Instruments, his major chamber works include Allegro and Arioso (woodwind quintet, 1942), *Concertino a Tre* (clarinet, violin, and cello, 1946), Piano Quartet (1957), Serenade (four flutes, 1960) and Piano Trio (1962). The Music for Brass Instruments is not only significant in Dahl's oeuvre, it also triggered a new interest in writing for these instruments, which had been languishing for about 200 years before his pioneering work.

Music for Brass Instruments

I. Chorale Fantasy.   II. Intermezzo.   III. Fugue.

A slow, solemn fanfare summons the listeners to pay attention, much as a tolling bell calls the congregants to worship. Dahl devotes the body of the movement to a freely realized fantasia on Bach's Easter chorale, *Christ Lag in Todesbanden* (*"Christ Lay in Bonds of Death"*), the subject also of Bach's well-known cantata. By offering up an amazing range of musical and sonic effects from whispered passages to showy flourishes, from perfectly balanced chorale sections to long-phrased cantabile melodies, Dahl exploits the full range of each brass instrument. The movement ending is reminiscent of the opening fanfare.

The playful Intermezzo is permeated by a delightful short rhythmic phrase. Around this tune, Dahl embroiders a bright tapestry of countermelodies, lively chattering accompaniment figures, and contrasting episodes that effectively create a mood of jolly good humor.

The Fugue is not written in Bach's style, but is rather a highly dramatic three-part movement, with a number of fugal passages. After some introductory chords, Dahl brings in the sharply delineated five-note subject, which is treated in imitation by the individual instruments. A quieter and slower middle section introduces the second subject, characterized by its large melodic leaps. The third part closely resembles the opening in thematic content and spirit.

Music for Brass Instruments was composed in 1942 and was introduced at the 1944 Contemporary Music Festival in Los Angeles.

Franz Danzi

Born June 15, 1763, at Schwetzingen, Germany
Died April 13, 1826, at Karlsruhe, Germany

FRANZ DANZI, although a composer of great reputation and impressive achievement during his lifetime, might be all but forgotten today, were it not for his nine woodwind quintets. The works are of both historical and musical interest. They were among the first compositions ever written for the woodwind-quintet combination of flute, oboe, clarinet, French horn, and bassoon; and they helped to establish a style of writing characterized by vitality, clarity, and freshness of melody, that is perfectly suited to this instrumental group.

Danzi's father, a professional cellist, gave the boy his first instruction in cello, piano, and composition. Young Franz learned well, and at age fifteen he was accepted into the renowned orchestra in Mannheim, where he also began his composition studies with Abbé Vogler. Five years later he replaced his father as first cellist in the more prestigious Munich orchestra, and had his initial success as an opera composer. After leaving this position, he worked as court conductor, first in Stuttgart (from 1807), and then in Karlsruhe (from 1812).

The nine woodwind quintets were written during Danzi's stay in Karlsruhe, probably in the early 1820s. They were published in groups of three each, as Opp. 56, 67, and 68. Danzi organized them all in essentially the same four-movement form. The outside movements are weighty in concept, fast in tempo, and quite lengthy. The second is the slow movement, and the third is the dance, a minuet. In style, they are all rather firmly rooted in the Classical tradition, but with certain Romantic elements and emotional expressivity.

143

Woodwind Quintet in G Minor, Op. 56, No. 2

I. Allegretto. II. Andante. III. Menuetto: Allegretto. IV. Allegretto.

Danzi supplies the imposing first movement of this quintet, probably the most popular of the nine that he wrote, with an abundance of thematic material. Thus, even though the movement is organized in sonata form, one's attention is drawn more to the individual motifs—their sharply different characters and varying relationships. In quick order we hear the perky opening theme, followed by a very smooth, vocal melody and, after a few measures of virtuosic display, a highly rhythmic dancelike section. The remainder of the movement is then concerned with working out and returning this material.

The initial melody of the particularly striking Andante, which is delivered by the French horn, is especially warm and noble. The more active second theme, announced by the oboe, sets into even greater relief the burnished beauty of the horn melody. The themes are then repeated, but with the oboe taking over the horn subject, and the flute replacing the oboe for the second melody.

Danzi calls the third movement Menuetto, but its one-beat-to-a bar lilt and its rhythmic patterns make it sound much more like a waltz, or its precursor, the Austrian peasant Ländler. The trio, in major after the minor-key Menuetto, is simply a short, pleasant interlude that gives the flutist an opportunity to shine for a while before the Menuetto's return.

Formally the finale is related to the first movement with its manipulation of several different thematic fragments. It differs, though, in that all the motifs are cheery and jovial in character. To further confirm the optimistic feeling he has engendered, Danzi ends the movement with the final theme in the bright major mode.

Claude-Achille Debussy

Born August 22, 1862, at Saint-Germaine-en-Laye, near Paris
Died March 25, 1918, at Paris

IN 1889, just as he was entering his maturity as a composer, Debussy summarized his feelings on music: "Music begins where words are powerless to express. Music is made for the inexpressible, and I should like it to seem to rise from the shadows and indeed sometimes to return to them."

Debussy's music does, in fact, strive to convey the ineffable and to depict the mists and the darkness. Ever-shifting harmonies, brief snatches of melody, and a kaleidoscope of tone colors pulsate and shimmer through his music, following their inner logic and direction, without the clear, well-marked structural organization that characterized the music of the past.

The tonal world that Debussy created was not an outgrowth of the music that came before. As critic André Suares said of his music: "Before it happened there was no reason to suppose it ever would." Yet, if we look at the changes taking place in the years when the composer was growing up, we can understand the forces that shaped his music.

The prevailing philosophy in the middle decades of the nineteenth century in France was August Comte's positivism, which defined reality as only that which has an objective existence, subject to empirical proof. The leading painters, Millet and Courbet, were the realists, and the dominant literary figure, often called a naturalist, was Gustave Flaubert.

As the Franco-Prussian War of 1870 brought this era to a close, a group of painters, including Manet, Monet, Pissarro, Degas, and Renoir, came to the fore. Named the Impressionists, their goal was

145

to depict personal responses to the fleeting, evanescent atmosphere of objects in the real world. They wanted to suggest rather than state, to portray sensory experiences rather than demonstrate actual form and substance.

Paralleling the rise of Impressionist art in the 1870s was Symbolism, the literary movement of the 1880s. Baudelaire, Mallarmé, Verlaine, and Rimbaud were its leading lights. The Symbolists, along with the Impressionists, wanted their art to appeal to the senses rather than the intellect. They used words more as symbols and musical elements than for their literal meanings. Mallarmé once stated the artistic aim of the Symbolists: "To evoke in a deliberate shadow the unmentioned object by allusive words."

As a youngster, Debussy was little aware of the great intellectual and artistic foment of the time. His parents were poor shopkeepers, and he never even attended school but was taught to read and write by his mother. At the urging of an aunt, Debussy started piano lessons at the age of six. He advanced rapidly and entered the Paris Conservatoire at age eleven, where he garnered a number of prizes and graduated with the prestigious Prix de Rome in 1884.

Debussy returned to Paris in 1887, and spent much of his time with artists, poets, and musicians in the popular cafes discussing the major philosophic and artistic concerns of the time. He was a striking figure with his short legs and wide shoulders, curly black hair covering his large, prominent forehead, black beard, and swarthy complexion, all topped by a cowboy-style hat.

Throughout his student days he had fought against the traditions of the past. When asked why he had chosen certain chords in a harmony class, Debussy simply replied, "My pleasure." Now he began to forge an original musical style, spiritually akin to Impressionism and Symbolism and drawn from a number of different sources: the melodic practices of the Russian composers Borodin and Moussourgsky; the sounds, textures, and exotic scales of eastern music; the clarity, precision, and refined qualities of eighteenth-century French composers; and the decorative arabesques of Oriental melody. Informing and organizing these disparate elements was a keen musical intelligence and an amazingly sensitive and highly developed ear for sonority and nuance.

Debussy's startlingly original music is often called Impressionistic, although Symbolistic is probably more apt. In any case, it effectively set the stage for the development of twentieth-century music into its many new and varied forms.

146

Quartet in G Minor, Op. 10

I. Animé et très decidé.   II. Assez vif et bien rythmé.   III. Andantino, doucement expressif.   IV. Très modéré; Très mouvemente.

The period around 1890 was a crucial time in Debussy's life. The composer had just returned to Paris after a two-year Prix de Rome residency in Italy and was eager to rid himself of the restraints of the academicians. One of the first works in which he struck a new artistic direction was the Quartet in G minor, which, along with *"L'Après-midi d'un faune"* from the same time, established what is called the Impressionist style in music. Its varied tonal effects, soulful beauty, and freedom of form and structure provide an excellent musical counterpart to the Impressionist paintings and Symbolist poetry of the time.

The opening notes of the first movement are of overriding importance. They make up the germ, the melodic cell, from which the entire quartet unfolds and grows. This germinal motif is a rather rough-sounding motto; rhythmically complex and melodically convoluted, it zigzags back and forth within a comparatively limited tessitura. A distinguishing feature is the rapid three-note ornamental fillip at the central turning point.

Following the short motif and its repetition, three other melodies are heard. They come between restatements of the motif, each time, though, in a slightly different form. The various themes, and especially the opening motto, are then heard in an imaginative procession of transformed shapes and guises—now surging with great passion, now stated in stentorian splendor, now stretched and drawn out in length, now plaintively sung—until the movement races to its climactic resolution.

The second movement offers a profusion of sparkling tonal effects, led by the viola playing an obstinately repeated, quickened version of the motif. Above, beneath, and all around this *ostinato* figure, the other instruments furnish brilliant pizzicato flourishes and scintillating cross-rhythms. The cello brings this section to a close and establishes the murmuring accompaniment for the first violin playing the opening motif in leisurely augmentation. Sections of new and derived melodic material follow, including a rhythmically attractive pizzicato passage in which the original motto is transformed into five-beat meter. Then, just as the cello seems to be starting the murmuring accompaniment again, the movement fades away.

147

After false starts by the second violin and viola, the third movement starts with the first violin softly singing a languid melody that rocks gently back and forth in pitch. The viola next seizes one fragment of the melody and expands it into a slightly faster theme. Another theme, also introduced by the viola, includes the three-note figure of the opening motto. It is worked up to an impassioned climax before a return of the quiet rocking theme brings the movement to a subdued conclusion.

The introduction to the final movement, also based on the original motif, continues the quiet mood. The music grows somewhat more animated as the cello starts a fuguelike passage, using a further transformation of the germinal motif. The fast part of the last movement then starts with a rapid, cluster-of-notes theme in the viola. From the final notes of this theme, Debussy spins out another melody. The shared notes of both themes become the accompaniment for the motif, this time in grandiose elongation. A reminder of the opening theme of this movement leads to a coda and conclusion that provide a final, exciting glimpse of the considerably altered germinal motto.

Completed early in 1893, the quartet was dedicated to the Ysaye Quartet, which gave the first performance in Paris on December 29, 1893.

Sonata No. 2 for Flute, Viola, and Harp

I. Pastorale. II. Interlude. III. Finale.

With the outbreak of World War I in August 1914, fifty-two-year-old Debussy was thrown into the depths of despair. At the same time the Germans were bombarding his beloved Paris, he seemed to be losing his own battle with cancer. The combined drain of the French military defeats and his failing health left him unable to compose anything of consequence for almost a year.

Early in the summer of 1915, Debussy left Paris for the village of Pourville near Dieppe. It was here that his desire, if not his need, to compose was revived. He explained his motivation in a letter: "I want to work, not so much for myself, but to give proof, however small it may be, that not even 30 million *Boches* can destroy French thought."

Debussy determined to advance a national French music, free of all German influence. The course he followed was to effect a synthesis

148

between the new directions he had pioneered in his earlier music, and the clarity and refinement of France's two great eighteenth-century composers, Couperin and Rameau. "Where is French music?" Debussy asked. "Where are the old harpsichordists who had so much true music? They had the secret of gracefulness and emotion without epilepsy, which we have negated like ungrateful children."

Debussy planned a series of six sonatas for diverse instruments. Working "like a madman," as he put it, he produced the first, a Sonata for Cello and Piano, in August of 1915. The very next month he began the sonata for Flute, Viola, and Harp, finishing it just before his return to Paris on October 12. In 1917 he completed the Sonata for Violin and Piano, the last of the six sonatas that he was to write. And lest there be any doubt as to the genesis of these works, he signed each one Claude Debussy, *musicien français*.

Texturally, the second sonata is austere and lean; each instrument stands out in clear relief with its strikingly different timbre. The instrumental writing is highly decorated and ornamental, with many of the melodies little more than arabesques or filigrees. The style is improvisatory, with fluid rhythms. The composer described the mood of the sonata as ". . . terribly melancholy—should one laugh or cry? Perhaps both at the same time?"

The formal organization springs from the material itself. The first movement is highly episodic. Each of the several themes is briefly stated, subjected to elaboration, and allowed to fade away to make room for the next theme, which is treated in much the same way, with but few returns of previous melodies.

The second movement is an obvious reference to the French Baroque masters who served as Debussy's inspiration. Alternating with the triple-meter minuetlike sections are duple-meter passages, somewhat faster in tempo and characterized by an Oriental-sounding drone in the harp.

The melodies in the final movement seem related in style and character to those of the opening. To emphasize the affinity, Debussy closes with a section that recalls the opening melody of the work.

The sonata, which Debussy dedicated to his daughter, Claude-Emma, received its first performance on April 21, 1917, at a concert of the Société Musicale Indépendante, played by Manouvrier, flute, Jarecki, viola, and Jamet, harp.

Jacob Druckman

Born June 26, 1928, in Philadelphia

JACOB DRUCKMAN began studies on the violin and piano as a young-ster and soon was playing violin with his friends in chamber music groups. He also learned to play the trumpet well enough to join a jazz combo. At age twelve Druckman began composing and within a few years decided to devote all of his musical energies to that end. After studying composition with Aaron Copland at Tanglewood dur-ing the summer of 1949, he entered the Juilliard School of Music, where his composition teachers were Peter Mennin, Bernard Wage-naar, and Vincent Persichetti.

Recognition came early to Druckman. He was awarded a Ful-bright Fellowship in 1954 and went on to win two Guggenheim Fel-lowships, a Pulitzer Prize, and awards from Brandeis University and the Society for the Publication of American Music. In 1978 he was elected to the American Academy and Institute of Arts and Letters. Many of his compositions have been commissioned and premiered by leading performers, ensembles, and orchestras; a good number have entered the standard concert repertoire. As part of his distinguished career as educator, Druckman has taught at the Juilliard School, Bard College, and Brooklyn College, and presently holds the position of Composition Department Chairman at Yale University.

Druckman's first compositions were influenced by the musical idioms of Debussy and Stravinsky, as well as by the large-scale or-chestral works of Ravel, Mahler, and Schoenberg. As he began to develop his own musical voice, however, Druckman became inter-ested in more advanced compositional techniques characterized by rigorous control and organization of pitch material on the one hand and by aleatoric, or chance, techniques, on the other. These seem-ingly opposite approaches were reconciled in his String Quartet No. 2, composed in 1966.

151

Over the following years a strong new theatrical element entered Druckman's music, and he began to move toward a "new Romanticism." Stylistic borrowings and quotations from music of the past became part of his musical vocabulary, and he integrated these elements into a distinctive and personal manner of expression

In addition to several works dating back to the 1950s, Druckman's chamber music output includes "Dark Upon the Harp" (mezzo-soprano, brass quintet, and percussion, 1962), String Quartet No. 2 (discussed below), "Animus II" (mezzo-soprano, two percussionists and electronic tape, 1968), and "Other Voices" (brass quintet, 1976).

String Quartet No. 2

The String Quartet No. 2, the second of three essays in the form, was commissioned by the Juilliard Quartet, which gave the first performance in New York on December 13, 1966, one month after its completion. The quartet was written at a critical point in the composer's development, when he was concerned with resolving conflicting musical and philosophical views. Druckman was deeply absorbed with the twelve-tone method of Arnold Schoenberg, in which the music is based on a specific arrangement of the twelve notes of the chromatic scale and with the serial technique developed by Anton Webern, which goes beyond the twelve-tone method to impose a particular order on such musical elements as tone color, texture, dynamics, register, and pitch. At the same time, Druckman was composing his first electronic composition, "Animus I," for Trombone and Tape (1966), which caused him to reexamine his entire approach to instrumental writing. Exposure to Elliott Carter's first two string quartets led to an awareness of the full potential for the use of advanced rhythmic concepts in his own works. And he was adapting to his own purposes the aleatoric techniques associated with the compositions of John Cage.

While experimenting with these different musical tendencies, Druckman also found himself gradually shifting away from the intellectual approach that had predominated in his earlier music and moving in a more dramatic and humanistic direction. String Quartet No. 2, then, is an integrative work that balances several major musical influences and thus represents a signal junction point in Druckman's creative development.

Mr. Druckman has written this brief description of his string quartet:

> The work is played without pause, the major sections being marked by the recurrence of unisons. These moments of unison, both in pitch and rhythm, describe the generative set of the work; and the concept of moving toward or away from unison is extended to the areas of texture and dramatic intent.

The quartet falls into five sections, nearly equal in length, that are separated by four cadenzas, one for each player, each with its own assigned musical character, particularly as defined by the cadenzas. According to Andrew Jenning, second violinist of the Concord Quartet (as quoted in the record liner notes by Lejaren Hiller), the composer described for the players the basic temperament of each of the instruments: the viola is "rhapsodic," the first violin, "flamboyant," the cello, "dramatic in a stentorian sort of way," and the second violin, "whimpering."

The entire piece is based on a particular arrangement of the twelve tones known as a tone row. Druckman manipulates the row in various ways, playing it backwards, upside down, and *both* backwards and upside down (which proves to be the same as the original row!), but without consistently and rigidly following the rules of twelve-tone composition. Because of its great complexity, the quartet is usually performed from the score, so that each player can see, as well as hear, what the others are doing.

Mr. Druckman makes use of a number of special performance techniques, such as indicating that the players drum on their instruments with their fingertips and press harder with the bow than is usually necessary. Also, he employs aleatoric techniques—allowing chance to determine how and in what ways the various parts fit together. No matter how unusual the musical devices or how striking the sounds, Druckman uses them not as ends in themselves, but as a means to producing an original and imaginative musical statement.

Antonin Dvořák

Born September 8, 1841, in Nelahozeves, near Prague
Died May 1, 1904, in Prague

DVOŘÁK'S MUSIC is a clear reflection of the circumstances of his own life, of current musical trends, and of the major political movements of the time. Coming from Slavic peasant stock, Dvořák was born in the Bohemia area of what is now Czechoslovakia. His father, a poor butcher and innkeeper, played the zither at local weddings and other festivities and sometimes composed original dance tunes. Before very long, young Antonin was playing fiddle with his father.

Although his father planned for Antonin to follow his trade as a butcher, music won out, and by age sixteen the young man was in Prague getting a solid grounding in Classical musical practices. His models were such composers as Mozart, Schubert, and especially Beethoven. By the mid 1860s, though, the music of Bedřich Smetana, based as it is on the folk idiom of Bohemia, was making a powerful impression on Dvořák, and he realized that the tunes he learned from his father could be a wonderful source of inspiration for his own music. Dvořák, who felt a deep affection for his native land, now saw how this love of country could be expressed in music and how this nationalistic strain could become an integral part of his compositions.

While Dvořák was discovering musical nationalism, the Czech people, who had long been ruled by the Hapsburgs from Vienna, were struggling to break free and establish their own nation. Although Dvořák was a committed Czech patriot, he was not a revolutionary. "But what have we to do with politics?" he once wrote to his publisher. "It is well that we are free to dedicate our services to a splendid art." While not directly involved in the agitation for Czech freedom, however, Dvořák could not help being swept up in the patriotic political fervor of the time.

Dvořák's musical nationalism seldom took the form of quoting

155

folk song melodies, but rather found him incorporating the traditional turns of melody and rhythmic patterns of Slavonic folk music into his own works. His chamber music, for example, contains many movements based on a popular folk form, the Dumka (from the Slavic word *dumati,* meaning "to meditate or recollect"). These narrative-type folk songs, which are particularly popular in the Ukraine, originally referred to remembrances in verse or song of the lives and deeds of ancient heroes. Formally, they alternate slow, elegiac sections with refrains of gay vivacity. Dvořák adapted this style in the Dumka movements of his String Quartet, Op. 51; Piano Quintet, Op. 81; and "Dumky" Trio, Op. 90. His chamber works also contain a number of movements that obviously spring from the Furiant, a lively Bohemian dance (unrelated etymologically to the English word "fury") in which patterns of duple meter are superimposed on the already established triple meter.

The folk influence, as filtered through his own musical imagination, was a major factor in Dvořák's music, with some exceptions. Around 1870, Dvořák was strongly affected by Liszt and Wagner and incorporated certain aspects of their musical style into his own writing. Somewhat later he even considered turning his back on the Bohemian wellsprings and moving to Vienna to devote himself to the composition of German opera (instead of the Czech operas he had been writing). But perhaps the greatest time of stylistic change occurred while Dvořák was in America, from 1892 to 1895, serving as director of the National Conservatory in New York City. In the United States the composer listened with great interest to black plantation songs and spirituals and to the music of the American Indians. It was while spending his summer holiday of 1893 in Spillville, Iowa, a tiny farming community where many Bohemian families lived, that Dvořák wrote the "American" Quartet, Op. 96, and the Viola Quintet, Op. 97, two pieces that show the impact of American music on his style.

Dvořák's music has the sound of a composer at peace with himself, content with his lot in life. We know that he was successful and highly respected and free of the stress and anxiety that plagued so many other composers. His special strengths—the ability to create original melodies of great charm, beauty, and freshness and a highly developed musical intelligence—delight us to this day. A prolific composer, Dvořák produced a sizable body of works in every form. His considerable chamber music output includes fourteen string quartets, a piano quintet, four piano trios, two piano quartets, a viola quintet, a string sextet, a string trio, and a few miscellaneous works. Within this long list are a good number that are part of the modern repertoire, and these are presented below.

String Quartet in E Flat Major, Op. 51

I. Allegro ma non troppo. II. Dumka: Andante con moto; Vivace. III. Romanze: Andante con moto. IV. Finale: Allegro assai.

The year 1878 was particularly auspicious for Dvořák, both personally and musically. The birth of a daughter in June, following the earlier losses of two children, was truly a blessed event. His career was flourishing as his three *Slavonic Rhapsodies,* the first set of *Slavonic Dances,* and the string sextet scored great artistic successes. Dvořák was also lauded for capturing the directness, warmth, simplicity, and infectious merriment of native Czech folk music, without resorting to overt borrowing of national melodies.

On the basis of his growing fame, Jean Becker of the Florentine Quartet asked Dvořák to write a quartet in the Slavic style. The result was the very charming and beautiful Op. 51, in which Dvořák intergrates elements of Czech national music with his basically Classical approach to composition.

The first movement reflects the serenity and contentment that Dvořák was experiencing at the time. The radiant first theme proceeds calmly; of special interest are the little figures at the ends of each phrase that bring to mind the dance rhythms of the Czech polka. The second theme, slightly more intense than the first, maintains the lightness of mood with the reappearance of the polka rhythm. After a development devoted mostly to the first theme, Dvořák starts the truncated recapitulation with the second theme, reserving the opening theme for the coda.

Dvořák's Dumka movements are traditionally slow and melancholy in character, with one or more fast, lively contrasting sections. Over strummed harplike chords in the cello, the first violin, echoed by the viola, sings the sad lament. In time this gives way to the saucy interlude, which resembles the popular Czech folk dance, Furiant. Melodically, it is a fast, rhythmic refashioning of the slow Dumka melody. After a shortened review of the opening section, a coda based on the Furiant subject ends the movement.

Short and intimate, the Romanze is the most songlike and least nationalistic of the four movements. It derives essentially from one theme, which Dvořák, most imaginatively and with great ardor, transforms, ornaments, and develops.

The Finale theme, akin to the *skačna,* a fast, boisterous Bohemian reel dance, is stated initially by the first violin, but is soon taken up by the others. A slightly slower and more serious subsidiary subject in the second violin intrudes on the good time, but its playful aspects are soon brought out as Dvořák speeds up the tempo and later gives it to the first violin and cello, playing a full four octaves apart. The two subjects are developed in more or less conventional sonata form, before reaching an exuberant climactic close.

Although dedicated to Jean Becker of the Florentine Quartet, the premiere was given by the Joachim Quartet in Berlin on July 29, 1879.

Piano Quintet in A Major, Op. 81

I. Allegro, ma non tanto.   II. Dumka: Andante con moto; Vivace.   III. Scherzo (Furiant): Molto vivace.   IV. Finale: Allegro.

Dvořák composed his first piano quintet (A major, Op. 5) in 1872, but, unhappy with the results, destroyed the score shortly after its premiere later that year. Some fifteen years went by and Dvořák reconsidered his rash act. He retrieved a friend's copy of the music and made extensive revisions. Still not satisfied, he decided not to submit it for publication after all. Instead, he wrote the completely new Piano Quintet in A major, Op. 81, which is now one of the three acknowledged masterpieces in the form; the others are by Schumann and Brahms.

By 1887 Dvořák had achieved acclaim and acceptance for his nationalistic music, having passed through a few years of crisis in the early 1880s, a time when he was torn between his desire to continue incorporating national musical elements into his compositions and the urging of Brahms and other friends to live in Vienna and devote himself to the creation of operas in German. As part of his renewed devotion to the Bohemian folk idiom, Dvořák composed the piano quintet, the E flat piano quartet, and the "Dumky" Trio, works that have come to epitomize the composer's nationalistic style.

Fresh and lovely, gleaming with bright melodies, glowing harmonies, and piquant rhythms, the quintet opens with a wonderfully lyrical theme in the cello. Dvořák immediately puts the melody through a succession of transformations before the viola introduces the second subject, less cantabile than the first, and with a slight tinge of sadness. Here, too, Dvořák varies the melody at once, changing its serious character to one of increasing jubilation. After a full development of the two subjects, Dvořák has a free recapitulation that is much shorter than the exposition.

The Dumka is modeled on an old folk-ballad form, with repetitions of a sober, pensive melody separated by fast, happy interludes. It can be diagrammed as A-B-A-C-A-B-A. The A section consists of the refrain (piano) and variations on the melancholy principal theme (viola); B is a contrasting melody, fast and sunny, shared by both violins and the piano. After the return of A, the quick and vigorous C section, which is derived from the opening refrain, is announced by the viola. The overall elegiac tone, alternating with abrupt changes in mood and tempo, readily conveys the spirit of the Slavonic folk ballads that were Dvořák's source of inspiration.

Although Dvořák parenthetically adds *Furiant* after the title, Scherzo, this movement lacks some of the customary characteristics of the folk-dance form. It sounds rather like a fast waltz, with a slow middle section that is really a nostalgic reminder of the Scherzo section and a shortened repeat of the first part in conclusion.

The Finale is a high-spirited, lightsome cap to the entire quintet. Combining the vigor of a peasant dance with the playful badinage of a humorous folk song, the entire movement, including a fugal section in the development and chorale in the coda, coruscates brilliantly throughout.

Dvořák composed the quintet from August 18 to October 8, 1887, and it was first heard in Prague on January 6, 1888.

Piano Quartet in E Flat Major, Op. 87

I. Allegro con fuoco.   II. Lento.   III. Allegro moderato, grazioso.   IV. Finale: Allegro ma non troppo.

For some four years, starting in 1885, Dvořák's publisher, Simrock, pressed him to compose a second piano quartet. (The first, Op. 23 in D major, was written in 1875.) Finally on August 10, 1889, Dvořák acceded and in one month was able to write his friend, Alois Göbl, "I've now already finished three movements of a new piano quartet, and the Finale will be ready in a few days. As I expected it came easily, and the melodies just surged upon me, Thank God!'' The quartet was indeed completed on August 19, and the premiere was given in Prague on November 23, 1890.

Although the E flat piano quartet was composed during Dvořák's nationalistic phase, it does not show extensive use of folklike themes. The quartet opens with a bold, courageous unison statement by the strings that draws a capricious response from the piano. The strings quickly change their tune, making it sweet and tender. The piano, though, keeps to its willful and carefree ways, until all four players join in a jubilant statement of the original string figure. The music then quiets in a transition to the second theme, a soulful melody for the viola. Freely following the outlines of sonata form, Dvořák then presents a richly textured, highly imaginative musical voyage based on the introductory material. Of special interest is the effect Dvořák achieves in the final measures of the movement, as the violin and viola play fragments of the opening theme with rapid, tremolo bow strokes on each of the notes.

Like a painting in which each face in a crowd portrays a different emotion—anger, fear, defiance, love, disgust—the Lento consists of five distinct themes, each with its own particular quality. The first theme, played by the cello, is intense and romantic, hinting at some mysterious passion. The violin enters with the next melody, an aloof and poised air, that maintains its calm in the face of all the activity in the other instruments. Excitement, even agitation, is borne on the piano's statement of the third melody. The fourth melody's stormy character is unleashed by the entire group, before the fifth theme, heard in the piano, quiets the furor with a reassuring melody derived from the third theme. After stating the five melodies, Dvořák repeats them with almost no change.

The first theme of the delightful third movement introduces the swaying rhythm of the Ländler, the peasant dance that was precursor to the waltz. The second theme, entrusted to the piano, is reminiscent of an oriental or Middle Eastern folk dance, an influence occasionally heard in Bohemian folk music. Particularly striking are the piano repetitions of the principal theme, which are written to sound like a cimbalom, or hammered dulcimer, a favored folk instrument. A faster, dashing middle section appears before a literal repeat of the opening.

The vigorous and energetic Finale demands so much tone from the four performers that some critics claim that it requires the tonal resources of a full orchestra. The assertive first theme receives a tutti statement before the individual instruments have a go at the tune. Another melodic phrase, one that starts with repeated notes and ends with a descending scale, functions both as part of the first thematic group and then, in a different key, as the opening of the second subject, to be followed by an intense lyrical melody heard in the viola. Powerfully climactic at times, the movement builds to a brilliant conclusion.

Piano Trio in E Minor, Op. 90, "Dumky"

I. Lento maestoso; Allegro vivace, quasi doppio movimento. II. Poco adagio; Vivace non troppo. III. Andante; Vivace non troppo. IV. Andante moderato (quasi tempo di marcia); Allegretto scherzando. V. Allegro. VI. Lento maestoso; Vivace, quasi doppio movimento.

The "Dumky" Piano Trio, Dvořák's fifth and last work for this combination, was composed between November 1890 and February 12 of the following year, toward the end of the composer's nationalistic period, which ended with his departure for the United States in 1892. With Ferdinand Lachner, violin, and Hanus Wihan, cello, Dvořák gave the first performance in Prague on April 11, 1891, at a concert celebrating Dvořák's honorary doctorate from Prague's Charles University. The work was so well received that the performers presented it on a forty-concert tour just before Dvořák left for America. The "Dumky" was published in 1894, while Dvořák was still abroad. His good friend, Johannes Brahms, did the proofreading and, it is believed, made a few minor corrections in the music as well.

The "Dumky" Trio captures perfectly the melodic freshness and rhythmic verve of native Czech folk music in an original stylized composition. "Dumky" is the plural of "Dumka," a Slavic folk song with a pervasive melancholy or pensive quality that is relieved by sharply contrasting interludes, which range from serene to exuberant. The trio consists of six individual Dumka movements that are thematically unrelated but share a similarity of character and bear a loose structural unity. The movements roughly approximate that of a typical four-movement chamber work: the first three Dumky, played without pause, correspond to the first movement; the fourth Dumka, dominated by its deliberate, somber theme, functions as the slow movement; the bright, fast fifth Dumka resembles the scherzo; and the last Dumka is the rondo finale.

The beginning of the first Dumka, an impassioned, anguished recitative for piano and cello, gives way to the doleful principal melody that alternately ascends and descends the large melodic interval of the sixth. The second section, twice as fast and much brighter in mood, has the violin and piano gaily prancing through the dance rhythms, while the cello continues the opening theme as a counter-melody. Dvořák then repeats both sections, reversing the roles of the individual instruments.

In the second Dumka, the cello theme casts a funereal pall that is underscored by the slow, monotonous measured tread in the piano and the violin's muted echoes. The following piano melody, over a low, long-held pedal tone in the cello, seems to offer some solace, but the original character soon returns. When the fast contrast appears, with a trivial tune unworthy of the opening's seriousness, the cello resumes its low-pitched, sustained note. After a brief cello cadenza, both parts are repeated, although scored differently.

After a short introduction, the piano states the slow main theme of the third movement, a plaintive melody played, uncharacteristically, as single notes on the piano. Dvořák builds the fast contrast on motifs extracted from this theme and ends with a truncated review of the first section.

Calm resignation pervades the entire fourth movement. As the piano and violin repeat their *ostinato* accompaniment figures, the cello gives out the sad melody. The brief fast section is a gay, speeded-up refashioning of the cello tune. Both parts are then repeated, little changed from their first appearances. After the third hearing of the slow theme, though, Dvořák gradually accelerates to the fast refrain, now with new melodic content, which is followed by a final presentation of the slow subject and a coda.

The tempo of the lively, slightly nervous fifth Dumka is somewhat faster than that of the other movements. Dvořák, therefore, makes the contrasting middle section, which is derived from the same four-note ascending scale fragment, slower instead of faster than the opening. An elaboration of the first part follows and leads to an exultant ending.

After a lamenting introduction, the final movement presents a character of melancholy mingled with a gentle sweetness. The fast second part, which sounds like a child's play song, is essentially the first theme played faster. Both parts are freely repeated before a quick acceleration in the music moves to an abrupt conclusion.

String Quartet in F Major, Op. 96, "American"

I. Allegro ma non troppo. II. Lento. III. Molto vivace. IV. Finale: Vivace ma non troppo.

When Dvořák arrived in New York from Prague on September 17, 1892, he immediately took up his duties as director of the National Conservatory but also continued to compose and fulfill his many obligations as a visiting celebrity. By the end of the taxing season, he was delighted to accept an invitation to spend the summer visiting the tiny (population: 300) farming community of Spillville, Iowa, made up of Czech immigrants who preserved the language, culture, and customs of their native land. Dvořák arrived in Spillville on June 5 with his wife, six children, sister, maid, and secretary. Three days later he was already at work on a new string quartet. Although he usually composed quite slowly, he finished the sketches by June 11, writing at the end, "Thanks be to the Lord God. I am satisfied. It went quickly." As soon as the final score was ready, on June 23, Dvořák, playing violin, along with three students, read it through. The "official" premiere was given in Boston by the Kneisel Quartet on January 1, 1894.

Written just after the *"New World"* Symphony, his most famous symphony, this quartet became Dvořák's best known chamber music composition and acquired a similar nickname, the "American" Quartet. Many hear in the quartet strains of black spirituals and plantation songs, as well as elements of American Indian music. Others doubt that the quartet grew from the sounds Dvořák heard in America and hold rather that it is based on certain melodic and rhythmic similarities shared by both American ethnic music and the Bohemian-Slavic folk tradition. This difference of opinion really matters little in light of the "American" Quartet's enormous popularity and universal appeal.

Against a shimmering background that resembles the start of Smetana's E minor quartet (1876), the viola sings out the first jaunty tune. After the confident swagger of the viola melody, the second theme, played by the first violin, seems tentative and restrained. Both themes are based on the five-tone pentatonic scale (the black keys of a piano), a common feature of folk songs around the world. The following development is devoted to the first theme until a fugato based on the second subject acts as a transition to the restatement of both themes.

The Lento, widely considered the crowning movement of the quartet, is like a lovely emotional aria with the first violin and cello mostly involved with the melody and the second violin and viola sustaining a busy, flowing accompaniment. The movement's construction is arch-shaped, starting quietly and building gradually to an impassioned climax before fading to a subdued close, as the cello nostalgically goes through the melody for the last time, accompanied by alternate bowed and plucked notes.

Although cast in A-B-A-B-A form, the third movement is essentially monothematic, since B is little more than a slower version of the A tune. The middle part of the A section is based on the song of the scarlet tanager, which Dvořák heard and notated on his walks around Spillville.

The Finale immediately establishes a rhythmic pattern that may be an adaptation of native Indian drumming. The first violin dances its joyful tune with and around the continuing beat. Other melodies follow, all with the same high-spirited good humor. In the middle of the movement, the tempo slows, and Dvořák introduces a chorale, probably derived from one of the hymns that he enjoyed playing on the organ for services at Saint Wenceslas church in Spillville. Following the chorale is a shortened restatement of what came before, leading to a resolutely happy ending.

Viola Quintet in E Flat Major, Op. 97

I. Allegro non tanto.   II. Allegro vivo.
III. Larghetto.   IV. Finale: Allegro giusto.

During his stay in the United States, from 1892 to 1895, Dvořák wrote three major works that best exemplify his so-called American Style—the "New World" Symphony, the "American" String Quartet, and the E flat viola quintet. All three compositions were influenced, to some degree, by the folk and popular music he heard here, superimposed on his basic European musical vocabulary.

Since the folk music of many lands share certain features—the use of the pentatonic scale is a good example—it is often difficult to separate out the elements that characterize one country's music from another's. But in this case there is general agreement that some of the tunes were inspired by a traveling troupe of Iroquois Indians, who performed their songs and dances to attract crowds and sell their herbal medicines and whom Dvořák heard while visiting the settlement of newly emigrated Czech farmers at Spillville, Iowa, during the summer of 1893. The rhythmic drumming effects heard in several places throughout the quintet are thought to be Dvořák's evocation of Indian drumming.

Dvořák started work on the viola quintet on June 26, just after completing the "American" Quartet, and was finished in just over five weeks, on August 1, 1893. The Kneisel Quartet, with violist M. Zach, gave the premiere in Boston on January 1, 1894, on the same program that introduced the "American" Quartet.

The opening melody, first heard in highly expressive augmentation and then stripped down to its essentials, is indistinguishable from any Bohemian-inspired tune that Dvořák ever used. The second theme, though, more energetic and rhythmical, is heard over a drumming, dotted (long-short) rhythm, and is believed to be based on a known Indian melody. The treatment of this material follows the outline of traditional sonata form.

The second viola starts the Allegro vivo, really a scherzo, with an Indianlike drumbeat pattern. To this background Dvořák adds melodies and contrasting countermelodies of great freshness and charm. The pensive central trio, slightly slower and in the minor, features a soulful melody presented by the first viola. The last section is a literal repeat of the opening.

Formally, the Larghetto is a theme and five variations. The first part of the theme, which is heard at the outset, is characterized by a repeated descending motif; the second part, more lyrical and choralelike, is believed to be based on sketches for a new American national anthem that Dvořák had written in New York as a setting of the words beginning, "My country, 'tis of thee." The first two variations essentially decorate and ornament the original melody, the next one imaginatively divides the theme between the instruments, the fourth gives the leading part to the cello with a rapid tremolo in the others, and the fifth is an impassioned conclusion that quietly drifts away.

The Finale is an exhilarating rondo, with a rollicking principal melody built on the same dotted rhythm heard in the first movement. The first contrast, with its rapid repeats of each note and its percussive pizzicato accompaniment reminds us of traditional Indian music; the cantabile second interlude seems more Bohemian in character. Both contrasts and the original theme are now quickly reviewed, leading to a joyful and exciting conclusion.

String Quartet in A Flat Major, Op. 105

I. Adagio ma non troppo; Allegro appassionato. II. Molto vivace. III. Lento e molto cantabile. IV. Allegro, non tanto.

By early 1895, after having been in the United States about three years, Dvořák was eager to return to his native Bohemia. He missed his relatives and friends, the Bohemian countryside and cities, and yearned to see his country home in Vysoka, just outside Prague. While in this wistful mood, but still living in New York, Dvořák began composing a new string quartet, his Op. 105, on March 26, 1895. He finished exactly seventy measures of the first movement before sailing homeward in early April.

Dvořák spent the following months at Vysoka, but did no composing. In August he wrote to a friend, "My muse is now quite silent. For the whole four months I have not even taken up my pen." In the fall, though, when he returned to Prague to resume teaching at the Conservatory, he felt ready to start writing again. Instead of continuing with Op. 105, however, he began a new quartet, which he marked Op. 106. On December 12, three days after Op. 106 was done, Dvořák returned to Op. 105, finishing it on December 30, 1895. Op. 105 proved to be the last of the fourteen quartets that Dvořák wrote, his last piece of chamber music, and, in fact, his last piece of absolute music; the production of the following years consisted entirely of symphonic poems and operas.

In Op. 105 there are no overt traces of either the Americanisms he acquired from his stay in the United States or of the Slavonic character that infused so much of his earlier music. Rather, these elements are integrated into a wholly unified work that seems both a celebration of Dvořák's joy at being back home and his confident mastery of the quartet medium.

Before beginning the flowing, optimistic first movement, Dvořák inserts a sober, foreboding introduction. The gloom, though, is quickly dispelled by the first subject, which starts with an extroverted, rising phrase based on the melody heard in the introduction. After a bridge passage, the second theme is heard, a hunting horn call by the two violins over rushing triplets in the lower instruments, concluding the exposition (the only part that he wrote in New York).

Dvořák imaginatively works out the various themes in the development section and brings them back for a final review in the recapitulation.

The second movement, one of Dvořák's finest scherzos, is closely akin to a Furiant, the Bohemian folk dance, with its verve and irresistible rhythmic energy. Written in traditional three-part form, the melody for the songlike middle section Dvořák draws from the final bars of the opening part. The movement ends with a repeat of the opening.

Intentionally or unintentionally, the principal theme of the following Lento is somewhat similar in contour to the main theme of the first movement. The broadly conceived, romantic melody plays itself out before the highly chromatic subject of the middle section is heard above repeated notes in the cello. The music rises to an impassioned climax, and Dvořák then returns to the opening material. This time, though, the second violin plays a rapid little decorative figuration, which Dvořák marks *scherzando* ("playful"), adding a light touch to the predominantly serious character of the first theme.

Starting at the very bottom of the cello's range, the last movement appears to have some difficulty getting started and remains rather episodic throughout. The mood is one of warmth and geniality rather than of sparkling gaiety, of inner smiles rather than of joyful laughter. At the end, though, Dvořák's exuberance breaks through for an all-out happy conclusion.

At Dvořák's request the A flat quartet was introduced by four students at the Prague Conservatory on April 16, 1896, the first anniversary of his return home. Very shortly thereafter, though, it was taken up by professional quartets throughout Europe.

String Quartet in G Major, Op. 106

I. Allegro moderato. II. Adagio ma non troppo. III. Molto vivace. IV. Finale: Andante sostenuto; Allegro con fuoco.

Dvořák returned to Prague from his three-year stay in America in April 1895 but did not start to compose again until November. Instead of completing the quartet (Op. 105) that he had begun in New York, he started a new work, Op. 106, which he wrote from November 11 to December 9, 1895. After finishing this quartet, Dvořák completed his Op. 105, which explains why the opus numbers do not conform to the order of composition. The Op. 106 received its premiere in Prague on October 9, 1896, played by the Bohemian Quartet.

Most of the musical traits associated with Dvořák's so-called American style are no longer heard in Op. 106; the work is more Classical in outlook, and exhibits more of a Czech flavor. The playful opening theme is hardly a theme at all; two leaps up, a quick fluttering, and a descending triplet passage. Theme two is also very spare; a four-note, songlike phrase that is repeated several times. But Dvořák masterfully interweaves these brief motifs into a rich musical texture, with great flow, variety, and organic unity. The overall impression is that this is the work of a brilliant musical intelligence in full command of his materials.

The Adagio is one of the most perfectly realized and touching movements in Dvořák's chamber music. The single theme, an ardent, lyrical outpouring that seems to come from the very core of the composer's Slavic being, is first stated in major, then in minor. The form consists essentially of a free and richly varied alternation of the two major-minor musical paragraphs. As the movement reaches its climax, Dvořák presents a version of the theme marked *grandioso,* in which each musician plays two, three, or four notes simultaneously, creating a most impressive sonorous effect.

Although not so marked, the third movement is really a scherzo with two trios, A-B-A-C-A. The crisp, sharp first section (A) is vigorously rhythmical in balanced four-measure phrases. A gentle, flowing duet between the viola and first violin, based on the five notes of the pentatonic scale, starts the first trio (B). After a shortened return of the opening part, the slower and quieter second trio (C) appears like a gently rocking Czech folk song. A final return of the scherzo (A) concludes this simple and charming movement, which so happily blends sections of great strength and vigor with equally attractive interludes of lyrical beauty.

A slow augmentation of the principal theme of the rondo Finale is heard before it appears in the proper tempo; its syncopated opening and stamping conclusion are reminiscent of the Furiant style. Other contrasting themes follow—one soaring exultantly, another glowing with emotional intensity. In a slower interjected section, one that sounds improvisational, Dvořák introduces melodies from the first movement. We also hear the second theme and the upward leaps and descending triplet figure that appeared at the very beginning. After briefly reviewing the third and second subsidiary melodies and fleetingly recalling the first movement, the finale builds to an exciting conclusion based on the movement's principal theme.

Gabriel Fauré

Born May 12, 1845, in Pamiers, France
Died November 4, 1924, in Paris

FAURÉ'S LIFETIME spanned a period of remarkable and revolutionary advances in musical style: Berlioz, Chopin, and Schumann were forging new approaches to composition during his youth; Liszt, Wagner, and Debussy were making their contributions during his mature years; and Schoenberg, Bartók, and Stravinsky were establishing twentieth-century modes during his last decades. Through these many changes, Fauré maintained an essentially conservative and traditional course. Mostly confining himself to the smaller forms—chamber music, songs, piano pieces—which he fashioned with broad singing melodies and exquisite harmonic designs, Fauré achieved an intimacy, elegance, and sophistication that is, nevertheless, richly expressive and communicative.

Fauré's musical talent was manifested early when he improvised on the harmonium in the village church. A knowledgeable worshipper convinced the boy's father to send the nine-year-old to a boarding school in Paris that specialized in teaching music. By the time Fauré graduated, he was already composing and his music was being published, but he still had to play the organ in Parisian churches for many years in order to support himself. In 1896 he was appointed professor of composition at the Paris Conservatoire, and he served as Director from 1905 to 1920, when he resigned because of increasing deafness.

Fauré's six major chamber music compositions—the piano quartets Op. 15 (1879) and Op. 45 (1886); the piano quintets, Op. 89 (1906) and Op. 115 (1921); Piano Trio, Op. 120 (1923); and his final composition, the String Quartet, Op. 121 (1924)—extended over most of his creative life. Of them all, the first piano quartet probably holds the most secure place in the current repertoire.

169

Piano Quartet in C Minor, Op. 15

I. Allegro molto moderato. II. Scherzo: Allegro vivo. III. Adagio. IV. Allegro molto.

In 1872, Camille Saint-Saëns, Fauré's teacher and friend, introduced him to the Viardot family, which was extremely prominent in operatic circles. The twenty-seven-year-old composer soon became a regular visitor to their home, and his betrothal to their beautiful young daughter Marianne was announced in the spring of 1877.

By fall of the same year, though, the engagement was broken, probably by Marianne, leaving Fauré quite disconsolate. "Perhaps the break was not a bad thing for me," Fauré later wrote. "The Viardot family might have deflected me from my proper path." Some biographers suggest that Marianne's mother, Pauline, urged him to write grand opera instead of the personal music that he wanted, central to which was *musique de chambre,* or chamber music.

Once over *l'affaire Marianne,* Fauré did indeed turn to chamber music, starting work on the C minor piano quartet. Completed in 1879 and dedicated to Belgian violinist H. Leonard, the work was introduced in Paris that year at a concert by the *Société nationale de Musique Français.* Although it has become Fauré's most popular chamber work, he received no payment at all from the publisher.

The quartet opens with a unison string statement of the virile, vigorous principal theme, which Fauré quickly transforms into a lovely, tender melody. The undulating subsidiary theme, introduced by the viola, is promptly imitated by the other instruments. With many changes of mood and temperament, but maintaining a fluid, flowing piano part throughout, Fauré discourses on the two themes and brings them back for a comparatively conventional recapitulation and coda.

The graceful Scherzo emerges with gossamer delicacy; the piano plays the wispy melody over light pizzicato chords in the strings. For the string statement of the tune, the meter changes from 6/8 (six eighth notes to a measure) to 2/4 (four eighth notes to the same measure). The shift of meters and the occasional superimposition of one on the other add a sparkling piquancy to the rhythm. The smooth, suave trio gives most of the melodic burden to the strings, which are directed to play with mutes, lending them a particularly attractive tonal quality. A review of the opening Scherzo ends the movement.

It is easy to imagine Fauré working out his personal grief in the

Adagio. Organized in ternary form, A-B-A, the deeply emotional movement portrays great yearning and melancholy. Both themes are structured around different treatments of rising scale fragments; the first, weighty and burdened, struggles to reach upward, even as it falls back in failure; the second, more songful, is slightly more optimistic. The piano part is much elaborated for the return of the opening section.

The principal theme of the finale has the same rhythmic pattern as the first movement, and the same rising-scale melodic contour as the Adagio, an attempt, perhaps, to unify the separate movements. After the energetic opening subject, the contrasting cantabile, but agitated, second theme is heard in the viola before being taken up by the others. After building to an impassioned climax in the development section, the recapitulation starts quietly, leading to the brilliant conclusion.

Irving Fine

Born December 3, 1914, in Boston
Died August 23, 1962, in Boston

IRVING FINE's death in 1962 at age forty-seven tragically cut short the life of one of America's most gifted composers. Fine obtained his bachelor's and master's degrees at Harvard University, where his composition teachers were Walter Piston and Edward Burlingame Hill, and he also studied privately with Nadia Boulanger. Along with composing, Fine had an outstanding career as a pedagogue, teaching at Harvard University from 1939 to 1950 and at Brandeis University from 1950 to 1962. His accomplishments were recognized with two Guggenheim grants, a Fulbright award, a MacDowell Fellowship, and honors from the National Institute of Arts and Letters and the Society for the Publication of American Music.

The major influence on Fine's early composition was the so-called Neoclassical style that arose during the 1920s, with Igor Stravinsky and Paul Hindemith as its leading proponents. Like the movement's leaders, Fine rejected the overblown emotional baggage of the late romantics, favoring instead emotional restraint, balance, and clarity. He believed in adapting the forms and stylistic techniques from the past to create his own new music. In his later works, Fine employed the twelve-tone method associated with Arnold Schoenberg, integrating that approach with his underlying Neoclassicism.

Aaron Copland once extolled Irving Fine's music as having "quality, sincerity, and vitality" as well as "elegance, style, finish, and a convincing continuity." Fine was an excellent craftsman who worked very slowly to achieve these results; his strong sense of self-criticism, combined with a heavy teaching schedule, resulted in a regrettably small body of works. His major chamber music output is limited to Partita for Woodwind Quintet (1948), String Quartet (1952), Fantasia for String Trio (1956), and Romanza for Woodwind Quintet (1958). Of these, the Partita is probably the most popular.

Partita for Woodwind Quintet

I. Introduction and Theme: Allegro moderato. II. Variation: Poco vivace. III. Interlude: Adagio. IV. Gigue: Allegro. IV. Coda: Lento assai.

Irving Fine composed the Partita in 1948, and it was premiered in New York City in February of the following year by the New Art Wind Quintet. It won the 1949 New York Music Critics' Circle Award.

The Partita belongs to Fine's early Neoclassical period; its musical materials are concise and astringent, and its structure and organization are tightly controlled. Although cast in five separate movements, the entire piece is freely derived from the thematic content of the first movement.

The composer prepared these notes briefly describing the five movements.

The first has the character of a classical theme to be varied in the classical manner. The second movement is clearly a variation of its predecessor. The short meditative *Interlude* presents the basic material in its simplest form, but accompanied by warmer harmonies. [Only 20 measures long, the Interlude functions as an introduction to the Gigue, which follows without pause.] The Gigue occupies the central position in the entire work and is, at the same time, the most extended movement. It is in sonata form, but has an abridged recapitulation, which ends abruptly in a foreign key. The movement entitled Coda has the character of an epilogue and solemn processional.

César Franck

Born December 10, 1822, in Liège, Belgium
Died November 8, 1890, in Paris

WHEN ONLY fifteen years old, César Franck entered the Paris Conservatoire, where he astounded the judges by transposing an extremely difficult piece from E flat to C and performing it flawlessly at sight. Then, when given two themes on which to improvise a fugue and a sonata movement, Franck combined them so ingeniously that at first the judges were not even aware of the feat and only later awarded him a prize for the brilliance of his conception!

On leaving the Conservatoire in 1842, and for the following thirty years, Franck was mired in obscurity, although he did give some recitals, teach, and compose. In 1872 he was appointed professor of organ at the Conservatoire, where it was no secret that his classes were more concerned with musical composition than with organ instruction. To the adoring group of students and followers who surrounded him, Franck represented the one person able to reestablish an instrumental tradition of French music after decades of an operatic tradition dominated by Meyerbeer, Gounod, and other lesser composers for the lyric stage.

His serene, placid personality (he was called "Pater Seraphicus" by his students) little suited him to do battle with the musical establishment. But his personal vision and the great appeal of his music helped to forge an innovative style that combined highly chromatic harmonies and frequent modulations from key to key, with bold new formal organizations that grew from the melodic material, rather than from following the established patterns. Through a limited number of compositions, written when he was in his late fifties and sixties, Franck was able to establish a new direction for French music.

His chamber music works effectively frame Franck's musical output. The very first works to which he assigned an opus number were

175

the three piano trios, Op. 1 (1841). His last major work, composed in 1889, one year before his death, was his String Quartet in D major (1889). In between came the piano quintet, his best-known chamber composition, and one of the half-dozen most popular works for the combination.

Piano Quintet in F Minor

I. Molto moderato quasi lento; Allegro.   II. Lento, con molto sentimento.   III. Allegro non troppo, ma con fuoco.

Franck's piano quintet, composed in 1878–1879, is surely one of the most passionate, dramatic, and stormy works in the entire chamber music repertoire. Nadia Boulanger, for example, asserts that it contains more pianississimo (''very, very soft'') and fortississimo (''very, very loud'') markings than any other chamber work. Such a raging, impetuous statement, which reaches the extremes of musical expression, does not conform to the usual image of Franck, the staid, solid, bewhiskered organist of Sainte-Clotilde Church in Paris.

Biographer Leon Vallas finds evidence that, at the time of the quintet, Franck was deeply in love with his beautiful student Augusta Holmes, and he suggests that the quintet depicted his powerful feelings for the young woman. Madame Franck's remark, ''His organ pieces are everything that is admirable; but that quintet! Ugh!'' and her refusal to attend any performances, suggest that she well may have suspected that it was inspired by her rival.

But it was not only Madame Franck who objected to the quintet. After the premiere in Paris on January 17, 1880, by the Marsick Quartet with Camille Saint-Saëns playing piano, Franck came on the stage and asked Saint-Saëns, an old friend to whom the work was dedicated, to accept the manuscript in gratitude for his wonderful performance. Saint-Saëns abruptly turned and stalked out, leaving the music on the piano, thus most insolently expressing his disapproval of the piece. The public, in sharp contrast, responded with the greatest enthusiasm, insisting on an encore performance, which was given four months later.

The quintet opens with a slow introduction containing two motives. The strings declaim the first, an impassioned descending line, and the piano responds with a gentle swaying melody. These two ideas are transformed and become the first and second subjects of the fast body of the movement. Of special interest is the second theme, which can be described simply as a series of varying intervals above a pivotal note. This theme becomes very important. In various guises it is heard in each of the following movements, in what is known as cyclical form. The remainder of the first movement generally follows the sonata form organization.

The emotional temperature drops a bit for the second movement, also cast in sonata form. The opening theme is presented in short, disjunct phrases by the first violin over a repeated-note piano accompaniment. During the repetition of the theme, the three lower strings play a little rhythmic figure that presages the subordinate theme of the finale. The second subject is given out by the first violin, the cello, and the piano. As this theme fades away, Franck brings back a faint echo of the second theme, the cyclical subject, from the earlier movement. A much condensed development and recapitulation complete the movement.

An agitated perpetual motion in the violins ushers in the first theme of the last movement; it slowly gathers strength and volume as it moves from the piano to the unison strings. The motif from the Lento movement is then heard as the second theme. Both themes are fully developed and restated for the recapitulation. In the coda, though, Franck brings back the cyclical theme, this time in triple meter, effectively unifying the entire quintet.

Giovanni Gabrieli

Born 1557, in Venice
Died August 21, 1612, in Venice

Canzoni for Brass

GIOVANNI GABRIELI'S *canzoni* (plural of *canzone*) consists of over seventy works composed in the late sixteenth and early seventeenth century that form an important segment of the modern brass ensemble repertoire. The origins of the *canzoni* can be traced back to a type of troubadour song popular during the eleventh century in the Provence area of southeastern France. By the early sixteenth century these songs had become very popular in Italy, where they were called *canzon francese*. Italian composers began to transcribe these works for single instruments such as the organ or lute; later they arranged them for groups of instruments. In time, they were composing original instrumental works in the *canzon francese* style. These compositions became known as *canzoni alla francese,* or to differentiate them from vocal works, *canzoni da sonare.*

One of the leading composers of the older organ *canzoni* was Andrea Gabrieli (1520–1586), uncle of Giovanni, who was also organist at Saint Mark's in Venice. Young Giovanni studied with his uncle and continued the connection with Saint Mark's by becoming organist there in 1584, a post that he held until his death. This was in addition to his highly esteemed work both as a composer and teacher.

Gabrieli's *canzoni* display a few stylistic constants. In general they are moderately fast, light and lively in tone, in one movement, and quite brief. The texture is polyphonic; that is, a single melody is imitated by instrument after instrument in a fugal manner, with all the instruments treated as equals. The melody itself is usually very short, nothing more than a single phrase or motif, and the melodic motion is predominantly stepwise. A favored rhythm of the opening of the melody is the dactyl (a long or accented note followed by two short or unaccented notes), often with the same note repeated. The meter is usually duple.

The *canzoni* tend to be episodic, usually consisting of between five and ten separate sections. Sometimes all the parts are polyphonic, each one based on its own motif. In other works homophonic sections of block, chordal writing, often in triple meter, alternate with the duple-meter polyphonic sections.

Most of the compositions do not specify which instruments are to play the various parts. But since Gabrieli did score some for brass, and since the rich interplay of the individual parts is especially attractive when played on modern brass instruments, brass ensembles feel fully justified in treating this music as their own. The ringing, resplendent brass sound very effectively brings to mind the vibrancy and excitement of Gabrieli's Venice—at the time the wealthiest, most powerful city-state in the world.

Gabrieli's *canzoni* were originally published in three volumes. The first, *Sacrae Symphoniae* (1597), contains sixteen examples for large ensembles of six to sixteen players; the second, published by Alessandro Raverii (1608) has thirty-six works for groups of three and more; and the second volume of *Sacrae Symphoniae* (1615) is made up of twenty-one large-scale *canzoni*. Many are available today in modern performing editions.

Edvard Grieg

Born June 15, 1843, at Bergen, Norway
Died September 4, 1907, at Bergen

GRIEG'S EARLY life was not much different from that of most children of well-to-do, urban Norwegian families of the mid-nineteenth century. The family spoke Danish at home and followed Danish customs and traditions. The young boy was given piano lessons starting at age six and, because of his obvious talent, was sent to study at the Leipzig Conservatory when he was fifteen years old. On his return home in 1862, Grieg became very busy and successful as a conductor and pianist and as a composer, mostly of miniature pieces that were very much influenced by such German composers as Mendelssohn and Schumann.

Two years later, though, Grieg experienced a profound and abrupt change in his musical outlook. The shift was due to his discovery of the treasure trove of Norway's national music, dance, and folklore. Once he came upon this valuable material, he proceeded to draw inspiration from his homeland's poetry and legends and to infuse his music with its melodies and rhythms. Grieg became identified with the other musical nationalists—Smetana and Dvořák in Bohemia, Mussorgsky and Rimsky-Korsakov in Russia, Albéniz and Granados in Spain—as well as with the political nationalists who, in the late 1800s, were advocating independence and cultural self-determination for all peoples under foreign domination.

While championing Norwegian national music, Grieg realized the disadvantages of drawing solely on this source. Thus, he could write to a friend, "No chasing after nationalism. I will try to throw reflection to the winds and write from the heart, whether it turns out to be Norwegian or Chinese." But in a letter to his publisher about his string quartet he said, "It is true that it is not written in conformity with the requirements of the Leipzig school."

181

String Quartet in G Minor, Op. 27

I. Un poco Andante; Allegro molto ed agitato.   II. Romanze: Andantino.   III. Intermezzo: Allegro molto marcato.   IV. Finale: Lento; Presto al Saltarello.

From letters Grieg wrote while working on his string quartet, we know that he was particularly concerned at that time with the never-ending struggle to achieve musical excellence. "Day by day I am becoming more dissatisfied with myself," he wrote. "Nothing that I do satisfies me, and though it seems to me that I have ideas, they neither soar nor take form when I proceed to the working out of something big." The letters also indicate the lofty goal Grieg set himself in the quartet: "It . . . is not meant for small minds! It aims at breadth, vigor, flight of imagination and above all, fullness of tone for the instruments for which it is written."

Grieg also hints in his writings that the quartet has some autobiographical significance. We can, perhaps, gain some insight into his thinking by tracing the origin of the motto theme that opens the quartet and recurs in subsequent movements. The composer borrowed the theme from his song, "The Minstrel's Song." The words, by fellow Norwegian Hendrik Ibsen, tell of the *Hulder,* the spirit from Norse legend that dwells in waterfalls and lures minstrels with promises to reveal the art of music. But then, in return for the musical gifts he bestows, the *Hulder* robs the minstrels of their happiness and peace of mind. Could the motto, then, represent the sacrifices that Grieg would be willing to make to improve his art?

Grieg announces the borrowed motto theme at the very outset in a single, deliberate, bold statement, with all four instruments in unison, and with an accent on every note. A fast, scurrying theme launches the main part of the work. Almost orchestral in texture, it is thickly written, with much use of double stops, in which each of the instruments plays on two strings at the same time. Two *tranquillo* ("calm") statements of the motto theme, with loud, violent interruptions, lead to the second theme, which is little more than a faster, though quiet, version of the motto. Both themes are developed and returned as in traditional sonata form. A striking moment comes toward the end of the movement when the upper three strings are playing tremolo *ponticello,* while the cello sings a nostalgic augmentation of the motto.

The Romanze shows Grieg at his tuneful best. Essentially the movement is organized into an alternation of the opening melody and an agitated contrast, in which echoes of the motto theme are thinly concealed.

Grieg's great love for the national music of Norway comes to the fore most clearly in the third movement; the melodies all have the rhythmic verve and earthy energy of folk dances. Continuing the thematic unity of the quartet, the theme heard at the opening reminds us once more of the original motto.

The motto theme acts as a frame for the Finale—appearing in both the introduction and the coda. The main body of the movement is a bright, lively *saltarello,* its style set by the eponymous sixteenth-century Italian jumping dance.

Grieg completed the quartet in 1877 and dedicated it to Robert Heckmann, whose quartet gave the first performance in October 1878.

Franz Joseph Haydn

Born March 31, 1732, in Rohrau, Austria
Died May 31, 1809, in Vienna

EARLY IN his life Joseph Haydn was given the sobriquet "Papa" by the musicians working under him in the service of Prince Esterhazy. The name came not from his age or appearance, but because of the affectionate, kind, and compassionate way he cared for those in his charge. As time went on, and his musical accomplishments became widely known, the nickname also alluded to his central role in creating, or "fathering," the Classical symphony and the string quartet as we know them today. His is considered by many to be among the greatest accomplishments in the entire history of music.

Haydn was born in the small village of Rohrau, in Lower Austria, the son of a poor wheelwright. At the age of eight, he was taken into the cathedral choir of Saint Stephen's in Vienna, where he received some rudimentary instruction on the clavier and violin. Later Haydn said that he was "a wizard on no instrument, but I knew the strength and working of all; I was not a bad clavier player or singer, and could also play a concerto on the violin." Although he received no training in composition at Saint Stephen's, his exposure to vast quantities of music proved a valuable course of instruction. He wrote, "I listened more than I studied, but I heard the finest music in all forms."

When Haydn's voice changed at age seventeen, he was rather unceremoniously thrown out of the Saint Stephen's choir with one pair of trousers, three shirts, a coat, and no money. For the next several years he joined groups of itinerant musicians playing on the streets of Vienna for any coins the onlookers would toss them and, as he put it, "trailing wretchedly around giving lessons to children." But, most important of all, he spent every spare moment teaching himself to compose.

Around 1755, Haydn got his first position as a musician in a nobleman's employ, just about the only way composers could earn a living in those days. In 1761 he entered the service of Prince Paul Anton Esterhazy, the grandest of the Hungarian aristocrats, where he was to work as *Kapellmeister* until the death of Paul's successor, Prince Nicholas Esterhazy—"Nicholas the Magnificent"—in 1790.

As *Kapellmeister,* Haydn directed a music staff that included about twenty-five instrumentalists, five singers, and a choir made up from among the servants. Although Haydn, too, was a servant, he was of the highest rank, so that he was paid a handsome salary and had a footman and maid to see to his needs. He was responsible, during average weeks, for presenting two orchestra concerts and two opera performances, as well as arranging the music at church services and for chamber music evenings, often with the Prince as participant. Since a significant part of the repertoire was music composed for the occasion by Haydn, the position was exceedingly demanding, but it did give Haydn ample opportunity to experiment and to develop his very considerable talents.

When Haydn undertook his duties at the Esterhazy castle, the Rococo style was dominant, with its lightness of touch, superficial charm, and elegance, and his early works were written in this idiom. Very soon, though, he began to weave the pretty Rococo themes, designed only to please and entertain, into more serious, substantial musical fabrics, into which he introduced elements of the robust, virile peasant music he knew from his rural childhood. At the same time he moved from the accompanied melody so favored in Rococo music to a more polyphonic texture, tending more toward the so-called learned style.

In the late 1760s and 1770s Haydn entered his *Sturm und Drang* ("storm and stress") period, coming under the influence of those thinkers who were reacting against the Enlightenment and its belief in logic and reason and accepted instead the view articulated by Johann Georg Hamann that existence can only be apprehended by faith and the senses. During this time Haydn's music took on a new emotional intensity as well as a dramatic sense of urgency and energy.

The next two decades saw a shift in Haydn's style that paralleled the changes taking place in society, changes that climaxed in the American and French revolutions. Just as the power and wealth of the idle and frivolous nobility was declining and world leadership was passing to the scientifically oriented society of the rising middle class, so the graceful, highly decorated Rococo music intended for the aristocrats was giving way to the logical, well-ordered Classical music written for the merchants and shopkeepers. Haydn bridged the gap between the Rococo and the Classical by transforming the various elements that had already appeared in his music into a new mature style that actually came to define the Classical era and to look ahead to nineteenth-century Romanticism.

Haydn was an amazingly prolific composer, despite his disclaimer that he was "never a quick writer" and that he composed with "care and diligence." Over his half-century of creative life, his chamber music output alone included eighty-three string quartets, sixty-seven string trios, thirty-one piano trios, and innumerable miscellaneous pieces. Since his best known and most important chamber compositions are the quartets, and since almost every published edition includes the same so-called Thirty Famous Quartets, we have limited our discussion of Haydn's chamber music to these thirty compositions.

String Quartets, Op. 3, Nos. 3 and 5

The six quartets of Haydn's Op. 3 have long been regarded as the first *true* string quartets. Although earlier composers had written pieces for four string instruments, and Haydn himself had composed the twelve *Divertimenti a quattro* of his Opp. 1 and 2 for the same combination, Op. 3 was the first to establish the form and instrumental treatment of the quartet style as we know it today.

In July 1964, however, an article appeared in the *Musical Times*, titled "Who Composed Haydn's Op. 3?" that questioned the authenticity of the work. Authors H. C. Robbins Landon and Alan Tyson argued that the six quartets in Op. 3 were written by Roman Hoffstetter (1742–1815), a monk in the monastery of Amorbach. Since then, other experts have studied the question; some agree with Robbins Landon and Tyson, but others are convinced that the music is by Haydn.

Since the manuscripts have never been found, and there is little verified information available, it is doubtful that this controversy will ever be resolved. In any case, these are charming works, with some rather beautiful sections. It is believed that Haydn, if indeed he was the author, probably composed Op. 3 in the early 1760s, just as he was starting his lifelong career as *Kapellmeister* to the Esterhazy family. Of the six quartets of Op. 3, only numbers 3 and 5 are part of the modern repertoire.

String Quartet in G Major, Op. 3, No. 3

I. Presto. II. Largo. III. Menuetto. IV. Presto.

The G major quartet is a frolicsome, joyful work that calls to mind Haydn's famous quote, "Since God has given me a cheerful heart, He will forgive me for serving him cheerfully."

The Presto movement opens with a bouncy little tune in the first violin, which is immediately repeated in variation by the second violin. The second violin and viola then join together to state the smooth opening of the subsidiary subject, followed by some brilliant passage work in the first violin that concludes the exposition. This is followed by a short development section and a recapitulation that closely mirrors the earlier exposition.

The Largo is essentially an aria, or song, even though it is organized in the same sonata form as the first movement. With almost no exception, all of the melodic interest in this short but exquisite movement is concentrated in the first violin part.

The Menuetto gives the quartet its occasionally used nickname of "*Dudelsack,*" or "Bagpipe." At the opening the first violin, and later the viola, imitate the bagpipe's sound by sustaining a drone under a moving melodic line. The middle part of this movement is called "trio," a reference to the old practice of inserting a different three-voiced minuet between the statement and repeat of a full-orchestra minuet. In most quartet minuets, the trio is played by the entire group. In this case, though, it is almost a real trio in the sense that for more than half its length only three instruments are playing. At the conclusion of the trio, there is a shortened repeat of the Menuetto.

The first theme of the Presto finale is a bright, witty dialogue between the first violin and the other players. All come together to start the second theme, but then again the first violin goes off on its own in rapid passages over a bare-bones accompaniment. A traditional development and recapitulation round out the movement and conclude the quartet.

String Quartet in F Major, Op. 3, No. 5, "Serenade"

I. Presto. II. Andante cantabile
(Serenade). III. Menuetto. IV. Scherzando.

Some few quartets have slow movements that are such popular favorites they have taken on a musical life on their own apart from the rest of the quartet. The Andante Cantabile of Tchaikovsky's Op. 11 and the Notturno of Borodin's D major are good examples. The Serenade of this quartet is also an all-time "hit" and, in addition to the original quartet version, is heard in countless arrangements, from solo piano to full orchestra. Although not as well known, the other movements of Op. 3, No. 5 are equally worthy and attractive, contributing to a work of considerable ingenuous appeal.

The Presto starts with the first violin stating a short phrase, to which the others reply with *their* version of the same tune. Then the violin changes its phrase, slightly altered, but the response shows that there still is no agreement. At last a truce is declared, and everyone plays the remaining phrases of the first subject together. The second subject starts with the violins presenting the quiet, songlike melody, attended by laconic comments in the lower instruments. After building to a forceful climax and a concise development, the thematic material returns for the recapitulation, which includes a few playful variations of the first theme.

The second movement, the familiar Serenade, is a glorious extended song for the muted first violin. Simple, but intense, it is discreetly accompanied pizzicato by the others.

The robust, heavy-footed Menuetto harks back to peasant dances that Haydn knew from his youth. The delicate contrasting trio, true to its name, uses only two violins and cello; at its conclusion the Menuetto is repeated.

The impish, mischievous main tune of the Scherzando evokes the spirit of a comic aria in the Italian *opera buffa* style so popular at the time. The theme is cheerfully tossed back and forth between the first violin and the others. The subsidiary subject, similar in mood but in a new key, starts in the violins, before the viola and cello emerge for the stronger concluding episode of the exposition. The rest of the movement, in standard sonata form, holds no surprises as it moves with great vigor and inner drive to the energetic ending.

String Quartet in E Flat Major, Op. 9, No. 2

I. Moderato. II. Menuetto. III. Adagio; Cantabile. IV. Allegro molto.

Haydn was kept very busy through the late 1760s as *Kapellmeister* in the service of the large and very active Esterhazy musical establishment. His duties included rehearsing and composing music for twice-weekly orchestral concerts and opera productions, planning performances for special occasions, as well as providing a continuous stream of new works to be played by Prince Nicholas Esterhazy, an avid musician. But despite this demanding work load, Haydn found the time, between 1768 and 1771, to write the six quartets of Op. 9.

Haydn considered Op. 9 his first "real" quartets and later asked his publisher to ignore his earlier works (Opp. 1, 2, and 3) and start the numbering with Op. 9. These quartets represent a significant leap forward in a few areas. For one thing, they show a new emotionalism and subjectivity, termed *Empfindsamkeit,* or "sensibility". Also, by slowing the first movements down to a moderate rather than fast tempo, Haydn was able to expand the scale of the movement, making it more dramatic, imaginative, and harmonically advanced.

Among the other innovations are the brilliant, virtuosic parts Haydn wrote for the first violin, in what is known as *concertante* style. The composer was inspired by the outstanding Italian violinist, Luigi Tomasini, concertmaster of the Esterhazy orchestra. "No one plays my quartets like Luigi," Haydn once said. The textures also tend more to the polyphonic, with the instruments playing independent melodic lines, than the homophonic, accompanied melody of the older Rococo style. And finally, in the first movements, and sometimes the others as well, Haydn focuses most attention on a single theme, having it dominate throughout, rather than emphasizing the contrast between two totally different themes. This approach, known as monothematicism, remains important through all of Haydn's subsequent quartets.

The quartet opens with the first violin resolutely striding up and down the notes of a broken chord. A number of other motifs follow, but none of them is as weighty or important as the initial melody, giving the feeling of a single-theme, or monothematic, movement. The lengthy development section, a true working out of the themes, is intense, dramatic, and spacious, with significant parts for all the instruments. The recapitulation reviews the exposition with but little change.

Instead of following the big, dramatic first movement with a serious slow movement, Haydn places the lighter Menuetto next. Of particular interest is the ten-measure descending cello line that is repeated four times under the first violin melody. The trio, with its flashy violin runs, acts as the contrast before a shortened repeat of the Menuetto. Haydn must have had a special affection for the Menuetto melody, because he later made it the subject of a set of keyboard variations.

Nowhere is Haydn's admiration for Tomasini's playing more evident than in the Adagio, which is essentially a recitative and aria
for solo violin. The prominence and virtuosic brilliance of the violin
part has led some scholars to speculate that Haydn might originally
have conceived it as the slow movement of a violin concerto, especially since there are a few pauses that seem to invite improvised cadenzas. The melody is played twice, the second time with even more
embellishments and decorations on the already highly ornate solo
line.

The finale is the most lightweight of the four movements. The
syncopated, rhythmically exciting first theme predominates throughout the frisky movement, giving it a typically monothematic structure.

String Quartet in G Major, Op. 17, No. 5

I. Moderato.   II. Menuetto.   III. Adagio.   IV. Finale: Presto.

Haydn composed the six Op. 17 quartets in 1771, right after finishing the set of Op. 9 and while still employed in the demanding position of *Kapellmeister* for Prince Esterhazy. They are the first quartets
the autograph manuscript of which still exists, avoiding any question
of authenticity or date. They are warmhearted, romantic works that
clearly show the profound effect on Haydn of the concept of *Empfindsamkeit* (sensibility), which he learned from Karl Philipp Emanuel Bach. Other features of interest, particularly in comparison with
his earlier quartets are the length and importance of the first movement, especially the development section; an inclination to monothematicism; brilliant writing for the first violin; and the greater
independence and importance of the three lower parts, which are
treated much more contrapuntally.

The principal theme of the Moderato, played by the first violin,
features a succession of Scotch snaps, which are quick two-note, short-
long rhythmic figures. Even though there is a subsidiary theme and
it is in a different key, the movement sounds monothematic because
it also contains Scotch snaps reminiscent of those in the first theme.
The exposition concludes with some virtuosic writing for the first violin, including double stops (two notes played simultaneously) and
rapid runs in the upper register. The full and substantial development section elaborates on both themes before a truncated recapitulation ends the movement without a coda.

In the robust Menuetto, imitations of the first violin melody start in the other voices, as though launching a fugal treatment, but they quickly peter out. The trio divides the melodic interest between a crisp moving line in the first violin and the second violin and the cello's songlike melody. The movement ends with a return of the Menuetto.

The Adagio is an *arioso,* a song for solo violin. Twice, though, it is interrupted by recitatives, improvisatory-sounding declamatory sections, which add a special dramatic tension to the music. The recitatives are played very freely, with many pauses, held notes, and freedom of tempo in imitation of impassioned human speech.

High-spirited and witty, the Finale involves all four players in the fun, giving each one a part of melodic interest. Structured in sonata form, the two violins state the light first theme with asides from the viola; the first violin leads the second theme, playing forcefully high in its range. The quite short development and recapitulation follow in turn and move along very quickly to the abrupt, quiet ending.

String Quartets Op. 20, Nos. 4, 5, and 6, "Die Sonnen-Quartette" ("The Sun Quartets")

To Haydn's contemporaries, the six quartets of Op. 20 (1772) were known as *"Die Sonnen-Quartette,"* for the simple reason that the publisher decorated the cover of the first edition with a drawing of a rising sun. But for far better cause they were also called *"Die Grossen Quartette"* ("The Great Quartets"), since these are large, fully mature works, showing Haydn as a true master of the quartet form.

Deeply influencing this music were the new ideas of the *Sturm und Drang* ("storm and stress") movement, which began making their impact on the arts in Germany around 1770. The cultural change represented a strong reaction against French rationalism, which had been holding sway over German art and thought since about 1680. To break free, the Germans stressed the dominance of natural feelings over rational free will, originality over imitation, religiosity over secularism, passion over politeness. The leading literary figure of the movement was Johann von Goethe (1749–1832), whose works are characterized by exuberance, subjectivity, rich imagery, and powerful language.

Besides accepting the tenets of *Sturm und Drang,* Haydn reacted against the Rococo style, or *style galant* ("courtly style"), in music. This chivalrous approach favored a homophonic texture, with a pretty, ornate melody in the upper voice and a light, elegant accompaniment beneath. It was music designed more to please and entertain than to stimulate and move. The new style, which Haydn favored, tended to be more serious and meaningful and made much greater use of polyphony, with significant parts for all the voices. It has come to be known as *Der Gelehrte Style,* or the "learned style."

The most obvious results of *Sturm und Drang* and *Der Gelehrte Style* in Op. 20 are an increased passion and intensity, as well as a greater subjectivity. To broaden the music's emotional range Haydn adds "feeling" words—*affettuoso* ("affectionately"), zingarese ("in Gypsy style"), *scherzando* ("jokingly"), and *cantabile* ("in singing style")—to the tempo designations of the various movements. The individual parts are more nearly equal in importance, with the cello in particular liberated from its older exclusive role as the bass instrument with little melodic importance. And there is considerably more use of polyphony, with fugues and canons figuring prominently in each of the quartets, culminating in the fugal finales of Op. 20, Nos. 5 and 6.

Haydn composed the Op. 20 quartets in 1772 and dedicated them to Nikolaus Zmeskall von Domanovecz, a prominent Hungarian diplomat and chamber music lover.

String Quartet in D Major, Op. 20, No. 4

I. Allegro di molto.   II. Un poco Adagio affettuoso.   III. Menuetto: Allegretto alla zingarese.   IV. Presto scherzando.

The preternatural opening—a series of five uninflected six-measure phrases—creates a wondrously mysterious mood that is precipitously shattered by the completely unexpected outburst that follows. A transition leads to the second theme, starting with three repeated notes like the first theme, but going on to a sparkling cascade of rapid triplets played by the first violin. Bold and adventuresome in its harmonies, the development section ends at a climactic moment, which is followed by five beats of silence and then a straight-faced return of the first theme—but in the wrong key! Haydn quickly ends the false reprise and concludes the movement with a much shortened recapitulation.

A simple meditative theme in the minor, stated by the first violin, is the subject of the four variations that make up the slow movement. The second violin leads the first variation with a line that is melodically and rhythmically quite different from the original theme, although the underlying harmony remains the same. In Variation II, Haydn changes the traditional quartet scoring, giving the high melody to the cello and making the viola the bass. Variation III has the first violin playing a rhythmic elaboration of the theme, and Variation IV presents a kind of summation of what has come before. Predominantly soft, only rising slightly in dynamics at the end of each variation, all the pent-up feelings explode at the start of the coda, which includes a few more outbursts before its three soft final chords.

After two rather serious movements, Haydn relaxes. The Menuetto, marked *alla zingarese,* "in gypsy style," is based on the folk music he probably heard as a child and infused with rhythmic vitality by the liberal use of cross accents. The quieter trio, an extended running passage for the cello, is accompanied by the others with three repeated notes and an arrival note that Haydn might well have derived from the rhythm that opens the quartet. The composer brings the Menuetto back after the trio.

A tempo indication of Presto scherzando ("very fast, jokingly") aptly describes the ebullient finale, which is liberally sprinkled with good humor and unexpected melodic, harmonic, and rhythmic touches. After presenting the several motifs of the principal subject—bouncy, gliding, and bold in turn—Haydn introduces the phrases of the second subject, the first gently moving up and down through a narrow range, and the second dividing a fast, bright sixteenth-note figure between the violins. Both subjects are developed and restated before the music fades away.

String Quartet in F Minor, Op. 20, No. 5

I. Allegro moderato. II. Menuetto. III. Adagio.
IV. Finale: Fuga a due Soggetti.

The highly emotional *Sturm und Drang* ("storm and stress") tone of this quartet is established right from the start, as the first violin sings its ardent melody over throbbing, pulsating chords in the other instruments. A slight lessening in intensity comes with the second theme, which involves all four instruments in its statement and appears in the warm major mode after the dark minor of the principal subject. Following a rather conventional development, Haydn further expands the themes in the recapitulation. He saves the culmination of the movement, though, for the coda, which he brings to an intense, passionate climax.

The Menuetto has none of the good spirits that usually characterize this movement. Instead, the mood of unease and restlessness established in the first movement continues here. The contrasting trio, often played a bit faster than the Menuetto, exhibits a slightly happier visage. The Menuetto returns to end the movement.

The rhythmic background of the Adagio, an alternation of long and short notes, is derived from an old Italian dance, the Siciliano. In the foreground is a simple, rocking melody initially stated by the first violin. This melody dominates the movement, although occasionally shared with the second violin and presented with increasing elaboration.

The Finale most clearly illustrates Haydn's *Gelehrte* style. Basically, it is a fugue on two *soggetti,* short subjects that are easily identified by some distinctive melodic feature. In this case, the first subject is comparatively slow moving and characterized by large intervallic leaps; the second is made up of faster-moving notes that essentially proceed by step. Subject one is announced at the outset by the second violin, with the viola statement of subject two following on its heels. For exactly 109 measures Haydn manipulates these two melodies into ever-changing keys and relationships, but all *sotto voce* ("in an undertone") before quickly building to a climactic chord. The music resumes quietly again, in even more complex contrapuntal intricacy, rising to two forceful outbursts, the second one ending the movement.

String Quartet in A Major, Op. 20, No. 6, "Sun"

**I. Allegro di molto e scherzando.   II. Adagio.
III. Menuetto: Allegretto.   IV. Finale: Fuga a tre
Soggetti.**

All the quartets of Op. 20 are subtitled "The Sun Quartets" because of the cover of the first edition; in addition, the sixth quartet's cheery warmth and lighthearted grace have specifically earned it the nickname of "Sun" Quartet.

The first movement, which Haydn directs be played "very fast and jokingly," glows with high-spirited humor. A good supply of delightful motifs are divided by key into three groups according to the standard sonata form structure: the playful first group in the home key of A major; the more lyrical second in E minor; and the mock-military concluding theme of the exposition in E major. Still more new melodic material is introduced in the development, and the movement ends with a shortened recapitulation.

The *Sturm und Drang* emotionality of the Adagio is achieved by the simplest of means. In style, it is an aria sung by the first violin with a minimal Italian-opera accompaniment in the other instruments. It is in binary form, but the second part is little more than an elaborated repetition of the first. A particular challenge for the players in this movement is to project the music's expressive qualities while following Haydn's constraining direction to play everything *mezza voce,* literally ''half-voice,'' or softly.

The robust, highly rhythmic Menuetto presents a striking contrast to the subdued preceding movement. Based on custom, a second minuet follows the first without pause; it is called a trio because of the old practice of using just three players. In this instance Haydn omits the second violin, and to get the desired tone color, he instructs the three players to play only on their lowest strings, giving the trio a dark-hued, somewhat constricted tone. The movement ends with a return of the much more graceful, dancelike Menuetto.

In the scintillating finale, a brilliant example of his *Gelehrte Style,* Haydn eschews the traditional sonata or rondo form for a highly complex fugue and avoids all dynamic contrast by keeping it *sotto voce,* in an undertone, throughout. The fugue has three *soggetti,* or brief subjects: a bouncy line starting with three repeated notes that is introduced by the first violin; a slower-moving legato descending line played by the second violin; and a smooth little rushing figure also stated by the first violin. Haydn manipulates these three subjects in a highly imaginative way, finally bringing everyone together in the last four measures for a rousing unison conclusion based on the first subject.

String Quartets, Op. 33, Nos. 2, 3, and 6, "Russian"

Haydn's Op. 33 probably has more nicknames than any other set of quartets. The most common designation, ''Russian,'' arose because the composer dedicated the quartets to Grand Duke Paul of Russia, and some, or perhaps all six, received their first performance on Christmas Day, 1781, at the Vienna apartment of the Duke's wife, the Grand Duchess Maria Feodorovna. To some these quartets are known as *Gli Scherzi,* because they were the first chamber works in which Haydn substituted scherzos (*scherzi* in Italian) for the traditional minuet movements. And the occasional reference to Op. 33

as the *"Jungfernquartette,"* or "Maiden," Quartets stems from the drawing of an attractive young woman that appeared on the title page of an early edition.

The composition of the Op. 33 in 1781 followed a nearly ten-year hiatus after Haydn's Op. 20 quartets. It may be that after Op. 20 Haydn was searching for a new approach to the form. Or perhaps his duty to compose five original operas and mount some fifty opera productions for Prince Nicholas Esterhazy between 1775 and 1781, in addition to all his other musical administrative tasks as *Kapell-meister,* left no time for quartets.

In any case, after Haydn returned to quartet writing, he regarded his Op. 33 with pleasure and satisfaction. His several letters to patrons inviting them to subscribe to the quartets say that they are "written in a new and special way." The most striking characteristics are the themes themselves. Using quite distinctive intervals and complex rhythms, Haydn builds the melodies up out of individual phrases that are organically unified but contain contrasting elements. His treatment—he calls it "thematic elaboration"—of the subject is handled with deftness and imagination as he expands and develops individual fragments and then reassembles the parts at the end. In Op. 33, the only apparent change in calling the minuet movement a *scherzo* (which is Italian for "joke") is that it tends to be faster than the minuet and occasionally has some touches of playfulness and humor.

In Op. 33 Haydn achieved a synthesis of the melodic grace of the *style galant* ("courtly style"), the contrapuntal texture and formal logic of *Der Gelehrte Style* ("the learned style"), and the emotional intensity of *Sturm und Drang* ("storm and stress"). The overall lightness in spirit and happy nature of Op. 33 are attributed, by some biographers, to Haydn's gratifying affair with singer Luigia Polyelli and his realization that he was well on his way to mastering that most intractable of all musical forms, the string quartet.

String Quartet in E Flat Major, Op. 33, No. 2, "The Joke"

I. Allegro moderato, cantabile. II. Scherzo: Allegro. III. Largo sostenuto. IV. Finale: Presto.

The first movement of Op. 33, No. 2, is a fine illustration of Haydn's technique of "thematic elaboration," the growth of an entire movement from several microcosmic musical gestures, in this case those introduced in the first four measures. The subject starts with a rising and falling fanfarelike motto. The opening few notes are then immediately fashioned into a dialogue among the quartet members, which Haydn spins out into a first violin figure. After a literal repeat of the motto theme, he focuses on different facets and characteristics, which he explores and uses as the material for creating new themes. Instead of a contrasting second subject, Haydn takes a melody derived from the first subject, although in a different key, providing the tonal opposition basic to sonata form. The ongoing elaboration process continues in the development and even somewhat in the recapitulation, thus ending the essentially monothematic movement.

The next movement, although called a Scherzo, closely resembles similar quartet movements that Haydn named minuets. The rustic first part is a heavy-footed peasant dance in solid three-beat time. The more relaxed middle section, or trio, is light and graceful and tends toward a one beat in a measure meter. The movement concludes with a repeat of the first part.

The weight of the quartet is focused in the third movement, with Haydn using his command of the *Gelehrte* style to create a section of great beauty and expressivity. The calm and restrained principal subject is stated at the outset as a contrapuntal duet for the viola and cello, which is then repeated by the violins. A passage of sharp chords and accented syncopations acts as a contrast and transition to a varied statement of the opening subject, now using three players, the second violin and viola playing the duet and the first violin adding a countermelody. The transition is heard once more, leading to the final variant of the subject, this time played by all four instruments.

The quartet derives its nickname, ''The Joke,'' from the comical conclusion of the Finale. The principal theme of the sonata-rondo is a joyous, quicksilver tune tossed off with great aplomb by the first violin. The first episode, which is an outgrowth of the original tune, is somewhat more subdued and restrained. Both sections, the opening and the episode, are then brought back somewhat changed. It is now, when one might expect a final statement of the main theme to end the movement, that Haydn decides to have some fun. The statement starts as expected, but it is soon interrupted by a slow, exceedingly sentimental interlude. Once again the melody resumes, but this time each phrase is followed by a pause, until after an un-

sult—a movement that contains both weightiness *and* a happy ending.

String Quartet in D Major, Op. 50, No. 6, "The Frog"

I. Allegro.   II. Poco Adagio.   III. Menuetto: Allegretto.   IV. Finale: Allegro con spir'

The three great composers of the Viennese Classical school, H
Mozart, and Beethoven, dedicated major chamber works to Free
William II, King of Prussia from 1786 to 1797, who was a fine c
and an enthusiastic quartet player. The compositions—the six q
tets of Haydn's Op. 50; Mozart's last three quartets, K. 575, ;
and 590; and Beethoven's two cello sonatas, Op. 5—all provided
music-loving monarch with cello parts of interest and importan
Haydn composed the quartets from 1784 to 1786, and when he c
livered the manuscript to King Frederick, the ruler was so please
that he gave the composer a gold ring. Haydn treasured the ring mo
than any other gift that he received; he always wore it as a source o
inspiration while composing. Op. 50, No. 6, the last of the set and
probably the lightest in character, is the only one to be included in
the various editions of Haydn's Thirty Celebrated Quartets.

The first violin alone states the germinal motif of the Allegro—
a long note followed by four rapid descending notes. The rest of the
movement, in effect, grows from this terse musical idea. The theme
undergoes various transformations—some quite similar to the original, others much further afield. Haydn follows, in a general way, the
structural organization and key relationships of sonata form but always allows the musical material to dictate the actual shape of the
movement, with its underlying restlessness and sense of urgency.

The deeply felt, minor-key Poco Adagio is essentially monothematic, since the second theme is the same as the first, although in
major. The melody, too, is slightly altered, giving it a supplicating
air not present in the original. Around the relatively simple melody,
Haydn weaves a rich tapestry of fast-moving countermelodies, with
a particularly prominent and difficult cello part, a gesture, no doubt,
to King Frederick.

The Menuetto, in traditional three-part form, is most striking in
its contrasts. The first part is loud, forceful, and robust. The trio is
tender and graceful. Towards the end there are a few long pauses

that impart a feeling of tentative hesitancy just before the shortened repeat of the virile Menuetto.

The quartet derived its nickname, "The Frog," from the opening of the Finale, in which the violinist uses a technique known as *bariolage,* a quick back-and-forth playing of the same note on two strings. Someone, not Haydn, decided the effect resembled a frog's croaking, and the name stuck. After the light, tripping *bariolage* tune, Haydn introduces a smooth second theme that is remarkably similar to the opening of the first movement. But the *bariolage* remains the point, and it permeates the movement—even to the very last notes.

String Quartets, Op. 54, Nos. 1, 2, and 3, "Tost Quartets"

Two mysteries surround Haydn's Op. 54, which he composed around 1788, while still serving as *Kapellmeister* to Prince Esterhazy. The first is why he only wrote three quartets in this opus, instead of the usual six; the second has to do with Johann Tost, to whom these quartets, the three quartets of Op. 55, and the six quartets of Op. 64, are dedicated.

Most scholars explain away the first mystery by saying that Haydn did it to earn a larger fee. But the question of Johann Tost is much more difficult to understand. It is known that from 1783 to 1789 there was an excellent violinist named Johann Tost in Haydn's Esterhazy orchestra. In 1789 Tost went on a trip to Paris, and Haydn gave him the scores of two symphonies (Nos. 88 and 89) and six quartets (Opp. 54 and 55) to place with a publisher in that city. Tost is believed also to have taken along a symphony by Adalbert Gyrowitz that he passed off as Haydn's, and compounded his improbity by being terribly slow and not completely honest in forwarding the payments he obtained to Haydn. On Tost's return to Vienna, he married the housekeeper of the Esterhazy estate, a woman of some considerable means. The next year, one Johann Tost appears as a wealthy cloth dealer in Vienna and an excellent amateur violinist. And it is to "the wholesale merchant Tost" that Haydn dedicates his middle twelve quartets. Are the violinist and the cloth merchant one and the same? And, if so, why should the composer have inscribed these works to the scoundrel?

Despite these obscurities, the "Tost" Quartets remain among the finest works Haydn created in this form. They are graced with an abundance of wonderful themes, which are treated boldly, imaginatively and inventively, and with a new freedom of harmony and of form that considerably deepened and enlarged the potential of the string quartet medium.

String Quartet in G Major, Op. 54, No. 1

I. Allegro con brio. II. Allegretto. III. Menuetto: Allegretto. IV. Finale: Presto.

The essentially monothematic first movement is dominated by the opening subject—an energetic melody in the first violin, played over a vigorous repeated-note accompaniment. Haydn, though, does provide subsidiary material without stint; there are at least five distinct melodic phrases within the first subject alone. And he also includes a regular second subject, a quiet, brief pattern of descending and then ascending pairs of notes. It appears so late in the exposition, though, that it feels more like an afterthought than an equal of the first theme. Haydn devotes the remainder of the movement to working out the melodic material and bringing it back for a free recapitulation.

As in the first movement, Haydn calls on the lower instruments to furnish a repeated, pulsating accompaniment, quieter and slower this time, as the first violin sings the soulful melody that opens the Allegretto. And once more he produces a number of warm, tender melodies organized not according to any textbook formal scheme, but in a shape determined by the flow of the music itself.

Robust, vital, and crackling with rhythmic vitality, the Menuetto is a startling contrast to the predominantly quiet second movement. The middle trio features the cello in a wide-ranging melodic line with discrete comments by the upper instruments, after which the Menuetto is repeated.

The Finale is a high-speed frolicsome movement that provides a delightful ending to the entire quartet. The opening theme, starting with three repeated notes, comes back several times, as in traditional rondo form. But the fact that the interludes are closely related to the principal theme, and its returns do not follow a regular pattern, indicate that this is really a unique structure that Haydn created just for this particular movement. The playful handling of the initial three-note motto—the unexpected pauses and the sudden changes from loud to soft or high to low—seldom fail to bring a smile to even the most jaded listener.

String Quartet in C Major, Op. 54, No. 2

I. Vivace. II. Adagio. III. Menuetto: Allegretto. IV. Finale: Adagio; Presto.

The C major is, in several ways, the most important and advanced of the three quartets of Op. 54. With true flashes of genius, Haydn boldly strikes out in new directions and makes powerful and original contributions that look ahead to the expressiveness of the late Beethoven quartets—and beyond.

The opening phrase of the first movement, forceful and incisive, is five measures long instead of the standard four and ends in a dramatic measure of silence. It is only on the third statement that the phrase builds up enough momentum to spin out into a full melody. Hewing more closely to traditional formal practices than is his wont, Haydn has the first violin and viola introduce a proper second theme—in the right key (G major) and in contrasting character (light and jocular). In an extension of the second theme, the first violin climbs to a dizzily high note, a nod perhaps to Tost's abilities as a violinist. The development and recapitulation, including a few special Haydnesque touches, follow, and the movement ends with a rather lengthy coda.

The Adagio, one of the most poignant movements in all the Haydn quartets, begins with all four instruments playing low in their registers, introducing the brooding, intense theme in the dark key of C minor. Haydn then repeats the theme three more times, but this time confined to the three lower instruments, while the first violin sets off on an anguished Hungarian-Gypsy lament that embroiders the slow moving melody with free, passionate arabesques.

The light, rhythmic Menuetto, which follows without pause, presents a stark contrast to the profundity of the Adagio. The Menuetto was such a favorite of the Esterhazy court, where Haydn was *Kapellmeister,* that Prince Esterhazy had its tune built into the sounding mechanism of a musical clock. After the delicate grace of the Menuetto, the trio rudely interrupts with a forceful unison, which continues with bold, astringent harmonies, before returning to the charms and delights of the Menuetto.

The Finale finds Haydn flaunting custom by ending the quartet with a slow movement. Since there is one short fast section, Haydn scholar Karl Geiringer suggests that the composer originally planned only a brief slow introduction, but that it just kept on growing until it took over almost completely. The movement starts with an eight-measure introduction, after which each instrument assumes the role it will maintain throughout the slow section. The violin plays the poised, noble theme; the second violin and viola accompany with a throbbing, repeated-note accompaniment; and the cello sings a melodic line that moves slowly and with great dignity from the bottom to the top of its range, lending a very special spiritual quality to the music. Haydn inserts a quick, madly scurrying Presto, as though to let everyone know that he is aware of what a finale should be. The movement then ends with a brief, glowing reminder of the opening section.

String Quartet in E Major, Op. 54, No. 3

I. Allegro. II. Largo cantabile. III. Menuetto: Allegretto. IV. Finale: Presto.

Of the three Op. 54 quartets, the E major is probably the least well known, even though many, including writer Donald Francis Tovey, consider it one of Haydn's greatest works.

Instead of a first movement dominated by a single all-important theme, as in so many other Haydn quartets, the Allegro opens with four distinct musical gestures. First is the scalic idea, with the second violin and viola moving note to note at the very outset. The first violin responds with an arpeggiated, descending figure that moves by leaps as well as steps. After a repetition of this exchange, the cello starts a long, low note, a pedal tone, which it sustains for a full eight measures while the violins discourse on the descending figure. And then, even before the pedal tone is finished, the first violin introduces the fourth component, a passage of fast, running triplets. Each element seems to fulfill a particular function. The scalelike and arpeggio phrases from the first subject are transformed to create the second subject; the pedal tone adds stability and unity throughout the movement; and the rapid triplets enliven the musical pulse relative to the slower-moving melodies. After passing through the general divisions of sonata form, the movement ends with a wonderful example of Haydn's whimsy—the superimposition of the first violin's triplets (three notes to a beat) over the duplets (two notes to the same beat) of the other instruments.

The second movement combines two basic formal principles—variations and contrast. As soon as the opening theme is stated, Haydn immediately varies it. The following section, with a florid first-violin line over a pulsating accompaniment, acts as the contrast. And the movement concludes with an episode of further variations on the opening theme.

Briskly sparkling with rhythmic verve, the Menuetto starts by pitting the violins, playing in octaves, against the viola and cello, also in octaves. The first violin then takes the lead for a while before the opening phrases are brought back. All four instruments join together for the ringing opening of the trio, but the first violin quickly asserts its hegemony. The Menuetto is then repeated.

The presentation of the playful theme of the Finale uncharacteristically omits the first violin. Only in its repetition does the first violin appear, with little decorative touches that add glitter to the already bright tune. Organized into a unique structure that borrows from both sonata and rondo form, Haydn crafts this movement into a gay conclusion to the entire quartet—even throwing in a few pedal points to remind us of where our musical journey began.

String Quartets, Op. 64, Nos. 2, 3, 4, 5, and 6, "Tost Quartets"

The Op. 64 quartets were among the last pieces that Haydn wrote while still in the employ of the Esterhazy family. He worked on them during the spring and summer of 1790. In September of that year Prince Nicholas Esterhazy died, and his family dismissed the music staff, thus relieving Haydn of his duties as *Kapellmeister* after nearly thirty years of service. At the same time Haydn was given a handsome pension, in return for which he only had to supply music for a few ceremonial occasions. Now free to pursue his musical career in his own way, Haydn embarked on a trip to London at year's end for the first of two highly successful concert tours.

It was while Haydn was in London that the six quartets of Op. 64 were published with a dedication to Johann Tost, a former violinist in Haydn's orchestra who by then was known as a successful wholesale cloth merchant. One group of scholars holds that the set was dedicated to Tost because his wife, Maria Anna von Jerlischek, who had been housekeeper to Prince Esterhazy, commissioned it and Haydn chose this way of showing his appreciation. Some cynics believe that, in Haydn's absence, Tost lied to the publisher and named himself the dedicatee. Still others maintain that Haydn simply inscribed them to Tost out of admiration for his skill as a violinist.

Quartets 2 through 6 of Op. 64, which are discussed below, are a popular part of the modern quartet repertoire and are included in all editions of the Thirty Famous Quartets. The works mark a further advance in Haydn's technical mastery, scope of understanding, and inventiveness in relation to the quartet medium.

String Quartet in B Minor, Op. 64, No. 2

I. Allegro spirituoso.   II. Adagio ma non troppo.   III. Menuetto: Allegretto.   IV. Finale: Presto.

The B minor quartet recalls the *Sturm und Drang* ("storm and stress") style that was important in Haydn's music some two decades earlier. The piece is passionate, intense, and prevailingly dark in mood.

The first violin states the opening theme alone, with the others joining only for the closing measures and for the repeat before the dramatic unison statement of the theme's beginning. The second theme is lighter in character, as the two violins meander down the scale, finishing the descent with a series of trilled notes. More motifs follow, each with some hint of mystery and foreboding, until a cheerful codetta ends the exposition. After an uneasy chromatic opening, the development reworks the various themes building to the first violin's extended *concertante* passage, which leads to the recapitulation and an angry, defiant conclusion.

The second movement, according to Haydn scholar H. C. Robbins Landon, is "the most beautiful adagio movement Haydn ever wrote." Structurally, it is quite simple—a theme, followed by three linked variations, with the underlying melodic and harmonic integrity of the original melody maintained throughout. Musically, the theme is a lovely, slow-moving song for the first violin, played over a gently undulating accompaniment in the other instruments. In Variation I, the three lower voices continue the same wavy motion, while the first violin decorates and ornaments the melody. In Variation II, the cellist has the lead, transforming the accompaniment figure into the melodic line. In the final variation the first violin further embellishes the theme, while the second violin plays the accompaniment twice as fast as before. After sustaining a quiet, *mezza voce* (''half-voice'') dynamic level throughout, the movement fades out completely at the end.

Much more a scherzo than a minuet, the third movement projects a bitter, sardonic mood as it stubbornly reiterates one rhythmic cell— long-short-short-long—throughout. Haydn then treats us to a relaxed, songful trio. Sending the eloquent first violin high in its range creates an aura of ephemeral grace, a perfect foil for the more serious Menuetto that came before and is repeated at the end.

Following the exploration of many deep emotions in the first three movements, the Finale offers up a sampling of unabashed fun, with only the briefest flashes of seriousness. The movement is monothematic; the effervescent first theme is only slightly altered to create the second theme. Sparkling with wit and humor, the movement proceeds through the sonata-form structure to the concluding major key coda, which reinforces the pervasive gaiety.

String Quartet in B Flat Major, Op. 64, No. 3

I. Vivace assai.   II. Adagio.   III. Menuetto:
Allegretto.   IV. Finale: Allegro con spirito.

Rhythm was very much on Haydn's mind when he wrote the B flat major quartet. The outside movements fairly crackle with vibrant energy. The second movement is a paradigm of intricate rhythmic figures that are combined with a slow-moving, cantabile melody. And the Menuetto is chock full of dazzling cross accents and syncopations.

While many of Haydn's first movements are monothematic, with essentially one melodic gesture, here there is a plethora of themes; at least seven distinct melodies can be counted in the exposition alone! The melodies follow one another in happy profusion, all rhythmically active either in melody or accompaniment. The development is quite sectional, as though Haydn wanted to work out each theme before proceeding to the next. Haydn restricts the recapitulation a bit, shortening or eliminating some of the tunes before reaching the quiet ending.

No single instrument provides the leading voice in the Adagio.

Instead each one contributes generously to the richly textured effect so that the individual parts cannot easily be categorized as either melody or accompaniment. The theme is in two parts; each part is played twice, with some variation, essentially through rhythmic elaboration, in the repetition. Organized in a basic ternary, A-B-A form, the middle B section is a variation of the theme in the minor mode.

The metrical thrust of the Menuetto is very clearly three-beat time. But by including passages where the alternate notes have heavy accents, Haydn creates the illusion of two-beat measures. Back and forth the Menuetto goes between triple and duple meter, before firmly ending in triple. Then, instead of allowing us to relax with a nice triple-meter trio, Haydn peppers the middle section with syncopations, so that after a while we are totally confused about the underlying meter.

The high-spirited Finale continues the syncopations that enlivened the Menuetto. There are two themes in this movement: the first, gaily leaping; the second, smoother and more sedate. The treatment is quite traditional. After the exposition, both themes are varied and transformed in the development section; the recapitulation proceeds as expected (except for a surprise pause before the return of the second theme); and a short coda wraps it all up.

String Quartet in G Major, Op. 64, No. 4

I. Allegro con brio. II. Menuetto: Allegretto. III. Adagio. IV. Finale: Presto.

A notable feature of this quartet is its unusually prominent and difficult first violin part. Some connect this with the dedication to Johann Tost, a very accomplished violinist who was also an avid amateur quartet player. More likely, though, Haydn had Luigi Tomasini, the outstanding violinist and concertmaster of the Esterhazy orchestra, in mind, as he did for his earlier quartets.

The principal theme of the first movement, one of Haydn's finest, is bright, fresh, and bursting with vigor. Yet, for sheer musical interest, it is probably topped by the three motifs that make up the second group. The first one is simply the original theme raised up five notes to the key of D major. The second, and most remarkable, is a descending syncopated line played in octaves by the violins in the key of D minor, which injects a slight air of mystery and foreboding into the otherwise happy music. The third motif, which brings the exposition to an end, is played on the first violin's lowest string, giving it an unusual dark timbre. The development starts with an imitative section based on the final motif of the second group, but this proves to be no more than a springboard for the first violin's bravura passage work, which leads to the recapitulation. Instead of the standard return of the themes, though, Haydn develops the thematic material even further before ending the movement.

For the Menuetto, Haydn reverts to the simpler style of his earlier works. The first part has all the vitality and verve of a sturdy Austrian-peasant Ländler. The more delicate trio, essentially one long violin solo over a pizzicato accompaniment, is followed by a return of the rustic Menuetto.

The Adagio combines elements of ternary (A-B-A) and theme-and-variation form. After the presentation and repetition of the main theme in the A section, the B part is a variation in the minor key. The return of A is still another variation, back in the original major. The melody stays in the first violin, with a rolling accompaniment figure in the second violin and viola.

The Finale evokes the spirit of a *galop,* a high-speed round dance based on the old German *hopser* dance. The composer casts it in sonata form and fills it with some of his most playful and witty music.

String Quartet in D Major, Op. 64, No. 5, "The Lark"

I. Allegro moderato. II. Adagio
cantabile. III. Menuetto: Allegretto. IV. Finale:
Vivace.

Probably the most familiar of all Haydn quartets, Op. 64, No. 5, bears two nicknames, neither of which was suggested by the composer. Most often it is known as "The Lark," from the general association of the opening violin melody with the bird's soaring circular flight pattern. The other subtitle, "Hornpipe," refers to the Finale, which has the seemingly inexhaustible flow of notes that characterizes this old English sailors' dance.

The quartet opens with a repeated staccato figure in the lower instruments, over which the first violin glides up in the beautiful "Lark" melody. The mood darkens somewhat as the viola begins a syncopated passage in which everyone joins with increasingly sharp dissonances and growing intensity. A cascade of falling triplets announces the second subject and a return of the joyous character. The development starts with the first theme—on a lower pitch and with a smooth accompaniment that gives it a more earthbound feeling—and ends in a forceful unison passage leading directly to the restatement of themes one and two. Haydn, though, continues to expand the second theme until the music stops on a long, held note, after which he goes through another complete, though concise, recapitulation to end the movement.

The Adagio cantabile is one extended song for the violin. Following the initial statement, which contains some development of the melodic material, Haydn modulates to the minor for a middle section based on the principal theme. The movement ends with the opening theme in variation.

The confident swagger of the Menuetto immediately breaks the pensive spell cast by the Adagio cantabile. It struts forward, robust and virile, until the minor-key trio interrupts with its busy scurrying, after which the contrasting Menuetto is repeated.

The Finale is a perpetual motion reminiscent of a spirited hornpipe dance. The rushing sixteenth notes are heard in one instrument or another throughout the entire movement. Organized in three-part, A-B-A form, the middle section is a fugato in which the tune, starting with a characteristic syncopation, is stated by the first violin and imitated by the others—but without disturbing the stream of fast notes. The movement ends with a coda of great dash and verve.

String Quartet in E Flat Major, Op. 64, No. 6

I. Allegretto. II. Andante. III. Menuetto: Allegretto. IV. Finale: Presto.

The key of E flat major seems to call forth from Haydn a particularly contemplative and lyrical style of music, which the Allegretto of Op. 64, No. 4, illustrates perfectly. The first violin announces the cantabile, gently flowing principal theme, which, slightly changed, also serves as the subsidiary subject. The beatific mood is essentially sustained throughout; but within this atmosphere, there are several unique and interesting touches. One striking passage, halfway through the development, sets up what Cecil Gray calls "a ghostly, chattering little staccato figure" in the second violin, while the other instruments hold a "mysterious colloquy" on the final notes of the theme. Then there is a false recapitulation, the first theme returning as though for the restatement—but in the wrong key. Haydn sustains this "joke" for several measures, before a transition passage takes us back to the true recapitulation. But even then, Haydn further develops and varies the two themes, finally building them up to a full-voiced conclusion.

The principal theme of the glorious Andante consists of a rapidly rising arpeggio and a slow descent in the first violin, with a richly textured contrapuntal web woven around the melodic line by the other instruments. The calm ends abruptly with the agitated middle section—throbbing repeated notes in the lower instruments and a highly dramatic, impassioned miniconcerto for the first violin. The excitement quickly quiets down for a shortened return of the opening.

The character of this fine Menuetto varies with the performers' interpretation of how it is to be played. If they put equal accents on every beat, which is perfectly acceptable, the music sounds forceful, rhythmic, and aggressive. On the other hand, if they only accent the first beat of each measure, which is equally valid, the character is much more dancelike and less intense. No matter how the Menuetto is played, however, the trio always presents a contrast. It is lighter in spirit, very soft throughout, and clearly with only one accent to each measure. The trio ends with the second violin playing the melody and the first violin soaring to the stratospheric regions before a return of the Menuetto.

The Finale, in rondo form, is essentially a theme repeated a number of times with contrasting interludes between the repetitions. The individual episodes are sometimes hard to hear because they are little more than transformations of the main theme. This whirlwind movement is varied and interesting, with many humorous touches.

String Quartets, Op. 74, Nos. 1, 2, and 3, "Apponyi Quartets"

In 1790, after twenty-nine years of service, Haydn left his full-time position as *Kapellmeister* to the Esterhazy family. The following year, at the invitation of impresario-violinist Johann Salomon, Haydn journeyed to England where he led and heard public concerts held in large halls, not intimate aristocratic salons; performed by highly trained musicians, not amateur nobles or servant-performers; and open to all, not just the high-born.

Upon Haydn's return from London, Count Anton Apponyi, a friend of the composer and a relative of the Esterhazys, asked Haydn to write a set of quartets for him. The composer produced six quartets during the summer of 1793, dividing them into the three of Op. 71 and the three of Op. 74. These "Apponyi Quartets" represent a major transformation in Haydn's style. More experimental and innovative than earlier compositions, they are generally considered the first written by a major composer with the public concert hall in mind and are regarded as being less for Count Apponyi and his musical soirees than for Salomon and his concerts at London's Hanover Square Public Rooms.

Several features in the music signal this change of purpose. The quartets have attention-catching introductions, considered necessary for the larger and less sophisticated public audiences. The part writing is more brilliant and demanding than before, and the melodies are catchier and easier to recall. The tempos are exaggerated (faster fast movements, slower slow movements); many intimate details are replaced by grand gestures; and there is a general intensification of all aspects, particularly of the emotional content of the music. Evidence of the stronger feelings and greater expressivity in these compositions led scholar Karl Geiringer to comment: "The dawn of Romanticism is noticeable in the string quartets of Op. 74."

While the three quartets of Op. 71 are rarely played, the Op. 74 are popular favorites and are performed widely.

String Quartet in C Major, Op. 74, No. 1

I. Allegro moderato. II. Andantino grazioso. III. Menuetto: Allegretto. IV. Finale: Vivace.

The first pages of Op. 74, No. 1 sound fully as orchestral as the London symphonies that Haydn composed around the same time. Two chords of powerful sonorous introduction are followed by a rather serious first subject, with amazing breadth, length, and motivic interest. Two important characteristics can be noted here and throughout the entire quartet. One is the use of chromaticisms, notes that fall between the notes of the diatonic scale. For example, the first notes of the diatonic scale are C-D-E, but in the first measures of the quartet the first violin plays C-C sharp-D-E flat-E. The other is the brilliant instrumental writing, the dazzling range of pitches and dynamics, the speed of the passage work, and the intricacy of the interrelationships. Essentially monothematic, the movement's second theme, played by the three lower instruments, is obviously derived from the first theme; it is coupled with a distinctive countermelody in the first violin. After developing the abundance of motifs, Haydn starts the recapitulation in a traditional manner. But he soon interrupts for a short canonic expansion of the theme, before proceeding to the second theme and coda, which features a forceful unison variant of the principal theme.

The graceful, balanced four-measure opening phrases of the second movement seem distinctly Mozartean until Haydn puts his unmistakable stamp on the music with a concluding five-measure phrase that looks wrong on paper, but that sounds perfectly proportioned in performance. He immediately continues with the violins playing the second theme, a sighing melody that again could easily have been penned by Mozart. The closing theme of the exposition is a dialogue between pairs of instruments. The development, which considers only the first and third themes, leads to the slightly decorated recapitulation. A coda follows, in effect another development, which ends the movement with a puissant unison that recalls the conclusion of the Allegro moderato.

The Allegretto tempo indication of the Menuetto is the same as most earlier Haydn quartet minuets, yet this music seems to call for a rather brisk one-to-a-bar meter instead of the more deliberate three-beats-to-a-bar of the previous works. The robust, rhythmic C major Menuetto is followed by a startling modulation to the distantly related key of A major for the lyrical trio. The trio theme, which sounds like an Austrian folk melody, seems to be derived from the generally ascending line of the Menuetto theme. Following a transition passage back to the original key of C major, the Menuetto is played again, this time without repeats.

Although basically monothematic, the brilliant Finale has a plenitude of individual motifs, much like the first movement. Near the end of the exposition are some rustic, peasantlike melodic fragments played over a bagpipe drone. The highly contrapuntal development section fully exploits the tonal and technical resources of all four instruments, individually and as a group. The recapitulation is much shortened; in the coda, Haydn creates sonorities that are orchestral in effect.

String Quartet in F Major, Op. 74, No. 2

I. Allegro spirituoso. II. Andante grazioso. III. Menuetto: Allegro. IV. Finale: Presto.

The F major quartet starts with what appears to be a forceful unison statement of the first theme. Only after it comes to a stop on a held note do we realize that this was really a fast, instead of the typically slow, introduction. The first theme proper then follows, a clone of the introductory melody. As the exposition continues, we also become aware that the movement is monothematic, with the first theme completely dominant. To forestall any danger of dullness, though, Haydn introduces a number of varied subsidiary subjects along with the principal one. He also makes considerable use of trills to add interest and call special attention to particular notes. A massive development section of great tension and intensity follows, replete with virtuosic passages for all the instruments and amazing contrapuntal interweaving of the various parts. After the recapitulation, the movement ends with another stentorian unison statement like the introduction, but this time of the first theme proper.

After the tension and intensity of the first movement, Haydn offers a few moments of quiet relaxation with the Andante grazioso. The two violins state the suave and elegant theme, while the viola and cello share a complementary countermelody. Haydn then subjects the theme to three variations. In the first he gives the melody to the viola and cello and sends the first violin off on decorative roulades. The next variation is quite novel in that the leading voice is the second violin, which Haydn marks *Solo*. And the final variation starts like the original theme, but Haydn soon introduces a rapid figure in the viola and cello that runs through the remainder of the movement.

The peasant-style Menuetto is marked in a faster tempo than most of Haydn's previous minuets (Allegro vs. Allegretto), and the rapid three-note figure that appears several times in the melody makes it seem slightly comical. The central trio is much darker in color and is in a startlingly distant key relationship (D flat major after F major) to the Menuetto. An added transition section modulates back to F major, and the Menuetto is repeated.

The gaily percolating theme of the Finale, typical of the popular melodies Haydn wrote for the "Apponyi Quartets," is so attractive and appealing that it has been published as an independent piano piece. After stating and discoursing on this flippant tune for some time, Haydn introduces the subsidiary subject, a smooth, slow-moving melody that provides a very strong contrast to the opening. The rest of the movement alternates these themes, or their close derivatives, in a lighthearted, spirited diversion.

String Quartet in G Minor, Op. 74, No. 3, "Reiterquartett" ("The Rider")

I. Allegro. II. Largo assai. III. Menuetto: Allegretto. IV. Finale: Allegro con brio.

Struck by the galloping rhythm of the first movement and even more by the driving vigor of the last movement, someone, not Haydn, nicknamed this the "*Reiterquartett*," variously translated as "The Rider" or "The Horseman." While this is a perfectly apt subtitle, it unfortunately calls extra attention to the quartet's outer movements, perhaps leading to some neglect of the Largo assai, the true soul of the quartet.

A brusque, gruff introductory eight-measure phrase opens the quartet, followed by an abrupt, dramatic silence. The first theme is then heard, neat and dainty by comparison, starting with a rising cello arpeggio, after which a motto of two repeated upbeats and a long note passes through the quartet. Following several repetitions, Haydn replaces the long notes with strings of rapid notes. This section builds to a climax and then grows suddenly quiet for the second theme, which uses the two repeated notes as the entree into a swinging mazurkalike dance tune. These two themes, and the introduction, too, are the subjects of the comparatively short development section, which ends with a climactic held note. The recapitulation starts not with the introductory bars, but by going right into a truncated review of the two main themes of the movement.

The spiritual and noble Largo assai is often cited as the most emotionally moving movement of all three Op. 74 quartets. Haydn's publisher must have recognized its special qualities, since he also put it out in five different piano arrangements. The movement is simply described. It starts with an unadorned melody in the major followed by a contrasting middle section in minor, in which the basic melodic contour is inverted. The original melody is then returned, with some additional filigree in the first violin. About halfway through this section, in an absolutely magical moment, all the instruments play many rapid repeats of the notes, creating an otherworldly effect. The ending is very quiet.

Although the Menuetto that follows is thought to be based on an old dance tune, the legato melody seems more songlike. The movement demonstrates Haydn's remarkable skill as a contrapuntalist, hiding the complex polyphony behind the easy flow of the music. The somewhat somber trio is heard before a shortened repetition of the Menuetto.

As soon as the highly energetic Finale starts, it is obvious where "The Rider" quartet got its nickname. Haydn achieves the powerful driving effect by having the three lower instruments play on the beats, with the first violin playing afterbeats. The subsidiary tune is a light, flirtatious, folklike melody heard against the same rhythmic pattern. Following the structure of sonata form, the movement provides an exhilarating conclusion to the entire quartet.

String Quartets, Op. 76, Nos. 1, 2, 3, 4, 5, and 6, "Erdödy Quartets"

By the time Haydn returned to Vienna in 1795, after his second immensely successful visit to London, several new elements had become integrated into his writing. His new style reflected his experience of composing for public performances by highly accomplished musicians in large halls. Also the realization that he was widely regarded as the greatest living composer (Mozart had already died, and Beethoven had not yet made his mark) had imbued him with great boldness and self-assurance.

When Count Joseph Erdödy asked Haydn for a set of quartets, probably early in 1796, the sixty-four-year-old composer brought to the task his newly developed musical outlook, along with forty years of continuous growth and maturation in writing for the medium. Among the new features he incorporated into these quartets are more profound and emotional slow movements that move at an extremely deliberate pace and, as Haydn biographer H. C. Robbins Landon finds, "are also bathed in a curiously impersonal and remote melancholy." The minuets, on the other hand, are now more like scherzos, faster in tempo and lighter in mood in comparison with the older, dignified minuet-style movements. Haydn also experimented with new formal schemes in the first movements of Quartets 5 and 6, instead of holding to the traditional sonata form. And the finales, which had tended to be light and humorous in character, became more serious and intellectually challenging.

Composed in 1796 and 1797, the six quartets of Op. 76 were dedicated to Count Erdödy and published in 1799.

String Quartet in G Major, Op. 76, No. 1

I. Allegro con spirito. II. Adagio sostenuto. III. Menuetto: Presto. IV. Allegro ma non troppo.

The quartet opens with three powerful chords, a symbolic summons perhaps for the public concert audiences. The statement of the first theme, a single line of melody, is made by the cello alone, answered by the solo viola. After two further statements by isolated pairs of instruments, there follows a tutti continuation of the theme. Haydn then expands and extends this subject until a rapid, violent unison passage acts as the transition to the delightfully ingratiating second subject. The development begins with a viola statement of the first theme along with a countermelody in the second violin. The countermelody comes to play a major part in the development and then again in the recapitulation, where the first violin plays it as the cello repeats the principal theme.

In the Adagio sosenuto, the focal point of the entire quartet, Haydn molds and fashions three distinct musical gestures into a solemn movement of deep significance. The first, which proves also to be most important, is a sustained theme played in chorale style by all four instruments. The second idea is a dialogue between the cello and first violin conducted against repeated notes in the second violin and viola. And finally, the three lower instruments play short repeated notes, above which the first violin adds a long, unbroken stream of afterbeats—a passage that requires a keen rhythmic sense and intense concentration from all the players. Through the statement and varied repetition of this simply described material, Haydn creates a most moving and effective movement.

Although Haydn called the next movement a Menuetto, the faster tempo, the single strong beat in each bar instead of three, and the much lighter character identify this movement as a scherzo, probably the first *echt* scherzo in the Haydn quartets. In another departure from tradition, the following trio, with its roots in the old Austrian Ländler dance, is obviously intended to be played very much slower than the opening and concluding Menuetto parts.

Not light and fluffy like earlier Haydn finales, this last movement has the necessary weight and importance to balance what came before. Although the quartet is in G major, Haydn starts the last movement in a unison G minor. After a long trilled note ends the unison, the viola alone plays the tune, while the violins add a countermelody. Haydn develops this material and then makes the outlook grow even darker as he slows down the propulsive forward motion for the second theme, an ominous-sounding transformation of the violin's countermelody from near the beginning of the movement. The development section tries to generate a more joyful spirit but never quite succeeds. Then, after coming to a complete stop, the recapitulation starts with the principal theme in the cheerful key of G major; the second theme, though, keeps its same dour expression. In the coda Haydn suddenly introduces a flip, happy tune. Some hear this as a successful attempt to achieve a sunny, cheerful ending. Others regret what they consider the trivialization of the work's final measures.

String Quartet in D Minor, Op. 76, No. 2, *"Die Quinten" ("The Fifths")*

I. Allegro. II. Andante o più tosto allegretto. III. Menuetto: Allegro ma non troppo. IV. Finale: Vivace assai.

The quartet's subtitle, "The Fifths," comes from the principal theme of the first movement, which starts with two descending melodic intervals of the fifth. Since these same four notes start the melody marking the third quarter of the hour on Big Ben, the quartet is also nicknamed "The Bells." The concentration of musical material and the impelling logic of its construction make Op. 76, No. 2, in the words of noted Haydn scholar H. C. Robbins Landon, "One of the most serious, learned and intellectually formidable works he ever wrote." Every note, every musical gesture, is used for a telling, expressive purpose.

219

The quartet opens with the bold, dominant, four-note motif from which the composition derived its subtitle. As soon as the theme is stated, once loudly and once softly, Haydn introduces a series of new motifs, all related, closely or distantly, to the two pairs of descending fifths. This constitutes the spacious exposition, without a formal second theme, but with built-in contrasts growing out of the original musical concept. The development and recapitulation that follow seem compressed by comparison and give way to a driving, relentless coda that plunges on to the powerful concluding chords.

The slow movement is faster and less emotional than comparable movements in other Op. 76 quartets, focusing more on grace and charm than on depth of feeling. The movement, though, serves as the perfect interlude between the intensity of the first movement and the ardor of the following Menuetto. The first violin states the simple, poised melody over an extremely thin accompaniment. The same theme, melodically varied in minor, serves as the contrasting middle section and is then embellished for the return of the initial major-key part.

For the Menuetto, Haydn reduces the quartet to only two voices—the two violins, and the viola and cello—with both pairs playing in octaves. And from beginning to end the lower instruments faithfully echo the violins three beats later, creating a note-perfect canon. This most striking effect earned the movement the subtitle "*Hexen-Menuett*" ("Witches' Minuet"). The trio is as different from the Menuetto as it can be. It is exclusively chordal, compared to the faultless two-part counterpoint; it changes dynamic level gradually from soft to very loud, compared to the consistently loud dynamic level; it feels like it is faster and should be played with only one heavy beat in each bar, compared to the previous three slow, heavy beats to a bar. The canon returns to round out the ternary form.

The syncopated main theme of the Finale, with its two held notes right in the middle, effectively captures the spirit of Hungarian peasant music, even though its full strength and vigor is not apparent until the second violin rings it out loudly. Haydn next presents a section that can be interpreted as a free development, after which he brings back the principal theme and, in an absolutely inspired way, transforms the minor-key theme to major. By simultaneously stopping all rhythmic motion in the accompanying second violin and viola, he gives this comparatively rough-hewn theme an exceptional spiritual quality. From here he proceeds to a wonderfully gladsome ending.

String Quartet in C Major, Op. 76, No. 3, "Kaiser" ("Emperor")

I. Allegro.   II. Poco adagio cantabile.   III. Menuetto: Allegro.   IV. Finale: Presto.

Most interest in this quartet focuses on its second movement, the expressive center of the work. The theme comes from a hymn Haydn wrote to honor Emperor Franz II, "*Gott erhalte Franz den Kaiser*" ("God Protect Emperor Franz"). In addition to its use in the quartet, the universally appealing melody became the national anthems of both Austria and Germany, a religious hymn, and a Masonic anthem.

Bearing the notable second movement in mind, Haydn probably decided to start with a less weighty opening section. The Allegro is essentially monothematic; the melody heard at the very beginning dominates throughout. The theme, though, undergoes several especially interesting transformations—from a bright, sunny first statement, to a murky, low-pitched appearance later in the exposition, to a rough peasant dance in the middle of the development section. The writing for all four instruments, especially the first violin, is uniformly brilliant and virtuosic.

Haydn subjects the simple and dignified, though highly emotional, theme of the second movement to four variations. In a departure from his usual variation technique, he keeps the melody essentially the same throughout, giving it to different instruments and varying the setting and accompaniment against which it is heard. After the first violin statement, the melody passes to the second violin, while the first violin embroiders around it a delicate lacery of sprightly runs and leaps. In the second variation, the cello has the melody and the other instruments pursue richly textured contrapuntal lines in the background. The viola is entrusted with the lead in Variation III, while the violins and cello contribute their rather spare countermelodies. The final variation is the apotheosis; the entire quartet plays the theme in a hauntingly beautiful and evocative setting.

To avoid competing with the preceding movement, Haydn created a simple, undemanding Menuetto. The first section is a heavy-shoed peasant dance, played loudly throughout. The contrasting trio is much smoother, quieter, and more songlike. It is followed by a shortened repeat of the Menuetto.

The grave Finale is the counterweight to the serious second movement. The opening measures contain three musical gestures that pervade the entire movement: three powerful chords, a smooth answering phrase that is rhythmically reminiscent of the first movement, and running triplet passages. While Haydn imaginatively transforms and develops these motifs with great vigor, the total effect is perhaps more anxious than cheerful. At the end he moves into major, presumably a happier key, but the concluding mood is still not entirely joyful.

String Quartet in B Flat Major, Op. 76, No. 4, "Sunrise"

I. Allegro con spirito. II. Adagio. III. Menuetto: Allegro. IV. Finale: Allegro, ma non troppo.

In the view of many, Op. 76, No. 4 is the finest among Haydn's eighty-three quartets. Rarely, if ever, did he equal its luminous spirituality and depth of feeling. Perhaps Haydn intended this quartet, with its prominent viola part, for his own use, since he was also an avid quartet violist.

The nickname, "Sunrise," widely accepted in America and England but seldom used elsewhere, comes from the very opening of the quartet where the first violin traces a loving curve of ascent above a soft, sustained chord, much as the sun gloriously rises to bathe the earth in its radiance. There are two more motifs in the first group: one stated by the viola, amidst long held notes in the violins and cello; the other, a repeated rhythmic figure combined with running sixteenth-note passages. The second subject starts with the cello playing what is essentially a mirror image—descending instead of ascending—of the first subject opening. It continues with an outgrowth of the first subject's last motif. The concluding theme of the exposition is a witty interplay of notes on and off the beat. Although the remainder of the movement can be divided into the customary development, recapitulation, and coda, Haydn creates such a strong feeling of inner cohesion that the overall musical effect is one of sustained, unified flow.

The second movement is one of the slowest and most morose of all Haydn adagios. Not conforming to any standard structural organization, it is best described as a free fantasia on the opening five-note motif. Uniformly soft, with only occasional accents, the movement provides little solace and ends in bleak despair.

After two such strong movements, the unsophisticated peasant charm of the Menuetto offers a welcome respite. With great rhythmic verve, Haydn builds this entire section on the opening motif. The trio that comes in the middle apparently also has its origin in folk music, but the outlook is not nearly so sunny and cheerful. Over a sustained drone in the viola and cello, the violins play the rather oppressive melody with its heavy accents. The Menuetto returns at the end of the trio.

The Finale is written in the carefree style of Haydn's earlier quartets. The melody is believed to be an adaptation of an English folk song, perhaps one he heard on his trip to London. Organized in three-part form, the middle section is in minor, but with no lessening of the Finale's overriding vivacity. To heighten the movement's exhilaration and good humor, Haydn marks the coda (which is a technical minefield for the players) *Più allegro,* or "faster," and then *Più presto,* "faster yet," for a thrilling conclusion.

String Quartet in D Major, Op. 76, No. 5

I. Allegretto. II. Largo: Cantabile e mesto. III. Menuetto: Allegro. IV. Finale: Presto.

In the opening measures of Op. 76, No. 5, Haydn establishes the mood that prevails, with but few exceptions, for the entire first movement. The moderate tempo, soft and lyrical melody, and gentle rocking motion produce the typical character of a Siciliano, a dance of Italian origin widely used by seventeenth- and eighteenth-century opera and cantata composers to suggest tranquil pastoral beauty. After some expansion, Haydn transforms the theme by going into an agitated minor section, in which the cello starts the melody and the others join in, creating a dense contrapuntal texture. In the final section of the ternary form Haydn returns to a major-key variant of the opening melody. For the lengthy coda, he picks up the tempo and further develops both the major and minor themes with great energy and vigor.

The deeply felt and recondite Largo is the gravitational center of the quartet. Written in F sharp major, an unexpected key after the D major opening movement, its first notes invariably startle the perceptive listener. This key, when played on string instruments, seems to impart a shiny radiance to the music and, because it is a particularly difficult key, tends to concentrate and intensify the performance. Further, this Largo is also much longer than any of the other movements; in fact, it is almost equal in length to all the other movements combined! Haydn fashions this lengthy movement from a single theme that contains two distinctive musical gestures. The first, a pure, noble vocal melody, is played by the first violin at the opening. The second, also played by the first violin, is a more active line, with dotted (long-short) rhythms against throbbing repeated chords. As soon as the two ideas have been presented, Haydn combines them, giving the opening phrase to the cello and the dotted notes to the first violin, with stunning results. Working essentially with only the two ideas, Haydn skillfully transforms them, invests them with ever-changing tone colors, and presents them in new combinations and relationships until the movement fades away.

The Menuetto looks back to the Largo; its legato opening melody is a quickened transposition of the Largo's first theme. Enlivened with occasional cross accents, this theme dominates the Menuetto. The trio features the cello in a mini-perpetual motion. The other instruments are mostly restricted to two-note interjections, a preview of the opening of the next movement. The Menuetto is heard again after the trio.

Haydn starts the Finale with a series of three concluding cadence figures, a wonderfully comic touch. Only after he arrives at a decisive ending does he speed off with the principal theme—fleet, light-hearted, and folklike—but interrupted by any number of cadences. The spirited music races along with great humor, until Haydn finally ends the movement just as he began it, an ironic touch that he surely must have relished!

String Quartet in E Flat Major, Op. 76, No. 6

I. Allegretto. II. Fantasia: Adagio. III. Menuetto: Presto. IV. Finale: Allegro spirituoso.

The final quartet of Op. 76 is the most enigmatic and abstruse one of the set. In it Haydn goes off in new directions not often encountered in eighteenth-century music. Although it is generally considered a difficult piece, those who make the effort to become familiar with it are amply rewarded.

The quartet opens with a series of terse, laconic phrases arranged in a sort of question-answer sequence. This theme, though, is not the first subject of conventional sonata form; rather, it proves to be the theme of theme and variations, which is rare, if not unique, as a first movement form. The four variations are also unusual in that the theme remains virtually intact. It is, though, passed from instrument to instrument—second violin, cello, first violin, and finally everyone—with fresh countermelodies and new harmonizations for each variation. For the players, Haydn's variations pose a difficult interpretative dilemma: Which is the leading voice of each varia- tion—the already familiar theme, or the countermelody?

Haydn's title for the second movement, Fantasia, has two pos- sible musical references. One is a general description of music written in a free and improvisatory style. A more specific reference is to Henry Purcell's seventeenth-century fantasias for strings, free-form pieces in intricate contrapuntal style, which Haydn might have heard while visiting England. Haydn seems to adapt elements from both defi- nitions of fantasia in this movement. He states the theme twice and then, as though rambling in an improvisatory way over the keyboard, makes a scalelike transition to a slightly varied statement of the theme in a different key. Four times he goes through the scalic preparation and variants of the melody. With the theme's fifth return, though, the music settles down into a serene contrapuntal fantasia on the original theme that sounds as though it might have been written by the English master.

The high-speed, humorous Menuetto lowers the emotional tem- perature and tension raised by the first two movements. Although in the traditional triple meter, funny cross accents at times obliterate the music's underlying pulse. The middle section, called *alternativo* instead of trio, is witty in another way. Melodically it is nothing more than descending and ascending iambic scales. The musical interest is found in the amazing things that Haydn does under, over, and around the plodding up and down motion. Finally the Menuetto comes back to end the movement.

The Finale is the third example in this quartet of scalic melodic figures playing a particularly important role. The principal and just about only theme of this frisky, high-spirited sonata-form movement is a series of slightly offbeat descending scale fragments. A fun move- ment, the Finale sparkles with Haydn's many droll touches.

String Quartets, Op. 77, Nos. 1 and 2, "Lobkowitz Quartets"

The two quartets of Op. 77, Haydn's last complete works in this form, were written in 1799 for the excellent violinist and amateur chamber musician, Prince Franz Joseph Lobkowitz; but no one knows why the set includes only two instead of the usual three or six quartets. Most commentators believe that it was because Haydn was in poor health and occupied with his massive oratorio, *The Seasons*. H. C. Robbins Landon, though, in his biography of the composer, ascribes the change to a musical confrontation between Haydn and Beethoven.

From the time Beethoven arrived in Vienna in 1792, he generally avoided writing in forms such as the string quartet, with which Haydn was associated. But just before the turn of the century, Prince Lobkowitz commissioned quartets from both Haydn and Beethoven. The results were Haydn's Op. 77 and Beethoven's Op. 18. As the first of these quartets were heard in performance, the reactions were far more approving of the younger composer's works than the older master's. Therefore, Robbins Landon conjectures, Haydn decided to avoid any more comparison with Beethoven, whom he already distrusted and disliked, by ceasing to write string quartets altogether. (There is precedent; much earlier in his career Haydn had stopped writing piano concertos and operas after hearing Mozart's triumphs in these forms.) Haydn devoted the remaining years of his life, with the single exception of the two movements of the unfinished quartet, Op. 103, to the composition of large-scale vocal and orchestra works, a genre that Beethoven generally avoided until many years later.

While the Op. 77 quartets may seem pale in comparison with Beethoven's forward-looking Op. 18, they do show Haydn at his most masterful. Thematically, the Op. 77 quartets are extremely strong, the texture is a perfect blend of homophonic and contrapuntal writing, and the expressiveness reaches new heights.

String Quartet in G Major, Op. 77, No. 1

I. Allegro moderato. II. Adagio. III. Menuetto: Presto. IV. Finale: Presto.

The Op. 77, No. 1 quartet is a fine example of a synthesizing work that integrates a number of disparate elements present in Haydn's style. Many of the motifs, though obviously of folk-song extraction and endowed with great directness of expression and simplicity of means, are treated with his own sophisticated, learned compositional approach. Also, while fully aware of all the standard formal structures, Haydn nevertheless allows the musical content to determine the final organization. And finally, Haydn strikes a new balance between such opposite tendencies as chordal writing and counterpoint, accompanied melody and equality of the voices, and a predominant first violin and active, interesting parts for all four instruments.

The opening theme, thought by scholar Bence Szabolcsi to be based on an old Hungarian recruiting song called a *bokazo,* has a marchlike lilt to it. As the first theme continues, Haydn introduces a running triplet passage in the form of a dialogue between the two violins. A modification of this triplet figure in the viola along with a smooth melody in the second violin start the subsidiary theme. The following development section barely gets started before there is an apparent recapitulation; we hear what sounds like the first and second themes (even though the latter is in the ''wrong'' key). After following this false direction for a while, Haydn brings everyone together for a loud unison measure in triplets to get into the true recapitulation, which omits the second theme in this final go-around.

The second movement, the only one that seems completely free of folk influence, is deeply personal and seems to come straight from Haydn's heart. After stating the short, impassioned opening phrase, which might be an anguished cry, Haydn devotes the rest of the movement to an exploration of its musical and emotional connotations in a structure that is partly theme and variations and partly sonata form. The character varies—from carefree to foreboding, from exultant to tender, from relentless to sentimental—until the movement ends with a quiet final statement of warmth and consolation.

The spirited Menuetto quickly sends the first violin running and leaping up from its lowest note to the very top of its range. (It is believed that the high D reached by the violin near the end of the Menuetto is the highest note in the standard string quartet repertoire.) The trio, which seems to have a folk dance origin, sustains the high-energy level of the Menuetto and features sharp changes in dynamics, with sudden bursts of fast (eighth) notes bursting in on the slower (quarter) notes. The Menuetto is repeated after a measure of silence.

The Finale theme, believed to be a *kolo,* a Croatian round dance that Haydn knew from his youth, is a gleeful, witty tune that provides the musical impetus for the entire movement. Although organized in sonata form, it is essentially monothematic; the second theme is nothing more than a transposition of the first. The part writing throughout is virtuosic, making it a true display piece for all four performers.

String Quartet in F Major, Op. 77, No. 2

I. Allegro moderato. II. Menuetto: Presto, ma non troppo. III. Andante. IV. Finale: Vivace assai.

The F major, the last quartet that Haydn completed, was written when he was in his late sixties, in failing health, and deeply involved in composing his great oratorios and masses. Unaware that the F major was to be his last quartet, Haydn did not use it for any great summing up. Instead he composed a meticulous work that has all the characteristic drive and vigor of his more youthful works, yet is imbued with a certain wistful melancholy.

The main theme of the first movement is essentially a melancholy descending F scale, but with many interruptions of its downward motion. To intensify the doleful impression, Haydn starts with a strong phrase, which fades away to a number of soft, weak extensions. Other motifs follow until the first violin introduces the new subsidiary melody while the second violin plays the opening of the principal theme. After a rather lengthy development section, which ends with a measure of silence, Haydn brings both subjects back for a truncated recapitulation.

There can be little doubt that Haydn wrote the humorous Menuetto with tongue in cheek. The first clue is the gay and skittish melody. Then, although the movement is in the traditional triple meter, Haydn goes out of his way to create duple-meter rhythmic patterns that go in and out of phase with the underlying beat. He also writes a cello part that at times makes the instrument sound like a timpani. After the high spirits of the Menuetto, the Trio, in a distant key, is quite unexpected. Smooth and sober, almost hymn-like, it is a sharp contrast to the impish playfulness of what came before. But Haydn's high jinks are not yet over. In the transition back to the Menuetto, he throws in a few "wrong" beat entrances, just for fun.

In the strange, striking opening of the Andante, the violin plays the staid, deliberate theme while the cello moves it forward with a slow, implacable tread. Basically there are three quite freely realized variations on the theme (featuring the second violin, the cello, and first violin respectively), which are separated by contrasting episodes between the variations. A tremendous crescendo and climax precede the final variation, which nonetheless starts very quietly, much as the movement began, and ends just as quietly.

The Finale theme captures all the dash and fire of a fast folk dance. A slightly more subdued second theme, characterized by misplaced accents, on the third beat instead of the usual first, follows. With great rhythmic vitality, Haydn then builds the rest of the movement almost exclusively on the first theme, although he brings both ideas back for the recapitulation. A few soft measures in the midst of the bustling coda heighten the impact of the exciting conclusion.

Paul Hindemith

Born November 16, 1895, in Hanau, Germany
Died December 28, 1963, in Frankfurt

ALTHOUGH HE was born into an uncultured, working-class family (his father was a poor house painter), Hindemith managed to become one of the most learned, skillful, and multifaceted musicians in recent times. Starting violin lessons at the age of seven, Hindemith left home just four years later to support himself by playing in beer gardens, dance halls, theaters, and night clubs. By age fourteen he began the serious study of composition. When he was drafted into the army near the end of World War I, he had the good fortune to be assigned to a colonel who detested military music and had organized his own string quartet! After the war, Hindemith performed as soloist on the violin, viola, and viola d'amore, conducted, taught, played piano and every other orchestra instrument, organized concerts of ancient music, authored a number of books on music, and above all, produced an impressive amount of music for solo instruments, chamber ensembles, symphony orchestras, and the operatic stage. So natural and easy was his musicianship that Paul Bekker once said, "He doesn't compose, he musics."

From about 1920 on, Hindemith's work reflected his sympathy with an emerging artistic movement known as *Neue Sachlichkeit* ("New Objectivity"), a form of Neoclassicism in which there was a great emphasis on the rules that governed the various arts. Hindemith, as well as composers Ferruccio Busoni and Max Reger, among several others, revived the forms and styles of earlier periods, especially of the eighteenth century. Hindemith's aesthetics are often linked with the German painter Max Beckmann, who displayed in works such as *The Departure* the use of shocking details organized with merciless clarity to demonstrate his belief in an orderly universe.

The new trend represented a reaction against the lush Romanticism, so popular at the time. For Hindemith, logic, organization, and formal restraint replace the expression of emotion as a primary concern. He avoids programmatic connections, and favors abstract, linear, polyphonic style, in which each voice is clear and independent. Most of his music is tonal, based on the major and minor scales.

Paul Hindemith also espoused *Gebrauchmusik,* or "music for use," as opposed to "music for music's sake." "A composer," he said, "should write today only if he knows for what purpose he is writing. The days of composing for the sake of composing are perhaps gone forever." And he stressed mastery of musical craft: "When a composer writes, he must be able to do so without any consciousness of technique. A great novelist . . . never thinks of grammar."

As he grew older, Hindemith became less rigorous in his adherence to the principles of system and order. His work became more expressive and lyrical—even Romantic. His lifelong feelings about contemporary music, though, remained the same; as he put it, he strove to "minimize the word *new* in the term 'new art' and emphasize rather the word *art.*"

Hindemith's chamber music output includes six string quartets, a clarinet quintet, the *Kleine Kammermusik,* a septet for winds, and two string trios.

String Quartet No. 3, Op. 22

**I. Fugato: Sehr langsame Viertel.   II. Schnelle Achtel-
Sehr energisch.   III. Ruhige Viertel-Stets
fliessend.   IV. Mässig schnelle Viertel.   V. Rondo:
Gemächlich und mit Grazie.**

At the start of the 1920s, Germany was a country in great turmoil, as Communists, royalists, army groups, and Hitler's National Socialists were all struggling to overthrow the weak Weimar Republic and assert their own power. Inflation raged out of control, causing widespread economic chaos and disorder, and an air of hopelessness and disillusionment pervaded the nation.

Hindemith's Third String Quartet, which dates from 1922, is very much a product of those times. In the words of Harold Schonberg, it "reflects a period as only great art can." The music also shows the composer's deep involvement with the *Neue Sachlichkeit* or New Objectivity, particularly in the dry harmonies and in the clear and logical formal structures, with easily heard repetitions and sharp contrasts.

The first movement is a fugato, in which a serene melody, ambiguous in tonality and meter, slowly passes in imitation among the four instruments. The movement builds to a fervid climax and then quiets down to end much as it began.

A barbaric explosion of sound launches the second movement, with its savage, disjointed rhythms hammered out by the entire quartet. A quiet, almost tender interlude follows, but it is soon overwhelmed by a return of the opening character. The coda brings back brief reminders of the middle section and of the opening.

Over the soft, gentle strumming of the viola and cello, the second violin sings the haunting melody of the third movement. An extra piquancy comes from the polytonality, with the lower strings in the key of A and the violin in C. Hindemith introduces other melodic material before presenting a free repeat of the opening.

The fourth movement is little more than a short, forceful introduction to the finale. It begins as a cadenza for the cello, with the viola joining in, and proceeds without pause to the fifth movement.

Hindemith treats us next to a charming two-part invention, one that Bach could have written—had he been composing in the 1920s. As in the first three movements, there is a contrasting middle section before the composer ends with a highly condensed reminder of the opening.

The premiere was given by the Amar Quartet, in which Hindemith played viola, at Donauschingen, Germany, on November 4, 1922.

Kleine Kammermusik, Op. 24, No. 2

I. Lustig. Mässig schnelle Viertel. II. Waltzer. Durchweg sehr leise. III. Ruhig und einfach. Achtel. IV. Schnelle viertel. V. Sehr lebhaft.

Hindemith had an impish sense of humor. He often drew funny caricatures for his friends and students and enjoyed decorating his manuscripts with ferocious-looking dragons and lions. He delighted in practical jokes. And several of his compositions, including his Kleine Kammermusik, contain parodies and other comical touches. Although the Kleine Kammermusik is sprightly and droll it does have an undercurrent of bitterness and irony, perhaps a reflection of the social and political unrest in Germany at the time. Hindemith composed the work early in 1922 for Frankfurt's Blaser-Kammermusik-vereinigung, which gave the first performance in Cologne on July 12, 1922.

A jaunty little tune on the clarinet immediately sets the lively character of the first movement; gaily tripping along, the melody is tossed from instrument to instrument. While the clarinet and bassoon continue the opening's rhythmic pattern, the oboe comes in with a more lyrical, legato melody. The first theme returns to round out the movement.

The Waltzer is a somewhat satirical imitation of a waltz, with fragmented melodies and awkward leaps in the first theme. There is a contrasting middle section with prominently repeated notes. For this movement only, the flutist switches to the higher-pitched piccolo.

Hindemith grows a bit more solemn in the third movement. Especially striking is the middle section where three of the instruments play a repeated mocking figure, marked *nicht scherzando!* (''not joking!'') on the score, against an extended cantilena line.

The brief fourth movement essentially serves as an introduction to the fifth movement. It consists of several terse tutti statements, separated by equally brief cadenzas for each instrument.

The last movement, continuing without pause, is a bright and bouncy, rhythmically delightful romp. A slightly more subdued central section acts as a contrast to the surrounding jocularity.

Jacques Ibert

Born August 15, 1890, in Paris
Died February 2, 1962, in Paris

IN THE early years of the twentieth century, French music was largely under the influence of two outstanding composers, Debussy and Ravel, exemplars of the so-called Impressionist style. There arose, however, a maverick group in Paris that largely rejected French Impressionism, as well as the contrary movements of German Post-Romanticism and Expressionism. This new school of musical thought drew its inspiration more from Stravinsky's and Hindemith's Neoclassicism, with its attempt to express Classical eighteenth-century musical concepts in twentieth-century terms. Further, they placed a premium on craftsmanship and technical polish and sought to imbue their music with clarity, Gallic wit, virtuosity, and sophistication. Jacques Ibert was one of the most creative members of this group, eclectically combining these diverse elements, including Impressionism, to create sparkling music of undeniable charm and delight. "All systems are valid," Ibert said, "provided that one derives music from them."

Since Ibert's father wanted him to become a businessman, the boy received only the most perfunctory early music instruction. Nevertheless, he was able to enter the Paris Conservatoire at age 20, where Gabriel Fauré and Paul Vidal were his major composition teachers. Four years later he graduated with prizes in harmony, counterpoint, and fugue. In 1919 he was awarded the Prix de Rome and, while living in Rome, completed *Escales* ("Ports of Call"), the first highly successful work of his very considerable output. Ibert also served as director of the Académie de France in Rome from 1937 to 1960, and for a while also directed the Paris Opéra, dividing his time between the two cities.

Ibert left three major chamber works: a string quartet

(1937–1942), a trio for violin, cello, and harp (1943–1944), and Trois Pièces Brèves for Woodwind Quintet (1930). The latter is by far the most popular of the three.

Trois Pièces Brèves for Woodwind Quintet
I. Allegro. II. Andante. III. Assez lent; Allegro scherzando.

In 1930 Ibert composed the spirited *"Trois Pièces Brèves"* ("Three Short Pieces"), a witty, virtuosic composition that impresses both with its irresistible *joie de vivre* and its excellent mastery of technique. The first piece, Allegro, opens with a splash of tone color from which inchoate melodic fragments bubble to the surface and then fade away. Out of this unfocused introduction, the oboe emerges with a cheerful, lilting dance tune. A middle section develops the melody, followed by an even more jubilant restatement and a high-speed brilliant conclusion.

Bach's contrapuntal two-part inventions were the obvious source of inspiration for the very short (twenty-six-measure) second piece. Essentially a pensive, reflective duet for clarinet and bassoon, the other instruments only join in for the final few measures.

From the very start of the mock serious introduction to the third piece, Ibert puts us on notice to expect a fun-filled satirical romp— and he does not disappoint. Over a repeated-note accompaniment, the clarinet sweeps up to the frolicsome main theme of the faster section. The others join in the good times, until Ibert interrupts with a brief parody waltz. Then once more he brings back the clarinet and waltz tunes, wrapping it all up with a short, flashy coda.

Charles Ives

Born October 20, 1874, in Danbury, Connecticut
Died May 19, 1954, in New York City

ON ONE level, the life of Charles Ives is the great American success story. Born into modest circumstances, he played on the Yale University football team while in college and then went on to a business career that brought him incredible wealth. But even more spectacular than his financial success is the reputation he attained as one of America's most experimental, iconoclastic, inventive, original, and distinguished composers.

Charles Ives was born in a small New England town just after the Civil War. Although he studied music at Yale University, after graduation, out of a sincere belief in the value and importance of life insurance, he accepted a five-dollar-a-week position with the Mutual Life Insurance Company in New York City. In time he opened his own insurance agency, which he built up to be enormously successful and which made him a rich man.

Throughout his life—as a youngster, during his business career, and for the twenty-five years he lived after retirement—music was Charles Ives's major, all-consuming interest and passion. The musical sounds of his childhood made a particularly strong impression on him and played a role in almost every piece he wrote. He heard little so-called art music. Much more familiar was the music of a typical small town near the turn of the century—church hymns and parlor songs and the popular dances, theater songs, and marches of the day. Since his father, George, was the local bandmaster and music teacher, Charles came to know all this music very well.

George gave Charles his first music instruction. Although he stressed the basics of music, he also taught his son to challenge the sacred canons of musical composition. The older man tended to ignore the accepted "rules" of music, preferring to let his imagination range freely, and to let his ears decide on what sounded good and what did not. His father's experiments, which included playing music in quarter tones instead of the usual half tones, placing musicians at the four corners of the town square to create special sonic effects, and trying to capture the tonal quality of an echo or of a church congregation singing out of tune, fostered Ives's own lifelong search for the new and innovative in music. To this was added the solid grounding in traditional musical practices that Ives acquired from his years of study with Horatio Parker at Yale.

Another determinant in shaping Ives's music was his philosophical acceptance of transcendentalism, a way of thinking that developed in America during the middle 1800s and was associated with such figures as Ralph Waldo Emerson and Henry David Thoreau. Transcendentalists believe that the human mind can go beyond what is seen or experienced; they emphasize the spiritual and intuitive over the empirical. For Ives, transcendentalism supported his belief that even the most ordinary things are suffused with an essential spirit, which he considered the only true reality. And since this essence pervades the entire universe, there is a unity, a singleness, to all that exists. This belief contributed to the unique spiritual quality of the music of Ives. It also allowed him to venture beyond the usual limits of musical composition, to quote popular songs and to juxtapose seemingly unrelated material in his works. It even justified his involvement with life insurance at the same time he was so fully committed to music. "All things are one," said Emerson. Ives lived by this dictum, embracing both the ordinary and the sublime, both art and business, and in so doing was able to combine them all into a transcendental unity.

Another factor in Ives's music is his use of a sort of musical stream-of-consciousness technique. Rather than adhering to predetermined structural forms, Ives allows his musical ideas to emerge chainlike in a free association that is loosely linked in one extended outpouring. Embedded in the musical flow are quotations of everything from patriotic songs and marches, to solemn church melodies, to snatches of Beethoven and Brahms. Each borrowing probably holds some particular extra-musical meaning or memory for the composer and adds a special interest for the listener.

According to critic Harold Schonberg, Ives has been "canonized as the saint of American music." Although one can easily imagine crusty old Charles Ives sneering at the designation of "saintly," it is a fitting recognition of his preeminent position in the music of our nation, both as a composer and as a pioneer anticipating many of the most advanced compositional techniques of the twentieth century.

String Quartet No. 1, "A Revival Service"

I. Chorale: Andante con moto. II. Prelude: Allegro. III. Offertory: Adagio cantabile. IV. Postlude: Allegro marziale.

During his four years at Yale University (1894–1898), Ives's musical activities were channeled in two different directions. At school he studied composition with Horatio Parker, an American-born, German-trained composer who was musical, competent, intelligent, and overwhelmingly conservative. Outside the regular course of study, to help pay for his education, he held the position of organist at New Haven's Centre Church.

The experiences with Parker and at the church influenced the creation of the string quartet, the young composer's first major work, which he completed in 1896. He fashioned the first movement from a fugue he prepared for Horatio Parker's composition class; the remaining movements he originally composed for church use. The subtitle is derived from the second and fourth movements, which were written for a revival meeting, and the other melodic material, which either comes from Protestant hymns or at least sounds as though it does.

The first movement is based on two hymn melodies: "From Greenland's Icy Mountains" and "All Hail the Pow'r of Jesus' Name." The tunes themselves are extremely simple, essentially made up of notes of equal duration. The writing is academically sound and technically secure, with little to distinguish it from that of any other talented student.

The second, third, and fourth movements, written for church use, show more of the musically adventuresome side of Ives. As church organist, he was growing bored with the elementary harmonies of the hymns and began "gussying up" the music he played or composed for church occasions. The minister, Dr. Griggs, encouraged this experimentation, saying, "Never you mind what the ladies' committee says, my opinion is that God gets awfully tired of hearing the same thing over and over again." So the second movement, which Ives originally wrote for a church revival meeting on October 2, 1896, retains its overall hymnlike character while displaying some of the freedom of treatment that was to characterize Ives's future output.

The hymn "Come, Thou Fount of Every Blessing" is the theme of the third movement and was also first intended for church use. Here the writing grows even freer and more daring, with greater use of dissonance and several interruptions of the rhythmic flow.

The Postlude, from the October revival meeting as well, is a rousing climax to the quartet. It starts with a quotation from the march-like hymn "Stand Up, Stand Up for Jesus!" Between the statements of this tune, Ives recalls the melody of the middle part of the Prelude. Just before the end, he pulls out all the stops, combining the three-beat middle-section melody with the ongoing four-beat meter, to soar to a climactic conclusion.

Although Charles Ives is now accepted as one of the truly great pioneers of contemporary American music, the first string quartet was not performed until 1957 and had to wait until 1961 for publication.

String Quartet No. 2

**I. Discussions: Andante moderato.   II. Arguments:
Allegro con spirito.   III. "The Call of the Mountains":
Adagio.**

The Second String Quartet was begun in 1907 while Ives was living in New York, working hard at his job of selling life insurance, and composing evenings and weekends. One of the goals he sought to achieve in this music was to unsettle the listeners, to make them sit up and listen and react strongly. He always railed against "nice" or "pretty" music. The following passage from his autobiographical writings explains how the need to express himself in striking and original ways led Ives to compose this quartet.

> It used to come over me—especially after coming from some of those nice Kneisel Quartet concerts—that music had been, and still was, too much of an emasculated art. Too much of what was easy and usual to play and to hear was called beautiful, etc.—the same old even-vibration. Sybaritic apron-strings, keeping music too much tied to the old ladies. The string quartet music got more and more weak, trite, and effeminate. After one of the Kneisel Quartet concerts in the old Mendelssohn Hall, I started a string quartet score, half mad, half in fun, and half to try out, practice, and have some fun with making those men fiddlers get up and do something like men. . . . It is one of the best things I have, but the old ladies (male and female) don't like it anywhere at all.

Ives composed the quartet in a spirit of spontaneity and improvisation. He left large sections of the score without dynamic markings and without identifying the leading voice, giving the performers considerable freedom to make their own musical decisions and work out their own interpretations. His vision of the quartet is conveyed through remarks inscribed on the manuscript: "String quartet for four men who converse, discuss, argue (politics), fight, shake hands, shut up, then walk up the mountainside to view the firmament." In keeping with this scheme, the three movements are titled Discussions, Arguments, and "The Call of the Mountains."

Discussions is indeed a musical conversation among the four relatively independent players. As the talk quickens there are moments of more heated interchange and times when the players meet in grinding dissonances. Fleeting quotations from "Dixie," "Hail, Columbia," and "Turkey in the Straw" suggest to some that the debate may concern the Civil War. The movement ends quietly and in much the same mood as it began, with Ives's written comment over the final measure, "Enough discussion for us!"

Musical tempers flare in the second movement, Arguments. Only the second violin, a fictitious character the composer dubbed Rollo, who is sensible, sane, conservative, and well-mannered (all traits that Ives absolutely could not abide), tries three times to impose order on the chaos. One time he interrupts with a short solo bit marked *Andante emasculata;* on another occasion Ives instructs Rollo to play *Largo sweetota.* Ives also makes little scribbled comments to Rollo throughout the movement: "Too hard to play—so it just can't be good music, Rollo," "Cut it out, Rollo," and "Beat time, Rollo." Again there are many brief quotes, including "Columbia, the Gem of the Ocean" and the "Ode to Joy" from Beethoven's Ninth Symphony. At the end of the movement is a brief section, "*Andante con scratchy (as tuning up),*" and for the final two brutal chords, Ives wrote "*Allegro con fistiswatto (as a K.O.).*"

The final movement is much more serious and tranquil than anything heard hitherto. It creates a mood of expansive sublimity. The quotes here are mostly from church hymns, and an imitation of pealing church bells leads to the quiet, contemplative close.

Composed in New York intermittently from 1907 to 1913, the second quartet was first performed at the Yaddo Music Festival in Saratoga, New York, by the Walden Quartet on September 15, 1946. It was not published, though, until 1954.

Leon Kirchner

Born January 24, 1919, in Brooklyn, New York

BROOKLYN-BORN Leon Kirchner moved to Los Angeles with his family when he was nine and received most of his musical training in California. Starting with piano lessons, Kirchner went on to composition studies with such notables as Arnold Schoenberg, Ernest Bloch, and Roger Sessions. Since capturing the highest music award (the George Ladd Fellowship) on graduation from the University of California at Berkeley, Kirchner has garnered a number of other honors: two Guggenheim Fellowships, two New York Music Critics' Circle Awards, a Pulitzer Prize, the Naumburg Award, and the National Institute of Arts and Letters Music Award. Following a teaching stint from 1946 to 1961 on the West Coast (at the San Francisco Conservatory, University of Southern California, and Mills College), Kirchner accepted a position at Harvard University, where he is currently Walter Bigelow Rosen Professor of Music.

Considering the musical bent of his principal composition teachers, it is not surprising that Kirchner writes music of strong expressivity and deep feeling. According to Aaron Copland his compositions "are charged with an emotional impact and explosive power that is almost frightening in intensity." Many of the most significant compositional approaches and techniques of the twentieth century—the rhythmic momentum associated with Bartók or Stravinsky, the tight organization and intense expressivity of Schoenberg's school, and the utilization of sounds generated by computer or synthesizer favored by electronic composers—have been assimilated into Kirchner's compositional style. Yet, despite these influences, he has developed a unique musical voice and maintains throughout his ability to stir and move audiences.

Composer Lejaren Hiller points out that "Kirchner works intuitively in composing by seeking a form through organic growth of a musical idea, rather than seeking appropriate musical substance to fill a preconceived structure." Put another way, Kirchner's basic approach is to start with a germ cell, a brief musical idea or gesture, and by extending this motif and by balancing other material against it, allow the pithy source to grow into a full-length, unified composition.

In addition to the Quartet No. 3 discussed below, Mr. Kirchner's major chamber music output includes two earlier quartets (1949 and 1958) and a piano trio (1954).

Quartet No. 3 for Strings and Electronic Tape

The Third Quartet is really a quintet, with parts for the customary four instruments and another part of electronically generated sounds prerecorded by Kirchner on audio tape and played back through loudspeakers at the time of performance. The reason for the tape, according to the composer, is "to produce a meaningful confrontation between 'new' electronic sounds and those of the traditional string quartet—a kind of dialogue idea in which the electronics are quite integral."

Kirchner prepared the tape on a Buchla synthesizer, a device that produces musical tones or non-musical sounds by electronic means. With the synthesizer, Kirchner was able to create the sounds he wanted electronically and to record them directly onto an audio tape. The tape Kirchner produced for Quartet No. 3 has eleven separate cues that are heard at various times during the piece. Sometimes, the tape sounds alternate with the string sounds; other times the tape is heard while the live musicians are also playing.

The score is divided into three broad sections. The first part is essentially a dialogue between the strings and the tape, although with considerable overlap worked in. Toward the end of this section, the music becomes aleatoric, based on chance. The score directs the live performers, in general, in when and what to play but does not specify the exact rhythms or notes to use. With such chance music, the results are never the same twice.

The middle part, for strings alone, is also in three parts. It opens with an assertive, rather angry passage; the central portion is slower, quieter, and more lyrical; a return of the active character comes at the end.

The final section of the quartet is reminiscent of the opening. An obvious carry-over is the tapping sound on the tape. At first the strings and tape alternate, followed by an extended stretch for strings alone, which gives way to a lengthy tape part before the quartet ends.

Kirchner wrote Quartet No. 3 in 1966 for the Beaux Arts Quartet, and the group introduced the work in New York City on January 27, 1967. Later that year, Quartet No. 3 was awarded the coveted Pulitzer Prize for Music.

Leo Kraft

Born July 24, 1922, in Brooklyn, New York

PIANO LESSONS as a child and listening experiences with his father's records encouraged Leo Kraft to make his first efforts at composing, but it was not until he began the serious study of composition with Karol Rathaus at Queens College of the City University of New York that he really decided to become a composer. His subsequent composition teachers, Randall Thompson at Princeton University and Nadia Boulanger in Paris, under a 1954 Fulbright Fellowship, served to further this ambition.

Kraft's early works, dating from the 1950s, show two main sources of inspiration: the Neoclassicism associated with Stravinsky, Bartók, and Hindemith, and the so-called American idiom, particularly the rhythmic and harmonic patterns that he heard in the music of Aaron Copland and William Schumann. By the end of the decade, though, Kraft began to explore new compositional approaches, trying to break free of the limitations he felt the older style had imposed on his creativity and seeking ways to increase the expressive content of his music. Familiarity with the works of Elliott Carter helped Kraft formulate his own personal vocabulary, and starting in 1959, his works showed a new intensity and emotionality, with a heightened chromaticism that moved beyond tonality. His melodies became more instrumental, instead of vocal, and there emerged more varied rhythmic patterns. His String Quartet No. 2 is the signal piece in this change of musical direction.

Around the mid 1960s, Kraft started to pursue an interest in electronic music and, after studying with Vladimir Ussachevsky at Columbia University, wrote a number of compositions that combine live and electronic sounds. Kraft recently summarized his dynamic approach to composing in this way: "I have chosen to follow a certain line of development growing out of earlier twentieth-century prac-

247

tices that appeal to me. I keep my ear and mind open to what is new in music and keep trying to incorporate new acquisitions into my stream of musical thought.''

Kraft's chamber music *oeuvre* includes two string quartets (1950 and 1959); Short Suite, for flute, clarinet, and bassoon (1951); Trios and Interludes, for flute, viola, and piano (1965); "Spring in the Harbor," for soprano, flute, cello, and piano (1969); Partita No. 4, for violin, double bass, flute, clarinet, and piano (1975); *Dialectica,* for flute, clarinet, violin, cello, and electronic tape (1976); and Inventions and Airs, for violin, clarinet, and piano (1984).

String Quartet No. 2

Leo Kraft's Quartet No. 2, although in one uninterrupted movement, is actually divided into five distinct sections that altogether describe a symmetrical arch shape. The opening and closing parts share the same melodic material and are essentially slow, quiet, and lyrical in character. The segments that follow the opening and precede the ending are fast in tempo and are thematically similar, although the order of presentation is reversed for the second appearance. The expressive heart of the quartet is the slow center section; its powerful impact comes less from its forceful climactic moments than from the inner intensity and fervor of the writing.

The quartet starts softly at the lowest extreme of the cello's range, with the moving, cantilena main melody. One at a time the other instruments enter in imitation, but with slight variants. When all four instruments are playing, the intensity builds up, until it abruptly gives way to a new, well-defined rhythmic figure introduced by the viola. The rhythm soon fades into the background as the first violin sings out the second melody, as lyrical as the first but with a greater sense of agitation and urgency, a feeling enhanced by the ongoing rhythmic pattern.

A quick acceleration leads to the fast, *Allegro* section, its high-speed theme loosely related to the second melody. While the other instruments continue expanding and developing this new material, the viola and then the first violin come to the fore with a variation of the main melody played against the continuing fast flow of the Allegro. Toward the end of this section there is a passage in which the two violins play the high, soft, scurrying music that is interrupted by sturdy chords in the viola and cello.

After the fast section comes to an abrupt conclusion, the slow, keystone section of the quartet starts with a series of alternate strong declamatory chords and impassioned cadenzalike passages for individual players. Then, over an implacable pizzicato cello line, the three upper voices discourse briefly, but ardently, on the original main melody.

The remainder of the quartet is, in effect, a mirror image of what has been heard to this point. The fast section, now starting with muted strings, comes first, with its various episodes mostly presented in reverse order; it is followed by the parallel to the opening slow part. The quartet ends with the cello playing an inversion of the main melody against hushed, sustained notes in the other voices, finally fading away to silence on the exact same note with which the quartet began.

Kraft composed his String Quartet No. 2 from February through April 1959, and it received its first performance in New York City in November 1961, played by the Phoenix String Quartet.

Ezra Laderman

Born June 29, 1924, in Brooklyn, New York

EZRA LADERMAN started composing at an early age, and the opportunity to play the solo part of a piano concerto that he wrote while still a student at New York City's High School of Music and Art helped him decide to devote his life to music. He began formal music studies after completing service in the United States Army during World War II, obtaining degrees from Brooklyn College and Columbia University. His major composition teachers were Stefan Wolpe and Otto Luening.

While Laderman's music resists easy categorization, we can find in it adaptations of several twentieth-century techniques, which he personalizes and transforms in order to create his own distinctive and original style. Expression, communication, and form dominate all other concerns, and one measure of his success is the frequency with which his works are performed, as well as the many commissions he receives for new pieces. Among the prestigious chamber music groups that have asked Laderman to write for them are the Lenox, Audubon, Composers, Vermeer, Sequoia, Alard, and Colorado quartets. The symphony orchestras of Philadelphia, New York, Chicago, Los Angeles, Pittsburgh, Minnesota, Denver, and Dallas have also requested major works.

A prolific composer, Laderman's output to date encompasses seven symphonies; seven string quartets; concerti for violin (two), viola, piano; a double concerto for flute and bassoon; and a concerto for string quartet and orchestra, along with an impressive body of dramatic works and film scores. Over the years he has taught at Sarah Lawrence College and at the State University of New York at Binghamton, where he was Composer-in-Residence. Other posts of distinction include Director of the Music Program for the National Endowment for the Arts and President of the American Music Center.

Among the honors Laderman has gained are three Guggenheim prizes (1955, 1958, and 1964), the American Prix de Rome (1963), and, twenty years later, an appointment as Resident Composer at the American Academy in Rome (1982–1983).

String Quartet No. 6, "The Audubon"

Laderman's Sixth String Quartet has a most striking opening, with all four musicians playing in forceful unison the active motif that will, in several forms and guises, permeate the entire one-movement work. By alternately plucking and bowing the notes, the instrumentalists create a unique tonal ambiance. No sooner is this statement made than the motif itself undergoes four dramatic transformations that, in effect, create four new themes. The first is a tender, lyrical melody that Laderman marks, "With gentle, caressing sound"; it is played by the second violin over a flowing cello line and follows the same melodic contour as the opening.

In the second section, which Laderman describes as "dissonant, acerbic," the composer introduces a number of instrumental effects that heighten its impact. First the violins play *flautando,* a flutelike tone produced by bowing lightly over the fingerboard. They then switch to *ponticello,* bowing near the bridge, for a glasslike, whistling effect. All the while the viola and cello play harmonics, which are also flutelike in timbre but are created by touching the strings lightly with the fingers of the left hand.

In the following passage of great rhythmic vitality, the first violin and cello play the wide-ranging syncopated melody in contrary motion. At the same time the second violin continues playing a figure in harmonics that is related to the opening motif, and the viola trills its short interjections. After building to a powerful climax, the music quickly quiets, and an intense, richly harmonized melody based on the first motif appears, marking the end of the quartet's exposition-like opening section.

What comes next bears little resemblance to a traditional development and recapitulation. Instead Laderman juxtaposes and layers the musical material in various new and interesting ways: he repeats some sections; others he subjects to further transformations. The mood also undergoes a number of marked changes—anger, rudeness, passion, uneasiness, tension, and finally reconciliation and relaxation.

Then, after some isolated notes tapped out *col legno,* with the

252

wood of the bow, and a soft, sustained passage, the first violin starts a series of hushed, rapid, scalelike runs. Losing its momentum, the music becomes, in Laderman's words, "amorphous and enigmatic," a conscious effort to approach disintegration. At this point, six highly dissonant tone clusters are heard. They start slowly and softly and grow faster and louder, signaling a reinvigoration of the music. Over the tone clusters Laderman wrote, "Damn it, I will survive!" The "I," he explains, refers to the sixth quartet and its survival; it also affirms his faith in the continued growth and success of the Audubon Quartet. (The hidden clue here is that the tone cluster is repeated six times, the number of years the Audubon Quartet had been playing together.)

The music now surges ahead with new strength and virility. The opening part is played again, with all the notes bowed this time, leading to a triumphant conclusion.

Completed in Washington, D.C., on December 17, 1980, the Audubon Quartet gave the first performance in New York City on April 23, 1981.

String Quartet No. 7

Ezra Laderman's seven string quartets were written over a span of about a quarter century—the first one dating from 1959 and the seventh from 1983. These works have included, in the words of musicologist Philip Friedheim, his "most personal music." A highly emotional utterance, the String Quartet No. 7 appeals to listeners through its strong expressivity, as well as through the impelling logic of its construction.

The quartet, in one extended movement lasting about twenty-two minutes, is built on two contrasting musical gestures presented in five distinctive, yet related, transformations. The first idea, heard at the very opening, is a jagged, leaping line that sends all the instruments, save the second violin, vaulting upward in wild agitation. The other musical idea, introduced by the cello, is a lyrical, waltzlike melody that moves by step and half step up the scale, with some octave jumps disguising the note-by-note ascent. The basic rhythmic cell is a long, sustained note followed by a quick upbeat to the next held note.

In the following section, the viola has the opening notes of the leaping melody, but plays them smoothly and quietly as it repeats the figure several times with subtle changes in note length and ac-.

centuation. After rising to a climax, all four instruments join in a rhythmic unison, pulsating on repeated notes that slowly move up or down and that simultaneously push ahead and hold back in tempo. The opening section, a sort of exposition, concludes with both violins playing the notes of the first theme, but in the rhythmic pattern (long note/quick upbeat) of the cello second theme, this time over a solemn march beat.

The remainder of the quartet is concerned with the material that has already been introduced. The working out takes the form of literal or similar restatements of previous material, further transformations of the thematic content, and presentations of the musical gestures in new contexts and relationships.

The coda is a summary, a synthesis, of all that has come before— but on an even deeper and more expressive, emotional level. It starts with a viola melody that suggests the two basic thematic thrusts; rhythmically, it is closely allied to the long note, quick upbeat pattern. The accompaniment is a repeated figure played *quasi col legno,* bowing with both the bow hair and the stick. The quartet ends quietly with a barely audible pizzicato note.

The Seventh Quartet is dedicated to the Colorado Quartet, who were able to commission the work as part of their 1983 Naumburg Chamber Music Award. Laderman finished the composition on August 19, 1983, at his summer home in Woods Hole, Massachusetts. The premiere was given in New York on May 2, 1984, by the Colorado Quartet.

Witold Lutoslawski

Born January 25, 1913, in Warsaw

THROUGHOUT HIS career, Witold Lutoslawski, considered the most significant of contemporary Polish composers, has been driven by the desire "to give the most faithful expression of a constantly changing and developing world that exists within me." From the very beginning he has explored various ways to find his own inner voice and to communicate it to others. He has described his creative life "as a kind of soul fishing, and the 'catch' is the best medicine for loneliness, that most human of sufferings."

To date, Lutoslawski's compositional style has followed three distinct paths. Between 1936, when he graduated from the Warsaw Conservatory with a degree in piano (a degree in composition followed in 1937), until 1955 or so, Lutoslawski was mainly influenced by Béla Bartók. Like Bartók, Lutoslawski sought to capture the essence of the folk idiom in his own compositions, but without quoting actual folk melodies. In 1958, Lutoslawski emerged with a new style, exemplified by his Funeral Music for String Orchestra, that resembles Schoenberg's twelve-tone method.

Around 1960, Lutoslawski heard some music by John Cage, which "provided a spark that ignited a powder keg in me" and inspired his latest stylistic direction. He was particularly struck by Cage's chance, or aleatoric, music, in which the notes and rhythms are selected in a random manner within some prearranged framework, so that no two performances are ever identical. Lutoslawski adapted the aleatoric technique to his own personal music style, producing some arrestingly original works, one of the most outstanding being his String Quartet.

String Quartet

I. Introductory Movement. II. Main Movement.

Given Lutoslawski's interest in human possibilities for expression, it is not surprising that around 1960 he embraced the aleatoric (from the Latin, *alea*, "game of chance") style of composing. In aleatoric music, the effects are not calculated and planned by the composer, as in traditional music, but are the result of the player's creative impulse, for example, how fast the first violin plays its notes, how long the viola pauses for its rests, the number of times the cello repeats its phrase, and so on. "Each of [the performers] is gifted with a much greater abundance of potentialities than those required by a purely abstractly conceived musical score," writes Lutoslawski. "And it is this abundance of potentialities concealed within the individual psyche of each performer that I wish to include in the repertory of my compositional methods."

Along with the musical notes of the score, Lutoslawski provides instructions on how they are to be played. For example, the first violin is told to repeat the opening phrase ad lib "until the audience has become completely quiet" and to wait "circa 2 seconds" between notes. At another point the viola is told to continue playing a passage until the cello makes its entrance. Elsewhere, the cello can only go on after the second violin has finished. And throughout, the tempo, lengths of notes and silences, number of repeats, and the precise moment of starting and stopping the individual sections are left very much to the discretion of the individual performers. Lutoslawski has compared this quartet to a Calder mobile. The random elements of the music create ever-changing relationships between the four players, much as the separate segments of the artwork form into varying visual patterns.

Although the string quartet is aleatoric, the overall architecture is carefully planned. In general, the music progresses from great independence of the various parts at the beginning to a close bonding and fusion toward the end.

The function of the shorter Introductory Movement, according to Lutoslawski, is "to create a sort of low pressure, after which the very substantial Main Movement will seem inevitable." The movement presents a number of different pitch, textural, and rhythmic motifs that are subsequently heard in a musical kaleidoscope of evolving contexts and relationships.

The longer Main Movement, which follows without pause, contains three major divisions. It starts with the introduction of a number of different, juxtaposed rhythmic fragments, which are then expanded in a sort of development section. The second part, the emotional and musical climax of the quartet, is further divided into an opening "Appassionato," a choralelike section played *senza vibrato* ("without shaking the left hand") and *indifferente* in style, and the final *Funebre,* a term that Lutoslawski says defines only the style, without any extra-musical association. The concluding section is a brief coda.

The quartet was given its first performance in Stockholm by the LaSalle Quartet on March 12, 1965.

Felix Mendelssohn

Born February 3, 1809, in Hamburg
Died November 4, 1847, in Leipzig

FEW COMPOSERS were born with as much musical aptitude, if not genius, as Felix Mendelssohn, and few achieved as much success and recognition during their lifetimes.

Mendelssohn started life as part of a wealthy and cultured family; his father, Abraham, was a prominent banker and his grandfather, Moses, a noted philosopher. When Felix was three years old the family fled French-occupied Hamburg and settled in Berlin, where their lavish home became a gathering place for the world's most outstanding artists, intellectuals, and social leaders. As a very young child, Mendelssohn displayed amazing musical ability—perfect pitch, the ability to recognize any note or combination of notes that he heard, and a phenomenal musical memory. His mother gave him his first piano lessons, and at age nine he made his concert debut. In the same year, his choral setting of the Nineteenth Psalm was performed in public. From that time on, he began composing in earnest.

In 1825, the sixteen-year-old Mendelssohn decided to make his career in music. The work he was composing at the time—the Octet (age sixteen) and the Overture to *A Midsummer Night's Dream* (age seventeen), for example—show an outstanding creative gift that far surpassed even that of Mozart at a comparable age. Mendelssohn's studies at the University of Berlin between 1826 and 1829, in addition, gave him a broad and extensive education not common to most composers of his time. The year he finished his university courses, he conducted a performance in Berlin of Johann Sebastian Bach's *St. Matthew Passion,* the first time this monumental work was presented since Bach's death in 1750. Not only was Mendelssohn credited with the concert's great success and recognized for his ability as a conductor; he was also praised for sparking a renewed interest in Bach's music.

Mendelssohn followed the Bach triumph with a leisurely three-year Grand Tour of Europe, one year later gaining an appointment as general music director for the city of Düsseldorf. In 1835 he became the director of the very prestigious Gewandhaus Orchestra at Leipzig and eight years later founded the Leipzig Conservatory. By the time he settled in Leipzig, he was widely accepted as an outstanding composer, the greatest living conductor, and one of the finest violinists and pianists of the day. Furthermore, he was known for the excellence of his drawings and paintings and for his intellectual achievements, which included the ability to speak several languages fluently. He traveled often to Great Britain, and it was shortly after his 1847 visit that his sister Fanny died. Mendelssohn was very deeply affected by her death and, after a short visit to Switzerland, returned to Leipzig, where he died of a stroke in November 1847, at the age of thirty-eight.

Oddly enough, despite his phenomenal attributes and accomplishments, Mendelssohn may have fallen short of reaching his full potential. Some say that Mendelssohn's failure to mature fully as an artist was due to his upbringing among the wealthy bourgeoisie, a class that generally inclines toward the safe and conservative and avoids the new and experimental. Although he lived at a time when the Romantic revolution was inspiring composers to think and write with increased freedom and expressivity, Mendelssohn clung to such older Classical ideas as clarity and emotional restraint. While his music is usually described as being logically ordered, precise, elegant, and superbly well-crafted, all Classical traits, there is no mistaking the many Romantic elements that do appear in his music.

Mendelssohn produced eleven mature pieces of chamber music: six string quartets, two viola quintets, two piano trios, and the Octet. His juvenile compositions comprise three piano quartets, a string quartet, and a sextet for piano and strings.

String Quartet in E Flat Major, Op. 12

I. **Adagio non troppo; Allegro non tardante.** II. **Canzonetta: Allegretto.** III. **Andante espressivo.** IV. **Molto allegro e vivace.**

Mendelssohn started his three-year post-university tour of Europe by sailing to England in April 1829. In a letter written to his sister Fanny on September 10, he said, "My quartet [Op. 12] is now in the middle of the last movement, and I think it will be completed in a few days." The work carries the lowest opus number of his quartets because it was published before Op. 13, which was actually written two years earlier.

The first movement of Op. 12 is a gentle outpouring of intimate, ingratiating melody. There are four significant musical ideas. In the slow introduction, a motto of three short upbeats leads to a longer note that comes back later in this and the third movements. The faster principal theme is a cantabile melody that starts loudly but immediately wearies of the effort and fades away. The subsidiary theme has the same rhythmic pattern as the first theme, and its descending contour corresponds to the drop in dynamics of the earlier subject. And then, early in the development section, the second violin introduces a new melody, also somewhat related to theme one. For the remainder of the development section and through the recapitulation, Mendelssohn does nothing to violate the warm, tender quality of all this thematic material, creating a movement of rare poetic beauty.

Mendelssohn models the second movement on the sixteenth-century *canzonetta,* a short, light vocal piece often in the character of a dance song, and substitutes it for the more traditional scherzo. The movement's fairyland charm and daintiness have probably made it the most popular single movement of all six Mendelssohn quartets, particularly favored as an encore piece. Written in ternary form, the first part features a delicate, bouncy melody with definite folk-music overtones. The middle section is faster and has the luminous transparency that Mendelssohn may have achieved better than any other composer. The movement ends with an abridged version of the first part.

The three-note upbeat motto from the first movement introduction is heard at the outset of the cantabile theme that opens the Andante espressivo. The theme statement ends with a brief, improvisatory recitative for the first violin that Mendelssohn marks *con fuoco,* "with fire." He then simply repeats the whole statement, although somewhat elaborated, ending with even more prominent appearances of the three-note motto.

Going ahead without pause, the high-spirited finale starts out like a spirited tarantella, a fast wild dance that was once believed capable of curing the bite of the tarantula spider. Prancing along with gay abandon, Mendelssohn weaves a number of motifs around the onrushing flow of notes. About halfway through, after a held note, the mood grows a bit more serious as the second violin intones the melody that it introduced in the first movement. But the vivacity of the tarantella is not to be denied, and the animation quickly returns. In the concluding coda, the character changes once more, as Mendelssohn transforms the first movement introduction into a marchlike melody, along with other references to first movement themes.

String Quartet in A Major, Op. 13, "Ist Es Wahr?" ("Is It True?")

I. Adagio; Allegro vivace.   II. Adagio non lento.   III. Intermezzo: Allegretto con moto.   IV. Presto.

Mendelssohn drew part of his inspiration for this quartet from Beethoven's monumental late quartets, which he had just heard and which overwhelmed him with their many advanced features and their amazing scope and spirituality. He paid these works the greatest possible compliment by adapting several of the techniques Beethoven used—integrated movements, fugal textures, new tonal effects, and more adventuresome harmonies—into his own quartet writing.

The composer was also stimulated by the poem *"Ist Es Wahr?"* ("Is it True?"), written by his close friend Johann Gustav Droyson, with the first line, "Is it true that you are always waiting for me in the arbored walk?" In the spring of 1827, after falling in love while on holiday, the eighteen-year-old Mendelssohn decided to set the poem to music. The opening three-note phrase of the song, published as Op. 9, No. 1, became the germinal melodic cell of the Op. 13 quartet. This motto permeates the entire quartet, sometimes in direct quotation, more often by recalling its rhythms or intervals. But even more incredible than the work's bold conception and brilliant execution are its passion and poignancy, which may well surpass in sincerity the feelings expressed in many of his later works.

The quartet starts with a slow introduction. After two mood-setting phrases, Mendelssohn presents the all-important three-note motto *"Ist es wahr?"*—long/short-long—a question he endows with great yearning and pain. The Allegro vivace then starts with busy sixteenth-note filigree until the viola starts the principal theme, based on the motto rhythm, which is expanded before the cello, playing high in its range, launches into the intense, impassioned second theme. The development, which starts exactly like the fast section, is highly contrapuntal, dissonant, and continually surging with musical electricity. The recapitulation is quite free, and the coda continues and builds on the already high energy level to reach a climactic ending.

The extremely emotional Adagio non lento starts with what might be termed a very loose paraphrase of the rhythm and feeling of the original song. A dark, somber fugato follows, its melody introduced by the viola and then imitated by the other instruments. The mood lightens as the tempo picks up slightly, and the first violin plays a distinctive rhythmic figure over a pulsing accompaniment. The fugato theme and its inversion are heard in this section before a brief violin cadenza acts as a transition back to a free, shortened reprise of the slower first part.

The guileless Intermezzo offers a welcome change from the Adagio's emotionally and intellectually charged atmosphere. The first violin sings the folklike theme, while the others supply a simple pizzicato accompaniment, with only the merest touches of countermelody. The much faster, whispered middle section recalls the fleeting, delicate scherzos from Mendelssohn's Octet and *A Midsummer Night's Dream*. After a repeat of the opening section, he combines the two musical ideas for the evanescent coda.

Mendelssohn starts the Presto with a dramatic opening reminiscent of the recitative from the fourth movement of Beethoven's Op. 132. Everyone plays tremolo except the first violin, who plays an agitated *ad libitum* recitative based on the fugato theme of the second movement. Once past the recitative, Mendelssohn puts forth a multitude of motifs, many of which bear a kinship of some sort with material from previous movements, and particularly the *"Ist es wahr?"* motto. At the very end of this vigorous movement, Mendelssohn brings back the introduction to the entire quartet. But this time, he allows it to continue with a melody that comes closest to the actual *"Ist es wahr?"* song setting—thus integrating the entire quartet and bringing the music full circle.

Completed on October 26, 1827, the Op. 13 quartet was actually written before the quartet in E flat, Op. 12, but published later. Although there is general agreement that Op. 13 is in the key of A minor, one frequently sees it listed as A major, probably because the first movement introduction is in that key.

Viola Quintet in A Major, Op. 18

I. Allegro con moto. II. Intermezzo: Andante sostenuto. III. Scherzo: Allegro di molto. IV. Allegro vivace.

In 1826, when he was seventeen years old and a student at Berlin University, Mendelssohn composed his first viola quintet. It consisted of four movements—Allegro con moto, Scherzo, Minuet, and Allegro vivace. On January 23, 1832, however, Eduard Rietz, Mendelssohn's former violin teacher, dear friend, and collaborator in the famous revival of Bach's *St. Matthew Passion*, died. As a farewell tribute to Rietz, Mendelssohn, who was in Paris at the time, wrote a *Nachruf*, or memorial, and put it in place as the second movement of the quintet, making the Scherzo the third movement, and discarding the original Minuet. The reworked quintet was published in 1833 in this form and was designated as Op. 18.

The pleasant and amiable Allegro con moto shows that even as a teenager Mendelssohn had the requisite skill to conceive and realize a movement of major dimensions. The rhythmic lilt of the principal theme is reminiscent of a Mozart minuet, although set in a contrapuntal texture that masks its dancelike qualities. The composer seems to find the animated transition section that the cello initiates very attractive, since he makes it longer even than the principal theme, thereby delaying the second theme and diminishing its importance. A fast, repeated staccato figure in the first violin concludes the exposition. The principal and concluding themes are the prime subjects of the development section, where they build to a furious climax. The music quiets for the recapitulation, which also ignores the second theme as it heads for the quiet ending.

The Intermezzo is the *Nachruf;* it is clearly the emotional peak of the quintet. Without becoming cloying or sentimental, Mendelssohn conveys a feeling of warmhearted sincerity. The challenging *concertante* first violin is the leading voice almost all the time, doubtless in recognition of the violinist it was written to honor. The principal subject, a tender, poetic melody, grows from the four-note descending figure with which it starts and which is heard several times subsequently. Mendelssohn then introduces the subsidiary subject, a smooth though wide-ranging melody played by the first violin while the others sound three-note pulses on every beat. Cast in sonata form, the music rises to great intensity in the development section. The recapitulation starts like the beginning, but as it progresses, Mendelssohn enriches the texture with intricate contrapuntal lines, an effect that heightens the movement's projection of poignancy.

Most scherzos are happy and playful. But this one, despite a surface glitter, seems unable to rid itself of a certain heaviness of spirit. It is written as a *moto perpetuo,* with only a few much-needed breathing places breaking the onrushing flow of notes. The theme starts in the second viola and is exposed in fugal entrances by the others, with much imitative counterpoint throughout. This treacherous movement requires of the players the ultimate in bow control, a metronomic sense of rhythm and the ability to play a high-speed, five-way game of musical catch, without ever dropping the tune when it comes their way.

The last movement is busy and active, with each part contributing sharp, staccato notes and cascading runs to the scintillating first theme. The second theme is a quieter cantilena line in the first violin, but the continuing sixteenth notes in the other parts prevent it from diminishing the overall breathlessness. Despite many passages of sparkling brilliance, the music often becomes very blustery, as though Mendelssohn were straining to get more sonority than a quintet can provide. This movement, like the Scherzo, makes extreme technical demands on the players as they negotiate the virtuosic passages, and challenges them to give it shape (it is in sonata form). When well done, though, it can be a truly exciting experience for player and listener alike.

Octet in E Flat Major, Op. 20

I. Allegro moderato con fuoco. II. Andante. III. Scherzo: Allegro leggierissimo. IV. Presto.

The Octet, written during the summer and fall of 1825, when Mendelssohn was but sixteen years old, is considered the most outstanding major composition in the entire history of music by one so young, far surpassing comparable efforts of such famous child prodigies as Mozart and Schubert. But the Octet is more than an example of precocity; it is a consummate work of art, able to hold its own with the finest pieces of chamber music.

While Mendelssohn was growing up, his lavish home was the setting for weekly Sunday morning musicales, with the most distinguished Berlin musicians as well as touring performers taking part in the informal music-making. It is believed that young Felix wrote the Octet for one of these gatherings, and that he made the score a birthday present to his violin and viola teacher Eduard Rietz. The composer probably played viola (he was reputedly an excellent violist, even though he never practiced) at the first performance. The piece came to occupy a special place in his affection; he later called it ''my favorite of all my compositions'' and said, ''I had a most wonderful time in the writing of it.''

Mendelssohn opens the first movement with a thickly textured carpet of orchestral sound. Above this deep, rich surface the first violin soars aloft with the nobly striving principal theme. As he expands the melody, Mendelssohn's scoring creates a palette of tone colors that approximates an orchestra in range and variety. Additional motifs and a transitional section lead to the subsidiary subject—a sedate, smooth melody presented initially by the fourth violin and first viola. Mendelssohn extends this theme with several snippets of the first subject tossed in. Near the end of the concise development, the instruments join in one after the other in continuing syncopations that build up to a *fortissimo* unison passage, leading to the abruptly quiet start of the recapitulation. The movement ends with a fiery coda.

The elegiac, dreamlike Andante derives its shape more from the interplay and patterns of its tone colors than from any memorable melodies or striking formal design. The sonorous music proceeds by its own unerring inner logic; the complex polyphonic interweavings add a true depth of feeling.

The light, gossamer Scherzo is a wondrous fantasy that seems to spin forth effortlessly. The ease of flow, of course, is deceptive; it actually rests on a solid foundation of brilliant compositional technique. Mendelssohn's sister, Fanny, wrote this about the movement: ''The whole piece is to be played *staccato* and *pianissimo* with shivering tremolos and lightning flashes of trills. All is new, strange, and yet so familiar and pleasing—one feels so close to the world of spirits, lightly carried up into the air. Indeed one might take a broomstick so as to follow the airy procession. At the end the first violin soars feather-light aloft—and all is blown away." The last phrase is a reference to the *Walpurgisnacht* scene from Goethe's *Faust*, which Fanny knew was her brother's source of inspiration. The quote comes from the concluding lines.

> *Flite of clouds and trail of mist*
> *Are lighted from above,*
> *A breeze in the leaves, a wind in the reeds,*
> *And all is blown away.*

Mendelssohn follows the elfin good spirits of the Scherzo with the Presto's more down-to-earth humor. The opening theme in the second cello sounds like it might be a continuation of the Scherzo—except that it is at the lowest, most awkward part of the cello *tessitura*, a passage that Mendelssohn surely meant as a joke, since no cellist, then or now, can possibly play it with grace and clarity. Up through the instruments the melody goes in imitation, climaxing with the second theme, a series of thundering, reiterated unison notes. The opening theme easily dominates the movement, but Mendelssohn occasionally applies the brakes with the repeated stamping notes—and even offers us a tantalizing glimpse of the Scherzo tune. The work closes with a long, slow buildup of the first theme to an ending of unbridled vehemence.

String Quartets, Op. 44, Nos. 1, 2, and 3

During 1837 and 1838, when he was composing the Op. 44 quartets, Mendelssohn was enjoying a time of personal happiness and international recognition, both as a composer and conductor. His marriage on March 28, 1837, and the birth of his son less than one year later gave him a great deal of pleasure. Highly esteemed as a composer, his every piece was eagerly awaited and immediately performed. And the Leipzig Gewandhaus Orchestra, which he had been conducting since 1835, had become known as the best orchestra in Germany.

Following an arduous performing and touring schedule, Mendelssohn nevertheless managed to complete the three quartets of Op. 44 and dedicate them to the Crown Prince of Sweden. As is the case with his earlier quartets, the opus numbers do not conform to the order of composition; they were actually written in the sequence 2, 3, and 1.

String Quartet in D Major, Op. 44, No. 1

I. Molto Allegro vivace. II. Menuetto: Un poco Allegretto. III. Andante espressivo ma con moto. IV. Presto con brio.

The manuscript of the D major quartet, the last of the three in Op. 44 to be completed, is dated Berlin, July 24, 1838. In a July 30 letter to violinist Ferdinand David, Mendelssohn suggests that it is one of his favorites, which may explain why it appeared first in the published version. "I have just finished my third Quartet, in D major," he wrote, "and like it much. I hope it may please you as well. I rather think it will, since it is more spirited and seems to me likely to be more grateful to the players than the others."

The first movement is particularly "spirited" and "grateful" in its writing; it fairly crackles with energy and exuberance. After the first violin statement, all the players share in the extension of the lusty principal theme. The second subject is much more restrained and introverted, a sharp contrast to the free-flying opening. The development, with great verve and dash, works over the various motifs of the main theme. Then, with no diminution of the high tension and but few moments of repose, the recapitulation and coda carry the movement through to the end.

To act as a calming, moderating influence after the high-powered first movement, Mendelssohn replaces the scherzo with a gentle Menuetto. The middle section features a ceaseless flow of eighth notes against either long sustained notes or little snatches of countermelody. The Menuetto, much shortened, returns to end the movement.

There is a poignancy and intimacy in the third movement that one rarely encounters in Mendelssohn's chamber music. Written in sonata form, both themes are constructed in the same way—a lovely, lyrical melody in the first violin and an equally important, and attractive, faster-moving countermelody in the second. The development is simply a brief transition from the second theme back to the first. In the recapitulation, the viola adds another countermelody to the return of theme one; the reprise of the second theme, though, is little changed.

After the two quiet inner movements, Mendelssohn obviously felt the need for a brilliant finale, and the Presto con brio more than fills the bill. It is a fiery *saltarello,* his version of a high-spirited sixteenth-century Italian dance form. There are two parts to the principal theme, one potent and forceful, the other more gentle and tender. The second theme, a soft, lyrical descending line similar to the second motif of the first theme, offers a pleasant contrast to the bustle but does little to make up for a certain lack of melodic interest and tendency to ramble. Although some may complain that the movement outlasts its welcome, there is no denying its irresistible sweep and drive.

String Quartet in E Minor, Op. 44, No. 2

I. Allegro assai appassionato. II. Scherzo: Allegro di molto. III. Andante. IV. Presto agitato.

It was while Mendelssohn was on his honeymoon in Freiburg that he composed the E minor quartet, finishing it on June 18, 1837. Although it was the first of the three Op. 44 quartets that he wrote, it was published second.

The main theme of the first movement, a tranquil, even bland, melody, is given a sense of urgency by the continuing syncopations in the second violin and viola. Another motif in the first group, a soft, unison sixteenth-note passage, acts as a unifying feature, running through the several other motifs that Mendelssohn introduces. A songlike second theme in the first violin follows, well-supported by contrapuntal lines in the other parts. The cello continues the theme in a range that takes it above all the other instruments, creating a unique tonal effect. The exposition ends with a strong concluding theme, after which Mendelssohn returns the opening melody. The development, and the recapitulation, which closely parallels the exposition, follow. The coda uses the two main themes for the final powerful buildup.

The Scherzo theme is more a rhythmic figure—four rapid notes (sixteenths) followed by a string of slower notes (eighths)—than a distinctive melody. To start the contrasting middle section, Mendelssohn shortens the time between the four-note bursts, so that they are heard on every beat, while the first violin holds long, sustained notes. Near the end of this section, the viola introduces a completely new theme, which it later repeats just before the conclusion of the movement. This is a particularly attractive Scherzo, lithesome, grace-ful, and one of the best examples of this form that Mendelssohn ever wrote.

The Andante movement resembles many popular nineteenth-century salon-type compositions, such as Mendelssohn's *Songs Without Words,* which are known as character pieces. Mostly short piano works, they have a distinctive melodic line, usually express one par-ticular mood or emotion very clearly, undergo a brief change of feel-ing in a middle section, and then return to the original character. In this case, the opening of the Andante is like an ardent love song that borders on the sentimental. Mendelssohn protects it from becoming gushy by instructing the players *nicht shleppend* ("do not drag") and by giving the nonmelodic voices interesting, active roles to play. At the end of this section the first violin takes over the flowing six-teenth notes as a transition to the slightly more angular middle part. After but a few measures, the fervor of the opening returns as the cello warmly sings the repeat of the first theme.

The buoyant Presto agitato pits the first theme, a rhythmic dance melody, against the second, a lyrical song melody. The two ideas are introduced sequentially. During the course of working them out, though, they are heard simultaneously, one superimposed on the other. At the end the rhythmic force proves the stronger, and the music dances to a boisterous conclusion.

String Quartet in E Flat Major, Op. 44, No. 3

I. Allegro vivace. II. Scherzo: Assai leggiero vivace. III. Adagio non troppo. IV. Molto Allegro con fuoco.

Although listed as Op. 44, No. 3, the E flat major was completed second of the three Op. 44 quartets, on February 6, 1838. In some ways it is the most interesting of the three and one that best realizes the possibilities of writing for the string quartet medium.

The quartet starts with a bold dramatic opening—four fast notes as the upbeat to a long-held note. After an expansive discourse on this theme, there is a loud measure of unison sixteenth notes, which the first violin continues softly as the others play a hiccupy, upbeat-downbeat subsidiary theme. Further episodes follow before the three lower instruments start a repeated-note accompaniment over which the first plays the opulent concluding theme. With a feeling of spontaneity that hides the craft, Mendelssohn then works through the various motifs in the development. The second violin sneaks in with the recapitulation at the end of a long chain of first violin sixteenth notes, while the first violin continues the running figure. The coda is really another short development section, distinguished by its brilliant exploitation of the quartet's varied timbres.

Widely acclaimed for his scherzo movements, Mendelssohn surely outdoes himself here. This Scherzo starts with rapid, light, fleeting notes that John Horton, in his perceptive book on Mendelssohn's chamber music, hears as a musical evocation of hunters riding off into a magical forest, a frequent theme of German music and folklore. Rather than continue in this character, though, Mendelssohn has the viola start a little fugato, a learned musical device very far removed from enchanted woodland scenes. The opening section then returns in a modified repeat, to be interrupted once more, this time by a double fugue, with a brisk rhythmic tune and a smooth descending chromatic line as the subjects. The movement ends with a final review of the opening, including a literal unison passage in which all four instruments play the exact same notes!

Although very much slower, the Adagio non troppo has a four-note upbeat figure that recalls the opening of the first movement. Despite the theme's solemn, treadlike quality, Mendelssohn brings it up to a high level of fervid expression. Two features stand out as he extends the melody: the first violin's occasional fast-rising arpeggio and the rocking accompaniment line. The latter continues as the link to the second theme, a sighing melody that gently goes its two-beat way over the underlying three-beat meter. After Mendelssohn brings back elisions of the two themes, he further integrates the quartet movements by concluding with the rising arpeggio from the first subject, which then becomes the opening of the finale.

In the bravura last movement, the high-speed sixteenths at the beginning are given extra energy by the slightly awkward three-and-one articulation of the alternate groups of four. Mendelssohn adds a touch of humor through the second motif—three repeated notes and an octave leap. Several times during the movement, one instrument or another plays the same figure, but overshoots the mark in a simulated mistake. A quiet, cantabile subsidiary theme calms the furor somewhat. But the vivacity of the principal theme prevails and easily dominates the rest of this exuberant movement.

Piano Trio in D Minor, Op. 49

I. Molto allegro e agitato.   II. Andante con moto
tranquillo.   III. Scherzo: Leggiero e
vivace.   IV. Finale: Allegro assai appassionato.

Mendelssohn evidenced an early preference for piano chamber music by composing, between 1822 and 1824, three piano quartets and a sextet for piano and strings, but only one string quartet. Later, in 1832, when he again felt the urge to write in this form, he confessed to his sister Fanny, "I should like to compose a couple of good trios." Even though it was not until the spring of 1839 that he set pen to paper, the D minor trio, Mendelssohn's first of two works for the combination, was finished by the end of that summer.

The D minor trio scored a great and immediate success. Robert Schumann considered it outstanding and, in an article in the *Neue Zeitschrift,* called it "the master trio of the age, as were the B flat and D major trios of Beethoven and the E flat trio of Schubert in their times." Among Mendelssohn's most popular chamber works, it is still applauded for its inspired melodies, incredible mastery of form, rich and idiomatic part writing, and warm emotional character.

The first movement, a glorious outpouring of melody, presents two memorable themes that express ardor and nobility in equal measure. Both themes are introduced by the cello, and both follow an arch shape—the first theme rising and falling over its entire length, the second moving up and down within each phrase. Written in sonata form, the exposition is completed with an agitated triplet passage in the piano. The piano writing here and in the subsequent movements is in virtuosic, *concertante* style, due in part to Mendelssohn's friend, pianist Ferdinand Hiller, who urged him to incorporate some of Liszt's and Chopin's advanced technical effects into the piano part. Despite some lush harmonies and melodies, Mendelssohn's Classical tendencies prevail in the development section, which is remarkably translucent, making it easy to follow the musical logic that guided him. In the recapitulation, the added violin countermelodies heighten the effect of the themes' restatement.

The conception of the second movement is remarkably similar to that of Mendelssohn's *Songs Without Words.* These short, intimate piano pieces feature a prominent melody over a pianistic accompaniment, are ternary in form, with a contrasting middle section, and tend toward the sentimental. The second movement starts with a piano statement of the melody, sounding very much like a piano introduction, before the strings enter with the same theme. The middle section, a minor-key variation of the original melody, introduces a note of unease. At the end the original returns in a somewhat altered version.

The Scherzo is a movement of delicacy, charm, and elfin grace, which challenges the skill of every performing trio. It requires a light, staccato touch, perfect ensemble, the ability to play cleanly at whirlwind speeds and to keep an absolutely steady beat. The movement is essentially monothematic, without the usual trio section in the middle. Throughout the gay, sparkling movement, there are contrasting episodes, but the opening theme clearly reigns supreme.

The rhythm of the dactyl, a poetic foot of one accented syllable followed by two without accents, runs throughout the entire Finale. The two main themes feature this particular rhythm, and there is scarcely a measure that does not include this figure in some melodic configuration. Although the repetition is effective in fixing the tunes in the listener's mind, the uniformity can become a little dull. The only true variety comes with the third theme, the cello's impassioned, cantabile melody. Nevertheless, the movement is an exhilarating instrumental tour de force, especially for the piano.

Piano Trio in C Minor, Op. 66

I. Allegro energico e con fuoco. II. Andante espressivo. III. Molto allegro, quasi presto. IV. Allegro appassionato.

Mendelssohn wrote two piano trios; the second, in C minor, was completed in 1845, with a dedication to the violinist and composer, Ludwig Spohr, who was known to have joined Mendelssohn in performances of the work. Although less familiar than the first trio, in D minor, this is in all respects a worthy composition and surely deserving of more performances than it currently receives.

In John Horton's book on the chamber music of Mendelssohn he says, in reference to the broadly singing first movement of this trio, "Mendelssohn never wrote a stronger sonata-form allegro." The piano gives out the restless, urgent first motif of the principal theme, a flowing eighth-note figure that rises and falls in each measure. Another motif within the same theme is a sweeping melody for strings in the same arch shape, against which the piano scampers up and down the keyboard in sixteenth-note runs. After a brief recall of the opening motif, the violin sings out the magnificent second theme.

The remainder of the movement is devoted to treating and trans-forming the melodic material in a variety of original and inventive ways and finally bringing it back for the recapitulation.

The Andante espressivo is one extended glorious song. The first of the three sections adheres closely to the iambic pattern of unac-cented upbeats followed by accented downbeats. The middle part, signaled by repeated piano notes, is slightly heavier in spirit than the opening. The freely realized return of the opening gives the melody to the violin and cello and is in essence a lovely vocal duet for the two instruments.

This movement carries on the tradition of Mendelssohn's fairy-land scherzos, capturing all the delicacy and sparkling élan with which he invests these movements, in this instance perhaps a bit more virile than customary. A middle section that tends to the robust intrudes for a short interlude before a return of the opening.

The first theme of the finale is somewhat paradoxical. It starts with an extended upward leap (a minor ninth), which is often as-sociated with music of great passion. Yet Mendelssohn continues by lightly dancing down the scale, robbing it of the usual emotional connotations. Various motifs of charm and elegance follow. After briefly reviewing the principal theme, Mendelssohn introduces a sol-emn chorale, which Eric Werner has traced back to *"Vor Deinen Thron,"* from the 1551 Geneva Psalter. The climax of the movement combines the chorale with the principal theme in a passage that strains to the utmost the trio's resources and provides a most appropriate cap to the entire work.

String Quartet in F Minor, Op. 80

I. Allegro vivace assai.   II. Allegro assai.   III. Adagio.   IV. Finale: Allegro molto.

This quartet, Mendelssohn's last completed piece of chamber music, is a powerful, impassioned utterance, with more deep feeling than any of his other works. If there is any criticism, it is that the emotions he tried to contain within the confines of a string quartet really re-quire a symphony orchestra for their full expression.

The circumstances attendant on its conception were tragic: On May 17, 1847, Mendelssohn's older sister, Fanny, to whom he was extremely devoted, died suddenly at the age of forty-one. Mendels-sohn collapsed on hearing the news and remained so distraught that he was unable to attend the funeral. To help him recover, his wife

Cécile convinced him to spend the summer months in Switzerland. At Interlaken Mendelssohn went on solitary walks and made drawing and watercolors of the beautiful landscape, but found it difficult to compose. On July 29, he wrote his younger sister, Rebecca, "I force myself to be industrious in the hope that later on I may feel like working and enjoy it."

By September he had managed to complete his F minor quartet, a sorrowful, yet angry piece that expresses some of the grief and bitterness Mendelssohn must have been feeling. Sadly enough, this profound work, which may have portended the start of a new phase in the composer's musical development, preceded his own death on November 4 by less than two months. The only subsequent chamber music he composed was two movements for a string quartet, which were combined with two individual movements written earlier and published as "Four Pieces for String Quartet," Op. 81.

The motoric passage that opens the first movement builds to an aggressive motto that hurtles down through the quartet. Once again the agitated opening phrase clamors up to the motto theme, but this time arrives as a warm, tender presentation of the same motto. A thematic extension carries the music to the first part of the subsidiary theme, a calm, sedate descending line. As the theme continues, all forward motion seems to cease as the instruments sustain long-held notes in highly chromatic, advanced harmonies. The motifs of the main theme are the subject of the development, in which they steadily rise in pitch and grow in volume before giving way to the recapitulation. Although the coda starts quietly, like the opening, it quickly reaches a high level of concentrated intensity, which it maintains to the end.

Instead of being light and effervescent like Mendelssohn's other scherzos, the second movement is savage and sardonic. The first part is a bizarre dance, with hammered syncopations and harsh dissonances. The brief middle section has the viola and cello playing an implacable *ostinato* line, to which the violins add a macabre waltzlike tune. The opening section is then heard again.

The most personal movement of the quartet is the elegiac Adagio. Growing from the opening phrase, which is shared by the cello and first violin, the music expresses, with great power and conviction, Mendelssohn's deep despair and anguish. The forceful climax is followed by a precipitous drop to the quiet level of the opening and a short final statement of the initial part.

The sonata-form last movement projects a restless anxiety that offers little in the way of solace or acceptance. Despite some loud outbursts in the exposition, the two themes, the first a continuing syncopated line, the second with a drooping cadence at the end of every short phrase, are held under tight control. Mendelssohn's wrath, however, emerges in the development, but is mostly muted in the much-shortened recapitulation, only to rise again in the coda.

Viola Quintet in B Flat Major, Op. 87

I. Allegro vivace. II. Andante scherzando. III. Adagio e lento. IV. Allegro molto vivace.

In the spring of 1845, biographer William S. Rockstro visited Mendelssohn in Frankfurt. He reported that the composer said he was not "writing much now: but sometimes . . . I know that I must write." That summer Mendelssohn composed his second and last quintet for two violins, two violas, and cello.

The two themes of the broad, expansive first movement are quite traditional. The first is strong, muscular, and thrusting; the second, lyrical, passive, and languorous. After a full measure of development of both themes, there is a long, exciting buildup to the recapitulation, which presents both themes in short order, but is followed by a coda that is really a second development.

The second movement is a scherzo, but not of the fast, sprightly variety. Tending toward the slow and lyrical, it nonetheless projects a wonderful delicacy and charm and is adorned with some intriguing fugal passages and particularly attractive cantabile countermelodies.

The dramatic Adagio e lento is highly emotional and written in a style that verges on the operatic. Formally quite free and rhapsodic, the work is scored with a wealth of tone colors and rich harmonies, including telling moments of shuddering and trembling. The heartfelt themes portray genuine pain and longing. Amidst the generally somber and despondent mood, however, there are lighter passages of grace and hope, such as near the ending, when the first violin plays in its highest register over a tremolo in the others.

The finale, which follows without a break, is a rhythmically vital, busy movement. After the *concertante* first theme, the two violas introduce the tranquil second theme. Driving forward with great energy, the music proceeds through the various sections of a modified sonata form. The last pages are uniformly loud and forceful, except for a short reminder of the second theme just before the final rush to the powerful ending.

276

Olivier Messiaen

Born December 10, 1908, at Avignon, France

OLIVIER MESSIAEN is a person who has always gone his own way. Starting at age eight, he taught himself to play the piano and to compose. At the Paris Conservatoire, he garnered all the traditional prizes, even as he devoted himself to the study of complex Hindu rhythmic patterns and became proficient in recognizing and notating bird songs and sounds—two skills that profoundly influenced his musical style. But the overriding inspiration for many of his most important compositions derives from Messiaen's profound religiosity, his deep, mystical attachment to the Catholic Church.

After graduation from the Conservatoire in 1930, Messiaen took a position as church organist and then added teaching to his schedule. He served in the French Army during World War II, was captured, and spent two years in a German prisoner-of-war camp. On his return to France, he was appointed a professor at the Paris Conservatoire, and resumed his duties as organist at the Trinité Church.

Through all these years as organist and teacher, though, Messiaen continued to compose. He produced an impressive list of major orchestral works—perhaps his Turangalîla-Symphonie (1948) is best known—along with many choral, piano, and organ compositions. His two essays in chamber music are *La Morte du nombre* (1930), for soprano, tenor, violin, and piano, and *Quatour pour la fin du temps* (1941), for violin, clarinet, cello, and piano. His complex rhythmic concepts, use of bird calls, and spirituality stamp his works as among the most original and unique of our time.

Quartet for the End of Time (*Quatour pour la Fin du Temps*)

I. Liturgie de cristal. II. Vocalise, pour l'Ange qui annonce la fin du temps. III. Abîme des oiseaux. IV. Intermède. V. Louange à l'Éternité de Jésus. VI. Danse de la fureur, pour les sept trompettes. VII. Fouillis d'arcs-en-ciel, pour l'Ange qui annonce la fin du temps. VIII. Louange à l'Immortalité de Jésus.

Messiaen's Quartet for the End of Time is judged by many to be his finest work, one of the most important of all twentieth-century chamber compositions, and perhaps the most significant piece of music to come out of the experience of World War II. While an inmate in the German prisoner-of-war camp at Görlitz, Silesia, from 1940 to 1942, Messiaen turned to composing to help him survive what he termed the "cruelty and horrors of the camp." The unusual scoring of this piece—violin, clarinet, cello, and piano—was determined by the fact that among his fellow prisoners were violinist Jean Le Boulaire, clarinetist Henri Akoka, and cellist Etienne Pasquier; Messiaen himself played piano. The four men gave the first performance of the quartet in Stalag VIII-A, before an audience of 5,000 other inmates on January 15, 1941. "Never," Messiaen later said, "was I listened to with such rapt attention and comprehension."

Messiaen found his musical source not in "the cataclysms and monsters of the Apocalypse, but rather [in] its silences of adoration, its marvelous visions of peace." In particular, he focused on the words of the Angel: "There shall be time no longer." Messiaen explains: "When we are freed from before and after, when we enter into that other dimension of the beyond, thus participating a little in Eternity, then we shall understand the terrible simplicity of the Angel's words, and then indeed there shall be '*Time no longer.*'"

Another stimulus came from what Messiaen calls "sound-color . . . the inner colored visions that I experience when listening to and reading music." The brutal life of the camp—the lack of food, the snow, the "wooden drawers that served us for beds"—made him dream of sound colors, which he tried to capture in his music.

Following the quotation from the Revelation of Saint John, Chapter X, verses 1 to 7, on which the quartet is based, is the composer's description of the music:

I saw a mighty angel descend from heaven, clad in mist; and a rainbow was upon his head. His face was like the sun, his feet like pillars of fire. He set his right foot on the sea, his left foot on the earth, and standing thus on sea and earth he lifted his hand to heaven and swore by Him who liveth for ever and ever, saying: *There shall be time no longer;* but on the day of the trumpet of the seventh angel, the mystery of God shall be finished.

I. *Liturgie de cristal.* (Liturgy of crystal.)   Between the morning hours of three and four, the awakening of the birds; a thrush or a nightingale soloist improvises, amid notes of shining sound and a halo of trills that lose themselves high in the trees. Transpose this to the religious plane: you will have the harmonious silence of heaven. The piano provides a rhythmic ostinato based on unequal augmentations and diminutions—the clarinet unfolds a bird song.

II. *Vocalise, pour l'Ange qui annonce la fin du temps.* (Vocalise, for the Angel who announces the end of time.)   The first and third parts (very short) evoke the power of that mighty angel, his hair a rainbow and his clothing mist, who places one foot on the sea and one foot on the earth. Between these sections are the ineffable harmonies of heaven. From the piano, soft cascades of blue-orange chords, encircling with their distant carillon the plainchant-like *recitativo* of the violin and cello.

III. *Abîme des oiseaux.* (Abyss of the birds.)   Clarinet solo. The abyss is Time, with its sadness and tediums. The birds are the opposite of Time; they are our desire for light, for stars, for rainbows and for jubilant outpourings of song! There is a great contrast between the desolation of Time (the abyss) and the joy of the bird-songs (desire of the eternal light).

IV. *Intermède.* (Interlude.)   Scherzo. Of a more outgoing character than the other movements, but related to them nonetheless by various melodic references.

V. *Louange à l'Éternité de Jésus.* (Praise to the Eternity of Jesus.)   Jesus is here considered as one with the Word. A long phrase, infinitely slow, by the cello, expiates with love and reverence on the everlastingness of the Word. Majestically the melody unfolds itself at a distance both intimate and awesome. "In the beginning was the Word, and the Word was with God, and the Word was God."

VI. *Danse de la fureur, pour les sept trompettes.* (Dance of fury, for the seven trumpets.)   Rhythmically the most idiosyncratic movement of the set. The four instruments in unison give the effect of gongs and trumpets (the first six trumpets of the Apocalypse attend various catastrophes, the trumpet of the seventh angel announces the consummation of the mystery of God). Use of extended note values [and] augmented or diminished rhythmic patterns. Music of stone, formidable sonority; movement as irresistible as steel, as huge blocks of livid fury or icelike frenzy. Listen particularly to the terrifying *fortissimo* of the theme in augmentation and with change of register of its different notes, toward the end of the piece.

VII. *Fouillis d'arcs-en-ciel, pour l'Ange qui annonce la fin du temps.* (Cluster of rainbows for the Angel who announces the end of time.) Here certain passages from the second movement return. The mighty angel appears, and in particular the rainbow that envelopes him (the rainbow, symbol of peace, of wisdom, of every quiver of luminosity and sound). In my dreamings I hear and see ordered melodies and chords, familiar hues and forms; then, following this transitory stage I pass into the unreal and submit ecstatically to a vortex, a dizzying interpenetration of superhuman sounds and colors. These fiery swords, these rivers of blue-orange lava, these sudden stars: Behold the cluster, behold the rainbows!

VIII. *Louange à l'Immortalité de Jésus.* (Praise to the Immortality of Jesus.) Expansive violin solo balancing the cello solo of the fifth movement. Why this second glorification? It addresses itself more specifically to the second aspect of Jesus—to Jesus the man, to the Word made flesh, raised up immortal from the dead so as to communicate His life to us. It is total love. Its slow rising to a supreme point is the ascension of man toward his God, of the son of God toward his Father, of the mortal newly made divine toward paradise.

—And I repeat anew: All this is mere striving and childish stammering if one compares it to the overwhelming grandeur of the subject!

Wolfgang Amadeus Mozart

Born January 17, 1756, in Salzburg, Austria
Died December 5, 1791, in Vienna

WOLFGANG AMADEUS MOZART was one of the most amazing musical prodigies of all time. At age three, he was making up little tunes at the piano; when he was four, he was able to recognize any music tone; and by the time he was six years old, he was already an accomplished pianist. Recognizing the youngster's incredible talent, his father, a violinist and assistant *Kapellmeister* at the court of the Archbishop of Salzburg, took him on lengthy tours of the courts of Europe where the young Mozart astounded everyone with his brilliant attainments as pianist, organist, violinist, and composer. At these performances the tyke would also sometimes play the piano with a cloth covering the keys, execute the most difficult pieces at sight, improvise at the keyboard, identify any note or combination of notes, and recall perfectly any work after but one hearing.

Although these childhood tours were immensely successful, Mozart was far less effective when it came to finding a permanent situation that would allow him to develop and put these extraordinary abilities to use. Perhaps the fact that he had grown from a precocious little child into a rather unpleasant young man contributed to the difficulty. Impulsive and crude, young Mozart showed little tact in dealing with others and criticized mercilessly those who failed to meet his extremely high musical standards. Physically, too, he had a somewhat unappealing presence, being short of stature, with an overly large head, a yellowish, pockmarked complexion, bulging eyes, and a prominent nose.

In January 1769, at the age of thirteen, though, Mozart entered the employ of the Archbishop of Salzburg, Hieronymous Colloredo, as concertmaster of the orchestra and court organist, an appointment that took little account of Mozart's already considerable capabilities

281

as a composer. Chafing under the restrictions of his position, Mozart annoyed the Archbishop with endless requests to undertake lengthy concert trips. The situation grew less and less endurable for both men until finally, in May 1781, Mozart was dismissed from his position, his ejection sealed with the notorious kick in the backside from the Archbishop's secretary, Count Karl Arco.

If Mozart had stopped composing after he left the Archbishop's court, he would be known as a gifted composer, but not as one of the world's most remarkable geniuses. Most of his works through that time are in the prevailing Rococo style, or *style galant,* with its emphasis on elegance, grace, and charm. The music, which is characterized by simple melodies often highly ornamented and with subservient accompaniments, is entertaining and delightful but generally frivolous and superficial. It was music that suited perfectly the idle, pleasure-seeking nobles who were Mozart's chief patrons and his main source of support.

But the days remaining to these aristocrats were numbered. The Absolutist beliefs that had assured their power were being replaced by the new ideas of the Enlightenment; rule by authority was slowly giving way to rule by reason. And the arts, of course, were undergoing a significant transformation in the process, influenced both by the emerging *Weltanschauung* and by the rise of the middle class, with their own special artistic needs and tastes.

Mozart was not nearly as musically innovative as his contemporary, Haydn, but he did respond to the changing musical world in his own inimitable way. While preserving the Rococo foundation of tuneful melodies, simple forms, and clear textures in his compositions, he found methods that infused them with great drama, expressivity, and emotional content. He also perceived manners of integrating counterpoint and other so-called learned methods into his compositional technique. It was only during the ten years between leaving the archbishop's service in 1781 and his death in 1791 that Mozart fully realized his inborn musical talent, creating a series of indisputable masterpieces for chamber ensemble, orchestra, solo performer, and the operatic stage.

Neither Mozart nor his publishers ever bothered to use opus numbers for his compositions; for many years it was difficult to arrange his works in accurate chronological order. Finally, in 1862, an Austrian musician and naturalist, Dr. Ludwig Kochel (1800–1877), prepared a *Chronologisch-thematisches Verzeichness* (''Chronological Thematic Catalog''), listing all of Mozart's music in order of composition. Today the title of each piece is followed by a K number, a reference to Kochel's catalog number. In 1937 Alfred Einstein prepared a revision of Kochel's catalog, and, when different, that number is given as well.

Flute Quartet in D Major, K. 285

I. Allegro. II. Adagio. III. Rondo.

The opening months of 1777 held little promise for Mozart. Employed by Salzburg's Archbishop Hieronymus Colloredo as concertmaster and organist, the twenty-one-year-old felt stymied in his artistic development. Due to financial difficulties, Colloredo had reduced his staff and cut back on the court's musical activities. Yet, in March, when Mozart asked for leave in order to perform at other courts, the noble refused, saying that he did not want his servants "running around like beggars." Furthermore, the Archbishop began exhibiting a strong antipathy to the young man. He told Mozart's father that Wolfgang "knows nothing" and "ought to go to a conservatory in Naples in order to learn music." Conditions grew increasingly worse until August, when Mozart became desperate and resigned. On September 23, accompanied by his mother, he set out on a lengthy trip that he hoped would advance his career and obtain for him a court position more in keeping with his abilities.

While the trip was mostly unsuccessful, the young composer did manage to pick up a few commissions as he made his way across Europe. In Mannheim, an amateur flutist, identified only as De Jean, offered Mozart 200 gulden for "three small, easy, brief concertos and a few flute quartets." The composition did not go easily. "You know how stupid I am," Mozart wrote his father, "when I have to compose for one instrument (and that one that I dislike)." Nevertheless, despite his protestations, Mozart completed two concertos and three quartets. (De Jean, though, was not satisfied, and just paid him ninety-six gulden.) Of the quartets, only the first, in D major, completed in Mannheim on Christmas Day, 1777, has won a place in the modern repertoire. A charming miniature, it perfectly expresses the Rococo, *galant* worldview of the time.

The first subject of the Allegro movement has at least three themes, all light and airy, and led throughout by the flute. The somewhat subdued second theme is introduced by violin and viola before it is repeated by the flute. The brief development considers only the first subject before leading to a condensed recapitulation and a brilliant coda.

The short second movement is a serenade, a pleasant diversion designed for an evening's pleasure. The flute sings a lovely, unbroken cantabile melody, while the strings furnish a discrete pizzicato accompaniment.

Following without pause is the last movement, a rondo. The perky opening theme is heard three times, with contrasting episodes that maintain the same high spirits coming between the repetitions.

Oboe Quartet in F Major, K. 370
I. Allegro. II. Adagio. III. Rondeau: Allegro.

After a trip of several months, during 1777 and 1778, which took him as far as Paris, Mozart had to return to Salzburg and take up his post once again as violinist and court organist to the hostile Archbishop Colloredo. In 1780 he was invited to Munich by Elector Carl Theodor who wanted him to compose an opera for the carnival celebration. Colloredo was very reluctant to allow Mozart to leave, but he was equally fearful of offending the Elector. He finally granted Mozart a six-week leave of absence, which the young man stretched out to four months.

While in Munich, Mozart renewed a friendship with Friedrich Ramm, the superb oboist of the Munich orchestra. And it was for Ramm that Mozart wrote the quartet for oboe, violin, viola, and cello, probably during the first two months of 1781.

From accounts of that time, and from the virtuosic demands of the quartet part, we assume that Ramm was a brilliant instrumentalist. The oboe predominates, probably because Mozart wanted to display Ramm's abilities to the fullest, but also because the oboe's assertive tone makes it difficult to blend with the string sound.

Mozart refashioned the traditional sonata form for the first movement. He opens with a sparkling theme stated by the oboe, but with considerable melodic interest in each of the instrumental parts. After playing a fast upward scale, the first violin starts the second theme, which proves to be the first theme in a different key and differently scored, with an added countermelody in the oboe. The concluding theme of the exposition is initiated by a series of four repeated notes. After the easy charm of the Rococo-style exposition, the development seems to begin as a learned fugue, but the lighthearted mood quickly returns, including several flashy passages for the individual players. Mozart defies tradition in the recapitulation, bringing back only the principal theme, subjecting it to further development, and then moving on to the coda and a quiet ending.

The thirty-seven-measure Adagio is a poignant and soulful small-scale masterpiece. Mozart interweaves and varies the minimum amount of melodic material to achieve an extraordinary level of emotional expression.

The saucy principal theme of the Rondeau (French spelling of Rondo) restores the jolly good humor of the quartet after the moving Adagio. Melodically, especially in the opening interval and the use of ornamental grace notes, it harks back to the main theme of the first movement. The first contrast introduces a somewhat sterner feeling, but the mood softens to get back to a shortened repeat of the opening. The second contrast includes perhaps the most striking moments of the entire quartet, as the strings maintain the same 6/8 meter while the oboe switches to 4/4 meter; in one section the oboe is playing eight sixteenth notes against three eighth notes in the strings, the musical equivalent of patting your head and rubbing your stomach at the same time! The final statement of the first theme follows. The oboe climbs to the very top of its range in the coda, concluding with three rising notes that echo the ending of the Adagio movement.

String Quartets, K. 387, 421, 428, 458, 464, and 465, "Haydn Quartets"

The genesis of Mozart's so-called "Haydn Quartets" dates back to the year 1781, when Mozart met Haydn for the first time and heard the older composer's string quartets, Op. 33. The effect on Mozart, in the words of scholar Alfred Einstein, was "one of the profoundest Mozart experienced in his artistic life." Haydn's approach to quartet writing found resonance in Mozart's subsequent chamber works in many ways, including the building up of melodies from individual phrases, the expansion, independent development, and later reintegration of these melodies, the reappearance of the developing themes throughout the sonata-form movements (not just the development section), and the treatment of all four instruments as equally important.

Inspired by Haydn's models, Mozart composed three quartets between December 1782 and July 1783 and three more from November 1784 to January 1785, dedicating the six quartets, as a set, to Haydn. That Mozart found these quartets difficult to work out is attested to by the many erasures, changes, cross-outs, and corrections he made on the manuscript—more than on any of his other works. Not written for any of Mozart's usual reasons—a commission, a nobleman's pleasure, some personal or professional need—the quartets' main purpose was to pay homage to Haydn, for as Mozart said, "I have learned from Haydn how to write quartets."

Mozart sent the six quartets to Haydn on September 1, 1785, with the following letter of dedication (in Italian).

To my dear friend, Haydn.

A father who had decided to send out his sons into the great world, thought it is his duty to entrust them to the protection and guidance of a man who was very celebrated at the time and who, moreover, happened to be his best friend.

In like manner I send my six sons to you, most celebrated and very dear friend. They are, indeed, the fruit of a long and arduous labor; but the hope that many friends have given me that this toil will be in some degree rewarded, encourages me and flatters me with the thought that these children may one day be a source of consolation to me.

During your last stay in this capital you yourself, my dear friend, expressed to me your approval of these compositions. Your good opinion encourages me to offer them to you and leads me to hope that you will not consider them wholly unworthy of your favor. Please, then, receive them kindly and be to them a father, guide and friend! From this moment I surrender to you all my rights over them. I entreat you, however, to be indulgent to those faults that may have escaped a father's partial eye, and, in spite of them, to continue your generous friendship toward one who so highly appreciates it. Meanwhile, I remain with all my heart, dearest friend, your most sincere friend.

W. A. Mozart

It is believed that the premiere of the first three quartets (K. 387, 421, and 458) was on January 15, 1785, at Mozart's Vienna apartment, probably with Wolfgang playing viola. The remaining quartets (K. 458, 464, and 465) were first heard on February 12, 1785, at the same location played by a quartet made up of father and son, Leopold and Wolfgang Mozart, and the Barons Anton and Bartholomaus

Tinti. Haydn was present at both performances and afterwards told Mozart's father, "Before God, and as an honest man, I tell you that your son is the greatest composer known to me, either in person or by name. He has taste and, what is more, the most profound knowledge of composition."

Although inspired by Haydn's Op. 33 quartets and showing their influence in several respects, there is no mistaking Mozart's gentle spirit and distinctive style in these quartets. They are fresh in melodic invention and subtle in treatment, but above all, they exhibit a perfect amalgam of the Rococo and Classical spirits.

String Quartet in G Major, K. 387

I. Allegro vivace assai. II. Menuetto: Allegro. III. Andante cantabile. IV. Molto allegro.

Despite great diversity between the movements of the G major quartet, there are some connecting threads that run throughout the entire piece. One unifying factor is the abrupt alternation of *forte* ("loud") and *piano* ("soft") in the first movement (measure by measure), in the Menuetto (note by note), and generally in the third and fourth movements, (with several sharp changes from one to the other). Also, fragments of the chromatic scale (moving by half steps only, instead of by whole and half steps as in major and minor scales) are found in the first movement (extension of the first theme), Menuetto (the forte/piano passages), and last movement (start of the development section).

The first violin presents the principal theme at the very outset, its forceful, determined character compromised somewhat by alternating soft measures. After a repeat, with the melody in the second violin, the chromatic scales weave their way through the four instruments and lead to the subsidiary theme, a jocular, graceful tune introduced by the second violin. As the theme continues, we hear flashes of chromatic runs and alternating fortes and pianos. After a rather lengthy development Mozart brings the themes back for the recapitulation, hewing quite closely to their original presentation, but with slight changes to vary the tonal coloration.

Although traditionally the minuet is an easygoing, undemanding movement, Mozart invests his Menuetto with a good deal of musical weight and significance and organizes it in sonata form, instead of the more usual ternary form. The first theme includes the alternately loud and soft chromatic line. Starting in the first violin and then cello, it passes next to the second violin and viola, which play it together but out of phase, the second's loud notes coming with the viola's soft notes and vice versa. The second theme, a one-measure downward-leaning motif, is played by the first violin over a rolling accompaniment. And a theme built around three repeated notes and a descending chromatic line concludes the tightly planned exposition. After the briefest development section, Mozart returns all three themes. The grim trio starts off with an ominous minor-key unison passage. Cast in ternary form, the middle section is a short interlude of downward melodic movement before the forbidding unison is heard again. The Menuetto returns after the trio.

The slow movement is an outpouring of serene, though concentrated, melody. Following a rising and falling contour, the main theme gradually grows louder and then suddenly drops to a soft dynamic level near the end as Mozart extends the final phrase of the theme with its three repeated-note upbeats. This motto goes on to become the impetus for the subsidiary theme. Further episodes conclude the exposition, after which Mozart skips any development, bringing back and developing the opening theme, followed by the second and third themes and a quiet close.

The finale is the most remarkable movement of the quartet, as Mozart effortlessly moves back and forth between learned polyphony, starting both themes with extended fugal passages, and *galant* homophony, ending the same themes with straightforward accompanied melody. The first theme fugato is based on a four-note phrase that Mozart later used, almost intact, in the last movement of his ''Jupiter'' Symphony. The homophonic continuation is a running eighth-note line, which includes a few loud-soft alternations. The cello initiates the second fugal theme, which is then combined with the first fugal theme, before the dancelike homophonic sequence ends the exposition. Mozart weaves in some short chromatic stretches at the beginning of the development. The following recapitulation is much shortened with the two fugal themes brought back simultaneously and the first homophonic theme not returned at all. A short coda, referring to the chromatic bit and the first fugato, ends the movement.

According to his notation on the manuscript, Mozart completed the quartet in Vienna on December 31, 1782.

String Quartet in D Minor, K. 421 (Einstein No. 417b)

I. Allegro. II. Andante. III. Menuetto: Allegretto. IV. Allegro ma non troppo.

Mozart was composing his D minor quartet on June 17, 1783, in the same room in which his wife, Constanze, was giving birth to their first son, Raimund Leopold. According to biographer Otto Jahn, "When she complained of pain, he would come to her to cheer and console, resuming his writing as soon as she was calm." Although many have searched in vain for a correlation between the immediate situation and this profoundly melancholy and intensely expressive quartet, most have concluded with Eric Blom that Mozart shows here his "amazing power of emotional detachment" and the "callousness of genius." Perhaps the D minor quartet, again in Blom's words, can best be understood as "a personal confession that is kept within the bounds of pure art only because its expressive intensity is matched by the utmost tact and the keenest discernment of a perfect balance between technique and design."

The Allegro, a short, concentrated movement, is deeply passionate despite its overall restraint. The principal theme in the first violin is characterized by leaps, both down and up, and by a plenitude of individual motifs. The subsidiary theme, more confined in range, sounds agitated and uneasy, partly because of the faster-moving notes in both the melody and accompaniment. At the end of the exposition the first violin plays once and then again a little isolated figure ending with three repeated notes. This motto, Reginald Barrett-Ayres points out in his book on Haydn's quartets, is heard in every movement and acts as a unifying device. While the following development, recapitulation, and coda fall into traditional sonata form patterns, the actual music is anything but ordinary, making this a very affecting movement.

The Andante, in A-B-A form, is almost tender, but with a bustle and agitation that stand in the way. Likewise, it is almost serene, but with too many individual motifs and changes of dynamics to provide the necessary tranquility. Soon after the opening, and several times in the course of the A strain, the first violin plays the three-note motto heard in the last movement, albeit in a slower tempo. The B section is dominated by the three repeated notes. Those, like Wolfgang Hildesheimer in his biography of Mozart, who say that the composer wrote the cries of Constanze in labor into the music think that the two loud outbursts heard in this part are her screams. A shortened A section concludes the movement.

The three-note motto forms an important part of the defiant Menuetto's main theme. In a striking *volte-face,* the trio is all sunshine and light, with the first violin playing a jesting tune over a simple pizzicato accompaniment. But the good times do not last long, as the movement ends with a repeat of the bold Menuetto.

The mood brightens considerably for the finale, a set of four variations and coda on an ingenuous-sounding theme with the rhythm of a Siciliano, an old, moderately fast Italian dance of pastoral character. In the first variation, the first violin substitutes a florid elaboration for the rhythmic pattern of the dance tune. The two violins share the lead in the next variation, enlivening the melody with sharp, offbeat accents. The viola, sounding as plaintive and doleful as can be, sets the tone for Variation III; early on it recalls the three-note motto from the previous movements. After three variations that move further and further away from the starting theme, the fourth variation shifts back toward the original, smoothing out the rhythms, modulating to the major, and adding a flowing countermelody in the cello and viola. The coda, which is slightly faster in tempo and back in minor, comes even closer to the opening theme. The three-note figure appears here again and grows in importance so that the entire quartet ends with three determined repetitions of that unifying motto.

String Quartet in E Flat Major, K. 428
(Einstein No. 421b)

I. Allegro non troppo. II. Andante con
moto. III. Menuetto: Allegro. IV. Allegro vivace.

Composed within weeks of his previous quartet, K. 421, Mozart probably completed K. 428 by the end of July 1783. Although concise and compact, it very successfully projects a reflective, pensive personality.

Instead of a straightforward first theme, the four instruments play an unharmonized melody in octaves replete with many notes alien to the home key of E flat. A warmer, harmonized passage with an insistent little rhythmic figure in the second violin establishes the E flat tonality. Mozart then loudly repeats the opening phrase, this time harmonized with lush, romantic-sounding chords. After expanding this idea, Mozart thins out the texture and has the first violin and then the viola state the second theme. A spate of scampering scales ends the exposition. The brief development, mostly concerned with the start of the second theme, leads to the recapitulation, which includes a few measures of development of the principal subject. The movement ends without a coda.

The melodies of the Andante con moto are not particularly distinctive or memorable. Far more musical interest is attracted by the advanced, chromatic harmonies that Mozart employs throughout the movement. Particularly striking to modern audiences is the passage in the development section that bears an uncanny resemblance to the famous motif from Wagner's *Tristan und Isolde,* which was written seventy-six years later! The music has a dreamlike, yearning quality, as well as a slight sense of urgency that comes from the frequent use of suspensions—one instrument holding on to a note while the others change to a new harmony.

The vigorous opening of the Menuetto provides the quartet's first forceful rhythmic impulse. While not especially dancelike, the Menuetto does have a good, strong swing to it. The smoother, rather melancholy strains of the trio, though, bring back the work's somber character before the music is reinvigorated by the Menuetto's return.

The impish opening of the finale, however, completely changes the quartet's mood to one of cheerful good humor. The attractive tunes, the unexpected silences, the alternation of forte (loud) and piano (soft) passages, the witty treatment, and the overall sturdiness show Haydn's influence very clearly. In form the movement is a rondo. The principal subject is stated three times with slight variations, the first violin countermelody in the final statement providing a most felicitous touch. Between the repetitions there are two appearances of slightly more lyrical contrasting episodes that differ more in key than in character.

String Quartet in B Flat Major, K. 458, "Hunt"

I. Allegro vivace assai. II. Menuetto: Moderato. III. Adagio. IV. Allegro assai.

The subtitle of this quartet, "Hunt" (*Jagd* in the original German), is not Mozart's invention and is, in fact, a particularly poor choice. The obvious reference is to the fanfarelike opening of the quartet, despite the fact that the sound produced by the two violins is a far cry from the ringing tones of a brace of hunting horns. The notion of Mozart involved with a hunt also strains credulity; his indoors personality seems much better suited to sitting in stuffy salons than to riding off into wild forests. And if the performers bend the music, in style or tone, to conform to the nickname, it can only destroy the work's essential spirit.

The familiar opening phrase and the following episodes immediately establish the playful, good-humored mood of the first movement. The second theme, little more than a shake, a slow, measured, back-and-forth trill, is tossed from player to player in a game of four-way musical catch. As though to make up for the lack of a strong subsidiary theme in the exposition, Mozart starts the development with a new cantabile melody. After repeating this tune he engages the listener's attention in a brief argument based on the second theme shake, which leads directly to the recapitulation. Apparently still making amends, he balances the short development with a long coda, in reality a second development section.

The broad, deliberate Menuetto has a certain antique air about it. The carefully measured phrases conjure up visions of bewigged nobles carefully working their way through the intricate moves of this poised, dignified dance. The light airy trio sounds like the dancers are now *sur les pointes*. It is the perfect foil for the heavier Menuetto, which is repeated to end the movement.

The fervid, even sentimental, Adagio is the slowest movement in all the "Haydn" quartets. While most of the melodic burden is borne by the first violin playing a florid, much-ornamented line, the other instruments are sometimes involved with presenting independent contrapuntal melodies; more often they play an accompanying role. The lower three voices establish a pulsating, repeated-note figure as the background for the second theme, a simple melody introduced by the first violin and repeated by the cello. Without any development Mozart brings back the two themes and adds a short quiet coda at the end.

The final movement reestablishes the cheerful mood with which the quartet started. Cast in sonata form, the movement has three winning themes: the principal one, a four-square motif that some trace back to an old Austrian folk song; a similar-sounding subsidiary theme presented by the second violin, with mercurial roulades played by the first violin at the end of each statement; and the concluding theme of the exposition, a quiet, sustained melody with significant parts of all four instruments. A succinct development, in which Mozart mixes, matches, and modifies the three tunes, is followed by an equally concentrated recapitulation and a quick conclusion.

Mozart finished the "Hunt" Quartet, probably the most popular of all the "Haydn" quartets, on November 9, 1784, less than two months after he began work.

String Quartet in A Major, K. 464
I. Allegro. II. Menuetto. III. Andante.
IV. Allegro non troppo.

Mozart is quite remarkable in the A major quartet for the amazing way he is able to present music that is extremely emotional and expressive, but in a detached, objective manner. He also achieves feats of technical brilliance, fashioning entire movements out of minimal melodic material and moving with ease between passages of pure homophony and intricate fugal and polyphonic sections. It is an eloquent, mellifluous, graceful piece, that hides, in Haydn's words, "the most profound knowledge of music."

The exposition of the first movement, a model of carefully planned organization, is presented with the utmost clarity and lucidity. The first subject contains a number of distinctive motifs that are heard one after the other. The most important motif is heard at the very outset, played softly by the first violin and neatly framed by the others who join in to start and end the four-measure phrase. The next motif, only two measures long and presented twice in a loud tutti-unison, comes next. Two more motifs follow: a derivation of the first that is passed consecutively down through the quartet and finally a tender, extended first violin melody. After coming to a complete stop Mozart introduces the several motifs of the subsidiary subject, equally clear in outline and amenable to analysis in the same phrase-by-phrase manner. The rather lengthy development section confines its attention exclusively to motifs one and two, which contribute an overall single-theme quality to the movement. The recapitulation contains a precis of all the motifs, and the movement ends with a short summarizing coda.

Mozart wrote the Menuetto (the second, not third, movement, as in some modern editions) without a tempo designation. It shows the greatest economy of means, growing from a pair of strikingly different two-measure phrases. The first is played in unison and moves by leaps up the notes of an arpeggio. After a repetition one note higher, the second is heard, harmonized and starting with three repetitions of a note before descending by step. As soon as the second phrase is repeated, one note lower, Mozart combines the two phrases, setting off on a fascinating exploration of their musical potential, singly and together. In the trio Mozart transcends the usual melody-accompaniment division of voices. There is a melody line mostly in the first violin, but all the other instruments are playing parts that are well integrated into the total musical fabric. The Menuetto is repeated after the trio.

The Andante is a theme and six variations. The angular theme, more complex than most variation movement subjects, nevertheless lends itself well to elaboration. Among the particularly interesting effects are the sounds Mozart achieves in Variation II where some instruments play accents while the others continue with unaccented notes, the darkening of mood in Variation IV with the change from major to minor, the eerie character of Variation V, which some quartets intensify by playing in an expressionless manner and without vibrato, and most familiar of all, the cello's military tattoo in the final variation that has earned the entire quartet the occasionally used subtitle, "The Drum." The coda rounds off the movement by recalling the theme in its original form between snatches of the tattoo pattern.

The quartet reaches a climax in the last movement. Using the merest wisps of melody and treating them in the most learned way, Mozart creates a movement of easy fluent charm. Essentially mono-thematic, the mottos from the opening are dominant throughout; the only competition comes from a flippant little tune Mozart uses to conclude the exposition. There is a striking moment when Mozart introduces a slow-moving, solemn chorale in the middle of the development section, a few measures of chordal repose amidst all the polyphonic intricacy. A short transition then leads to the recapitulation and the coda, which ends like a glowing ember that flickers and then gradually grows dark.

According to the autograph copy, Mozart completed the A major quartet on January 10, 1785, in the same burst of creative endeavor that saw the completion of the "Hunt" Quartet two months earlier and the "Dissonance" Quartet four days later.

String Quartet in C Major, K. 465, "Dissonance"

**I. Adagio; Allegro. II. Andante
cantabile. III. Menuetto: Allegro. IV. Allegro.**

As is so often the case, the subtitle of this cheerful and generally consonant quartet is not only inappropriate but actually misleading. Music lovers in the 1780s, though, gave it the appellation "Dissonance" because they thought they heard "wrong" notes in the twenty-two-measure introduction. Some did even more: performers in Italy returned the parts to the publisher for corrections. When Prince Grassalkovics heard the music, he considered it a personal insult and ripped up the parts. Even Haydn expressed some shock, although he finally defended the music by saying, "Well, if Mozart wrote it, he must have meant it."

Although Mozart never explained the introduction, others have opined that the dissonance and obscurity was Mozart's way of setting the bright radiance of the rest of the movement, indeed the rest of the work, into bold relief. In actual fact, the first subject of the Allegro body of the movement, a group of lively themes, is all the more telling because it follows the tense opening. The forward motion slows a bit for the second theme, which starts with three repeated notes played by both violins. Mozart imparts a vigorous, buoyant quality to the following development section, even though the texture is thick with polyphonic interweaving. The recapitulation is somewhat shortened and rescored, and the amount of contrapuntal activity is increased. At the end the movement disappears like a puff of smoke in the air.

The second movement, among Mozart's most intimate and personal creations, provides an extremely touching listening experience. After presenting the several individual phrases of the leading theme, Mozart makes the transition to the second theme by means of a simple but sublime conversation between the first violin and cello. The very pure new theme is essentially a repeated note that resolves by going down one step. From the repetitions of this phrase, the movement proceeds through a reminder of the violin/cello dialogue right to the recapitulation, without a development section. Near the end of the recapitulation, though, Mozart introduces a completely new lyrical countermelody against echoes of the violin/cello duet.

The Menuetto crackles with the energy of the startling contrasts of harsh unisons cutting in on gentle melodies and sharp staccato notes following smooth cantilena lines. The trio is in the minor, and its melody of rising and falling widely spaced intervals over motoric, relentless eighth notes seemingly yearns to reach some elusive, unattainable goal. The Menuetto is repeated at the end.

The finale abandons itself to bubbling good spirits. Again Mozart delights the listeners with a plethora of happy motifs, one more charming and joyful than the next, and all presented with wonderful touches of wit and mischievous good humor. A brief development section leads to a return of the thematic sequence and a coda that brings the movement and quartet to a glorious conclusion.

The "Dissonance" Quartet is the last of the set of six that Mozart dedicated to Haydn and is a fitting climax to the series. Mozart finished it on January 14, 1785, four days after completing the previous A major quartet, K. 464.

Viola Quintet in C Minor, K. 406 (Einstein No. 516B)

**I. Allegro.   II. Andante.   III. Menuetto in Canone;
Trio al Rovescio.   IV. Allegro.**

Mozart's C minor viola quintet, K. 406, of 1787, is known to be a reworking of his Serenade for Winds in the same key, K. 388, composed five years earlier, but no one can explain a couple of the mysterious circumstances that surround the work. First of all, since Mozart always composed with a specific purpose in mind, what was his object in writing the Serenade (no reason has been found)? And secondly, having written the Serenade for eight players—two oboes, two clarinets, two bassoons, and two horns—why did he choose to transcribe it for viola quintet?

According to Alfred Einstein, Mozart planned to write a set of six viola quintets and dedicate them to King Frederick William II either for a gift of money or a court appointment. His reason for adapting the serenade was merely to speed the project along. If this was the plan, nothing came of it either in terms of cash or position. A. Hyatt King, on the other hand, argues that Mozart made the transcription in order to earn some money quickly and repay his many outstanding debts. Support for this view comes from evidence that he offered the C minor and two other quintets for sale to a publisher in April 1788, but without success. In either case, the C minor quintet proves to be an exceptionally powerful work and perfectly suited to the five-player medium.

The first movement's stark, forbidding opening motif is played in unison. Once it is stated, though, Mozart immediately introduces four other distinct motifs—in order they may be characterized as beseeching, defiant, flirtatious, and stubborn—before the cello repeats the opening phrase. A transition leads to the contrasting subsidiary theme, a long, arched melody of exquisite beauty. A rhythmically incisive third theme played by violins and cello concludes the exposition. After the presentation of some material little related to the exposition, the development centers around the large downward leap (a seventh) that ends the exposition's first phrase. In the recapitulation, the first subject gets a straightforward reprise, but the second theme is presented as a variant. There is no coda.

The Andante, calm in mood and in major, serves to release the tensions built up in the first movement. There are two main themes, both stated by the first violin. The first theme is an extended lyrical line; the second theme contains a four-note descending figure reminiscent of the subsidiary theme in the previous movement. The short development deals only with the first theme, after which both themes are returned in the recapitulation. The second theme, though, is first heard in the dominant key (B flat major) instead of the expected key (E flat major), but Mozart sets everything right in its repetition.

The Menuetto is a stunning display of contrapuntal brilliance that is used to serve purely musical and expressive ends. The first part is a veritable lexicon of intricate and complex imitative polyphonic devices. The *Trio al Rovescio* ("Trio in Reverse") goes even further; it shows all the contrapuntal sophistication of the Menuetto but adds the complication of having the melody appear both in its original form and upside down! That Mozart could conceive and carry out such a conception is admirable; that he could, at the same time, make it seem so musically telling and so effortless is truly awesome.

The last movement starts with a rather sober, introspective theme, which Mozart then subjects to seven variations plus a substantial coda. As the variations progress, the connection with the original theme becomes increasingly tenuous. The seventh variation is farthest removed; it is very quiet and simple yet has anguished chromatic harmonies. The coda is a beam of sunlight that bathes the final bars in a joyful radiance.

Horn Quintet in E Flat Major, K. 407

I. Allegro. II. Andante. III. Allegro.

Mozart wrote his horn quintet, which was completed on the last day of 1782, for Ignaz Leutgeb, a horn player in the Salzburg orchestra from 1763 to 1777. After leaving Salzburg Leutgeb moved to Vienna and opened a cheese shop, financed in part by a loan from Mozart's father, Leopold. Although there is sufficient evidence that Leutgeb was an excellent player, Mozart made him the butt of innumerable childish jokes and pranks. The dedication on the Horn Concerto, K. 417, is one notorious example: "Wolfgang Amadeus Mozart takes pity on Leutgeb, donkey, ox and fool . . ." While no one knows just why Mozart ridiculed Leutgeb, music lovers everywhere are grateful to the horn-player-turned-cheese-merchant for eliciting four concertos and this quintet from the composer. Written for the odd combination of horn, violin, two violas, and cello, the quintet seems more like a miniature horn concerto than a true piece of chamber music, with the *concertante* horn part making extraordinary demands on the player and the strings essentially relegated to an orchestralike, accompanying role. Modest in conception, the horn quintet is nonetheless a work of great charm.

The first subject of the Allegro is a study in contrasts—loud-soft, staccato-legato, lyrical-rhythmic, horn-strings. There is much more unity in the second subject, one long cantabile line introduced by the horn and repeated by the first violin. The following development and recapitulation sections are conventional, except that Mozart varies theme two on its return.

Despite the difference in tonal quality between the horn and the strings, Mozart makes the Andante an intimate conversation among the five players. He establishes a mood of dreamy, mellow peacefulness, as the instruments discuss the principal theme, which is heard at the very beginning and prevails throughout.

Mozart's mischievousness surfaces in the last movement, as he makes a joke of the rhythmically ambiguous opening. The principal theme clearly starts on the downbeat, or does it? The fact that soon becomes clear is that the first note is really an upbeat! Mozart may have also been having fun by giving the start of this theme the same melody, but not identical rhythm, as the second movement theme. As one enjoys the wholesome good spirits of this rondo-form movement, it is easy to lose sight of Mozart's wickedly difficult horn part.

Quintet for Piano and Winds in E Flat Major, K. 452
I. Largo; Allegro
moderato. II. Larghetto. III. Rondo: Allegretto.

During the incredibly busy early months of 1784, Mozart completed three of his best known piano concertos, K. 449 in E flat (February 9), K. 450 in B flat (March 15), and K. 451 in D (March 22), performing them at concerts on the last three Wednesdays in March (17, 24, and 31). Moreover, he finished his Quintet for Piano and Winds, K. 452, on March 30 and played the piano part for the premiere at the Imperial and Royal National Court Theater, Vienna, two days later. Afterward he wrote to his father about the quintet: "It had the greatest applause. I myself consider it the best thing I have written in my life. I wish you could have heard it, and how beautifully it was performed. To tell the truth, I grew tired of the mere playing at the end, and it reflects no small credit on me that my audience did not in any degree share the fatigue."

Most everyone agrees with Mozart that the quintet was "the best thing" he had yet written. Perhaps most significant is that he succeeded in creating a highly emotional work in the most intimate style and with the simplest of means. He also mastered the difficulties involved in composing a chamber work that includes a brilliant piano part, but one that is perfectly integrated with the other instruments. And finally, he demonstrated his remarkable skill in writing for the wind instruments, exploiting each one's distinctive tone quality and taking into account the players' need for time to breathe.

The dignified and majestic slow introduction to the first movement introduces each of the performers by means of a short solo turn. In their presentation, the two main themes of the body of the movement are stated quietly by the piano, with loud counterstatements by the entire quintet. The concluding theme of the exposition, though, a descending syncopated figure, belongs almost exclusively to the winds. The very short and simple development section is essentially four statements of the first theme, each statement a step higher than the one before. This treatment builds inner tension that finally finds relief in the recapitulation, where the themes are further developed. Without a formal coda, the movement ends with two brilliant flourishes in the horn.

The richly sonorous Larghetto gives a first impression of long, singing melodies, but careful listening shows that the extended cantabile line is really built up of much shorter fragments. Structurally, the movement is in ternary form. The winds state the first motif of the opening section, and the piano presents the second against pulsed, repeated notes. Mozart then gives the French horn a particularly attractive new melody to start the middle section. The return of the first part is differently scored and includes a hauntingly beautiful sustained chromatic line in the winds that functions as an extension of the first theme. The movement ends in much the same way as the first part.

The sparkling, high-spirited Rondo is made all the more appealing by the deliberate Allegretto tempo and Mozart's playful treatment of the enchanting tunes. Rondos are traditionally diagrammed as A-B-A-C-A; A is the principal theme, B and C are contrasts. Mozart dutifully follows the first four parts of this scheme, but then, instead of bringing back A, he reintroduces B. As a further surprise, Mozart next inserts a *Cadenza in tempo,* improvisational sounding parts written out for all five players, before finally providing the final statement of the A theme that ends the quintet.

Piano Quartets, K. 478 and K. 493

Georg Nicolaus von Nissen, who married Constanze after Mozart died, wrote a biography of the composer in which he gave some background information about the piano quartets. According to Nissen's account, the composer had contracted to write a set of three piano quartets in 1785 for the publisher Franz Anton Hoffmeister, although this particular combination—piano, violin, viola, and cello—was still rather unusual. A substantial amount of keyboard and string music had been written during the seventeenth and eighteenth centuries; most, though, used the keyboard as the *continuo,* to provide a filled-out bass part to the solo string lines. The two sons of Johann Sebastian Bach, Karl Philipp Emanuel and Johann Christian, who had published quartets, had given the keyboard a part that was more than just a *continuo,* but neither had made it an equal member of the ensemble.

Mozart's first piano quartet, the G minor, completed on October 16, 1785, treated the four instruments as equals; the concertolike piano part was balanced by equally strong and interesting string parts, to create a unified, well-integrated chamber work. Hoffmeister, however, complained that the work was too difficult and that the public

300

would not buy it. "Write more popularly, or else I can neither print nor pay for anything of yours!" he told Mozart. Mozart released the publisher from the contract, saying, "Then I will write nothing more, and go hungry, or may the devil take me!" Freed of the obligation to continue the series, Hoffmeister allowed the composer to keep the money that he had already been paid. Although there was no prospect of having the works published, Mozart wrote another piano quartet, the E flat major nine months later, completing it on June 3, 1786. Artaria, a publisher with considerably better judgment than Hoffmeister, issued both quartets the following year.

Piano Quartet in G Minor, K. 478

I. Allegro.   II. Andante.   III. Rondo (Allegro).

The key of G minor always had a special meaning for Mozart, as witness his Symphony No. 40, K. 550 and his Viola Quintet, K. 516. Alfred Einstein in his outstanding book on Mozart says that it is the composer's key of fate, and he describes the opening of the piano quartet's first movement as the fate theme, fully as powerful and trenchant as comparable fate themes from Beethoven's Fifth or Tchaikovsky's Fourth Symphony. The terse motif is rendered in unison by all four instruments and is immediately extended, transformed, and developed before leading to the subdued second subject, which is introduced by the piano alone. In a daring departure, Mozart uses accents superimposed on the basic four-beat meter to start the second theme with two measures of five-beat meter. The third subject, the only one with traces of lightness, is stated by the piano with echoes in the violin. After a comparatively short, though passionate, development, Mozart follows with a recapitulation in which he continues to develop the thematic material. In the coda, though, he hammers away at the fate motto, driving to the inexorable conclusion.

The Andante is a tranquil foil to the fervid expression of the first movement. Written in the less connotative key of B flat major, the movement starts with a lovely, slightly melancholy melody, which is first stated softly by the piano and then more forcefully by the quartet. The closing phrases of the first theme are heard against long streams of rapid notes, which continue as the background for a transitional motif in the piano. This leads to the string statement of the second theme, one that is weighed down with pain and hopeless resignation. The transition motif functions as the concluding theme of the exposition. Replacing the development section with two scant measures of transition, Mozart then proceeds to restate all the themes, little changed except in scoring.

Few movements in the chamber music repertoire contain such an incredible abundance of melody as the Rondo movement (there is no minuet). Exhibiting as much jubilant strength as would be fitting after the despondency of the first two movements, it sets a confident, vigorous tone that maintains throughout. Although it is organized in a modified rondo form, the details of structure are eclipsed by Mozart's melodic profligacy.

Piano Quartet in E Flat Major, K. 493
I. Allegro. II. Larghetto. III. Allegretto.

The dark, dramatic opening phrase of the E flat quartet is scant preparation for the several delightful motifs that Mozart soon introduces to round out the first subject. The second theme, stated by the piano after two powerful chords, has but one melodic strain, with a particularly memorable mottolike opening. A number of brief new motifs bring the exposition to a close. The second-theme motto dominates the development section, appearing about twenty times in various keys, instrumental combinations, dynamics, and musical meanings. The somewhat shortened recapitulation closely mirrors the exposition, and the final coda features a tight, fugal reworking of the by now very familiar second-theme motto.

Mozart wrote the Larghetto with a wonderfully light and delicate touch. The entire movement is distinguished by immediate echoes of almost every phrase—sometimes in exact repetition, sometimes elaborated or modified in some way. The overall feeling is wistful and tender, but with strong hints of great inner tension.

Mozart usually planned compositions completely in his head, without writing out preliminary sketches. But two preparatory versions of the last movement's principal theme have been found, which suggest that it required a mighty effort to create what Alfred Einstein enthusiastically called ''the purest, most childlike and godlike melody every sung.'' The movement is structured in a combined rondo and sonata form with the first theme followed by a second rather militant theme that soon relaxes into a more lyrical mood, as Mozart brings in additional motifs. After a brief section featuring virtuosic runs for the piano that can be considered the development, the second and first themes come back, and the work concludes with a short coda.

Trio for Clarinet, Viola, and Piano in E Flat Major, K. 498, "Kegelstatt" ("Skittles")

I. Andante. II. Menuetto. III. Allegretto.

This trio has the fanciful subtitle *"Kegelstatt"* ("Skittles"), presumably because it was written while Mozart was playing skittles (similar to bowling) with his friend, clarinet virtuoso Anton Stadler. If this story is true, nothing in the music betrays the place of its composition. The trio also has an unique instrumentation, probably chosen for the use of his favorite piano student Franziska von Jacquin, the clarinetist Stadler, and Mozart himself playing viola.

Mozart completed the *"Kegelstatt"* Trio on August 5, 1786, in Vienna, during a particularly productive period of chamber music composition. He had finished the K. 493 piano quartet just two months earlier and exactly two weeks later the K. 499 string quartet was done. The trio is small-scaled and intimate in character, showing particularly affectionate part writing for both the clarinet and viola, instruments for which Mozart had a great affinity.

The slow-tempo opening of the Andante can be thought of as doing double duty, serving both as the fast and slow movements. The motto heard at the very outset, and that prevails throughout, can be identified by its *gruppetto,* a fast, ornamental group of notes that goes up, down, and then returns to its starting pitch. Although the motto is heard over and over, by placing it in fresh settings, Mozart manages to keep it interesting and attractive. The second theme is simply the last five notes of the motto, rhythmically transformed. (The continuation of this melody, a rising and falling scale line, later serves as the basis of the finale's principal theme.) Even though the development section is quite short, Mozart continues working out the material through the recapitulation and coda.

The Menuetto, a long, serious, and intense movement, is a far cry from typical eighteenth-century minuets. Its emphatic bass line and sharp contrasts in dynamics project a feeling of smoldering defiance. The strange trio is a conflict between two antithetical musical ideas—a short, sensitive legato phrase that the clarinet introduces, and the viola's gruff, overeager triplet response. Back and forth these two gestures flow, with neither gaining the ascendancy, until Mozart returns to the Menuetto and ends the movement with a quick reminder of the trio motifs.

The glorious songlike main theme of the rondo, as mentioned, comes from the Andante's second theme. Following an A-B-A-C-A-D-A rondo form, each A is a repetition of the principal theme, with the others contrasting interludes. Perhaps the C episode, in minor and featuring an impassioned outburst from the viola, is most striking. Although the clarinet and piano seem to offer consoling homilies to the viola, the dark-voiced string instrument persists in its heavy sorrow. When the viola's *angst* finally subsides, Mozart gently slips into the third statement of the A section. With only short interruptions, warm, good spirits obtain for the rest of the movement.

String Quartet in D Major, K. 499, "Hoffmeister"

I. Allegretto. II. Menuetto:
Allegretto. III. Adagio. IV. Allegro.

Of Mozart's ten mature quartets, the first six make up the set of "Haydn" quartets and the last three are the "Prussian" quartets. Only the D major, K. 499 stands alone. Subtitled "Hoffmeister" for Mozart's friend, benefactor, and publisher, Franz Anton Hoffmeister, the work was either written on commission from Hoffmeister or to repay a particular debt that Mozart owed the publisher. Despite a determinedly optimistic outlook, the quartet conveys a sense of despondency beneath the surface glitter, which Mozart biographer Alfred Einstein described as "despairing under a mask of gaiety." We hear sections of light, cheery, Rococo music giving way to heavy and solemn passages of serious "learned" writing.

The first movement illustrates well the coexistence of both gravity and lightness within the music. The gay, insouciant unison theme that opens the movement holds the promise of some merry music-making to come. But as Mozart introduces new motifs—intricate little contrapuntal dialogues between pairs of instruments, a section of sharp contrasts in the midst of impassioned outbursts and timorous responses, an extended canonic passage for first violin and cello—we perceive the theme's darker side. The prominence of the triadic opening motif obscures the formal second theme, which is heard more as an episode within the exposition. Running through the short development section is a continuing eighth-note figure like a ticking clock that accompanies the working out of the first theme. Finally the instruments come together for a unison statement that signals the recapitulation. The clock motif reappears in the coda and gently disappears to end the movement.

In isolation, the theme of the Menuetto would seem happy and innocent. But the dense texture, the chromatic lines in the other parts, and the extensive imitative writing give it a special depth of feeling. The trio is in minor with a somber gray cast, despite the lively running triplets. The Menuetto returns after the trio.

The Adagio continues the style of the first two movements. Its outside warmth seems to hide what Einstein calls "past sorrow." Less intimate and expressive than other Mozart chamber works, the movement combines personal reticence with superb compositional skill. Reminiscent of an Italian opera aria, the long, vocal melodies all but obliterate the movement's underlying sonata form.

Mozart starts the finale by parceling out short scraps of the first theme before launching into a full-length presentation. While the abrupt pauses are humorous, the gaiety is unaccountably restrained. After the theme comes to a full stop, the violins introduce the light and bouncy second theme, but with viola interruptions rudely compromising the merriment. Theme I acts as the transition to the concluding theme of the exposition, an awkward rising triplet figure in the cello that is answered by the viola's descending run. A short development leads to the direct and forthright recapitulation and coda.

Mozart completed the "Hoffmeister" Quartet in Vienna on August 19, 1786, and it was published about one month later. Nothing is known of the first performance.

Piano Trio in B Flat Major, K. 502

I. Allegro. II. Larghetto. III. Allegretto.

Mozart called his B flat trio a *terzett,* originally a "vocal trio," but by Mozart's day signifying any three-voiced composition. He probably used the term to distinguish it from his earlier trios, which he called *divertimenti.* In these works he treated the cello as a *continuo* instrument, mostly reinforcing the bass line of the piano, and also gave the violin a role subservient to the keyboard. In K. 502, while not completely freeing the cello of its *continuo* role, Mozart gave greater independence to all three instruments, including a virtuosic part for the violin. By combining splendid part writing with the most personal expression and forming a perfect union between the intellectual stimulation of learned counterpoint and the charm of the *style galant*, Mozart created a true masterpiece. The composer indicated that the trio was to be played in "friendly, musical, social circles," and it has been widely assumed that he wrote it for the congenial family group of Franziska von Jacquin, Mozart's talented piano student.

The opening theme's fragile and sensitive quality requires the greatest control and delicacy of touch from the performers. The second theme is essentially the same theme, moved up five notes from the key of B flat to F, making the movement essentially monothematic. Even the concluding theme of the exposition is a derivative of that same all-important theme. After his exclusive devotion to the one musical idea, Mozart begins the development section with a completely new theme, which soon gives way to a working out of motifs from the exposition. The process of development continues through the recapitulation, and the movement ends as daintily as it began.

The Larghetto can be likened to a leisurely, intimate dialogue between three very good friends. The leading voice belongs to the piano; it introduces the various topics that are discussed. The violin is second in importance; most of the time it echoes the views expressed by the piano; occasionally, though, it utters its own thoughts. The cello takes a lesser role; it seldom goes off on its own, but offers support, now to the piano, now to the violin. The opening theme, stated by the piano and then the violin, pervades the entire movement, with two rather similar interludes coming between its repetitions.

The chameleonlike principal theme for the last movement is light and dancing in the soft opening piano statement. But in the violin's loud repeat it takes on the character of an exhortation, a powerful call to action. As the subject continues, though, the buoyant aspect dominates. Over a repeated accompaniment figure in the cello and piano, the violin plays a countersubject, a brief motto extracted from the principal theme. The rest of the movement, then, is basically an alternation of these two musical ideas.

Mozart completed the B flat trio in Vienna on November 18, 1786.

Viola Quintet in C Major, K. 515

I. Allegro. II. Menuetto:
Allegretto. III. Andante. IV. Allegro.

When Mozart added a viola to the string quartet, as he did for his six viola quintets (K. 174, 406, 515, 516, 593, and 614), he vastly increased the harmonic possibilities and exposed new scoring and grouping opportunities. But even more, the viola quintets opened up for Mozart a world of broad scope and deep expression. They called forth some of his most grandiose conceptions and most emotional outpourings. Of the six, the C major quintet most gloriously combines exhilarating high spirits with a sense of seriousness. Longer than any of the other quintets, it brings together the monumentality of the symphony with the intimacy of a string quartet.

The first movement opens boldly and dramatically with the cello on its lowest note leaping upward through an arpeggio for over two octaves to a first violin resolution. Three times the statement and response are made, against a throbbing in the three middle voices, before there is a pregnant measure of silence. The same motif then returns three more times, but with two significant differences: it is now in C minor instead of C major, and the violin has the arpeggio followed by a cello conclusion. After some transitional material, Mozart briefly brings back the opening motif, now compressed into four-measure phrases instead of the more awkward five-measure phrases heard before. The second theme, given out initially by the first violin and then the two violas, is a flowing eighth-note line, not nearly as striking as the principal subject. Other motifs follow to conclude the exposition. Full of all sorts of harmonic surprises, the development manages to address each of the exposition motifs before proceeding to the recapitulation in which Mozart further amplifies the basic melodic material.

The Menuetto, the most untraditional of all the movements, starts ambiguously with a lyrical melody of uncertain tonality in the violins, which is further compounded by its unbalanced four- and six-measure phrases. The trio, rather than being the conventional undemanding interlude before the repeat of the Menuetto, is exceptionally long and provides the expressive focus of the movement, with its several highly emotional chromatic sections.

The Andante particularly exploits the harmonic richness provided by the extra viola. The movement, essentially an intimate dialogue between the first violin and first viola, contrasts the light, clear violin timbre with the viola's darker, denser sonority. Structurally the movement is made up of three themes—the first tender and warm, the second more flowing, and the third passionate and urgent—which are stated and then repeated with only the necessary adjustment of keys. The simplicity of the organization serves to heighten the emotional impact of this very touching movement.

By measure count the finale is probably the longest movement in Mozart's chamber music, but rare is the listener who does not find it delightfully short because of its speed, rhythmic flow, and vivacious melodies. Sometimes Mozart presents the bare themes simply as an expression of sheer joy; other times he presents them in complex contrapuntal settings, as he weaves them together in combined rondo-sonata form.

Mozart completed the C major quintet in Vienna on April 19, 1787.

Viola Quintet in G Minor, K. 516

I. Allegro. II. Menuetto: Allegretto. III. Adagio ma non troppo. IV. Adagio. V. Allegro.

Twice in his career, Mozart conceived major pairs of works in the keys of C major and G minor, completing both at about the same time. On April 19, 1787, he finished the C major viola quintet and one month later, on May 16, the G minor quintet. The summer of the following year, he finished his Symphony No. 40 in G minor on July 15 and his "Jupiter" Symphony No. 41 in C major, just over two weeks later. All four compositions proved to be peak achievements for Mozart, with the major-key works basically cheerful and happy in outlook and the minor-key works generally projecting poignancy and yearning.

The sorrowful character of the G minor quintet is apparent right from the start. The first theme is built up of broken sighs and gasps that give a feeling of unease made all the more plaintive by the many fragments of descending melodic line. The second theme, starting in the same dark key (G minor), further intensifies the despair, especially when the opening melodic leap is expanded to a minor ninth, an especially agonized interval. The compact development section works through both subjects, with the treatment creating the impression that all the melodic movement is downward in direction. The recapitulation is quite regular, and a brief coda recalls the two themes. Then, instead of following tradition and appending a more cheerful, major-key ending, Mozart carries through to a despondent conclusion in minor.

It would be hard to imagine a less dancelike minuet than the second movement. An oppressive cantabile melody lacking a strong rhythmic component is interrupted by ungainly heavy third-beat chords and is treated with considerable chromatic alteration. The last four measures of the Menuetto, in minor, become the first four measures of the trio, in major, establishing a much brighter and consoling character for this middle section, before the heaviness returns with the repeat of the Menuetto.

The third movement, which is played with mutes, does little to dispel the prevailing melancholy. The first theme starts as a lovely cantilena, but breathless fragments of melody recall the sighs of the first movement. The second theme is a descending scale line in the first violin with a wistful concluding comment from the second viola. The major key (B flat) third theme, with its energetic offbeat accompaniment, brightens the mood somewhat. The second half of the movement is essentially a repeat of the sequence of melodies heard in the first half.

The fourth movement, a slow cavatina, is really just an introduction to the finale. A dirge or lament, it is slower in tempo than the third movement. The voicing stays the same throughout: melody in the first violin, an inexorable pizzicato line in the cello, and slow pulsing chords in the three inner voices.

An ominous pause signals the break between the lyrical though palpably despondent Adagio and the start of the faster and carefree Allegro. Based on what sounds like a free transformation of the opening theme of the first movement, this section clears away all remnants of despair with its zestful lightheartedness. While some critics find the Allegro trivial in this context, most admire its insouciant gaiety. Amidst the plethora of carefree motifs one can easily surrender to the movement's high spirits and forget all the pathos that came before.

Piano Trio in E Major, K. 542

I. Allegro. II. Andante grazioso. III. Allegro.

In a June 17, 1788, letter to his friend, fellow Mason and benefactor, Michael Puchberg, Mozart added the postscript: "When shall we have another little music-making at your house?—I have written a new trio!" He was referring to the Piano Trio in E major, which he actually finished five days later, on June 22. The trio came just before the three great final symphonies; it finds Mozart at the very height of his powers. One indication that he recognized the trio's outstanding quality was his decision to play it at the Court of Dresden the following year when he was hoping for an appointment there. And the fact is that others appreciated its worth, too. Chopin, for example, made it a practice, decades later, to open all of his trio concerts with Mozart's E major. In this trio, Mozart creates some less-than-inspired themes yet, by working his musical magic, fashions them into a work of radiant beauty and great inner joy.

The principal theme of the Allegro, stated by the piano, is rather static, as compared with the usual flow of Mozart melodies, and the transition, a little phrase that moves back and forth between the violin and piano, is not much better. The second theme is more appealing, with a nice lilt and a pleasing contour. After the violin and piano statements (in B major), the drama is heightened by the drastic and exciting modulation (to G major) for the cello's turn at the tune. During the remainder of the movement Mozart treats us to a succession of intriguing harmonic and melodic touches that raise the Allegro far above its rather humble origins.

A single folklike theme prevails throughout the fresh and charming Andante grazioso. Music scholar Alfred Einstein described the movement, in which the solo piano alternates with tutti passages, as "poetic and pastoral, like a Watteau." The wonder, though, is not the quality of the melody as much as Mozart's miraculous, but subtle, transformations of the basic theme, making this a very special, hauntingly beautiful movement.

Mozart wrote out sixty-five measures of a restless, agitated finale before he stopped, started again, and composed the present version, with its simple relaxed melody that is so like a nursery song. It is a glittering movement in combined sonata and rondo form in which he introduces sections of sharply contrasting character and mood and provides ever-fascinating melodic and harmonic changes. Part of the movement's compelling brilliance comes from the many virtuosic passages for the piano and violin.

Divertimento for String Trio in E Flat Major, K. 563

I. Allegro. II. Adagio. III. Menuetto: Allegretto. IV. Andante. V. Menuetto: Allegretto. VI. Allegro.

Mozart used the term *divertimento* to call to mind a style and form of music that was popular in the second half of the eighteenth century. A divertimento traditionally has some of the characteristics of a Baroque suite—lightness of mood, simplicity of construction, and a good number of short, dancelike movements—as well as some elements of the symphony (or quartet or trio), with some serious movements and, in particular, a sonata-form first movement. The E flat major divertimento pays obeisance to the suite aspect of the form by including six movements, with two minuets, but it shows even more affinity to the symphony from the viewpoint of depth, expressivity, and seriousness of purpose. With good reason, many commentators consider this the most outstanding string trio ever written.

The light, singing melodic content of the first movement suggests a genial entertainment. The first theme is a placid cantabile melody, interrupted by joyous rising and falling scales. The second theme, first given out by the violin and cello, has a quality of soaring lyricism. The development section, though, ushers in a change of mood as these seemingly happy themes become restless and almost foreboding. Following tradition, Mozart ends with a recapitulation, which recaptures the winsome innocence of the exposition, leaving some uncertainty as to the movement's *real* musical message. Is it one of lightness or of gravity?

The intent of the long Adagio is also not too clear. The two rising, major-key arpeggios in the cello with which the movement opens connote a certain optimism and resolve. Yet, the scoring and lugubrious tempo give the theme a reflective, if not mournful, character. Instead of a proper second theme, Mozart transposes the cello melody to a new key and presents it to the violin in a slightly elaborated form, thus giving it a more affirmative cast. The compact development returns the theme to the cello for three more repeats before a transition leads back to the recapitulation. Here the single, all-important theme builds up to a powerful climax, followed by an abrupt ending, as the violin climbs up in a final echo of the arpeggio.

The divertimento spirit comes to the fore in the third movement. Lighthearted in character, the movement is cast in the traditional three-part form: Menuetto, contrasting trio, repeat of the Menuetto.

The inspiring Andante, the emotional peak of the divertimento, starts with a rather lengthy theme of beguiling simplicity that might well be of folk origin. Mozart then subjects this theme to four continuous variations, not of elaboration and decoration, but of meditation and transformation. Perhaps most striking is the final variation in which the viola boldly asserts a slow-moving skeletal outline of the theme amidst rapid counterpoints in the violin and cello. Having moved by now so far from its source, the return of the opening theme in the short coda is a fresh, welcome reminder of the original innocence.

The second Menuetto is a true dance movement, filled with great charm and rhythmic verve. In the opening section Mozart hints at sounds of paired hunting horns. The trio entrusts the viola with a robust, peasantlike dance tune before Mozart directs that the repeat of the Menuetto be played piano ("softly") throughout. This is followed by a second trio, gay and bouncy, with the melody all in the first violin. Once more the Menuetto returns, now in full dynamics, and a short coda based on the Menuetto caps it all off.

The ebullient and affectionate last movement can only delight listeners with its winning melodies and perfection of detail. The captivating principal theme is introduced by the violin over a rolling viola accompaniment and a rudimentary cello bass line. Toward the end of this theme, Mozart introduces a drumlike, repeated-note figure that grows increasingly important through the movement. Organized in a combination rondo and sonata form, the Allegro has repetitions of the principal theme separated by contrasting episodes, but with a developmentlike section in the middle. The coda briefly develops the drumbeat figure, and two insistent repeats of the pattern by the viola and cello bring the movement to a close.

Mozart completed the divertimento in Vienna on September 27, 1788, dedicating it to his friend, Michael von Puchberg. The trio received its premiere in Dresden on April 13, 1789, with Anton Teiber (Teyber), violin, Mozart himself playing viola, and Anton Kraft, cello.

String Quartets, K. 575, 589, and 590, "Prussian" Quartets

While on a trip to Berlin in the spring of 1789, Mozart performed for the accomplished cellist and great patron of music, Frederick William II, King of Prussia, who asked him to compose a set of six quartets. But on his return to Vienna on June 4, circumstances made it extremely hard for Mozart to get to work, even though be knew the King would have paid him well. Mozart's letters speak of the physical pain he was suffering from rheumatism, toothaches, headaches, and insomnia. Further, his wife's agony with a foot condition at the same time she was pregnant for the fifth time added to his worries. And to compound matters, he was desperately short of money. The humiliating, pleading letters he wrote begging to borrow a few more *gulden* from friends who had already lent him considerable amounts of money went largely unheeded. And when he tried to promote a series of concerts to get back on his feet, he sold a grand total of one subscription! Is it any wonder that he was despondent and had little enthusiasm for writing the quartets?

Nevertheless, despite his most burdensome situation, Mozart began to work on the D major quartet (K. 575) and somehow managed to finish it the month of his return. The fact that he did not bother to list the day of its completion in the account of compositions that he kept, only the month, is considered a measure of his depressed and apathetic state. Following a hiatus just short of a year, Mozart wrote two more quartets, in B flat major (K. 589) and in F major (K. 590), in May and June 1790—the last quartets he ever composed. Since he was not occupied with other projects, it would seem that his deteriorating physical condition and dejection prevented him from completing the six quartets for the king. Eager for immediate income, Mozart sold the three completed quartets to a publisher and later complained that he had had "to dispose of the quartets (all that toilsome work) for a mockery of a fee, only to lay my hands on some money to keep myself going."

Although originally published during such a difficult period, the three graceful and happy "Prussian" Quartets, as they are called, betray little of Mozart's difficult straits. Perhaps less inventive or expressive than Haydn's quartets written for the same monarch or Mozart's earlier quartets, these works nevertheless delight with their simplicity and joyfulness. Although published without a dedication to King Frederick, later editions did honor the Prussian head of state.

String Quartet in D Major, K. 575

I. Allegretto. II. Andante. III. Menuetto: Allegretto. IV. Allegretto.

Nowhere is it more clear that Mozart was able to separate his troubled physical and emotional condition from the spiritual and musical side of his life than in the melodic, optimistic D major quartet. Even though Mozart was suffering from the greatest adversity at the time, the work achieves a rare buoyancy of spirit. In one regard, though, the quartet bears the imprint of the immediate circumstances. Since it was written at the urging of King Frederick of Prussia, who was an excellent cellist, the cello plays an important role throughout. Then, to balance the prominent cello, Mozart wrote parts of greater consequence for the two inner voices, the second violin and the viola.

The principal theme of the first movement is essentially a rising arpeggio and a descending scale. Stated by the first violin, it is repeated by the viola, and its extension features both the first violin and cello. The second theme, a rising arpeggio followed by a long held note, is introduced by the cello, but with turns for all four players. Either by calculation, or because the rising arpeggio is so common a figure, both first movement themes—and the main theme of the finale, too—share the same melody, although in completely different rhythms. The development and recapitulation are conventional, and continue the movement's buoyant good spirits through to the very end.

The second movement is in ternary form, A-B-A. The contrast between the two sections comes from the melodic contour of A, an earthbound line, and B, a soaring phrase that passes from instrument to instrument. It is also heard in the difference between the thick texture of A, with the violins doubled, and B, which is a single melodic line, well-distanced from the repeated-note accompaniment. In the very short coda, the first violin has a rapid, rising run that the second violin answers with a long note and a four-note turn; the cello and first violin echo this exchange to conclude the movement.

The sprightly Menuetto starts with the four-note turn that came at the finish of the Andante. Perking along in one-beat-to-a-bar pulse, the music glitters with sharp contrasts—soft and loud, staccato and legato. The trio is a showcase for the cello, which sings out the cantabile melodies (with that same four-note turn), very high in its range. The Menuetto is repeated after the trio.

The cello introduces the main theme of the serenely happy last movement; it starts with the same rising arpeggio as the themes of the first movement. The contrasting interludes of the movement's rondo form spring from the ascending arpeggios as well, but in different keys, settings, and scorings, so that they truly sound like new material. Tightly organized and highly contrapuntal, this movement is probably the most interesting one of the entire quartet.

The premiere of K. 575 was given at Mozart's lodgings in Vienna on May 22, 1790, very likely with the composer playing viola.

String Quartet in B Flat Major, K. 589

I. Allegro. II. Larghetto. III. Menuetto: Moderato. IV. Allegro assai.

This quartet was written when Mozart was just thirty-four years old, but it sounds like the work of someone at a much later stage of life.

Not only does Mozart display all the consummate mastery of technique and profundity that is commonly associated with maturity; he also conveys some sense of the acceptance and resignation that so often accompanies old age.

There are several distinctive motifs in the first, mostly quiet, contemplative subject group; the initial one heard at the very outset, rhythmically a long note (half-note) followed by four rapid notes (sixteenths), is most prominent. The cello, which plays a leading role in presenting this theme, also introduces the second theme, a wide-ranging melody enlivened with several chromatic touches. Linking the two themes and accompanying the first theme at the end of the exposition are slightly awkward running triplet passages that add a touch of rhythmic spice to the cantabile brew. The triplets play an important part in the development section and lead to the recapitulation that ends the movement.

The cello and first violin divide the melodic lead in the Larghetto. The former states the songlike first theme, which is echoed by the latter, and the violin introduces the lovely, passive subsidiary melody, to be followed by a cello repeat. After delivering the two themes, Mozart brings them both back in an almost literal repeat for the second half of the movement.

Most listeners agree with musicologist Reginald Barrett-Ayres, who calls the Menuetto "one of the most interesting movements in the quartets of Mozart." In several ways it transcends all the others in terms of originality, imaginativeness, and brilliance of writing. Deliberate in tempo, the opening section gives the first violin a *concertante* part and the others subservient roles. The mood becomes more mellow for the short middle part, although it contains quicksilver runs in the cello and then the viola. Mozart ends the Menuetto with an elaboration of the opening section. One of the outstanding features of the dark trio is the insistent rhythm played by pairs of instruments—one playing eighth notes, the other sixteenths—while fragments of melody flit around the quartet. The central part of the trio brings in a new, highly chromatic melody with unexpected second beat accents and a long silence right in the middle. It is followed by an expansion of the first part of the trio and a shortened return of the Menuetto.

The opening of the Allegro assai sounds at first like a bit of fluff that will lead to a light, happy ending. Instead, while never losing its elfin enchantment, the movement proceeds quite seriously, full of contrapuntal wonders and unexpected harmonic twists and turns, to reach a surprisingly quiet conclusion. Formally it is a rather free rondo.

Mozart completed K. 589 in May 1790 and gave the premiere in his apartment in Vienna on the twenty-second of that month.

String Quartet in F Major, K. 590
I. Allegro moderato. II. Allegretto. III. Menuetto: Allegretto. IV. Allegro.

The F major is Mozart's last quartet, written in June 1790, a year and a half before his death. The tenth of his mature quartets, it is actually the twenty-third that he wrote.

The opening theme of the quartet can be simply described as an ascending arpeggio followed by a descending scale. Yet Mozart immediately transforms this basic material, changing the dynamics, the individual notes, and the scoring, thereby effecting a metamorphosis of the character it originally presented. To start the second theme the cello moves up in a broken chord from its very lowest note over two octaves to the new lyrical melody. The first theme returns to end the exposition. A concise development section leads to the recapitulation, which is little changed from the exposition. The coda starts just like the development but quickly winds down to a delightfully attractive, witty ending.

Alfred Einstein, the noted Mozart scholar, says of the Allegretto: "One of the most sensitive movements in the whole literature of chamber music, it seems to mingle the bliss and sorrow of a farewell to life. How beautiful life has been! How sad! How brief!" The basis of this movement is not so much a melody as a rhythm, a plain, rhythmic figure played at the outset by the entire quartet. Mozart then reflects and meditates on this basic cell, plumbing its emotional depths and setting it forth in any number of different guises and postures, allowing it to permeate the entire movement.

The opening of the Menuetto—and, even more, the central trio— is rich in the use of *appoggiaturas,* quick ornamental notes that are played just before main notes. While there are those who dispute whether *appoggiaturas* should be played before the beat (so the main note is on the beat) or on the beat (delaying the main note), most experts now agree that Mozart's *appoggiaturas* should be played squarely *on* the beat. In the Menuetto the *appoggiaturas* precede long notes; in the trio they come before short notes. In addition to the extensive use of *appoggiaturas,* the irregular phrase lengths, seven measures in the Menuetto and five measures in the trio (instead of the customary four measures), contribute to the movement's overall eccentric quality.

The finale, a high-speed, vivacious frolic, unstintingly gives all four players flashy passages that test even the most secure techniques. Cast in a combined rondo and sonata form, this irresistible, appealing movement has intricate fugal and contrapuntal sections, unexpected pauses and silences, harmonic surprises, and even a brief imitation of a bagpipe, making it a brilliant cap to Mozart's tragically short string quartet-writing career.

Clarinet Quintet in A Major, K. 581, "Stadler's Quintet"

I. Allegro. II. Larghetto. III. Menuetto. IV. Allegretto con Variazioni.

Mozart wrote his clarinet quintet for Anton Stadler, friend, fellow Mason, and extremely gifted principal clarinetist of the court orchestra in Vienna, giving it the subtitle, "Stadler's Quintet." From all accounts, though, Stadler was a scoundrel who lived like a parasite in the Mozart home, never repaid the money he borrowed from his host and even stole and sold some of the composer's pawn tickets! But apparently a combination of Mozart's refusal to acknowledge Stadler's failings, his admiration for him as a musician, and his great love for the clarinet was enough to inspire this superb chamber work. Mozart finished the manuscript on September 29, 1789, and gave the first performance, along with Stadler and others, at the Imperial and Royal Court Theater in Vienna on December 22, 1789.

Three distinctive motifs make up the first thematic group of the opening movement: a sedate, lovingly shaped melody for the strings, the clarinet's athletic rejoinder, and a flowing eighth-note figure combined with a derivative of the string opening. After a full stop, the first violin presents the ingratiating second theme, also built on moving eighth notes, but with a more wistful character. As though this were not enough, Mozart presents still another glorious theme, shared between the first violin and clarinet, before the end of the exposition. In the development section, each string instrument plays the clarinet's opening phrase. After a while the clarinet joins in, going in broken chords from its lowest to highest notes. While the treatment may seem mechanical to some, there is no denying the amazing sonorities Mozart achieves. All three themes, slightly modified, are returned for the recapitulation.

The Larghetto is a quiet, soulful *arioso* for the clarinet, its prominence assured by Mozart's instruction that the strings be muted. After presenting the extended principal theme, Mozart introduces as a contrast a slightly more agitated duet for first violin and clarinet. The remainder of the movement is a repeat of these two sections.

Mozart goes far beyond tradition in the third movement; this minuet is much more intense and expressive than the usual dance movement, and it also has an additional trio. After the ardent, emotional Menuetto section, Mozart moves to minor key and strings alone for the somewhat anxious and breathless first trio. The Menuetto, without repeats, returns next, followed by the second trio, a rustic, peasant dance with the clarinet in the lead. The movement ends with another brief review of the Menuetto.

A delightful bit of insolence seeps into the folklike theme of the last movement, which is stated by the strings with afterthoughts from the clarinet. Mozart then puts the theme through six variations: Variations I, IV, and V playfully decorate or ornament the original tune, while II, III, and VI dig deeper into the melody, bringing out various aspects of its basic character. Of particular interest are Variation III, a mournful viola lament in minor key, and the slower Variation V, with its lyrical, but somber, melodic line. Good cheer, though, returns for the final variation, a sprightly close to a gentle and beautiful work.

Viola Quintets, K. 593 and 614

Mozart's last two viola quintets (K. 593 in D major and K. 614 in E flat major) were posthumously published in 1793, but it is still not certain for whom they were written. The newspaper announcement at the time said that they were composed "at the earnest solicitation of a musical friend," and the music itself is inscribed *"Composto per un Amatore Ongarese"* ("Composed for a Hungarian Amateur"). After Mozart's death, his widow, Constanze, offered the opinion that they were written for Johann Tost, a wealthy cloth merchant and excellent amateur violinist of Hungarian extraction, who had commissioned a number of string quartets from Haydn at about the same time.

In any case, these two fine compositions, profound and rich in detail, contain little to betray the fact that they are Mozart's final chamber works, written within one year of his death on December 5, 1791.

Viola Quintet in D Major, K. 593

I. Larghetto; Allegro. II. Adagio. III. Menuetto: Allegretto. IV. Finale: Allegro.

The slow introduction to the first movement is an intimate conversation between the cello and the others. The cello, with its broken chords, tentatively poses the questions, and the others magisterially pronounce their answers. Then the Allegro takes over, sturdy and marchlike, enlivened with the liberal use of cross accents. For the contrasting theme, Mozart merely changes key and writes a canon on the same melody, with the second violin and viola chasing after the first violin and viola at the distance of one measure. Comparatively regular development and recapitulation sections follow. But then, instead of heading toward an ending, Mozart brings back the introduction and a literal repeat of the first eight measures of the Allegro, ending the movement very abruptly at that point.

The first section of the Adagio seems to be the struggle of an optimistic, lyrical phrase to establish itself, only to fall away in despairing, descending sighs. Without resolving this conflict Mozart opens a new section, an enraptured dialogue between first violin and cello, against a throbbing background in the others. An expanded return of the opening focuses even more determinedly on the falling figure and is followed by a review of the duet section. At its conclusion, Mozart appends a coda that bespeaks a strengthened confidence and the dissipation of all weakness and pessimism.

The brisk Menuetto surges with great vitality, despite its rhythmic intricacy. It ends with a climactic canon that pits the two violins against all the others, who lag one measure behind. The trio is based on two musical gestures, a rapidly rising staccato arpeggio and a lyrical phrase of response, with repeated pizzicato notes in the background. At first Mozart confines the melodic activity to the violins but soon allows all the instruments to join in the fun. The Menuetto returns after the trio.

The Finale sports a witty, peppy first violin tune as the principal theme. Without allowing it to lose any of its appeal, Mozart gracefully puts it through some amazing learned contrapuntal paces. Although freely structured as a rondo, the delightful main theme is so frequently heard in its various forms, shapes, and fragments that it easily dominates the entire movement.

Mozart completed the D major quintet in December 1790, exactly one year before he died.

Viola Quintet in E Flat Major, K. 614

I. Allegro di molto.   II. Andante.   III. Menuetto: Allegretto.   IV. Finale: Allegro.

The E flat viola quintet is Mozart's last major chamber work, finished on April 12, 1791, less than eight months before his death. The piece is radiant, sparkling, untroubled, and confident, with no hint of the imminence of Mozart's demise.

The violas open the quintet (unconventional for Mozart) with a bold, declamatory statement that is immediately given a coquettish answer by the two violins. After some highly contrapuntal expansion of the forceful two-viola motif, Mozart transforms the motif into the more lyrical second theme. Brilliant part writing, liberal use of trills, and occasional angry interjections from the cello make this a particularly lively and arresting exposition. With great wit and abandon, Mozart works through the initial motif in the development section. The recapitulation starts like the beginning and proceeds, little changed from the exposition, to an exultant coda with the opening motif triumphant.

A lovely, sensitive melody is the basis of the four freely realized, interconnected variations that make up this movement. After introducing the theme, though, and before starting the variations, Mozart inserts an intense, highly chromatic transitional interlude. In the variations themselves, Mozart treats the original theme in a highly expressive Romantic manner, imbuing the melody with deep meaning and beautiful imagery.

The overriding melodic gesture of the Menuetto is a vigorous, staccato line, descending throughout the section but ending with the two violas playing its inversion. The trio is a startling contrast, legato and sinuous, with strong melancholic overtones and a waltzlike accompaniment. In a particularly adroit bit of cumulative scoring, the first violin states the melody alone, the repeat and extension are played by the first violin and first viola in octaves, and the final statement is played by both violins and the first viola. The movement ends with the return of the crisp, joyful Menuetto.

320

From everything that we know about Mozart, the Finale is an excellent reflection of his personality—boisterous, zesty, full of life, and bubbling with mischievous humor. A jaunty first theme, obviously derived from the coquettish countertheme of the first movement seldom strays from view as Mozart races through this combined rondo-sonata-form movement. The complexity and intricacy of the polyphonic writing are concealed by the gusto and verve of the musical flow.

Carl Nielsen

Born June 9, 1865, at Norre Lyndelse, Denmark
Died October 2, 1931, at Copenhagen

MANY COMPOSERS of Nielsen's time—Edvard Grieg (Norway), Nicolai Rimsky-Korsakov (Russia), Leoš Janáček (Czechoslovakia), Isaac Albeniz (Spain), Jean Sibelius (Finland), Ralph Vaughan Williams (England)—were nationalistic composers who borrowed the melodies and rhythms of native folk music and drew their inspiration from the legends, heroes, and landscapes of their homelands. Nielsen was surely influenced by Danish nationalism and by the folk songs and dances he heard in childhood. Much more than the others, though, he found his musical models in Johannes Brahms, Gustav Mahler, and other German Post-Romantic composers.

Born to a poor house painter, who also played fiddle for local dances and celebrations, Carl received his first music lessons at home. He went on to more formal violin instruction with the local schoolmaster and, by age fourteen, had learned to play the bugle well enough to join a military band. Five years later he entered the Royal Conservatory in Copenhagen where his major composition teacher was Niels Gade. After graduation he became extremely active in the musical life of Denmark's capital city—playing violin in, and later conducting, the opera orchestra and teaching at, and later directing, the conservatory. He also composed an impressive body of works, including two operas, six symphonies, three concertos, four string quartets, and a woodwind quintet.

In Denmark he is revered as the nation's greatest composer; in America and elsewhere, his name was virtually unknown until the mid 1960s when three conductors—Leonard Bernstein, Eugene Ormandy, and Erich Leinsdorf—began performing and championing his symphonies and concertos. Their interest brought Nielsen's music to the attention of the public and has resulted in more frequent exposure to his compositions in concert and through recordings. Although his string quartets are not frequently played, his Woodwind Quintet, which some have hailed as the most distinguished piece of Danish chamber music, appears regularly on concert programs.

Woodwind Quintet, Op. 43

I. Allegro ben moderato. II. Menuet. III. Preludium: Adagio; Tema con variazioni.

In the fall of 1921 Carl Nielsen heard the Copenhagen Wind Quintet perform at a friend's house. He was so impressed with the quality of their playing that he promised to write a piece for them, which he completed early in 1922.

The composer, writing in the third person, prepared this brief description of the warm, gentle quintet.

> The composer has here attempted to present the characteristics of the various instruments. Now they seem to interrupt one another and now they sound alone. The theme for these variations is the tone of one of Carl Nielsen's spiritual songs, which is here made the basis of a number of variations, now gay and grotesque, now elegiac and solemn, ending with the theme itself, simply and gently expressed.

The first theme of the quintet, leisurely and deliberately stated by the bassoon, descends through the notes of a broken chord, pauses, and then rises in scalic motion. The other instruments then join in with playful little phrases until the horn repeats the theme, which is again followed by some more lighthearted banter. The flute and oboe next introduce the second theme, played in octaves and imitating bird calls and nature sounds. After the music comes to a stop, the flute and clarinet share a repeated *ostinato* figure, against which the horn sings out the concluding theme of the exposition, a theme the general contour and feeling of which is not much different from theme one. A brief development then precedes a much-shortened recapitulation stated by flute and oboe.

The principal theme of the Menuet, introduced by the clarinet over a brisk accompaniment in the bassoon, bears a definite stylistic resemblance to Danish country dance tunes. After Nielsen repeats and expands this idea, the oboe starts the contrasting middle section, much more typical of the concert hall than of the village green. The opening section then is heard once more, and the movement ends with a coda built on a scalic figure reminiscent of the first movement's initial theme.

The third movement, the soul of the quintet, was chosen to be played at Nielsen's funeral. A dark, somber prelude comes first, with anguished cadenzalike passages for flute, English horn (played by the oboist), and clarinet. This is followed by Nielsen's setting of the hymn, "My Jesus, make my heart to love Thee." Through the eleven variations of the theme, the composer explores a wide range of moods and characters, from melancholy to comic, before ending with a restatement of the hymn tune, now marked *Andante festivo,* "moderate in speed, festive in character."

Walter Piston

Born January 20, 1894, in Rockland, Maine
Died November 12, 1976, in Belmont, Massachusetts

WALTER PISTON, one of America's most outstanding twentieth-century composers, resists easy classification. His early works, from about 1926 to 1938, are best described as Neoclassical, with clear tonalities, transparent textures, and carefully planned structures. During the years of World War II, 1939 to 1945, Piston was more experimental, adapting elements of the compositional styles of such pioneers as Schoenberg and Stravinsky into his own musical vocabulary. The major portion of his creative life, from about 1946 to 1960, found him consolidating the classical and innovative tendencies into a new synthesis. And during his final period, 1961 to 1976, his music grew even more romantic, personal, and complex. Throughout these somewhat arbitrarily defined periods, two characteristics have infused all of Piston's music: appealing, attractive melodies, and complete command of the craft of musical composition.

Although Piston studied violin as a child, his first love was art, and it was only after graduation from the Massachusetts Normal Art School in 1916 that he began to feel a growing attraction for music. After playing saxophone in a Navy band during World War I, he enrolled as a music student at Harvard, graduating summa cum laude and Phi Beta Kappa. Following graduation he was awarded the John Knowles Paine Fellowship for two years of study in Paris, where he worked with Paul Dukas and Nadia Boulanger. On his return to the United States he was appointed to the faculty at Harvard, a position he held until his retirement in 1960.

Piston was always an active composer, producing an impressive body of works. A list of just his chamber music compositions indicates his fecundity: Three Pieces for Flute, Clarinet, and Bassoon (1925), five string quartets (1933, 1935, 1947, 1951, 1962), Piano

Trio (1935), Quintet for Flute and Strings (1942), Piano Quintet (1949), Woodwind Quintet (1956), String Sextet (1964), and Piano Quartet (1964). Among these works, the "Three Pieces" and the Woodwind Quintet are probably the most popular and are discussed below.

Three Pieces for Flute, Clarinet, and Bassoon
I. Allegro scherzando.   II. Lento.   III. Allegro.

In 1924 Walter Piston received a fellowship for two years of music study in France and enrolled at the École Normale in Paris, where he studied composition with Paul Dukas, while also taking private lessons with Nadia Boulanger. Piston completed "Three Pieces," his first published composition, in Paris in 1925, and the premiere was given there on May 8 of that year, by a trio made up of Blanquart, Coste, and Dherin.

Piston, at that time, was very much influenced by a new artistic movement led by Stravinsky and Hindemith, termed Neoclassicism. Neoclassicism was an attempt to recapture in contemporary music some of the classical and pre-classical qualities found in the music of the distant past. Arising in reaction against late nineteenth-century Romanticism, it favored spare polyphonic texture and an objective, detached approach to writing music. Many composers, including Piston, found Neoclassicism very congenial to their musical conceptions and outlook. When asked about the influences on "Three Pieces," Piston replied, "Certainly Hindemith had something to do with it . . . but no, it may sound corny, but Bach had a great deal more to do with it. More than that, I would say it was in the air."

Piston once said that the "Three Pieces are intended simply as pleasant and mildly diverting pieces to play and listen to. The first playful, the second nostalgic, and the third more dancelike." He compared them to "concise pencil drawings." Woodwind players and audiences alike enjoy them for their abstract qualities, technical excellence, and superb craftsmanship.

Over a four-note repeated bassoon bass line, which is thrown awry by the underlying triple meter, and an *ostinato* clarinet phrase, the flute gives out the rhythmically piquant main theme. The flute and clarinet then exchange roles for a repeat of the melody. All three instruments join together for the subsidiary theme, followed by a return of the opening tune. A brief slow, lyrical section comes next, followed by a literal repeat of the first part, giving the formal structure a classical clarity.

The Lento starts with a sinuous, tightly interwoven line in the flute and clarinet as the bassoon takes the leading role, singing an expressive, though restrained, melody. The melodic interest shifts to the flute for the middle section, with the bassoon echoing its phrases. The movement ends as it began, with the melody in the bassoon.

Over a murmuring flow of rapid flute notes and a syncopated rhythmic line in the bassoon, the clarinet announces the saucy principal theme of the last piece. A short slow interlude, introduced by chirping, birdlike sounds in the flute, precedes a repeat of the first part.

Quintet for Wind Instruments

I. Animato. II. Con tenerezza. III. Scherzando. IV. Allegro comodo.

The Quintet for Wind Instruments, the composer's major work of 1956, was commissioned by the Elizabeth Sprague Coolidge Foundation in the Library of Congress. It was first performed at the Library of Congress on January 24, 1957, by the Boston Woodwind Quintet, a group made up of players from the Boston Symphony.

Piston wrote the following brief note on the work.

> The makeup of the traditional woodwind quintet may be said, in a sense, to be ideal as chamber music, in which the individual voices' blend complement one another without giving up any of their distinction and independence. These five instruments differ strikingly in tone color, tone weight, intensity, dynamic range, expressive power and technical capability. Furthermore, each instrument by itself presents similar differences between the parts of its range. Difficult and fascinating problems arise from these physical facts, not only for the composer but for the performer as well.

The quintet opens with a brittle, rhythmically vibrant tutti theme, but with the flute emerging as the leading voice. After working through this melody, Piston has the French horn introduce the second theme, a lyrical, cantabile melody, considerably different from the previous theme. Following the dictates of classical sonata form, Piston develops the two subjects and brings both back for a restatement.

The second movement, *Con tenerezza* (''with tenderness''), is a theme and variations, in which the theme is varied both melodically and in tone color. The pensive, melancholy theme is introduced by the oboe. This is followed by continuous, interlinked variations for, respectively, the flute, bassoon and horn, clarinet and flute. They are set off by each instrument's individual timbre, as well as by the melodic changes that Piston introduces. The movement ends with the oboe again playing the original theme, but with some subtle rhythmic alterations.

Through some very sharp and crisp part writing, Piston achieves a wonderfully sparkling transparency in the Scherzando. Instead of a full-length contrasting middle section, the composer merely gives the flute a brief cadenzalike interlude before returning to the theme and character of the opening.

In keeping with his interest in the classical forms, Piston fashioned a perfectly constructed rondo as the final movement. It starts with the clarinet stating the principal theme. The entire quintet then plays the first interlude, which stays within a very narrow melodic range in comparison with the main theme's expansive quality. The flute is entrusted with the return of the opening melody, after which the tempo slows and the oboe starts the intricate, contrapuntal second interlude. After some introductory material in the original tempo, the flute sings out the first theme for its second return. Some passages reminiscent of the opening of the entire quintet are heard. The clarinet then reviews the rondo theme for a final time, before a unison playing of the head of the tune ends the movement.

Francis Poulenc

Born January 7, 1899, in Paris
Died January 30, 1963, in Paris

FROM AN early age, Francis Poulenc rebelled against the musical establishment. The first piece to bring him recognition, *Rapsodie Negre,* from 1917, was a setting of a series of nonsense poems, written in gibberish, for baritone and seven instruments. That same year Poulenc and five other young composers—Arthur Honegger, Darius Milhaud, Georges Auric, Germaine Tailleferre, and Louis Durey— came to the defense of Erik Satie, who had caused a sensation in Paris with his score for the ballet *Parade.* The score shocked audiences with its startling dissonances, passages of childlike simplicity, and quotations from music-hall songs and popular waltzes. By supporting Satie, Poulenc demonstrated his rejection of the prevailing Romantic and Impressionist styles, and asserted his support of music that advanced beyond the traditional forms and idioms.

The five young men and one woman who were involved in the Satie affair formed a little ad hoc group to try to advance their musical and esthetic ideas. They came to be known as Les Six. The members agreed that the future of music lay in infusing the musical practices from the past with the new "blood" of jazz and pop music and dedicated themselves to composing works that were simple, light, and entertaining. "We were tired," Poulenc said, "of Debussyism, of Florent Schmitt, of Ravel." In the process they discarded many of the traditional methods of formal organization and invented new structures to contain their music. Following a "back to basics" approach, liberally spiced with special effects designed to startle, amuse, and stimulate, they created music, as Poulenc later wrote, that was, "clear, healthy and robust—music as frankly French in spirit as Stravinsky's *Petrushka* is Russian."

At first Poulenc was not considered one of the leading composers of the group. Many critics refused to take him seriously and regarded his music as well-crafted, witty, and humorous, but lacking in substance and significance. As musicologist David Brew, who shared this negative viewpoint, wrote, "When he [Poulenc] has nothing to say, he says it."

But music history has vindicated Poulenc. Today he ranks high among twentieth-century composers and is generally considered the most creative figure of Les Six. His many songs have earned him a reputation as one of the great vocal composers of recent times. The Concerto for Two Pianos (1932), the Organ Concerto (1938), the opera *Les Dialogues des Carmelites* (1957), and the Gloria (1961), to mention but a few major compositions, are established works in the orchestral and operatic repertoires. And three of his chamber pieces—Sonata for Horn, Trumpet, and Trombone; Trio for Oboe, Bassoon, and Piano; and Sextour for Piano, Flute, Oboe, Clarinet, Bassoon, and Horn—are popular favorites.

Poulenc's chamber music, while generally more conservative in tonal and melodic language than many of the more experimental works being composed over those same decades, is still unmistakably modern. Sparkling with Gallic wit and sophistication, it catches us off-guard with unexpected modulations or stretches of wrong-note harmony. Its wonderful melodies often evoke the ambiance of the French cabaret, the dance hall, the circus, or the street fair. And it always clothes its musical message in sounds that charm, entertain, and delight.

Sonata for Horn, Trumpet, and Trombone

I. Allegro moderato: Grazioso.   II. Andante: Très lent.   III. Rondeau: Animé.

Francis Poulenc's upper-class parents insisted on giving their son a classical education which, despite an early interest in music, left him scant time for the study of composition. He had lessons with Maurice Ravel and Paul Vidal, but they provided little of the basic grounding that he sought.

It wasn't until after he had served in the French army from 1921 to 1924 that he received his only formal training in composition, with Charles Koechlin. And it was in 1922, while under Koechlin's tutelage, that Poulenc wrote the Sonata for Horn, Trumpet, and Trombone. (Modern performances use the revision Poulenc prepared in 1945.) The sonata, a work that dazzles with clever instrumental writing, delightful variety of tone colors, shocking dissonances, humor and elegant wit, melodic appeal, and rhythmic verve, also amazes with the composer's expert craftsmanship and deft handling of the musical material.

The episodic first movement opens with a little trumpet tune of folklike charm, which gives way in time to a cantabile melody in a slower tempo. A short, jolly third section, started by the horn at a faster tempo, is based on a rhythmic reworking of the first tune. Poulenc introduces still another melody played by the trumpet before a return of the opening melody leads to a joking, wrong-note ending.

The two principal lullabylike themes of the Andante are derived from the slow second theme of the first movement. The second theme's opening contour is essentially an inversion, a mirror image, of the shape of the first theme. The first theme returns to end the ternary form movement.

The trumpet and horn in unison state the principal theme of the mercurial Rondeau, with its indecision between major and minor. Poulenc presents various short episodes between appearances of the theme in this lightweight movement, ending it all with wonderfully comic touches in the coda.

Trio for Oboe, Bassoon, and Piano

I. Presto: Lento; Presto. II. Andante. III. Rondo: Très vif.

Poulenc composed the Trio for Oboe, Bassoon, and Piano from February to April 1926, while staying on the French Riviera at Cannes. A tight, concise piece, the trio very successfully captures the classical spirit of Mozart and decks it out in modern garb. Clear-cut and confident, it is considered Poulenc's first major chamber music work.

The musical burden for most of the trio is borne by the piano, with the bassoon contributing its comments and asides, and the oboe going off on its own flights of lyrical fancy. The first movement begins with a short, slow introduction. Written to be played very freely, it has the character of an operatic recitative, now grave and solemn, now wry and ironic. The following Presto is most scintillating and effervescent. Formally it is extremely episodic, with themes of wit and charm succeeding one another.

The brief, slow movement, a pure lyrical outpouring, is essentially one extended song.

The high-speed Rondo glistens on the surface with vivacious good humor, though the oboe imparts a slightly sardonic edge to the glitter. Varied interludes appear between the repetitions of the principal theme. Although melodically different, they maintain the same good spirit until the abrupt, unexpected ending catches us all by surprise.

Sextour for Piano, Flute, Oboe, Clarinet, Bassoon, and Horn

I. Allegro vivace: Très Vite et emporte. II. Divertissement: Andantino. III. Finale: Prestissimo.

A quick series of loud scales opens the Sextour, or Sextet, with an exciting flourish—except that it lands on the "wrong" note (a G sharp instead of the expected A)! Undaunted, Poulenc immediately tosses out a succession of rapid, vivacious, bubbly motifs and melodies, seasoned with occasional flutter-tongue passages in the flute. Suddenly everything stops, and the bassoon plays a cadenza, after which the tempo is halved, and the movement's merry character is dramatically and abruptly altered, as the piano introduces a somber melody that is basically an augmentation of the fast first theme. Other themes follow, all in the new serious mood, before Poulenc brings a short, freely realized return of the opening section, with the gaiety somehow not as convincing now as it was before the sobering middle part. The horn leads off the marchlike final section, and the movement ends with a flourish similar to the opening.

The title of the second movement, Divertissement, leads us to expect a lightweight entertainment; yet careful listening reveals that Poulenc had something a bit more serious in mind. In the first section, the oboe melody, marked *très doux et expressif* ("very sweet and expressive"), and other beautifully crafted melodies are passed around the group. But before we can grow too reflective, the tempo doubles for a gay, rollicking middle section that is believed to have its antecedents in an old circus song. A truncated reminder of the opening gives the movement its A-B-A form.

All instruments, except the bassoon, play happy chirping sounds to introduce the exciting Finale, in which lively, highly rhythmic passages alternate with smoothly sung lyrical phrases. The good-humored feelings that have carried over from the opening of the Sextour are maintained. But then, as if to underline the fact that this is more than a piece just for fun, the composer appends a rather solemn coda, melodically related to the first theme of the first movement. The work then ends with a stridently dissonant chord, which leaves us wondering whether the conclusion contradicts the previous joyful good humor.

Originally composed from 1930 to 1932, the Sextour was completely reworked in 1939.

Sergei Prokofiev

Born April 23, 1891, in Sontsovka, Russia
Died March 5, 1953, in Moscow

SERGEI PROKOFIEV once said, "And as far as politics, they don't concern me. It is none of my business." Ironically enough, his life was more affected by the political turmoil in the world around him than almost any other composer.

Prokofiev showed his amazing musical talent when still very young, and his mother, an excellent amateur pianist, started giving him lessons before he was five years old. By age thirteen he was enrolled at the Saint Petersburg Conservatory, where his fantastic mind and outstanding gift for music were often obscured by his harsh, abrasive personality, an obvious lack of respect for his teachers, and contempt for the other students. One of his least endearing traits reportedly was to compile lists of all the mistakes his fellow pupils made in class!

The Russian Revolution, a few years after Prokofiev's 1914 graduation from the Conservatory, disrupted the fabric of life throughout the country. Afraid that the new regime would be antagonistic to composers, Prokofiev went into self-imposed exile, first living in New York and then Paris. By late 1920, though, homesick and not unsympathetic to communist ideals, Prokofiev yearned to resume life in his native country. Twice he went on extended concert tours of the Soviet Union to see conditions for himself, but both times hesitated to move back, fearing the power of the Russian Association of Proletarian Musicians (RAPM), an organization formed in 1925 to rid Russian music of decadent foreign influence and to promote socially responsible, realistic music in the service of the Soviet state. In 1933, one year after the government dissolved the RAPM, Prokofiev finally returned home.

Over the remaining two decades of his life, Prokofiev's music was continually subject to official scrutiny and appraisal. When he was in favor with the politicians his music was widely performed. But at other times, such as in 1936 and even more in 1948, when he was under attack, he had to apologize humbly and compose music on themes that pleased the authorities.

In connection with the celebrations surrounding his fiftieth birthday in 1941, Prokofiev prepared a brief autobiographical sketch detailing the major trends he recognized in his music: Classical ("its origin lying in my early childhood when I heard my mother play the sonatas of Beethoven. It assumes a neoclassical aspect"); innovation (". . . the search for an individual harmonic language, but was later transformed into the desire of finding a medium in which to express the stronger emotions"); motor element (". . . it was probably influenced by Schumann's Toccata, which impressed me greatly at one time. This element is probably the least important"); lyrical (". . . appearing first as lyric meditation, sometimes unconnected with melos . . . but sometimes found in long melodic phrases. This lyric strain has for a long time remained obscured, or perceived only in retrospect, and, since my lyricism has long been denied appreciation, it has developed slowly"); grotesque (". . . merely a variation of the other characteristics. In application to my music, I should like to replace the word 'grotesque' by 'scherzo-ness,' or by three words indicating its gradations: 'jest,' 'laughter,' and 'mockery.'").

Prokofiev's four chamber works show the distinguishing characteristics he mentioned in his own analysis. Three compositions— Overture on Hebrew Themes and the two string quartets—are discussed below, omitting only the infrequently performed Quintet, Op. 39.

Overture on Jewish Themes, Op. 34

Just after the Russian Revolution of 1917, Prokofiev decided to emigrate to America, believing that there was no place or need for artists in the new Soviet society. While living in New York in the fall of 1919, he was asked by a group of former classmates from the Saint Petersburg Conservatory to write a piece for them based on Jewish themes. The group, called Zimro, consisting of a string quartet, clarinet, and piano, had come to America to raise money for a conservatory in Jerusalem by giving concerts of chamber music works by

Jewish composers. Since Prokofiev was not Jewish and did not know Jewish folk themes, they gave him a notebook filled with traditional melodies to use as a source.

Prokofiev refused at first; he did not approve of writing music based on borrowed themes. But one day as he was glancing through the book of Jewish songs, "to while away the time," he began improvising at the piano on a few of the melodies. Suddenly, he said, he "noticed that somehow whole sections began to take shape. I worked all of the following day and sketched out the entire overture." It took him ten more days to complete the score, and Zimro gave the highly successful first performance in New York on January 26, 1920.

The overture is based on two Jewish themes. The first, a playful, almost humorous, dance tune, is introduced by the first clarinet over a simple rhythmic accompaniment. The melody is characterized by the interval of an augmented second, which is so typical of Jewish and Middle Eastern music. The tempo picks up for a transition of sustained chords in the clarinet and strings and a murmuring repeated figure in the piano that leads to the second theme, a melancholy, plaintive lament, first given out by the cello high in its range. Prokofiev then proceeds to a brief development of the first theme, at one point fragmenting the melody in true *klezmer* style, another time playing the tune in a mirror inversion. After a short recapitulation of both themes, the coda slowly builds up momentum to reach the forceful final chords.

String Quartet No. 1 in B Minor, Op. 50

I. Allegro. II. Andante molto; Vivace. III. Andante.

During Prokofiev's fifteen years of self-imposed exile from Russia (1918 to 1933), he concertized widely as a piano soloist and at the same time continued composing. While he was on a tour of the United States in 1930, the Elizabeth Sprague Coolidge Foundation of the Library of Congress in Washington commissioned him to write a string quartet, his first. He completed the composition later that year, and it received its premiere at the Library on April 25, 1931.

The String Quartet No. 1 is a predominantly serious, deeply felt work, although there are extended sections in Prokofiev's light, witty, slightly sardonic style. The first movement opens with a wide-ranging saucy, thumb-to-the-nose tune in the first violin, which grows somewhat grotesque as the melody progresses. Both violins state the next theme, moody and brooding in contrast to the brilliant first theme. A brisk, marchlike theme, with a propulsive dotted (long-short) rhythmic figure in the second violin and viola, brings the exposition to a close. After a brief development section a string of sharp repeated notes in the first violin signals the start of the recapitulation with its varied return of the three themes.

Contrary to tradition, Prokofiev starts the second movement, which is really a scherzo, with a grave, melancholy introduction. The viola and cello open the fast Vivace section with a bright, catchy little tune that stays in the instruments' lowest registers, robbing it of some of its effervescence. The violin responds with a phrase taken from the introduction. Once launched, the movement drives forward with great motoric energy, featuring rapid bowed passages, moving pizzicato lines, and lyrical stretches of melody. The character changes as the three upper instruments play repeated notes at the bottom end of the bow and the cello contributes loud pizzicato accents. This leads to the high-pitched, forceful second theme, which is sung out by the cello. After coming to an abrupt stop, the music resumes quietly, with a shortened and somewhat altered return of the opening section.

Prokofiev, as well as most commentators on his music, consider the long, emotional Andante the quartet's crowning achievement. The composer communicates deep feelings and powerful passions through a direct and muscular approach, avoiding all sentimentality. The Russian-style melodies are treated quite rhapsodically, but with subtle interconnections and a softly throbbing accompaniment that unifies the entire movement. The Andante ends on a note of despair, but with a sense of inner strength and fortitude. Perhaps the firmness of spirit is related to the fact that Prokofiev, at the time, was planning to return to his beloved Russia.

String Quartet No. 2 in F Major, Op. 92

I. Allegro sostenuto.   II. Adagio.   III. Allegro.

In June 1941, Hitler tore up Germany's nonaggression pact with the Soviet Union and hurled his army into a *blitzkreig* attack on Russia. A succession of stunning military victories carried the Nazis deep into Russian territory. In August the Soviet government, fearing the advancing Germans, evacuated a group of leading artists, composers, and writers, including Sergei Prokofiev, from Moscow to the quiet little town of Nalchik in the Kabardino-Balkaria Autonomous Republic region of the northern Caucasus mountains.

At Nalchik Prokofiev met the local art administrator, who introduced him to the wealth of little-known folk music from the area. Prokofiev was inspired to use several of the melodies for a new string quartet, in which he aimed to achieve "a combination of virtually untouched folk material and the most classical of classical forms, the string quartet." He began work on his String Quartet No. 2 on November 2 and was finished some five weeks later. It is of interest that the start of the premiere performance in Moscow by the Beethoven Quartet, on September 5, 1942, was delayed because of a German air raid.

Most official critics praised Prokofiev for using the songs and dances of Kabardino-Balkaria, and for maintaining the color, character, and imagery of this folk material. At the same time, though, they criticized him for the excessive use of "barbaric" harmonies and "strident" timbres and for his severe and uncompromising emphasis on the music's primitive power. Nevertheless, the piece scored an immediate success, and its blend of folklore and modern harmony continues to attract listeners.

The forceful, aggressive principal theme of the first movement, which Prokofiev took from an authentic Kabardian folk song, combines childlike naivete with menacing belligerence. The unrelenting intensity holds until the three lower voices start a repeated two-note back-and-forth figure over which the first violin announces a sharply marked round-dance tune. The concluding, more lyrical theme of the exposition is the most cheerful of the three. The development section, harsh and grotesque at times, is a kaleidoscope of brilliant sonorities and tonal effects, and the recapitulation is a shortened, literal reprise of the exposition.

After a few introductory measures, the cello sings the melody of the Kabardian love song, *"Synilyaklik Zhir,"* against a murmured, oriental-style background. A stretch of subtly shifting tone colors intervenes, before the second violin and viola repeat the theme in unison, with the viola playing tremolo *ponticello*. For the middle section, Prokofiev very brilliantly transforms the motif of a folk dance, *"Islambey,"* into the accompaniment, imitating the sound of a native Caucasian instrument—the kemange. The melody here is a light-spirited free alteration of the original love song. The movement ends with a brief return of the opening.

A vital, vigorous mountain dance, *"Getigezhev Ogurbi,"* is the basis for the opening of the last movement. Its continuation bears some resemblance to the first movement's opening theme. The viola and cello start a fast, agitated passage that becomes the accompaniment to an uneasy lyrical violin melody. A reminder of the opening is followed by a slightly slower, more relaxed episode. The tempo picks up for a varied return of the opening. A cadenza for the cello leads to an excited development section, after which there is a return of the previously heard tunes, but in reverse order.

Maurice Ravel

Born March 7, 1875, in Ciboure, France
Died December 28, 1937, in Paris

MAURICE RAVEL had a distant or reserved manner that set him slightly apart, some say aloof, from the world around him. He was loath to form strong personal attachments and disinclined to espouse any one esthetic, philosophical, or political creed. Even in his music he did not invoke deep, personal feelings; while his tone is emotional, he maintains an objective rather than subjective approach.

Born in the Basque region of France, in the Pyrenees, near the Spanish border, Ravel moved with his family to Paris when he was just three months old, and it was in and around that city that he spent his childhood. At age seven, he began piano lessons, and at fourteen entered the Paris Conservatoire, where his major composition teacher was Gabriel Fauré. Ravel was not very successful at school; four times he applied for and was denied the coveted Prix de Rome. Nevertheless, by the time he left the Conservatoire in 1903, he had become a consummate composer, as his String Quartet (1902–1903) attests so well.

At about this time, Ravel became associated with a small, loosely organized group of young Parisian artists, poets, musicians, and intellectuals who took the name Apaches, because they regarded themselves as social outcasts. In the words of member Leon-Paul Farque, "Ravel shared our preference, weakness or mania respectively for Chinese art, Mallarmé and Verlaine, Rimbaud and Corbiere, Cezanne and Van Gogh, Rameau and Chopin, Whistler and Valery, the Russians and Debussy." An intellectual and a scholar, Ravel accepted the belief that music, painting, and literature were part of one art and that they differed only in their means of expression.

Ravel's music from these early years was considered revolutionary. Already he had achieved virtuosic control in his writing, enabling him to shock, enchant, or excite the ear as he desired. And deriving inspiration from the music of the Far East, as well as from Debussy, he did indeed explore a wide range of tonal possibilities. In later years he tended more to the Neoclassical, showing what was considered a conservative preference for clarity, logic, and overall restraint.

Ravel led a quiet life. Although he did some private teaching and occasionally performed or conducted his own music, he made everything subsidiary to his full-time preoccupation with composing. He crafted his music as fastidiously and carefully as he dressed, every note being cautiously weighed and considered before it was entered. As a consequence, he left only a small body of music, including some immensely popular orchestra works (such as *Bolero* and *La Valse*). His best-known chamber works are his Quartet in F and Piano Trio, which are discussed below. The other chamber compositions are Introduction and Allegro for Harp, String Quartet, Flute and Clarinet (1906), and Sonata for Violin and Cello (1922).

Opposed by his critics for being an imitator rather than an originator of styles, and championed by others for his extraordinary talent to create in several different styles, Ravel wrote music that, in his words, "continues to charm and remains always music." About his approach, Ravel once wrote:

> The fact is I refuse simply and absolutely to confound the *conscience* of an artist, which is one thing, with his *sincerity,* which is another. The latter is of no value unless the former helps to make it apparent. This conscience compels us to turn ourselves into good craftsmen. My objective, therefore, is technical perfection. I can strive unceasingly to this end, since I am certain of never being able to attain it. The important thing is to get nearer to it all the time. Art, no doubt, has other *effects,* but the artists, in my opinion, should have no other aim.

Ironically enough, near the end of his life, Ravel said that he would willingly exchange the technical perfection of his mature works, such as the piano trio, for the artless strength of his youth, as heard in his string quartet.

String Quartet in F Major

I. Allegro moderato—Très doux.   II. Assez vif—Très rhythmé.   III. Très lent.   IV. Vif et agité.

Even though Ravel worked on his sole string quartet from late 1902 to April 1903, while still a student at the Paris Conservatoire, it is far from a student work. The piece integrates the several styles that he had incorporated into his own musical vocabulary. A major influence was Debussy, and particularly Debussy's Quartet in G minor, with its Impressionist quality and fascinating tone colors. At the same time, the clear and transparent textures, the impelling logic, and tight control of the basic organization bear testimony to Ravel's strong Neoclassical proclivity and admiration for Mozart. Finally, some of the strange and unfamiliar tonal effects reflect an interest in the exotic music of the Far East.

The generally excellent initial reactions to the quartet included some sharp criticism, with a few commentators even suggesting that Ravel make extensive revisions. Debussy, a good if not intimate friend of Ravel, advised the younger composer, "In the name of the gods of music, and in mine, do not touch a single note of what you have written in your quartet." Despite this evidence of Debussy's support and approval, a comparison of the Debussy and Ravel quartets became a prime subject of newspaper and cafe debate in Paris, resulting in a breach between the two men. Eventually Ravel was moved to comment sadly, "It's probably better for us, after all, to be on frigid terms for illogical reasons."

The quartet opens with a thematic group that contains two distinctive ideas: a rich, warmly scored melody involving the entire quartet and a first violin melody of similar character over rapid figures in the second violin and viola. After speeding up to a climax, the music quiets, and the soaring second theme is stated by the first violin and viola playing two octaves apart, producing a most striking tone color. Although the rest of the movement follows the dictates of regular sonata form, the precise writing, the exciting tonal effects, and the powerful climaxes make this a most impressive movement.

Ravel conjures up the sound of a Javanese *gamelan* orchestra in the swift-moving pizzicato opening of the second movement by having the outer instruments playing in 3/4 meter (three groups of two eighth notes to a measure), while the inner parts play in 6/8 meter (two groups of three eighths in the same measure). Trills and tremolos create a lustrous sheen as the movement continues. The cello alone plays a transition to the slow, moody middle section. Although they are not exactly parallel, the extremely lyrical themes here seem to grow from the second subject of the first movement. A shortened reprise of the opening section concludes the movement.

Ravel achieves an improvisatory rhapsodic feeling in the slow third movement, with its continually shifting tempi and episodic construction. He is also able, with consummate skill, to weave the opening melody of the quartet in with the new melodic content. As in the previous movements, there is an ever-changing progression of new and imaginative tone colors, a remarkable achievement, considering the fact Ravel had at his disposal only the four instruments, not the strings, winds, and percussion of a symphony orchestra.

The vigorous finale opens with an angry snarl followed by a long, held note, repeated twice before the movement starts moving forward. Its awkward five-beat meter, possibly Russian in inspiration, lends it an unsettling character. The rest of the movement alternates the contrasting expressive and lyrical melodies, including returns of the first movement theme, with repeats of the opening outburst.

The quartet, which was dedicated to Fauré, was introduced in Paris by the Heymann Quartet on March 5, 1904.

Piano Trio in A Minor

I. Modéré. II. Pantoum: Assez vif. III. Passacaille: Très large. IV. Final: Animé.

When friend Maurice Delage asked Ravel about a piano trio he had been discussing for some time, but had not yet started to write, the composer replied, "My Trio is finished. I only need the themes for it." The jesting, offhand remark was probably quite accurate; Ravel had thought through the style of the instrumental writing and the formal structure he would follow. All that he lacked were the melodies with which to realize his conception.

Ravel began the actual composition of the trio during the summer of 1913 that he was spending at St. Jean-de-Luz, a city in the Basque region of France near where he was born. But he made little progress until the following year, when he began intensive work in April. As he struggled to complete the trio, the imminent outbreak of World War I drove Ravel to a frenzy. "I think that at any moment I shall go mad or lose my mind," he wrote to his friend, Cypa Godebski, on August 3, just before he finished. "I have never worked so hard, with such insane heroic rage."

Considering the great emotional turmoil that we know he was experiencing during this period, the music is remarkably remote and objective, with no reference to extra-musical events. True to his belief that "one can have a head and have guts, but never a heart," he kept his personal feelings to himself yet was able to make the trio an intense, expressive piece of music.

346

Ravel derived the rhythm for the Modéré first theme from a popular Basque folk dance with an underlying 3–2–3 rhythm. This folklike theme, stated first by the piano and then by the strings, undergoes several remarkable transformations in the course of the movement. The violin introduces the second theme, which is slightly slower but in the same 3–2–3 rhythm. It places incredible virtuosic demands on all three players, forcing them to exploit their instruments to the limit in order to obtain the amazing range of tone colors and effects that Ravel seeks.

The composer titles the bright and sparkling second movement Pantoum from *pantun,* a Malayan verse form that was used on occasion by Victor Hugo and Charles Baudelaire and also became the basis of a type of declamatory, guitar-accompanied song. Really a scherzo, the movement opens with a series of sharp, highly rhythmic motifs. After building to a climax, the music quiets and the violin plays a transition to a solemn chordal progression, which is played by the piano while the strings continue their sprightly patter. This middle section is actually polymetric; the strings remain in 3/4 time, while the piano switches to 4/2 time, creating a fascinating interplay of cross accents. The concluding section recalls the opening portion.

The Passacaille, or passacaglia, is based on a famous Baroque form in which a melody, usually in triple meter, is subjected to continuous variation. The eight-measure theme is heard first in the bass of the piano, and each of the variations that follows raises it in pitch and increases its textural density. The dynamics and intensity continue to build to the seventh variation, after which the music starts its descent, dropping in power and ending with the tenth variation played by the piano alone. Some of the most fervent, impassioned music of the entire trio is found in this movement.

The music proceeds without pause to the Final, a musical tour de force. The instrumental writing is spectacular, with Ravel using all sorts of technical devices to create an amazing range of sonic effects. The first theme is an inversion of the first theme of the Modéré; the subsidiary theme is an expansive outpouring by the piano while the strings sustain many measures of trills. With flashing virtuosic runs the music coruscates to a dazzling conclusion.

The trio, which was dedicated to André Gédalge, Ravel's counterpoint teacher at the Conservatoire, received its first performance in Paris on January 28, 1915, played by Alfredo Casella, piano, Gabriel Willaume, violin, and Louis Feuillard, cello.

Antonin Reicha

Born February 26, 1770, in Prague
Died May 28, 1836, in Paris

DURING HIS lifetime, Antonin Reicha was highly respected as an extremely gifted, successful, and prolific composer; his works extend to Op. 107! As a teacher, he numbered among his students such major figures as Berlioz, Liszt, Franck, and Gounod. And the four texts that he wrote on various aspects of musical composition brought him honor as a theoretician. Yet today Reicha's claim to fame rests almost exclusively on his twenty-four woodwind quintets and his friendship with Beethoven.

Reicha received his early training in flute, violin, and piano from his uncle, Joseph Reicha. In 1785 he secured the post of second flute in the orchestra at Bonn, where he became very friendly with a violinist, also fifteen years old, named Ludwig van Beethoven. According to some accounts, Reicha actually shared living quarters with the young Beethoven. With only minimal outside help, Reicha taught himself composition, and within ten years, he was well established as a composer, spending periods of time in Hamburg, Paris, and Vienna, overseeing performances of his music, as well as teaching. In 1808 he settled in Paris, becoming a professor at the Paris Conservatoire ten years later.

In his *Autobiography* Reicha discusses the process that led him to start composing woodwind quintets in 1811, compositions that are now considered the first significant works for this combination of instruments.

There was a dearth not only of good classic music, but of any good music for wind instruments, simply because the composers knew little of their technique. The effects that a combination of these instruments could produce had not been explored. Instrumentalists have made enormous strides in the past twenty years, their instruments have been perfected by the addition of keys, but there was no worthwhile music to show their possibilities. Such was the state of affairs when I conceived the idea of writing a quintet for a combination of the five principal wind instruments (flute, oboe, clarinet, horn and bassoon). My first attempt was a failure, and I discarded it. A new style of composition was necessary for these instruments, which are between the voices and strings. Combinations of a particular kind had to be devised in order to strike the listener. After much thought and careful study of the possibilities of each instrument, I made my second attempt, and wrote two very successful quintets. A few years later I had completed the six that make up the first book [Op. 88].

The first group of quintets created a demand for more, and over the following few years Reicha finished three additional groups of six each—Opp. 91, 99, and 100—making twenty-four quintets in all. Although each quintet is unique, they do share some general characteristics. Their texture is more contrapuntal than homophonic; even with today's more advanced technique, musicians find the parts quite difficult to play. They are all in four movements: typically a first movement with a slow introduction followed by the lengthy, fast section in sonata form; a slow second; a third-movement minuet that is usually quite short; and a cheerful virtuosic finale to show the players off to their best advantage.

Woodwind Quintet in G Major, Op. 88, No. 3

I. Lento; Allegro assai.   II. Andante.   III. Minuetto: Allegro vivo.   IV. Finale: Allegro vivace.

Antonin Reicha did not have a particular performing group in mind when he wrote his woodwind quintets, since no such organization existed at the time. But he was inspired by five of the leading instrumentalists in Paris—Joseph Guillou, flute, August-Gustave Vogt, oboe, Jacque-Jules Bouffil, clarinet, Louis-Francoise Dauprat, French horn, and Antoine-Nicola Henry, bassoon—who enthusiastically encouraged Reicha to write for the combination, expertly performed the works he wrote, and clamored for additional compositions. What more could any composer ask?

The G major quintet starts with a slow introduction after which the flute dashes up the scale to start the fast section with a bouncy, joyful theme. Other brief motifs follow and build up to a climax

before the subsidiary theme—a rising triplet figure in the bassoon—
is introduced. With great energy and verve Reicha then puts the several motifs through their paces, following the general outline of standard sonata form.

The clarinet starts the slow movement with a short, sighing, syncopated figure that imparts a gently rocking motion to the music.
The end of the phrase bears an unmistakable similarity to the first
theme of the previous movement. Reicha then varies the melody in
continuous, improvisatory-sounding variations. He ends the movement with the clarinet stating the theme as before, but this time in
a completely new contrapuntal setting.

The fast tempo, the one-beat-to-a-bar meter and the rhythmic
pattern of one note to a bar makes the Minuetto feel like a scherzo.
The following trio offers no great contrast to the first section. After
the trio, the Minuetto comes back again, and finally both the trio
and Minuetto are repeated one last time.

The Finale abounds in attractive ingratiating tunes, with a succession of fresh, delightful melodies following, one after the other. By
employing a form related to a rondo, Reicha gives the listener more
than one chance to enjoy each of several themes.

Reicha composed his G major quintet around 1815 in Paris, where
it was given its premiere by Reicha's five woodwind-playing friends.

George Rochberg

Born July 5, 1918, in Paterson, New Jersey

GEORGE ROCHBERG'S musical development shows a constant search to achieve what he describes as "the most potent and effective way to translate my musical energy into the clearest and most direct patterns of feeling and thought." He was trained at the Mannes College and Curtis Institute, and his early compositions, among them the String Quartet No. 1 (1952), tended to be vigorous and energetic, as well as highly emotional; they show the influence of such composers as Stravinsky, Bartók, and Hindemith.

Over the following years, Rochberg turned to atonality (lack of key or tonality) and serialism (applying the principles of twelve-tone music not only to pitch, but to rhythm, dynamics, and tone color as well), moving closer to the approach to composition associated with Schoenberg and his school. The composer, and others, consider the Second String Quartet (1959–1961) and Second Symphony (1955–1956) the best works from this period.

By the early 1960s, though, Rochberg found that, "the over-intense manner of serialism and its tendency to inhibit physical pulse and rhythm led me to question a style which made it virtually impossible to express serenity, tranquility, grace, wit, energy." He entered what he calls "the time of turning," and "engaged in an effort to rediscover the larger and more sweeping gestures of the past, to reconcile my love for that past and its traditions with my relation to the present and its often destructive pressures." The result of this reexamination is a style of composition that has been given the sobriquet "new Romanticism."

Mr. Rochberg has completed seven string quartets. He has enjoyed, over the years of their creation, a very close relationship with the Concord String Quartet, which has performed and recorded all of his works in that form, as well as his piano quintet (1975).

In addition to his rather considerable musical output, Rochberg spent several years as director of publications at Theodore Presser Music Publishers and taught at the University of Pennsylvania from 1960 to 1983, when he retired as Emeritus Annenberg Professor of the Humanities.

String Quartet No. 3

I. Introduction: Fantasia.
II. March. III. Variations. IV. March.
V. Finale: Scherzos and Serenades.

The String Quartet No. 3 represents a significant milestone in George Rochberg's oeuvre. It is the first major work in a style now loosely referred to as the "new Romanticism," in which he combines tonality, with an established key center, and atonality, in which there is no feeling of key. "The decision of which to use," Rochberg says, "depends entirely on the character and essence of the musical gesture." Rochberg feels that this approach to composition, which he evolved during the 1960s, gives him the freedom he needs and "denies neither the past nor the present."

The Third String Quartet was commissioned by the Concord String Quartet, which gave the premiere performance in New York City on May 15, 1972. In describing the work, Rochberg said, "In this quartet I draw heavily on the melodic-harmonic language of the nineteenth century (even more specifically on the 'styles' of Beethoven and Mahler)."

Rochberg has written the following analysis of his third quartet:

The fantasia-like introduction contains both atonal and tonal ideas, violent and tranquil gestures, directly juxtaposed to each other without apparent connection. While each of the two marches is a unit by itself, they share common ideas—tunes, accompaniments, gestural attitudes. The second March takes off, after its own introduction, from a tune barely suggested at the end of the first March and proceeds on its way to finally work back to common ground. The Variations (on a theme of my own) are clearly and unambiguously tonal (in A major) and embrace the harmonic/polyphonic palette of the Classical and Romantic traditions. The Finale develops out of the alternation of Scherzos and Serenades: the first Scherzo, highly chromatic and rhythmic, is followed by the first Serenade which is tonal (in D major); the center Scherzo (in B flat) is a *fugato* whose motivic ideas are derived from the initial Scherzo-Serenade confrontation: the Serenade is repeated with minor alterations and expanded somewhat; out of its last open-ended phrase comes the final Scherzo which extends and amplifies the first one, carrying the quartet to its conclusion.

Arnold Schoenberg

Born September 13, 1874, in Vienna
Died July 13, 1951, in Los Angeles

ARNOLD SCHOENBERG once characterized his position in music by say-ing, "I am a conservative who was forced to become a radical." Throughout his life he maintained a strong allegiance to the music of the past, even while introducing innovations that completely transformed the history of modern music. Although he had a large and varied musical output, it is his chamber music that most clearly reveals his metamorphosis.

Schoenberg's first exposure to music was through violin lessons, which led him to start composing chamber music while still very young. The earliest work to bring him recognition as a composer was the D major string quartet (1897). A charming, melodic piece, it shows its debt to Brahms's principles of motivic organization and to the harmonic freedom of Wagner. The most perfectly realized com-position in this early style is the string sextet *Verklaerte Nacht* (1899). This richly romantic work quickly became the most popular and fre-quently performed of all his musical efforts. He continued the di-rection he struck with *Verklaerte Nacht* for nearly a decade.

In his String Quartet No. 2, Op. 10 (1908), Schoenberg departed from the concept of tonal music that had prevailed for some 200 years. While the first three movements conform to the older style, the melodies and harmonies of the final movement destroy all feeling of key and tonality, making it the first example of atonality.

Over the following years, Schoenberg produced several atonal works, including the well-known *Pierrot Lunaire*. From 1915 to 1923, he composed nothing, due in part to the disruption of World War I, but also because he was formulating an approach to composition that would carry atonality even further. He called this new technique "method of composition with twelve tones."

The basic concept of twelve-tone music is that all the notes of the chromatic scale must be heard before any can be repeated. The tone row, which contains the twelve tones in a particular order, acts as a sort of replacement for the melody of traditional music. The row can be heard sequentially, as a melody, or simultaneously, as in chords, or in a combination of both. And it can be inverted, reversed, and altered in any number of different ways. In effect, twelve-tone music gives the composer a positive organizing principle to substitute for the negative avoidance of key that was the basis of atonality. Schoenberg's Piano Suite, Op. 25 (1925) was his initial twelve-tone composition.

The course that Schoenberg charted, first of atonality and then twelve-tone composition, brought him virtually no public recognition and precious little respect in the musical community. Yet he perserveved, probably because of a strong drive that came from within and an intense desire to move music beyond what had been written before. He said that composers have to write "various themes and melodies that incorporate intervals and rhythms that have not been heard before and in a new way."

Schoenberg's change in style was also a reaction to the political and intellectual foment of the era. By the early years of the new century the power of the Austro-Hungarian Empire, a stable, prosperous, and highly cultured nation at the time of Schoenberg's birth, was crumbling. The basic relationships of space, mass, and time were being questioned by Albert Einstein's special theory of relativity. And Sigmund Freud's newly enunciated theory of the unconscious was challenging the belief that people were masters of their own thoughts and actions.

"Supposing times were normal," Schoenberg later wrote, "normal as they were before 1914—then the music of our time would be in a different situation." Like much of the contemporary artistic production, Schoenberg's music was influenced by the cataclysmic political, social, scientific, and psychological upheavals of the time. Just as the Expressionist painters, such as Kandinsky, Nolde, Kokoschka, and Marc, were distorting perspective, using overly bright, jarring colors, and even dispensing with recognizable objects, so Schoenberg was replacing traditional harmony with atonality and twelve-tone writing, introducing sharp dissonances and doing away with the usual concept of melody.

Schoenberg was convinced that his mission in life was to forge new directions for music, thereby enriching the culture of his beloved

Germany. When he was ready to announce the twelve-tone system, he told a student, "I have discovered something that will guarantee the supremacy of German music for the next 100 years." Ironically, he was forced to flee his homeland and come to America during the Nazi era because he was born a Jew. And with equal irony he was able to say, when asked if he was really the composer Schoenberg, "Well, nobody else wanted to be, so I had to take on the job."

Verklaerte Nacht ("Transfigured Night"), Op. 4

The first large-scale work that Schoenberg wrote, *Verklaerte Nacht,* remains the most popular and accessible of all his compositions. It was completed in just three weeks of September 1899, when the composer was only twenty-five years of age. "The thematic construction," Schoenberg wrote, "is based on Wagnerian 'model and sequence' technique above a moving harmony, on the one hand, and on Brahms's technique of developing variation, as I call it, on the other."

Schoenberg drew his inspiration for the work from Richard Dehmel's eponymous poem of 1896. By portraying the full range of the poem's powerful emotional content with music of great passion and intensity, Schoenberg created a tone poem, a rare form in the chamber music repertoire. While the music of *Verklaerte Nacht* is well able to stand on its own, an extra dimension is added when the music and the poetry are correlated.

TRANSFIGURED NIGHT

Two people walk through the bare cold woods;
the moon runs along, they gaze at it.
The moon runs over tall oaks,
no cloudlet dulls the heavenly light
into which the black peaks reach.
A woman's voice speaks:

I bear a child, and not from you,
I walk in sin alongside you.
I sinned against myself mightily.
I believed no longer in good fortune
and still had mighty longing
for a full life, mother's joy
and duty; then I grew shameless,

then horror-stricken, I let my sex
be taken by a stranger
and even blessed myself for it.
Now life has taken its revenge;
Now I met you, you.

She walks with clumsy gait.
She gazes upward; the moon runs along.
Her somber glance drowns in the light.
A man's voice speaks:

The child that you conceived
be to your soul no burden,
oh look, how clear the universe glitters!
There is a glory around All,
you drift with me on a cold sea,
but a peculiar warmth sparkles
from you in me, from me in you.
It will transfigure the strange child
you will bear it me, from me;
you brought the glory into me;
you made my self into a child.

He holds her around her strong hips,
Their breath kisses in the air.
Two people walk through high, light night.

The music can be divided into five parts, corresponding to the five stanzas of the poem. Schoenberg first conjures up the couple's despair as they plod through the moonlit forest. The second viola and cello depict the heavy trudging steps beneath a descending melody in the other instruments. For the second stanza, as the woman recounts her tale, Schoenberg introduces and develops a number of motifs that very powerfully convey her agitation and anguish. A forceful recall of the opening's heavy tread and downward-moving theme signals the third section. For the fourth stanza, the man's reply, Schoenberg presents some new melodic material, and also expands some of the motifs heard in the second section; the overall character is warm and tender, even though it builds to an impassioned climax. The final section portrays the magical moment, the transfiguration of the unborn child. Musically Schoenberg represents this ennobling change by transforming the descending opening figure and giving it to the first violin at the very top of its range. The sublime exultation lasts but a brief moment before the music fades away.

The Rosé Quartet, with two extra musicians, gave the premiere of *Verklaerte Nacht* in Vienna on March 18, 1902.

String Quartet No. 1 in D Minor, Op. 7

Aside from violin lessons as a child and some informal instruction in counterpoint, Schoenberg was self-taught—some say the greatest autodidact in music. When asked, he always said that his teachers were Bach, Beethoven, Brahms, and Wagner. And it is indeed the latter two composers whose musical influence we most clearly hear in Schoenberg's richly romantic first quartet.

Schoenberg, however, did not merely accept and pass on the musical traditions of the past. The strength and intensity of his own musical vision and the emerging Expressionist artistic outlook, with its focus on the passionate presentation of powerful inner feelings and emotions, directed and shaped his creativity. "Music expresses all that dwells in us," Schoenberg said.

Schoenberg began work on the quartet during the summer of 1904. He described his method of composition: "I composed in my mind forty to eighty measures complete in almost every detail. I needed only two or three hours to copy down these large sections from memory." The quartet was completed on September 26, 1905, and the Rosé Quartet gave the premiere in Vienna on February 5, 1907, after holding forty rehearsals to master this extremely difficult work.

The quartet, which lasts approximately forty-five minutes, is probably the longest single-movement work in the entire chamber music repertoire. Within its unique structure, however, can be found the traditional four-string quartet movements—opening allegro, scherzo, slow movement, and finale.

In the initial section Schoenberg introduces a wealth of melodic material that reappears throughout the quartet. The first theme, a vaulting, intense melody, is announced at the very outset by the first violin. It is followed by several motifs that conclude the first subject group. After several measures of an improvisatory-sounding cello solo, the second, more chromatic theme is played by the first violin alone at a slightly slower tempo. Additional themes are introduced, and all of them are then varied, developed, and juxtaposed, in an amazing range of moods. The section is brought to a close as the four instruments join in a scalelike passage that grows increasingly louder until it reaches a climax.

Although there is no pause to set it apart, a syncopated rhythmic unison in triple meter marks the start of the scherzo section. The viola introduces the middle section or trio of the scherzo by playing the same rhythm at a slightly slower tempo and all on one note. Included here, also, is a recapitulation of the opening thematic group. Following the trio, a much-changed version of the original scherzo returns before an extended cadenzalike passage for the cello brings this part to an end.

Three soulful descending intervals played alone by the first violin indicate the beginning of the slow movement. Presently the viola introduces a particularly lovely lyrical theme, while the other instruments murmur discreetly in the background. A slightly faster reworking of the descending intervals comes back after this section, with a recall of melodies from earlier movements to end this slow part.

The finale is ushered in rather peacefully, with the descending intervals now played calmly and at a slightly faster tempo. The movement is basically a very free rondo, with many echoes of previously heard melodies. It concludes with a beatifically reposeful coda.

Schoenberg once described this quartet as a sort of symphonic poem. When asked, therefore, whether it had a program, he replied, "Oh yes, very definite—but private!" Although no one has discovered any specific extra-musical meanings, there is a remarkable resemblance between the descending intervals of the slow section and the opening melody of Smetana's quartet "From My Life," written about 30 years earlier. Smetana's autobiographical composition describes his life from youthful yearnings to the deafness of old age. Does the musical similarity perhaps suggest the possibility that reminiscences of Schoenberg's life lay buried within his quartet?

String Quartet No. 2 in F Sharp Minor, With Soprano Solo, Op. 10

I. Mässig.   II. Sehr rasch.   III. Litanei: Langsam.   IV. Entrückung: Sehr Langsam.

Few works in the chamber music repertoire are as filled with musical and personal significance as Schoenberg's second quartet. One major distinction is that it adds the human voice to the strings. But its chief musical importance derives from the fact that it is the first example of atonality, breaking a tradition of some 200 years in which almost every piece of music had been in a particular tonality or key (C major, G minor, or whatever). In the final movement of the quartet, Schoenberg makes the historic breach; he uses melodies and harmonies that avoid any sense of specific key, thus creating music that is atonal, without key.

Schoenberg came to atonality not as the result of a search for novelty, but from a strong inner need to expand and extend what had come before. As he once said, "The transition from composition that still emphasized key (while always containing many dissonances) to one where there is no longer any key, any tonic, any consonances, happened gradually, in accordance not with any wish or will, but with a *vision,* an *inspiration;* it happened perhaps instinctively." Further, he wrote, "The task of the creator consists in establishing laws, and not in following laws."

Schoenberg composed his second quartet from March 9, 1907, to July 11, 1908, which was also a time of great private anguish. His wife, Mathilde, had just left him and gone to live with Richard Gerstl, a young artist with whom the couple had studied painting. When Mathilde eventually returned and they were reconciled, Schoenberg dedicated the work to her.

Despite the radical nature of this quartet, the first movement is in traditional sonata form. Of particular interest is the opening theme. The rhythmic pattern—long, long-short, long—is based on the whistle signal Mathilde used to call Schoenberg when she came to pick him up in their car.

In the second movement, one hears a brief quotation from the old Viennese street ballad, *"Ach, du liebe augustin, alles ist hin!"* ("O, beloved Augustin, everything's lost!"). Most commentators read into this a reference to the end of tonality, as well as to the collapse of Schoenberg's marriage. The form is a scherzo and trio, with the quote coming during the transition between the two parts.

Stefan George's poem "Litanei," a prayer for relief from passion, which Schoenberg set for soprano and string quartet as the third movement, reflects the composer's marital despair. In setting the word *Liebe* (love) in the last line, the voice drops a chilling two octaves! Formally, the third movement is a theme and variations; the theme itself is constructed of motifs from the preceding movement. Although unique in its use of the soprano voice, the organization is fairly conventional.

LITANEI

Tief ist die Trauer, die mich umdustert,
Ein tret ich weider, Herr! in dein Haus . . .

Lang war die Reise, matt sind die Glieder,
Leer sind die Schreine, voll nur die Qual.

Durstende Zunge darbt nach dem Weine.
Hart war gestritten, starr ist mein Arm.

Gönne die Ruhe schwankenden Schritten,
Hungrigem Gaume bröckle dein Brot!

Schwach ist mein Atem rufend dem Traume,
Hohl sind die Hände, fiebernd der Mund.

Leih deine Kühle, lösche die Brände,
Tilge das Hoffen, sende das Licht!

Gluten im Herzen lodern noch offen,
Innerst im Grunde wacht noch ein Schrei . . .

Tote das Sehnen, schliesse die Wunde!
Nimm mir die Liebe, gib mir dein Glück!

LITANY

Deep is the grief that surrounds me,
I enter again, Lord, into thy house . . .

The journey was long, my limbs are weary
The shrines are empty, pain alone is full.

My thirsty tongue longs for the wine,
The battle was hard, my arm is numb.

Give rest to my faltering steps,
Break thy bread for the hungry mouth.

Lend thy coolness, quench the flames,
Away from all hope, send thy light!

Flames still burn fiercely in my heart,
From deep inside me comes a cry . . .

Death to my longings, close up my wound!
Take away love, grant me only peace!

The final atonal movement is a setting of Entrückung ("Remoteness") by the same poet. It follows the general outline of sonata form. Of particular significance are the soprano's opening words, "I breathe the air of another planet," which is usually taken as a reference to music's entry into the new world of atonality.

ENTRÜCKUNG

Ich fühle Luft von anderem Planeten.
Mir blassen durch das Dunkel die Gesichter
Die freundlich eben noch sich zu mir drehten.

Und Baum und Wege die ich liebte fahlen
Dass ich sie kaum mehr kenne und du lichter
Geliebter Schatten—Rufer meiner Qualen—

Bist nun erloschen ganz in tiefern Gluten
Um nach dem Taumel streitenden Getobes
Mit einem frommen Schauer anzumuten.

Ich löse mich in Tönen, kresiend, webend,
Ungrundigen Danks und unbenamten Lobes
Dem grossen Atem wunschlos mich ergebend.

Mich überfährt ein ungestümes Wehen
Im Rausch der Weihe wo inbrünstige Schreie
In Staub geworfner Beterinnen flehen:

Dann seh ich wie sich duftige Nebel lüpfen
In einer sonnerfüllten klaren Freie
Die nur umfängt auf fernsten Bergesschlüpfen.

Der Boden schüttert weiss und weich wie Molke . . .
Ich steige uber Schluchten ungeheuer.
Ich fühle wie ich über letzter Wolke.

In einem Meer Kristallnen Glanzes schwimme—
Ich bin ein Funke nur vom heiligen Feuer
Ich bin ein Dröhnen nur del heiligen Stimme.

REMOTENESS

I breathe the air of another planet.
The faces through the darkness I see fainter
Which only just so kindly turned toward me.

And trees and paths which I loved, now grow paler
So that I scarcely know them, and you lighter
Beloved shadow-causer of my torments—

Have in the deeper glow now fully faded
Only to cast round me after tossing turmoil
Of fights a spell of pious shuddering.

I am dissolved in music, circling, binding,
With boundless gratitude and praise unnamed,
Yet wishless to the grand breath yielding.

A wild and strong wind now overtakes me,
Enraptured by the solemn rites of service,
Where women, thrown in dust, cry pleading.

Then I see how the airy mists are lifting,
In sun-filled skies, in air so clear and free,
Which envelopes you only on farthest mountains.

The earth shakes white and soft as something curdled,
I climb across some deep ravines gigantic.
I feel as if I, past the last cloud floating,

Were in a sea of crystal-glittering splendor—
I am a spark, no more, of holy fire,
A thundering only of the holy voice.

The second quartet was given its first performance in Vienna on December 21, 1908, by the Rosé Quartet with soprano Marie Gutheil-Schoder.

String Quartet No 3, Op. 30

I. Moderato. II. Adagio. III. Intermezzo: Allegro moderato. IV. Rondo: Molto moderato.

Schoenberg's third quartet, which was commissioned by the American chamber music patron Elizabeth Sprague Coolidge, was completed in just one month, from February 4 to March 3, 1927. It was introduced in Vienna on September 19, 1927, by the Kolisch Quartet, which accomplished the amazing feat of performing the work from memory.

The third quartet continues the composer's progression: tonality in the first quartet; atonality in the second; and now the use of the twelve-tone system in the third quartet. According to this system, the music is based on a tone row, a particular arrangement of the twelve notes of the chromatic scale. The composer presents the notes of the row sequentially, simultaneously, backwards or inverted, with the single restriction that no note may be repeated until all the notes have been heard. In this quartet, however, Schoenberg treats the tone row rather freely.

Schoenberg insisted, though, that the row and its manipulations remain the concern of the composer, not the listener. In fact, when Rudolph Kolisch, leader of the Kolisch Quartet, excitedly wrote Schoenberg that he had discovered the quartet's tone row, the composer replied, "Do you really believe it's any use knowing it? I can't quite imagine so. I can't repeat often enough: my works are 12-tone *compositions,* not *12-tone* compositions."

Schoenberg recounts a very frightening experience he had while composing the third quartet. He saw an apparition of a sea captain's head nailed to the mast by his mutinous crew. The specter resembled an illustration from a book he recalled from his childhood, *The Ghost Ship,* by Wilhelm Hauff. Despite this alarming vision, the quartet is among Schoenberg's most lighthearted, cheerful, and melodious chamber works. And notwithstanding the advanced twelve-tone technique, the formal scheme is close to the classical model, modified only by the characteristics of twelve-tone music.

The first movement follows the general outline of sonata-allegro form, with a rapid *ostinato* rhythmic figure that is heard throughout against lyrical melodic lines. The serene slow movement combines elements of theme-and-variation and rondo forms; each time the melody returns it is somewhat transformed. A three-part Intermezzo, which is structured much like a scherzo and trio with a return of the scherzo, constitutes the third movement. The final movement combines elements of rondo and sonata form and contributes to the generally positive and optimistic character of the entire work.

String Quartet No. 4, Op. 37

I. Allegro molto; energico.
II. Commodo. III. Largo. IV. Allegro.

In 1933 Schoenberg fled from Nazi Germany to America, settling first in Boston. His poor health, though, sent him to the warmer climate of Los Angeles one year later. While in California, chamber music patron Elizabeth Sprague Coolidge offered him a thousand-dollar commission for another quartet, his fourth. The work occupied Schoenberg from April 27 to July 26, 1936, and the Kolisch Quartet gave the first performance on January 9, 1937, in Los Angeles.

The great popularity of the fourth quartet is probably due to the fact that it combines so well the emotional force of his early works with his supreme mastery of twelve-tone compositional techniques.

The twelve-tone row first appears in the bold opening melody given out by the first violin. A contrasting second theme, quiet, tender, and highly syncopated, follows. The rest of the first movement is mostly involved with an exploration of the initial subject's power and passion.

The viola states the theme of the second movement, but the cello soon takes the lead for a heavy-shoed Ländlerlike section. After a brief silence the viola begins the middle section of the movement in duple meter, as contrasted with the three-beat time of the opening. A very freely varied return of the original section in triple meter brings the movement to a close.

All four instruments join in the recitativelike unison opening to the slow third movement. The music at times recalls the drama and emotionality of an operatic *scena*. At other times, its chantlike, improvisatory character sounds more like the cantillations of Jewish liturgical music.

The final movement contrasts two styles—one sweet and amiable, the other excited and agitated. Overall the movement has a march-like quality that, near the end, quiets and slows down to a conclusion of gentle strength.

String Trio, Op. 45

On August 2, 1946, just before his seventy-second birthday, Schoenberg suffered a nearly fatal incident of cardiac arrest. The doctor had to give an injection directly into the heart in order to revive the critically ill composer. The dramatic treatment, though, was successful, and Schoenberg recovered.

During his recuperation, Schoenberg started composing his string trio, which had been commissioned by Harvard University. Using sketches he had prepared before the onset of his illness, he worked intensively on the trio from August 20 until it was completed on September 23. The first performance was given at Harvard on May 2, 1947.

Schoenberg's traumatic illness played an all-important role in shaping and forming the trio. Novelist Thomas Mann wrote of "a meeting with Schoenberg at which he told me of his new, just completed trio, and of the experiences of his life that he secreted in the composition—experiences of which the work was a kind of precipitate. He had, he said, represented his illness and medical treatment in the music, including even the male nurses and other oddities of American hospitals." To composer Adolph Weiss, Schoenberg confessed that the work even contains a literal description of the hypodermic injection that restored him to life!

The piece, written according to the twelve-tone method, is in one uninterrupted movement. Structurally, however, it is divided into five sections: Part One, Episode One, Part Two, Episode Two, and Part Three.

The melodic material of Part One contains little that fits the traditional definition of theme or subject. Frenzied and agitated, it is taken up mostly with explosions of sounds, eerie scrapings, and high-pitched whistles, and produces a wide variety of tonal and instrumental effects. There are also striking rhythmic outbursts that subside into trembling whispers. Some commentators consider this section the musical analog to the onset of Schoenberg's illness. The force of the music lessens, however, for Episode One, and a serene violin melody spins out over sustained notes in the viola and cello, a sharp contrast to the furor and delirium of Part One.

The subsequent two sections continue the alternation between violent dissonance and warm lyricism, although in the opposite order. Part Two maintains the tranquility of Episode One, opening with a rhythmic pattern that resembles a slow waltz. Despite several musical explosions, the calm prevails until the violent interruption of Episode Two, with its brash slides and disruptive ferocity.

Part Three is a shortened repetition, sometimes literal, sometimes freely varied, of Part One and Episode One. The tender and compassionate coda seems to represent a conquest of the pain and anguish that have come before, and the trio ends in an aura of serenity and acceptance.

Franz Schubert

Born January 31, 1797, in Vienna
Died November 19, 1828, in Vienna

SCHUBERT IS perhaps the best example of a composer who received little or no public attention during his lifetime, but who gained international acclaim after his death. Starting to compose in his early teens, Schubert produced a substantial number of compositions in an astonishing variety of forms; he left to posterity over 600 songs, nine symphonies, numerous operas, over twenty quartets, a good deal of other chamber music, and many solo pieces. But most of his music was rarely heard outside his small circle of friends, and almost none was published. It remained for future generations of music lovers to make up for the neglect Schubert suffered and to celebrate his extraordinary achievement as one of the greatest melodists in music history.

The son of a poor school teacher, Schubert received violin and viola lessons from his father, an amateur cellist, and piano instruction from an older brother. Many of his early quartets were written for the family group. By the time he was eleven, he became a choir boy in the chapel of the Austrian Emperor and studied at the Imperial and Royal State School, where he received his only formal musical training from 1808 to 1813. After teaching for a while in his father's school, a position he disliked intensely, he left in 1817 and gradually drifted into a bohemian existence in Vienna among other poor, struggling artists.

For the eleven years remaining to him, Schubert lived a free, communal life within a small circle of adoring friends who affectionately nicknamed him *Schwammerl* ("Tubby") for his appearance—short (just over five feet) and chubby, with curly brown hair, a round face, with dimpled chin and adorned with prominent wire spectacles. Although Schubert's music failed to bring in any money, and his few attempts to obtain a position as a court musician were unsuccessful, he never starved; because he and his friends shared their food, clothes, and living space, Schubert was able to devote himself to his composing.

In 1827 Schubert learned that Ludwig van Beethoven was gravely ill; he visited him shortly before his death and took part in his funeral. By this time, though, Schubert himself was a very sick man, having neglected his health and suffered several bouts of serious illness, including a case of venereal disease. On March 26, 1828, Schubert presented a concert of his own music that filled the hall to overflowing and was an immense artistic and financial success. Unfortunately, this high point in an otherwise uneventful career came only a few months before Schubert became bedridden, on November 14, 1828, and succumbed to typhoid fever a few days later.

When asked his method of musical composition, Schubert replied, "I finish one piece and begin the next." This workmanlike approach belies the exceptional freshness and originality that attend every note that Schubert wrote and the melodic inventiveness that characterizes all of his music. Schubert's unmistakable Romantic stamp moved music several giant steps away from the earlier Viennese school of Haydn, Mozart, and Beethoven and solidly into the nineteenth century.

Because so few of his works were published during his lifetime, for a long time they were not organized in sequential order. Starting in 1914, Otto Erich Deutsch began publishing a chronological catalogue that assigned a number (the D, or Deutsch, number) to each composition. For ease of use, the compositions discussed below are basically presented in Deutsch's chronological order, but with the works bearing opus numbers inserted in their own numerical order.

String Trios, D. 471 and D. 581

It was while Schubert was working as an assistant elementary school teacher (a job he detested) from 1814 to 1817 that he became a professional composer. In June 1816 he wrote the cantata *Prometheus*, the first composition for which he was paid. In September of that year he also wrote a single movement (D. 471) of what was probably intended to be a four-movement string trio and the following September finished an entire four-movement trio (D. 581)—his only two essays in the form.

The string trios have two important features in common: both look back more to eighteenth-century forms and styles than ahead to the nineteenth-century methods of composition with which Schubert later became identified. Also, both are rather slight, un-prepossessing works that succeed entirely on the basis of their ingen-uous charm, warmth, and wealth of melody.

String Trio in B Flat Major, D. 471

Just as Schubert left his "Unfinished" Symphony mysteriously in-complete despite many opportunities to finish it, so he broke off composing his first string trio in B flat major for some unknown reason. In September 1816, he wrote the first movement and thirty-nine measures of the second, an Andante sostenuto. And then, sud-denly and inexplicably, he stopped. One of the most plausible the-ories appears in Alfred Einstein's biography of Schubert, where he speculates that the composer ceased work "because he was not clear in his mind about the form."

The single complete movement that exists has long been recog-nized as a gem in the chamber music repertoire—a gentle, tender piece of great fluency and melodic beauty. The principal subject has a number of distinctive motifs—a lyrical, genial melody, a more ag-itated extension of that idea, a slightly more intense motif, and a final gesture that features forceful descending unison scales. The sec-ond theme is a legato melody that is initiated by two perky, repeated upbeats and is shared by all three instruments. After the easygoing good spirits of the exposition, the development is unexpectedly se-rious, introducing an emotional component that had not appeared before. But the recapitulation restores the original character, and all is well at the end.

String Trio in B Flat Major, D. 581

I. Allegro moderato. II. Andante. III. Menuetto: Allegretto. IV. Rondo: Allegretto.

Although the Second String Trio in the key of B flat major is a short piece, written for a small group of instruments and not containing any ringing climaxes or tearful laments, it nevertheless presents a wide range of musical and emotional expression within the confines Schubert set for himself.

The first theme sounds like someone (the violin) recounting a series of events, each one different, while the others (viola and cello) listen with interest and add comments from time to time. The second theme is structured as a musical conversation between various pairs of players. A final rhythmic motif played by the violin brings the exposition to a close. The development includes a brilliant part for the violin, written in the style of a coloratura Italian opera aria. A regular recapitulation follows, and the movement ends quietly.

Cast in simple ternary A-B-A form, the violin carries all the thematic burden in the first section of the slow movement with its highly ornamented melodic line. The cello starts the densely textured contrasting middle part. Schubert then brings back the opening, this time even more decorated and free.

The Menuetto is an outpouring of melody, beguilingly inventive with very original harmonic underpinning. The trio is the violist's chance to shine, having the leading voice throughout, after which the Menuetto returns.

The last movement is a jaunty rondo. The mostly staccato main theme is followed by an articulation that becomes generally smooth and legato for the first episode. After a shortened repeat of the prime melody, a new vitality enters with the second episode. The movement ends with a final statement of the opening theme.

String Quartet in A Minor, Op. 29, No. 1, D. 804

I. Allegro ma non troppo.
II. Andante.   III. Menuetto: Allegretto.
IV. Allegro moderato.

Schubert began composing string quartets for his own family quartet made up of his two brothers (the two violins), himself (viola), and his father (cello), when he was but fourteen years old. By the beginning of 1824 he had completed twelve such quartets, but had only performed them inside the home. But then, discouraged by the poor reception his operas were getting and inspired by the professional quartet playing of Ignaz Schuppanzigh, Schubert turned once more to quartet writing, this time producing the A minor, his first truly mature, "public" work in the form.

Schubert began work on the quartet during February or March of 1824, following a long hospitalization for treatment of the veneral disease he had contracted two years earlier. Soon after completing the composition, he wrote to his friend Leopold Kupelwieser. "I feel myself the most unfortunate, the most miserable being in the world. Think of a man whose health will never be right again, and who from despair over the fact makes it worse instead of better, think of a man, I say, whose splendid hopes have come to naught, to whom the happiness of love and friendship offer nothing but the most acute pain, whose enthusiasm (at least, the inspiring kind) for the Beautiful, threatens to disappear, and ask yourself whether he isn't a miserable unfortunate fellow?'' Surely some of the unrest, despair, and despondency that Schubert expresses in his letter is reflected in the achingly beautiful music of the quartet.

Each of the four movements has some connection outside the quartet. The flowing accompaniment the second violin plays at the very opening calls to mind Schubert's 1814 song, *"Gretchen am Spinnrade"* ("Gretchen at the Spinning Wheel"); it might be a specific reference to two lines from the song that he quotes in the Kupelwieser letter: "My peace is gone, my heart is heavy, I'll find it never, never again." The violin sings the wistful, almost forlorn, principal theme, first in minor and then in the slightly more hopeful major. An agitated transition leads to the subsidiary theme, introduced by the second violin, and with the same melancholic character as the opening. Schubert works over several elements of the exposition in the development section. The recapitulation starts with regular, though elided, versions of the principal theme and the transition, but he brings the second theme back in major, giving it a more cheerful character. The coda, though, reverts to the minor for a sorrowful ending.

Schubert borrowed the theme of the Andante movement from the incidental music he wrote for Wilhelm von Chezy's play *Rosamunda,* a disastrous presentation that was terminated in December 1823, after only two performances. Most likely he adapted the theme in part because he liked it and in part to rescue it from oblivion. In the play, this theme is heard as the *entr'acte* before the fourth act, in which Rosamunda tends her flocks in a lovely, tranquil valley. Schubert conceals the complex and intricate treatment he used in fashioning this entrancing movement behind the overall spiritual and contemplative serenity.

The playful, yet touching, Menuetto can be traced back to Schubert's 1819 song, *"Die Götter Griechenlands"* ("The Greek Gods"). The text, by Friedrich Schiller, expresses a yearning for the return of youth: "Fair world, where art thou, Come again glorious age of Nature." These words are sung over the same melodic-rhythmic figure that the cello introduces to open the Menuetto. Soon, though, this motto yields to a warm, lilting Ländler, the happy innocence of which reinforces the dream of recapturing the happiness of tender years. The trio is a brief elaboration on the opening motto; it serves as an interlude before the repeat of the Menuetto.

A marked change of mood occurs in the consistently cheerful last movement. The main subject is a jolly, peasantlike tune, obviously of Hungarian derivation. After some working out of this melody with its accented second beat, Schubert brings in a mock-conspiratorial contrasting theme, with its dotted (long-short) rhythm. Through brilliant writing for all four instruments, the composer devotes the rest of the movement to developing and returning this material, keeping the good spirits up right through to the very end.

The A minor quartet was dedicated to Ignaz Schuppanzigh and received its premiere performance in Vienna by the Schuppanzigh Quartet on March 14, 1824. It was published the following September, the only Schubert chamber work to appear in print during the composer's lifetime!

String Quartet in D Minor, D. 810, "Death and the Maiden"

I. Allegro.   II. Andante con moto.   III. Scherzo: Allegro molto.   IV. Presto.

The D minor quartet is subtitled "Death and the Maiden" because Schubert borrowed the theme for the second movement from his 1817 song, *"Der Tod und das Madchen"* ("Death and the Maiden"). The short, simple lied tells of death gently coming to claim the life of a young girl who urges him, "Go on, oh go on past me!" The melody that Schubert uses in the quartet is actually the piano introduction that represents the approach of death. The central role of this quotation in the quartet has led several commentators to regard the entire work as an exposition of Schubert's views on death, and the climax it reaches in the finale as a frenetic Dance of Death. More likely, Schubert borrowed the melody for musical rather than programmatic reasons; according to some evidence, the idea for basing the quartet on the song came from some friends who loved the melody.

The first movement starts with a tense, forceful motif, flung out twice like a bold, repeated challenge. The prominent triplet figure is heard throughout all of the motifs that make up the first subject group and furnishes the motoric energy that carries the music surging forward. The same rhythmic triplets underlie the lyrical, Italianate second theme, which is given out by the violins. After the spacious, leisurely presentation of the two subjects, Schubert goes on to a comparatively brief development section that is mostly concerned with the second theme. The recapitulation is quite freely realized and flows right into the coda, which builds to a stunning climax. The quiet ending echoes with the sound of the ever-present triplets.

In the somber second movement, Schubert uses the theme he took from the song's introduction as the foundation on which to build a set of five variations. The theme is perfect for the purpose; it consists of a simple repeated rhythmic pattern with minimal melodic and harmonic movement, allowing the composer to add musical complexity and new expressive content in the ensuing variations. Variation I passes the melody in the form of repeated triplets to the second violin, to which the first violin then adds its ennobling comments. The cello has the lead in the second variation with the others weaving a dense accompanying web in the background. The third variation bursts forth with unbridled strength and vigor, revealing still another character inherent in the original theme. In stark contrast, the following variation is all soft, with the first violin describing a delicate tracery in its upper register over a murmured reminder of the theme in the other instruments. Although it reaches a fervid climax, a general feeling of gloom and dejection suffuses the final variation. A short coda rounds off the movement.

The Scherzo opens with fierce, slashing syncopations, and the rhythmic drive does not slacken throughout the entire first part. There is an abrupt change of character in the trio with its tranquil, warmly sung cantilena line. Schubert brings the Scherzo back in a literal repeat to end the movement.

Although the finale starts with a bleak, distant unison, it mounts to several climaxes of feverish gaiety. The high-speed rhythmic pattern derives from the old Italian dance, the tarantella, the frenzied steps of which were believed to counteract the poisonous effects of the tarantula spider's bite. The movement is propelled forward with great energy and verve, culminating in the brilliant *prestissimo* coda.

Schubert composed the "Death and the Maiden" Quartet in March 1824. Its first performance, actually an unrehearsed reading, was on January 29, 1826, at the Vienna home of Karl and Franz Hacker, two amateur musicians. Schubert, who enjoyed playing viola in chamber music ensembles, could not participate since he was busy copying out the parts and making last-minute corrections. The quartet was not published until July 1831, nearly three years after Schubert's death.

Piano Trio in B Flat Major, Op. 99, D. 898

I. Allegro moderato. II. Andante un poco mosso. III. Scherzo: Allegro. IV. Rondo: Allegro vivace.

"One glance at Schubert's Trio (Op. 99)—and the troubles of our human existence disappear and all the world is fresh and bright again." So wrote Robert Schumann of this radiant and cheerful piece, with its wealth of melodic beauty, rhythmic inventiveness, and rich, Romantic harmonies. But what Schumann does not suggest in this quote are the many surprises that Schubert provides in this exciting musical journey. While following traditional forms, Schubert furnishes many twists and turns in the usual structural organization. Movement one, for example, is in sonata form, and he arrives at the recapitulation in the usual way—and then makes three false starts in wrong keys before finally turning to the "right" key. Likewise, in the second movement, organized in A-B-A form, he returns the opening A section, but bends the melody quite a bit out of shape when he finally reaches the expected key. And by calling the last movement a Rondo, he leads us to anticipate a principal theme that is repeated with contrasting episodes between each return of the melody, but instead makes each appearance of the refrain a transformation of the original melody.

Schubert probably composed the B flat trio, the first of two works in the form, during the summer of 1827. Although the work was not publicly performed nor published during Schubert's lifetime, there was a private performance in Vienna on January 28, 1828, given by Carl Maria von Bocklet, piano, Ignaz Schuppanzigh, violin, and Josef Linke, cello.

The trio opens with a noble theme played in octaves by the strings. The piano's right hand plays repeated eighth notes (two to a beat), which create a rhythmic tension with the triplets (three to a beat) of the melody. The swaggering figure in the left hand of the piano adds an extra dash of vitality to the proceedings. After allowing this theme to grow and expand, Schubert introduces the second theme, a lovely, cantabile melody played high in its range by the cello. The spacious exposition leads to a leisurely development. Then follows the three false recapitulations before the piano brings back the opening theme in the proper key, starting the regular recapitulation. A short, quiet coda ends with two abrupt, loud chords.

Schubert presents the exquisite cantilena theme of the second movement much as he does the vocal line of his songs; here the cello sings out the theme while the piano plays an accompaniment that contributes to its expressivity and sets it into clear relief. Violin and piano statements of the theme follow, each with countermelodies in the other instruments. A complex repeated accompaniment figure with syncopations in the strings signals the start of the contrasting middle section in which the new melody is first heard in the piano. At the conclusion of this section, the violin seems to be bringing back the principal theme—but in the "wrong" key. Finally, the music arrives at the expected key (E flat) and the piano plays a melody related to, but different from, the first theme, which seemingly completes the symmetrical feeling of the A-B-A structure.

The Scherzo finds Schubert impishly and playfully racing through the scintillating phrases to build to a climax at the very end. The wisp of a trio is an unabashed waltz—a brief, charming interlude before the Scherzo returns.

Although titled Rondo, the architecture of the buoyant last movement is closer to sonata form, with a substantial development section and no clear repetitions of the principal theme, the hallmark of a rondo. In his book on Schubert, Alfred Einstein points out the Rondo theme's resemblance to the composer's 1815 song, *"Skolie,"* which has these words: "Let us in the bright May morning take delight in the brief life of the flower, before its fragrance disappears." Undoubtedly, the same joyful impulse that led to the creation of the song melody influenced its use in the vivacious concluding movement of the trio.

Piano Trio in E Flat Major, Op. 100, D. 929

I. Allegro.   II. Andante con moto.   III. Scherzo: Allegro moderato.   IV. Allegro moderato.

Schubert completed the E flat major trio in November 1827, shortly after the one in B flat major, his only other effort in the form. Although some commentators criticize the piano trio in E flat major for being overly long and for having less-than-inspired melodies, it was Schubert's favorite (he programmed it as the major work on the March 26, 1828, concert devoted entirely to his music), and it was accepted by the public in his own time. Premiered at the Vienna Musical Society's hall on December 26, 1827, by Carl Maria von Bocklet, piano, Ignaz Schuppanzigh, violin, and Josef Linke, cello, the piece was published soon after. Robert Schumann said of the E flat, ''Some years ago, a Trio by Schubert passed across the face of the musical world like some angry comet in the sky. It was his hundredth opus, and shortly afterward, in November 1828, he died.''

The goal of unifying extended movements or lengthy works seems to have been on Schubert's mind in this trio, and the first movement is a good example of his problem-solving technique. The trio opens with a statement of the bold, dramatic unison motif. The counter statement, first heard in the cello, springs from a three-note motto—note, lower neighbor, note. Rapid chromatic scales in the piano and trills in the strings lead next to an episode dominated by a hesitating rhythmic pattern of one quarter note and four eighths (one long and four shorts). A quick reminder of the opening phrase leads to a passage based on the counter statement, which builds to a climax before giving way to a kind of second theme, an ascending line shared by the two string instruments. The concluding theme combines the rhythm of the opening with the melodic contour of the counter statement to create a soulful melody of ineffable beauty that ends the exposition. The development is exclusively concerned with the concluding theme, set off by cascades of rippling triplets in the piano. This section ends with faint echoes of the opening motif. The recapitulation, which essentially follows the thematic sequence of the exposition, concludes with a series of loud, ringing chords; the following coda is like another, short development, ending quietly with the hesitating rhythm.

According to Leopold Sonnleithner, one of Schubert's friends, the main theme of the second movement is a Swedish song that the composer heard sung by Issak Albert Berg, a tenor from Sweden who visited Vienna in 1827. Over a marchlike piano accompaniment, the cello sings the deliberate, perfectly symmetrical phrases of the melody, which is then repeated by the piano. The violin leads the transition to the second major musical idea, a theme based on the poetic iamb (an unaccented beat followed by an accented beat), which Schubert obviously derived from the descending octave leaps in that rhythm heard near the end of the principal theme. The rest of the movement grows from these two melodies, rising to peaks of impassioned heights between sections of ethereal loveliness.

The entire Scherzo is a canon, with the various tunes stated by one instrument and echoed by another one measure later. The main theme is light and delicate, with an appealing swagger, as it bounces back and forth around the trio. The much heavier trio is more like a stomping dance. After an abrupt cutoff, followed by two measures of silence, a section begins that is a reminder of the hesitating rhythmic pattern from the first movement. Schubert brings the more forceful Scherzo back after the trio.

The vast, sprawling finale opens with a graceful, perky tune played by the piano alone and then by the violin. The second theme is a sharp contrast, in key (E flat major to C minor), meter (six-eighths to alla breve), and character (from light and tripping to repeated, cimbalomlike strummed notes with definite Hungarian overtones). As episode after episode follows, Schubert modifies, develops, and interweaves the two musical gestures and, in a rare departure, has the cello bring back the principal theme of the second movement. Freely following sonata form structure, Schubert's giant movement proves the old adage, "Nothing succeeds like excess!"

Quintet for Piano and Strings in A Major, Op. 114, D. 667, "Trout"

I. Allegro vivace. II. Andante. III. Scherzo: Presto. IV. Thema: Andantino. V. Finale: Allegro giusto.

The twenty-two-year-old Schubert spent the summer of 1819 on a walking tour of Upper Austria, staying some while in the small town of Steyr, where he visited Sylvester Paumgartner, a wealthy music patron and amateur cellist. According to Schubert's friend, Albert Stadler, Paumgartner asked the composer to write a piece suitable for his home chamber music gatherings, but with two stipulations: the instrumentation should be the same as Johann Nepomuk Hummel's quintet (violin, viola, cello, double-bass, piano), which was a favorite among Paumgartner's friends; and the piece should include a variation movement based on the theme of Schubert's 1817 song, *"Die Forelle"* ("The Trout"). Having no objection to these conditions, Schubert set to work at once and finished the "Trout" Quintet, as it is universally known, in Vienna that fall. Suffused with the warmth and intimacy of *haus musick,* rather than the extroverted brilliance of a piece intended for concert hall presentation, it is, nevertheless, a great crowd pleaser.

The first movement opens with a dramatic, upward-sweeping arpeggio in the piano, followed by a leisurely legato string melody in seeming contradiction to the tempo marking, Allegro vivace ("fast and lively"). Soon, though, the viola and cello establish a forward-moving accompaniment figure that shows the true speed of the underlying metrical pulse. Schubert expands and develops the two distinctive musical gestures before leading into the subsidiary theme, a loving songful duet between violin and cello, with an arpeggio from the opening thrown in for special effect. The second motif of this theme is a highly rhythmic tune introduced by the piano. The sole focus of the development section, with its many modulations from key to key, is the first theme. The recapitulation is an almost literal repeat of the exposition, except for the necessary adjustments of key. There is no coda.

Over a gently flowing string accompaniment, the piano, playing in bare octaves, presents the lyrical first theme of the Andante. Other, varied statements follow, until a passage of arpeggios leads to the second theme, a rather morose melody in the viola and cello, which is heard against a busy background in the other parts. This section in turn gives way to the third theme, a quirky intricate, rhythmic melody in the piano. After coming to a full stop, Schubert literally repeats all three themes, three notes (actually a minor third) higher, but without any development—just giving listeners the welcome opportunity to hear these wonderful melodies again.

The high-speed Scherzo starts with a quick four-note motto, and all that follows flows from that original impetus. Gay and frolicsome, the Scherzo is filled with sharp contrasts of dynamics and unexpected accents. In an abrupt change of character, the trio sounds quiet and politely conversational, with voices raised only once to assert vehement agreement on a particular point. And then, as though embarrassed by the unseemly outburst, they return to their carefully modulated tones. The Scherzo comes back with its bristling electricity to shatter the calm and restore the energetic drive of the first part.

The fourth movement is a series of six variations on a quotation of the "Trout" theme from Schubert's own song, borrowed intact, but with slight rhythmic modification. The theme derives from the song's opening, which concerns the ease with which the fish escapes the fisherman: "In a bright stream the capricious trout darted along like an arrow." The first three variations are mostly decoration and ornamentation on the melody, which is heard, respectively, in the piano, viola and cello, and double bass. The fourth and fifth variations are more substantial transformations of the original melody. The faster sixth variation is a summation of what has come before, with the theme presented in its original form and the piano playing the same rippling figure accompaniment as in the song.

A single bell tone signals the start of the Finale and leads directly to the principal theme, a lively tune in the Hungarian style played by the violin and viola. Schubert immediately subjects the melody to a rather full development before introducing the second theme, a legato line in the strings against a prominent, attractive accompaniment figure in the piano. He then brings the first theme back and develops both melodies. To follow this with still more development would be redundant. Schubert, therefore, merely sounds another bell tone and proceeds to an exact repeat of the first part (with only some key changes). As in the second movement, some may feel deprived of a more traditional working out of the themes, but most merely enjoy the fresh, invigorating melodies, which never seem to pall no matter how many times they are heard.

Quartettsatz in C Minor, D. 703

Late in 1820, Schubert entered a new phase in his quartet writing, leaving the so-called sociable, domestic character of his earlier compositions to compose highly dramatic works that surge with passion and intensity. One reason for the change may have to do with the fact that Schubert was no longer writing for his more technically limited family quartet, brothers Ferdinand and Ignaz, violins, Franz, viola, and their father, cello. Now he had in mind professional players with a virtuosic command of their instruments. Also, it may be that Schubert's turn to a more revolutionary and Romantic style of writing was in reaction to an official reprimand he received that year for consorting with the radical poet Johann Senn.

In December 1820, Schubert completed the first movement and forty-one measures of the second movement of what seemed to be the beginning of a full-length quartet in C minor. And there the manuscript ends! As with the "Unfinished" Symphony, scholars speculate that Schubert probably planned to write four movements, but somehow circumstances intervened. It is also possible that he abandoned the task when he found himself unable to sustain the high-pitched intensity of the first movement. Although we will probably never know for sure why the work was not finished, we can savor the quartet movement *(Quartettsatz* in German) for what it is—a thoroughly satisfying and compelling chamber music composition, among the most outstanding in the entire repertoire.

The music opens mysteriously, with the first violin murmuring a repeated-note figure that is taken up fugally by the others. After quickly rising to a fervid climax, the same melody, but without the repeated notes, continues quietly. Another, more lyrical theme appears in the first violin, while the second violin and viola carry on the rocking rhythm that has been established. An abrupt change of mood intrudes as the lower instruments introduce a highly theatrical, tense section similar to the opening and the first violin sweeps up the scale, again and again, in portentous-sounding runs. Schubert then brings in still another theme, an air of lyrical innocence, but the initial melody insistently runs through the viola and cello, gaining in importance and finally taking over in a hushed, chilling episode. The exposition ends as the cello plays the last echo of the opening and the others go through the measured paces of the closing theme. Two violent outbursts signal the start of the brief development, which uses the contour of the opening theme as the springboard for fanciful flights of melodic creation. The recapitulation brings back all the themes in the proper order—except for the most important theme, the first; Schubert saves that for the final measures of the piece, the short, concluding coda.

String Quartet in E Flat Major, Op. 125, No. 1, D. 87

I. Allegro moderato. II. Scherzo: Prestissimo. III. Adagio. IV. Allegro.

Nicknamed the *"Haushaltung Quartett"* ("Household Quartet") because it is so well suited for home performance, the E flat quartet was composed as Schubert was completing his studies at the Imperial and Royal State School. It is the last of six comparatively immature works that the teenaged composer wrote for his family quartet. Pleasant in tone, the quartets are characterized by a "touch of Biedermeier," the solid, comfortable, rather humdrum design character so favored by the German and Austrian bourgeois in the early decades of the nineteenth century. Technically they are quite undemanding because of the limited performing abilities of the four players, particularly Schubert's father.

The E flat quartet, by far the best of the six, was composed in November 1813 and published posthumously in 1830, as Op. 125,

No. 1. It is the only one of these early works to have found a place in the modern repertoire as a pleasant, ageeable piece showing evidence of Schubert's mature quartet style.

The principal subject group of the genial and warm first movement has three amiable motifs, all introduced by the first violin. A two-measure bridge of repeated syncopations in the viola leads to the second theme, not much different in character, but in the dominant (B flat major) key. The concluding theme, heard over an ongoing dotted-note (long-short) accompaniment, is closely related to the last of the first subject themes. The development and recapitulation sections are concerned with this melodic material and maintain the same comfortable, *gemütlich* tone to the end.

The high-speed Scherzo whizzes by, a fun movement, full of wit and humor. The basic melodic and rhythmic figure is a quick grace note followed by a downward plunge. After dashing through this section with great verve, Schubert presents the trio, a short contrasting legato interlude that sounds folklike in origin. Then the Scherzo returns for a full-length repeat.

The Adagio casts a mood similar to that of the first movement and, like the Allegro moderato, is organized in sonata form. All four players join in presenting the first theme at the very opening. The first violin then states the second theme against a throbbing background. A short development section carries the music back to a restatement of the themes from the exposition, and the movement ends quietly without a coda.

Written with great flair and assurance, the bright, scintillating last movement is generally considered the high point of the quartet. The first theme consists of two delicate ascending staccato phrases with a series of three accented descending legato phrases that are truly captivating in style. After extending this idea, Schubert introduces the ingratiating second theme, played by the first violin over a brittle staccato accompaniment. A forceful unison starts the development section, which continues alternating loud and soft, until a regular recapitulation and short coda end this delightful movement.

String Quartet in G Major, Op. 161, D. 887

I. Allegro molto moderato.   II. Andante un poco moto.   III. Scherzo: Allegro vivace.   IV. Allegro assai.

Schubert's fifteenth and last quartet, the G major, was composed during ten days of intensive work, from June 10 to 20, 1826, following several weeks of inactivity. A work of impressive nobility and grandeur, but perhaps not personal or lyrical enough to become a popular favorite, the G major's true value was little noted nor much appreciated during Schubert's lifetime. The first private performance was given on March 7, 1827, by Schubert (playing viola) and three friends. The composer programmed just the first movement at a public concert of his music on March 26, 1828. Regrettably, the premiere of the entire quartet did not take place until 1850, and publication had to wait until the following year—a full twenty-three years after Schubert's untimely death.

The three musical gestures that make up the first theme leap to the fore in the striking opening: a long, sustained chord that comes from nowhere and quickly swells; the switch from the G major of the held chord to the G minor climax note; and the quirky, staccato response that follows. This presentation, which almost sounds like an introduction, is repeated before the three lower voices lay down a rich, soft tremolo carpet on which the first violin places what sounds like the "proper" first theme, based on the rhythmic figure. Schubert treats this material with great vehemence until he comes to a full stop. The second theme is based on the quirky rhythm now tamed, polished, and more songlike, but with a syncopation that adds a certain pathos and tension. The first violin statement of this theme is followed by three more utterances—second violin, cello, and viola—each with its own scoring and separated by what could be considered mini-developments of the theme. Some powerful unison passages act as a transition to the development section, which is mostly on the first theme, since the second theme was developed in the exposition. The development rises to two impassioned climaxes before quieting down for the rather free recapitulation and a short coda that quickly summarizes the three opening gestures.

The start of the second movement seems straightforward and easily understood as the cello plays a lovely, melancholic melody with supportive background murmurings from the others. With frightening suddenness, though, this quiet mood is shattered by a burst of uncontrolled ferocity. In a towering rage, the first violin impetuously whips up the scale again and again, ending each ascent with an alarming roar and a wild shriek. Then, just as abruptly, the violin, seemingly unaware of what has just happened, innocently takes up the cello's mournful song. But the feral strain, not to be denied, explodes once again—even fiercer and more savage than before. When its energy is spent, Schubert discourses quietly on the first theme, although some barbarisms lurk in the background. Out of this development emerges a shortened, ornamented reprise of the opening theme and a coda that brings the disquieting happenings of this provocative movement to a quiet end.

The Scherzo is swift and sprightly; a single melodic/rhythmic idea—six rapid and three slower notes—runs throughout, without any real contrast. Schubert treats the movement with the same deftness of touch that we associate with Mendelssohn's best scherzos. The trio introduces a completely different feeling; it is slower in tempo, legato in articulation and with the character of a warmhearted, genial Ländler, the peasant dance that predated the waltz. The Scherzo, minus its repeats, comes back to end the movement.

Schubert captures all the gay abandon and frivolity of a comic Italian *opera buffa scena* in the quartet finale. Moving along at a brisk clip, the music makes extreme demands on all four players, requiring perfect ensemble and absolute control in negotiating the sudden accents and mercurial changes in dynamics. Although cast in rondo form, the two contrasting interludes are not significantly different, so that it is up to the performers to sustain interest by the brilliance of their playing.

Cello Quintet in C Major, Op. 163, D. 956

I. Allegro ma non troppo. II. Adagio. III. Scherzo: Presto; Trio: Andante sostenuto. IV. Allegretto.

Music lovers are in general accord that Schubert's cello quintet is the greatest work in the chamber music repertoire. In his book, *Chamber Music,* Homer Ulrich writes of the quintet, "In nobility of conception, beauty of melody, and variety of mood it is without equal." William Mann's article on Schubert's chamber music describes it as "his masterpiece, and perhaps the greatest of all his works in range of emotion, quality of material and formal perfection." Pianist Arthur Rubinstein asked that the slow movement be played at his funeral, and violinist Joseph Saunders had the second theme of the first movement engraved on his tombstone. Through the loftiness of its conception, the spiritual quality of its melodies, and the masterfulness of its technique, the quintet touches listeners in a very special and personal way.

Musicologists have long wondered why Schubert chose to add a cello to the basic string quartet in this, his sole string quintet; the precedent, established by Mozart and Beethoven, was for an extra viola. The explanation probably lies in the vastly expanded range of sonorities that Schubert is able to elicit from the two cellos, and which he exploits to the fullest, particularly in his ever-changing pairings and combinations of instruments.

The quintet opens very simply. The four upper voices play a basic C major chord that swells from soft to loud and ends with a melodic extension in the first violin. Schubert then repeats the entire phrase with the four lower voices playing a D minor chord—producing a magical transformation of color and character, and serving notice that a most exciting musical journey is about to begin. The music grows more and more agitated until three ringing chords announce the appearance of the second theme, heard first as a duet for the two cellos. Schubert repeats and expands this exquisitely shaped melody until everyone joins in a marchlike rhythmic unison, the third theme, which concludes the exposition. The second and third themes furnish the motifs on which the spacious development section is based. After building to a climax that is orchestral in effect, the first violin starts a series of slow, deliberate arpeggios that hide the start of the recapitulation in the other instruments. The rather free recapitulation follows the general outline of the exposition, and the short coda whips itself up into a frenzy before fading away to a gentle ending, capped by two loud chords.

The principal subject of the Adagio combines sublime lyricism with dolorous *Weltschmerz* (''universal weariness'') in equal measure. This theme, which is played in rich harmonies by the three middle voices, moves so slowly that it seems suspended in time, isolated from all temporal concerns. Beneath it, the second cello supplies an underpinning of solemn pizzicato figures; above are the first violin's muted cries, heard in short fragments. The section closes with a second statement of the theme, shorter and softer than the first. With no warning, Schubert then unleashes a unique musical onslaught. The second violin and viola join in a convulsive syncopated pattern; the second cello stubbornly repeats its low-pitched growling; and the first violin and first cello sing out a vaulting lyrical line that binds together these disparate elements. The middle section perseveres, finding new strength when it seems to falter, until finally it grows too weak. There are long silences between the gasps of sound. The opening section then returns with the melody intact, but with decorative elaborations. Just before the end, there is a brief return of the fiery middle section, but the flame is quickly extinguished, and the movement ends in quiet resignation.

The Scherzo sweeps in like a fresh breath of country air dispelling the morose mood of the Adagio. The five players sound like a rough-and-ready rustic band playing a boisterous peasant dance. But the vigor and vitality do not last long; the mood alters from exultancy to hopelessness and despair as Schubert changes all the musical elements in the trio. The tempo goes from Presto ("very quick") to Andante sostenuto ("sustained moderate speed"); the major key switches to minor; the triple meter changes to duple; and the rhythmic melody is replaced by a wailing plaint. In what is surely the emotional high point of the piece, we glimpse the plight of the individual, victim of inexorable fate and inevitable death. Before things get maudlin, though, Schubert inserts a transition section, which reverts to the opening of the Scherzo, the irresistible triumph of life and hope over despondency and gloom.

The finale is a stirring paean to the indomitability of the human spirit; after two movements of soul-searching and torment, Schubert emerges hopeful and optimistic. The principal theme is a rollicking dance tune that seems to be of Hungarian origin. The equally positive subsidiary theme, though, is more suave and legato, slightly suggestive of Viennese cafe music. Falling between sonata and rondo form in organization, these two subjects provide the thematic framework for the last movement. Just in case there are any lingering doubts as to the movement's meaning, Schubert twice picks up the tempo in the coda, making for a brilliant, exciting finish.

Schubert composed the quintet in August and September 1828, completing it just weeks before his death on November 18. In a letter of October 2, he offered it to a publisher, who refused. The premiere did not take place until 1850; publication had to wait three years beyond that.

Octet in F Major, Op. 166, D. 803

I. Adagio; Allegro. II. Andante un poco
mosso. III. Scherzo: Allegro
vivace. IV. Andante. V. Menuetto:
Allegretto. VI. Andante molto; Allegro.

The beginning of 1824 found Schubert at a very low ebb. In poor health, he was suffering from anemia and a nervous disorder. Also impecunious, he was existing only with the help of his many loyal supporters. And his music, including his several operas, was not being performed. In a letter he wrote, "Every night when I go to bed I hope I may not wake . . . I live without pleasure or friends."

It was at this point that Count Ferdinand von Troyer, a high official in the court of Archduke Rudolph and a first-rate amateur clarinetist, approached Schubert with a commission. He wanted a companion work to Beethoven's highly popular Septet, Op. 20, something that would use the same instruments and that would, of course, include a part for him. Schubert started composing in February 1824, using the same instruments (clarinet, bassoon, French horn, violin, viola, cello, and bass) as Beethoven, but with the addition of a second violin to increase the sonority. In a letter written on March 6, 1824, Moritz von Schwind described the composer's absorption in the music: "Schubert has now long been at work on an octet, with the greatest zeal. If you go to see him during the day he says, 'Hello, how are you?—Good!' and goes on working, whereupon you depart." One of Schubert's longer chamber works, the octet is determinedly sunny and optimistic; it betrays little of Schubert's pain and suffering.

The octet, which was completed in March 1824, received its private premiere at the home of Count von Troyer on April 16; the public premiere was given three years later, on April 16, 1827. As an indication of the low esteem in which Schubert was held, the octet was not published until 1853, nearly three decades later.

The octet opens with a slow, broadly conceived introduction that contains foreshadowings of the themes that are to follow in the fast body of the movement; of particular importance is the dotted (long-short) rhythm that runs through the introduction, and the entire movement as well. Schubert starts the Allegro with a tutti statement of the vigorous, forthright principal theme, which he extends and expands before the clarinet introduces the subsidiary theme, much quieter and cantabile, but sharing the same dotted-note rhythmic pattern. The subsidiary theme is the main focus of the development. The music quiets before Schubert brings back a brief reminder of the introduction, leading directly to the formal recapitulation and a faster coda at the very end.

The second movement, Andante un poco mosso ("moderate speed with a little motion") in many performing editions, but Adagio ("slow") in Schubert's manuscript, is dreamy and lyrical in character. It starts with a beautifully written clarinet statement of the theme, an obvious nod to Count von Troyer, which is immediately repeated by the first violin with the clarinet adding a countermelody above. The violin is also entrusted with the second theme, which maintains the same mood, but with a sense of urgency lent by the pulsating viola accompaniment. Both themes, and the brief development section, include echoes of the dotted rhythm from the first movement. Schubert then ends quietly after reviewing the two melodies.

A soft, but robust, peasant dance played in unison by the strings announces the third movement; it is immediately followed by a forceful tutti response. This exchange goes back and forth until the clarinet emerges, executing its own perky rendition of the same tune. After fully working over this material with its characteristic dotted rhythm, Schubert goes on to the smooth, cantilena violin melody and walking bass line of the trio. At the end, the first part is repeated.

Schubert borrowed the melody for the following theme-and-variations movement from his earlier opera, *Die Freunde von Salamanka* (*The Friends from Salamanca*). He subjects it to seven variations, not to develop and transform the original melody so much as to decorate and embellish it. Essentially he replaces the sedate, slow-moving melody with rapid figurations and complex rhythms, reaching a climax in the final, seventh variation, with its bravura violin parts, before a quiet coda brings the movement to an end.

The Menuetto, which is not particularly dancelike, nevertheless exudes a feeling of comfortable warmth. Schubert effortlessly spins out the gentle, charming melody with the focus of interest alternating between the strings and winds. Except for a slight intensification of the rhythmic pulse, the middle section trio is little different in character and even has some turns of melody closely akin to the opening. As usual, a repeat of the Menuetto follows, and a short coda rounds out the movement.

The most foreboding, dramatic moment in the octet is the introduction to the last movement. Over a tremolo in the cello, the others give out the theme in breathless surges, this time in a double-dotted rhythm that makes the long notes longer and the short notes shorter, intensifying the tension and power. After two statements of the melody, the music fades away and the movement proper sets off with a rousing march melody, nonetheless causing a little discomfort with its three plus five measure phrases, instead of the more usual four plus four. As soon as the music comes to a full stop, the clarinet and bassoon introduce the jolly second theme, resembling an *opera buffa* tune. After developing and returning the two themes, Schubert interrupts with a reminder of the introduction before rushing headlong through the high-speed coda.

Gunther Schuller

Born November 22, 1925, in New York City

EVEN A very brief review of Gunther Schuller's career reveals both the depth and scope of his truly remarkable musical talent as composer, performer, and teacher. Born into a musically gifted family (his father was a violinist in the New York Philharmonic), Schuller's first instrumental studies were on flute, followed two years later by instruction on French horn. So amazing was his progress that, by age seventeen, he was playing the French horn in the Ballet Theater Orchestra and the same year was appointed principal horn of the Cincinnati Symphony. Two years later Schuller moved to the Metropolitan Opera Orchestra, where he remained until 1959, at which time he gave up his career as an instrumentalist to devote himself more fully to composing, conducting, and teaching.

Largely self-taught as a composer, Schuller has been writing music since age twelve. His approach, which might best be labeled syncretistic, is a joining or bringing together of various trends of twentieth-century music. The best example is his synthesis of the improvisatory approach and rhythmic freedom of jazz with the forms, styles, and vocabulary of contemporary serious music to create a new music language that he named Third Stream in 1957. (If jazz is one stream and serious music is the second, this merging of the two is the Third Stream.) In his own music we can hear, in addition to the Third Stream influence, adaptations of Schoenberg's twelve-tone method, Webern's serialism, and Stravinsky's metrics, all integrated into a distinctive and unique musical conception.

Even before resigning from the Metropolitan Opera Orchestra, Schuller had already begun his outstanding career as a pedagogue, which took him to the Manhattan School of Music (1950–1963) and Yale University (1964–1967), culminating in a ten-year tenure as president of the New England Conservatory (1967–1977). In addition to a highly successful career that has embraced composing, performing, and teaching, Schuller has been involved in numerous musical projects that range from conducting many of the world's greatest orchestras to bringing the ragtime music of Scott Joplin to public attention.

Schuller's achievements as a composer have been widely recognized and have earned for him two Guggenheim Fellowships, an award from the National Institute of Arts and Letters, the Brandeis University Creative Arts Award, and several honorary degrees. His chamber works, in addition to the Woodwind Quintet discussed below, include Quartet for Four Double Basses (1947), Five Pieces, for Five Horns (1952), *Symbiosis,* Music for Violin, Piano, and Percussion (1957), two string quartets (1957 and 1965), Fantasy Quartet for Four Cellos (1958), Music for Brass Quintet (1961), *Aphorisms,* for flute and string trio (1967), Octet (1979), *Sonata Serenata* (1978), a piano trio (1984), and a piano quartet (1984).

Woodwind Quintet
I. Lento. II. Moderato. III. Agitato.

The first movement of Schuller's Woodwind Quintet is based on two sharply contrasted ideas that the composer asks the players to delineate very clearly at the outset. One is a long lyrical melodic line with a pointillistic accompaniment that extends through the entire movement; the other Schuller describes as ''short outbursts of considerable violence and complexity,'' which periodically break into the extended melody. The particular quality of this melody is that it is passed, imperceptibly, from instrument to instrument (in succession, flute, oboe, clarinet, bassoon, and so on) much like a baton being handed from one runner to the next in a relay race. With each change, the melodic line undergoes a transformation of timbre and tonal quality, creating subtly evolving gradations of color. This technique, in which the tone color itself becomes the carrier of the basic musical idea, was first elaborated as a musical technique by Schoenberg and is known as *Klangfarbenmelodie,* or tone-color melody. As the movement proceeds, though, the originally calm melody grows more agitated and increasingly dense in rhythm and texture, until at the end the two underlying ideas have phased into each other, becoming indistinguishable.

The second movement is even more lyrical than the first and illustrates again Schuller's interest in instrumental sonorities. There is, for example, one short example of *Klangfarbenmelodie* as a single note is passed back and forth among the players. But the emphasis in this movement is on harmonic coloring, essentially homophonic and melodic music contrasted with the highly polyphonic first movement.

The jazz element in Schuller's musical vocabulary comes to the fore in the Agitato third movement. The opening and closing A sections of the simple A-B-A form are built on a steady, swinging jazz beat. Since many woodwind quintet players may not be familiar or comfortable with jazz inflection, Schuller includes comments in the score on the idiomatic playing of this style of music. The rhythm relaxes in the middle B section, which, as Schuller explains, is improvisatory "not in the sense used in jazz, but rather as used in cadenzas." "These 'improvisations,'" he says, "are not melodic in nature but textural, and serve as 'improvised' accompaniments to written out, freely interpreted cadenzas for several [clarinet, flute, bassoon, horn] of the instruments."

Schuller completed his Woodwind Quintet on August 7, 1958, and dedicated it to the New York Woodwind Quintet, who gave the first performance in Cologne, Germany.

Robert Schumann

Born June 8, 1810, in Zwickau, Germany
Died July 29, 1856, in Endenich, Germany

ROBERT SCHUMANN was an artist with a mission: "To send light into the depths of the human heart." From the very beginning, Schumann dedicated himself to overcoming the confining canons of eighteenth-century Classical music, and he along with Liszt and others helped to evolve the concepts and techniques of nineteenth-century Romanticism. "I am affected," Robert Schumann wrote, "by everything that goes on in the world—politics, literature, people—I think it over in my own way, and then I long to express my feelings in music." Because of this undeniable urge to connect his music with "distant" and "sometimes unorthodox" interests, many people found Schumann's pieces difficult to understand, and consequently they were seldom performed during his lifetime.

Schumann's parents were not especially musical. His father was a book seller and publisher, his mother, the daughter of a surgeon. Nevertheless, Schumann was drawn to the piano at the age of seven and, while developing his talent as a pianist, was soon trying his hand at composing. His musical sensibility is well illustrated by the account of how, one night while still a child, he stole to the piano and played a progression of chords that moved him so profoundly that he wept without being able to stop.

In 1828, at his mother's insistence and against his own wishes, he entered into the study of law, but managed to spend more time with music than in class. That same year, Schumann began piano lessons with Friedrich Wieck and met Wieck's nine-year-old daughter, Clara, already a successful pianist, whom Schumann adored. At twenty, Schumann decided to abandon his studies of law and to devote himself full-time to serious piano study. To accelerate his already

397

amazing progress, Schumann devised a mechanical contraption that he believed would strengthen his fingers. Unfortunately the contrivance permanently damaged a finger of his right hand, precluding the possibility of ever fulfilling a career as pianist. Undaunted, Schumann redoubled his efforts to compose, following what he now saw as his true musical calling, and by 1831 his first piano pieces appeared in print. Of his drive to write music, he said, "Often I feel such a compulsion to compose that even if I were on a lonely island in the middle of the sea I could not stop." Over the following years, he added songs, orchestral works, and chamber pieces to his growing list of piano compositions.

In addition to composing actively, Schumann engaged in literary efforts that gave voice to his new ideas about music. *Neue Zeitschrift für Musik* ("New Journal for Music"), which he launched in 1834, contained articles he wrote attacking the bourgeois taste of the time— the art of the Philistines, as he called it. Assuming two pseudonyms—Florestan, the free, exuberant artist who opposed restraints, and Eusebius, the more reflective and introverted individual who upheld the rules of order and form—Schumann carried into print the conflict that he and other artists of the time were experiencing between the Romantic freedom they sought and the strict Classical controls they had inherited.

Meanwhile, Friedrich Wieck was trying unsuccessfully to end the growing love relationship between his daughter and Schumann. Eventually the couple went to court to force his consent to their marriage, and after a bitter legal battle they were wed in 1840. Throughout their life together, Clara, one of the most celebrated pianists of her time, furthered her husband's career by championing his music and giving the first performances of many of his works.

Schumann's musical achievements and his great personal happiness with his beloved Clara and their large family (eight children) were overshadowed by the specter of mental illness. His father, August, had suffered from so-called "nervous disorders," and his sister Emelia had committed suicide. Despite signs of his own emotional instability, Schumann was able to continue teaching at the Leipzig Conservatory until 1844, when he suffered a severe breakdown. After he recovered, he became conductor at Düsseldorf in 1850, but recurring illness soon interfered with his duties in that position. He began to experience hallucinations and to show other symptoms of mental illness, climaxing with a suicide attempt in 1854. After he was rescued, he asked to be placed in a mental asylum, where he died two years later.

Introspective, impassioned, and innovative, Schumann represents the highest ideals of Romanticism. His personal, emotional music continues to impress listeners in a most affecting and direct way.

String Quartets, Op. 41, Nos. 1, 2, and 3

Schumann had a tendency to cluster his compositions. From 1831 to 1839, he wrote piano pieces; 1840 was mostly given over to songs; 1841 saw his first symphonies; and 1842 was the year for chamber music—three string quartets, a piano quintet, and a piano quartet. The entries in his "household book" show how he prepared for his first chamber music essays (discounting a few now-lost juvenile attempts):

April 1—Constantly quartets. Studied Mozart.

April 28—Quartets by Beethoven.

May 6—Studied quartets by Haydn.

June 4—Quartet in A minor begun.

The composer worked on the first two quartets simultaneously and then went on to the third; all were done within five weeks and were dedicated "To his friend Felix Mendelssohn Bartholdy." He arranged for the premiere of all three as a present for his wife Clara on September 13, her twenty-third birthday.

While much of the music is idiomatically written for quartet, some sections sound as though they were conceived as songs or miniature piano pieces and then transposed to the string quartet medium. Perhaps it is for that reason that, although Schumann regarded the Op. 41 quartets very highly, he never again wrote for strings alone; every subsequent chamber work included, or indeed featured, the piano. The most striking aspect of the Op. 41 quartets is the sharp contrast in style and mood and feeling among individual sections or movements. These abrupt changes may have to do with the conflict between the free, outgoing, Dionysian side of his musical personality (Florestan) and the restrained, pensive, Appollonian side (Eusebius).

String Quartet in A Minor, Op. 41, No. 1

I. Introduzione: Andante espressivo;
Allegro. II. Scherzo: Presto;
Intermezzo. III. Adagio. IV. Presto.

While Schumann prepared to write his quartets by studying the quartets of Mozart, Beethoven, and Haydn, he also spent time absorbing Bach's contrapuntal techniques. And it is the Bach influence that we hear most clearly in the introduction to the strangely impersonal A minor quartet, a highly contrapuntal section that Schumann added after the movement was finished. A brief transition leads from the polyphonic introduction to the homophonic pianistic Allegro (curiously in F major instead of the expected A minor) with its easy, fluid theme. Schumann spins out this theme before giving the subsidiary subject, an obvious derivative of the first theme, to the second violin with saucy comments from the first violin. Very neatly Schumann then works through the two themes in order and brings them back little changed for the recapitulation and a quiet ending.

The theme of the Scherzo appears in two starkly contrasting guises—Florestan and Eusebius. At times, it is light and delicate, much like a Mendelssohn fairyland scherzo; other times it is forceful and energetic, more in the manner of a charging cavalry brigade. The sweetly sentimental trio, a foil to the two facets of the Scherzo, acts as a brief, lyrical interlude before the return of the first part.

Three recitativelike measures lead to the principal theme of the Adagio, a beautiful love ballad that moves from sprituality to ecstasy as it is eloquently sung, initially by the first violin and then by the cello. After the two statements of the theme, an agitated middle section, based on the viola's accompaniment figure from the first part, intrudes. The interruption is followed by a final presentation of the main theme, and the movement ends with a recitative similar to the opening.

The entire last movement springs from the emboldened theme— rhythmically, short-short-long followed by a rapid run—heard at the very outset. The second theme merely turns the melodic direction of the first theme upside down and combines it with rising chains of eighth notes heard earlier. The exciting development section features a wide variety of sonorities, including some that are almost orchestral in effect. The recapitulation starts with an even more forceful return of the opening; the second theme, in its turn, now appears right side up. Then, in a brilliant stroke of imagination, Schumann suddenly cuts the tempo and presents the eighth-note chains in a slow-motion, bagpipe treatment, followed by a solemn choralelike episode. The high spirits of the principal theme will not be denied, though, and the lively gaiety quickly reestablishes itself in a brilliant coda.

String Quartet in F Major, Op. 41, No. 2

I. Allegro vivace. II. Andante, quasi variazioni. III. Scherzo: Presto. IV. Allegro molto vivace.

In 1838, when Schumann told his future wife Clara Wieck that he was thinking of writing some strings quartets, she replied, ''I'm very much delighted over your plan. Only, please compose more clearly. It hurts me too much when people fail to understand you.'' Although her answer got an angry response from Robert, one senses that in the F major quartet at least, he did try to downplay his individual and forward-looking style of writing and adapt to the rather reactionary public taste of German audiences of the time.

The first movement of Op. 41, No. 2 is clear proof that Schumann studied the quartets of Haydn in preparation for his Op. 41 quartets. Here, Haydn's monothematicism—a single theme dominating a sonata-form movement—is evident, despite Schumann's very distinctive handling of the formal technique. The principal theme is a warm, soaring melody that Schumann immediately subjects to an extensive development. Then, near the end of the exposition, he does indeed toss in another theme that moves in equal quarter notes and is treated in canon. But the theme is so short and lacking in profile that it hardly qualifies as a theme. Following one quick glimpse of this motif, the entire development section is devoted to the first theme. The recapitulation returns both themes, but with the focus still exclusively on the first. A brief coda ends the movement.

The second movement, in variation form, starts with a rather rambling, gentle love-song theme. Four variations follow. The first is sinuous and dusky with its chromatic eighth notes; the second doubles the speed of the notes (to sixteenths) and adds a good-humored pizzicato bass line; the third is slow and solemn; and the fourth has an innocent, childlike quality. The last two variations seem to move further and further away from the original theme and sound more like the salon-type character piano pieces of Schumann's *Scenes from Childhood*. Schumann next returns the theme, albeit shortened, and ends with a coda closely related to the second variation. Since this appears to be a straightfoward theme and variations, then why did he title the movement Andante, *quasi* Variazioni ("Slow, *almost like variations*")? The probable reason is that the effect is more like ternary form (A-B-A) than theme and variations—A: Theme, and Variations 1 and 2, B: Variations 3 and 4, A: Return of Theme and Variation 2.

Schumann most likely conceived the series of arpeggios that are the theme of the Scherzo at the piano, little realizing how difficult and uncomfortable they are to play on string instruments. Nevertheless, the composer follows the very demanding Scherzo with a humorous, almost burlesque trio, in which the cello introduces the lighthearted melody against an offbeat accompaniment, with each statement leading to an outburst of laughter in the others. After a repeat of the Scherzo, the short coda brings together the fun of the trio and the opening arpeggio figure.

The first theme of the brief finale is a coruscating *Moto perpetuo* in which all four players share. The forward movement slows for the subsidiary theme, which seems to lack a very clear melodic or rhythmic contour. The development, which is mostly focused on the second theme, leads to a truncated recapitulation. The coda, in a faster tempo, builds to a climactic conclusion.

String Quartet in A Major, Op. 41, No. 3

I. Andante espressivo: Allegro molto moderato. II. Assai agitato. III. Adagio molto. IV. Finale: Allegro molto vivace.

The A major, the favorite and probably most exceptional of the three quartets of Op. 41, opens with a slow, dreamy introduction in which the descending interval of a fifth, heard at the very outset, figures very prominently. The same interval appears subsequently as the head of the main theme and in the second theme as well. After introducing the tender, plaintive theme, Schumann moves on to an even more lyrical second theme, a sustained cantilena melody heard in the cello against a brisk offbeat accompaniment. Since the concise development is almost entirely devoted to the first theme, Schumann starts the recapitulation with the second theme, saving the first for a codalike appearance at the very end of the movement. The last two notes are an echo in the cello of the descending fifth interval.

The Assai agitato, which functions as the scherzo, is among the most imaginative and ingenious movements in the chamber music repertoire. In free variation form, the second movement is really a theme preceded by three variations and followed by a final variation. The first section, restless and hesitant (a variation on an as-yet-unheard theme), corresponds to the Eusebius aspect of Schumann's character. The two variations that come next are stronger and more agitated (representing Schumann's Florestan side). It is at this point that the tempo slows and we hear a canon for first violin and viola—the simple theme (Eusebius-like) of the movement and the source of the preceding transformations. A final variation follows (the triumph of Florestan), leading to a coda, in which echoes of the last variation end the movement.

Schumann rises far above the common and ordinary to scale the heights of Romantic expression in the deeply moving Adagio. He introduces a number of distinctive musical ideas. The introspective, yearning opening melody; a counter statement, introduced by the viola, with a dramatic upward leap before it falls away; and a first violin and viola dialogue around a throbbing second violin accompaniment figure. Then, giving this remarkable material free rein, Schumann allows it to expand, develop, and return rhapsodically, creating an impassioned and profound movement that is shaped more by content than by any prescribed formal construct.

The powerful, scintillating Finale is the apotheosis of rondo form, with each of thirteen individual sections clearly separated and delineated. The principal theme, a mere fourteen measures long, is characterized by syncopations and dotted (long-short) rhythm. After it comes to a full stop, the delicate tracery of the contrasting B theme is heard, another reference to Schumann's Florestan-Eusebius duality. The original A theme returns in all its vigor to give way to C, a slightly more earthbound derivative of B. The A theme comes back again, now condensed to eight measures. The tempo slows down a bit for the D interlude, a graceful, poised dance episode. At the end of the D section, Schumann pauses briefly and, in effect, starts all over again, going through each of the sections once more, this time with some modifications and changes in key. Following the second hearing of the D section, Schumann appends a rather lengthy coda that whips the original tune up into a furious climactic finish.

Piano Quintet in E Flat Major, Op. 44

I. Allegro brillante. II. In Modo d'una Marcia: Un poco largamente. III. Scherzo: Molto vivace. IV. Allegro ma non troppo.

Schumann's piano quintet is his most frequently performed chamber composition; it is also the pioneering quintet for piano and string quartet and the inspiraion for a line of great works for the combination, including those by Brahms, Franck, and Dvořák.

Schumann wrote this seminal work in September 1842, taking five days to prepare the sketches and two weeks to complete the score. He dedicated it to his wife, Clara, and scheduled the premiere for December 6 of the same year at the Leipzig home of Carl and Henriette Voigt. Clara, who was to participate, fell ill on the day of the performance, and Felix Mendelssohn stepped in, playing the difficult piano part at sight.

Mendelssohn's participation at the premiere left a lasting impact on the work; he found the second trio in the Scherzo movement lacking, and it was at his suggestion that Schumann wrote a livelier replacement.

Critics have faulted the quintet for what some consider an overly prominent piano part, with the strings relegated to the background. According to one explanation, offered by Homer Ulrich in his book on chamber music, Schumann conceived the piano as a counterbalance to the four strings and not as one part among five equals; therefore it bears one-half of the musical burden, not one-fifth. All too often, though, the fault lies not with Schumann but with the pianist, who plays too loudly. If the pianist allows the string tone to predominate when the piano and a string instrument are playing the same note, as is so often the case, most of the balance problems seem to disappear.

The bold, assertive first theme, played in a forceful tutti opens the quintet, followed immediately by its miraculous transformation into a wonderfully warm, cantilena melody. The cello and viola present the sensitive second theme as a conversational dialogue. A heavily accented third theme, an obvious outgrowth of the first, brings the exposition to its conclusion. Schumann ignores the second theme in the development section, which includes long strings of virtuosic piano runs against sustained string chords. The recapitulation brings back the exposition slightly modified, and the movement ends without a coda.

The second movement, In Modo d'una Marcia ("In the Style of a March"), clearly refers to a funeral march, not in any personal mournful sense but as an objective musical experience. Schumann structures the movement as a cross between rondo and sonata form. The first theme has the cadence of a solemn march. A tenuous, sustained first violin line over a busy, anxious accompaniment functions as the contrasting second theme and precedes the return of the opening. The faster-moving next section works over both the first and second ideas before the movement concludes with a final statement of the first theme.

The Scherzo is the glorification of the scale. Whether a single instrument or in combination, going up or down, loud or soft, in even notes or trochees, the subject is always scales. The lyrical, legato first trio with the first violin and viola in canon, offers a welcome respite from the relentlessly scalic Scherzo. The return of the Scherzo is followed by the second trio, a high-powered, heavily accented perpetual motion. Schumann ends the movement with a final review of the Scherzo and a summarizing coda.

The crowning last movement contains all the virility and sturdiness of the first movement. The pianist flings out the muscular principal theme with an accent on every note, backed up by the strings playing a tempestuous repeated-note accompaniment. A contrasting quiet and songlike subsidiary melody acts as a foil to the first theme. The short, subdued development is mostly concerned with the second theme, building up at the end to an exultant return of the first to start the recapitulation, which proceeds regularly through both themes. In the very spacious and remarkable coda, Schumann introduces two major fugal sections, the first based on the movement's principal theme, the second combining that melody with the main theme from the first movement in an overwhelming three-voice double fugue.

Piano Quartet in E Flat Major, Op. 47

I. Sostenuto assai; Allegro ma non troppo. II. Scherzo: Molto vivace. III. Andante cantabile. IV. Finale: Vivace.

Schumann wrote his Piano Quartet in E Flat Major in 1842 for Count Matvei Wielhorsky, an amateur but very accomplished cellist, judging from the difficulty of the cello part and its prominence throughout. In this way, then, the quartet may be said to look back to the eighteenth century, to the practice of dedicating music to aristocrats for their use and in the hope of receiving money or a gift in appreciation. But in most other ways, this piano quartet is a product of the nineteenth century; it is a lush, Romantic, impassioned work, fully committed to the expression of the composer's most intimate thoughts and feelings.

The principal theme of the first movement appears in three guises: soulful and melancholy when heard initially in the slow introduction; rhythmically incisive as played by the piano in the faster Allegro ma non troppo; and finally bright and songful as spun out by the cello. The more forceful subsidiary theme—an accented syncopated note and a rapid rising scale—is introduced as a canon between piano and strings. A repeat of the opening Sostenuto acts as a link to the development section, which is involved exclusively with working out the first theme. The music grows louder and more frenzied, leading to the climactic return of the themes (minus the introduction) for the recapitulation. Schumann, though, has a surprise in the coda. He increases the tempo and gives the cello a completely new theme, before capping the movement off with a quick recollection of the initial tune.

Despite the Scherzo's apparent happy and high spirits, it seems slightly reticent to give in to untrammeled joy. The effect is perhaps due to the opening, which is played in the cello and piano's lowest range, where it is especially hard to sparkle or scintillate, and then to some overall thickness in the subsequent writing. The first trio, a sweet, ingenuous legato melody, is treated in imitation, with each appearance set off by quick staccato flashes from the Scherzo. The Scherzo returns after the first trio, followed by a second trio, a sequence of piano and tutti chords with little wisps of the Scherzo peaking through. The Scherzo's last peroration brings the movement to a close.

The Andante cantabile is the emotional high point of the quartet. After two measures of introduction, the cello sings the impassioned, highly Romantic principal melody, which is imitated by the violin. The piano, with some help from the viola, concludes this section and leads to the middle part, a somber interlude, after which the viola and then the cello present the original melody. While the viola plays its part, the cellist lowers his or her C string one step to B flat, which is then sustained as a low pedal tone during the coda as the others play distant whispered anticipations of the Finale.

The exuberant joie de vivre of the Finale quickly dispels the fervid, ardent mood of the Andante cantabile; it is the reappearance of Florestan after Eusebius, so to speak. Theme after theme pours forth in wonderful abundance. The first, hinted at in the previous movement, becomes the subject of a strong, willful fugal section. The cello responds with a soaring cantabile melody. A flowing lyrical theme follows, passed gently back and forth between piano and viola. The opening fugal melody returns, this time, though, more legato. And finally a sprightly, staccato line appears, introduced by the cello and piano left hand. This plenitude of material, moving with great energy and élan, is interspersed with sections of contrapuntal intricacy that fit in perfectly, never impeding the ongoing musical flow.

With the piano quartet, begun at the end of October 1842 and finished a couple of weeks later, Schumann brought to a close his amazing burst of chamber music activity that started in June with the three quartets of Op. 41 and included the piano quintet. The works's well-received premiere was given in Leipzig on December 8, 1844, by Ferdinand David (violin), Niels W. Gade (viola), Count Wielhorsky (cello), and Clara Schumann (piano).

Piano Trio in D Minor, Op. 63

I. Mit energie und Leidenschaft. II. Lebhaft, doch nicht zu rasch. III. Langsam, mit inniger Empfindung. IV. Mit Feuer.

Of Schumann's four piano trios (D minor, Op. 63, F major, Op. 80, G minor, Op. 110, and *Fantasiestücke,* Op. 88), only the exceedingly Romantic D minor (1847)—passionate and surging with emotion—has won a place in the modern repertoire. Like other Schumann chamber music that includes piano, the trios are prone to balance problems unless the pianist is especially sensitive to the potential difficulty. Since the piano plays all the time, and the music is so often thickly written, with piano and string instrument doubling (playing the same notes), it is incumbent on the piano to underplay its part, thus protecting the violin and cello from being reduced to feeble background murmurings.

The first movement opens with a fervent, though slightly troubled, violin melody over busy, rolling piano accompaniment. Schumann's tempo direction, Mit Energie und Leidenschaft ("With Energy and Passion"), dictates the performance style. A sharply accented transition (an anticipation, perhaps, of the Scherzo theme) leads to the subsidiary subject, an intense, syncopated melody in the piano against a densely textured background. After setting out two such lengthy and emotional themes, what is left for the composer to do in the development? Schumann starts out in a traditional way, but then breaks off, introducing a completely new choralelike theme in a slightly slower tempo. Particularly striking is the tone color Schumann obtains by having the piano play its high-pitched chords staccato and *una corda* ("soft pedal"), while both strings double the piano's bass line, playing *ponticello*. The recapitulation follows, differing from the exposition in that the second theme is now in the bright major mode. The new material reappears in the coda, which slips back into minor for a somber ending.

The Scherzo, a movement of unflagging vitality, is very simply constructed. The theme grows from a rapid pattern of ascending long and short notes that must be played with great crispness and accuracy. The contrasting trio theme is a smoothed out, legato version of the Scherzo motif passed canonically from instrument to instrument. A shortened return of the Scherzo and a coda round off the movement.

In the somber, but beautiful third movement Schumann seems to be speaking to each listener from deep within his own troubled soul. One senses, though, that so much of his attention is focused on the expression of his inner feelings that perhaps a certain rhythmic laxness and lack of harmonic direction creep into the writing. The violin and piano share in the presentation of the principal subject, which is soft in dynamics, but turbulent at its emotional core. A slightly faster middle section is propelled forward by repeated triplets in the piano as all three instruments take turns presenting the somewhat more cheerful major-key melody. The minor key, though, returns for a truncated repeat of the morose opening section.

The vital and robust finale follows without pause, its strongly affirmative outlook derived in part from its major-key tonality. The piano gives out the exalted, upward-stretching first theme, which Schumann helps to define by directing it to be played Mit Feuer ("With Fire"). After subjecting it to some development, he moves on to the second theme, a moving scalic cello line in equal quarter tones, which he also expands at once. The development section is neatly divided; the first part deals with the first theme, the second part with the second theme. The recapitulation is quite short, but Schumann makes up for it with a lengthy coda, practically another development section, which grows faster for the brilliant conclusion.

Dmitri Shostakovich

Born September 25, 1906, in Saint Petersburg (Leningrad)
Died August 9, 1975, in Moscow

SHOSTAKOVICH WAS a product of the Soviet system, and all of his music was affected by the official interpretation of Lenin's famous dictum, "Art belongs to the people." His first major piece, Symphony No. 1, written when he graduated from the Saint Petersburg Conservatory in 1926, was an immediate success. Its brash, barbed writing satisfied the Soviet leaders, who were filled with revolutionary fervor and willing to encourage originality and experimentation in art.

By 1930, though, public policy had changed, and the new goal was "socialistic realism," art works that glorified the state, its heroes, and its accomplishments. Under the new esthetic, anything new, abstract, or strikingly original was condemned as being in conflict with the national ideals. Thus, Shostakovich's satirical opera, *The Nose,* was soundly denounced by the official Russian Association of Proletarian Musicians as "bourgeois decadence." While he returned to favor with his light, charming First Piano Concerto in 1933, an even more serious accusation followed in 1936 after Premier Joseph Stalin, furious at what he was hearing, stormed out of a performance of Shostakovich's opera, *Lady Macbeth of Mtsensk.* A denunciation that appeared in *Pravda* under the headline "Muddle Instead of Music" spoke of the opera's "quacks, grunts and growls" and threatened that its composer "could end very badly."

Shostakovich bounced back with his brilliant, popular Fifth Symphony (1937), which he called his "creative reply to just criticism." The official seal of approval came in 1940, when Shostakovich was awarded the extremely prestigious Stalin Prize for his Piano Quintet. The following years had their ups and downs, with another Stalin Prize for the 1941 Seventh Symphony, *Leningrad,* and criticism for

409

the 1945 Ninth Symphony, which was not the monumental commemoration of the Soviet victory in World War II that the government leaders had expected.

The climax—or nadir—came in 1948, when the Central Committee of the Communist Party charged a number of Russian composers, including Shostakovich and Prokofiev, with ". . . formalist perversions and antidemocratic tendencies in music, alien to the Soviet people and its artistic tastes." It is interesting to note that the same music that Stalin banned as imperialistic, capitalistic formalism, Hitler also banned—but as decadent Bolshevism!

Shostakovich, always shy, nervous, and somewhat sickly, became exceedingly contrite in his public posture. "I am deeply grateful," he wrote, "for all the criticism contained in the Resolution. I shall, with still more determination, work on the musical depiction of the images of the heroic Soviet people." The next year he wrote the oratorio, *The Song of the Forests,* which earned him a third Stalin Prize, followed by two symphonies dealing with the Russian Revolution. Spiritually, though, he turned inward and pursued at the same time the composition of "private" music, where the content was increasingly autobiographical, such as his Tenth Symphony and Eighth String Quartet. As the years passed and his health deteriorated, Shostakovich's musical imagination became increasingly occupied with thoughts of death, culminating in his deeply tragic Fifteenth String Quartet.

Shostakovich started his series of fifteen string quartets soon after the 1936 attack on *Lady Macbeth* and continued working on them until the end of his life. The chamber works contain Shostakovich's innermost thoughts and feelings and are judged by many critics to be among the towering accomplishments of twentieth-century music.

String Quartet No. 1, Op. 49

I. Moderato. II. Moderato. III. Allegro molto. IV. Allegro.

After being savagely attacked in a 1936 *Pravda* article for his opera *Lady Macbeth of Mtsensk,* Shostakovich returned to official favor with his Fifth Symphony in 1937 and the First String Quartet, which he wrote in the summer of 1938. "I began to write it," Shostakovich said of the quartet, "without any particular idea or feeling in mind, and thought nothing would come of it. The quartet is one of the hardest musical mediums. I wrote the first page as a sort of exercise in quartet form, without any thought of completing it. But then the piece took hold of me and I completed it very quickly. One shouldn't look for any great depth in this first quartet. I'd call it a 'springtime' work."

Written in a simple, relaxed, pellucid style, the quartet is pleasurable and delightful. The first movement starts with a tranquil, open-faced melody, to be followed by a second melody that is introduced by the cello's gentle sliding accompaniment figure. The remainder of the brief movement has time for little more than a few measures of development and a short, altered restatement of the two subjects.

Although the tempo of the second movement is the same as the first, the character is quite different. The theme, introduced by the viola, is reminiscent of a soulful Russian folk song. Shostakovich then subjects the theme to a number of continuous variations, some quiet and pensive, others quite warm and fervent, before bringing the movement to a quiet close.

The Allegro molto is a high-speed, whispered scherzo that races along with a rapidly repeated note being heard almost continuously. The catchy little tune of the middle section serves as a contrast preceding a final recollection of the opening.

A spirit of buoyant good humor runs through the last movement with an infectious merriment that cannot be resisted.

The quartet was introduced in Leningrad by the Glazunov Quartet on October 10, 1938.

Piano Quintet, Op. 57

I. Prelude: Lento. II. Fugue: Adagio. III. Scherzo: Allegretto. IV. Intermezzo: Lento. V. Finale: Allegretto.

Shostakovich had a close working relationship with the members of Russia's Beethoven String Quartet, and he entrusted the premieres of most of his fifteen quartets to them. Early on, while preparing the first quartet, the group asked Shostakovich to write a quintet for piano and strings that they might play together. Shostakovich readily agreed; he composed the quintet during the summer of 1940 and performed it with the group in Moscow on November 23, 1940. So enthusiastically was it received by the audience that the performers were forced to repeat the Scherzo and Finale, establishing a custom that is sometimes observed today and leading one wit to observe that the work has five movements—of which there are seven! That same year the quintet was awarded the Stalin Prize of 100,000 rubles, perhaps the largest sum ever paid for a piece of chamber music!

Clear in texture and classical in style, the quintet starts with a slow, declamatory Prelude. The opening solemnity soon gives way, though, to a light, charming, slightly faster middle section. But the dramatic intensity returns for a brief, free reprise of the opening.

The Bach-like Fugue, which follows without pause, is profound and moving. The subject, which sounds as though it might be a melancholy Russian folk song, is announced by the first violin alone. Shostakovich develops considerable tension as he allows it to unfold ever so slowly in an unbroken cantabile line with an overall arch shape. The melody passes through all the strings and the piano, and additional motifs are introduced. After building to an impassioned climax, the music relaxes and gradually fades into inaudibility.

Fiery and tempestuous, the Scherzo bursts forth with two repetitions of an almost naive, two-phrase piano tune against an aggressive accompaniment in the strings. This saucy, slightly impertinent character continues until some humorously jarring sharp dissonances introduce the contrasting middle section with its folk dancelike melody. The first section returns again, in altered form, to conclude the movement.

The Intermezzo is essentially a dialogue between a broad flowing melody and a crisp, "walking" staccato line. Exploring the full range of tone colors available from the five instruments, Shostakovich creates a most attractive tone painting.

Near the end of the Intermezzo, the piano foreshadows the theme of the Finale and then carries it, without stop, into the fifth movement proper. Slower, more subdued and restrained than a typical Shostakovich last movement, the Finale nonetheless is cheerful and optimistic. The structure is clean and simple; the rhythm hovers between dance and march. Lest there be any question of the movement's character, one theme is a quotation of the tune traditionally played at the entrance of the clowns in the Russian circus. Yet, despite the joyful, even raucous and boisterous moments along the way, the Finale ends calmly, with an indifferent shrug.

Piano Trio No. 2 in E Minor, Op. 67

I. Andante; moderato. II. Allegro con brio. III. Largo. IV. Allegretto.

At the November 9, 1944, premiere of Shostakovich's second piano trio, many audience members were shocked by the apparent stylistic inconsistencies in the music. Shostakovich had composed the work that summer in remembrance of his dear friend, the music critic and brilliant intellectual, Ivan Sollertinsky, who had recently died of a heart attack while still a young man. Some parts of the trio have the solemn character one would expect in a memorial tribute, but other sections are cheerful, have the sound of Russian folk songs, or, in the case of the last movement, seem to be inspired by the vigorous dances of eastern European Jews.

Dmitri Rabinovich, a close personal friend of Shostakovich and a leading Russian music critic, has proposed a theory that posits an underlying coherence to the trio. According to Rabinovich, "The whole first movement leaves the impression of a calm and clear poetic picture of everyday, specifically Russian, life." The elegiac, dolorous melody of the introduction resembles a melancholy Slavic folk song, a presumed reference to Sollertinsky's Russian heritage. Repeated staccato notes lead to the somewhat faster main body of the movement, in which the principal theme, derived from the introductory material, exhibits unmistakable folk qualities. Other tunes, all related by their folkloric roots, build to a powerful climax, before fading away to a quiet ending.

The bright, energetic second movement is propelled with great motoric force; it has no apparent connection to Russian folk music. But, again to quote Rabinovich, ". . . although these two movements employ different means of expression, they are connected by the unity of their optimistic coloring, they are one in character, in their emotional meaning."

The Largo, obviously a threnody on Sollertinsky's death, is formally a chaconne, a set of continuous variations on eight grave, ponderous chords given out by the piano. Five times the piano repeats the series of chords while the strings sing the somber lament—now bleak and desolate, now anguished and impassioned.

Rabinovich suggests that the final movement, which follows without pause, is where "the real tragedy is unfolded." The themes bring to mind frenzied Yiddish dance tunes, although sounding much more like macabre dances of death than celebrations of life. Shostakovich's choice of melodic material was probably a musical reference to grim reports just reaching Russia of how the Germans had forced Jewish concentration camp inmates to dig mass graves and then dance on the edge as they were machine-gunned to death. The composer develops and expands these themes before ending the trio with reminders of the earlier movements and a final, despairing return of the last movement's themes. With the closing notes Shostakovich completes the journey from "life, serene and peaceful, full of joy and beauty," to death—not only of Sollertinsky, but of all others who died tragically before their time.

String Quartet No. 8, Op. 110

I. Largo. II. Allegro
molto. III. Allegretto. IV. Largo. V. Largo.

"In memory of victims of fascism and war." So reads the dedication of Shostakovich's eighth quartet, completed in about three days during the summer of 1960, while the composer was in Dresden writing the score for a film on World War II, called *Five Days, Five Nights*. Deeply involved in the film's subject matter and surrounded by evidence of the dreadful violence and destruction of the war, Shostakovich was moved to compose a frankly autobiographical quartet reflecting on that tragic period. By using the acronym formed from his name, DSCH, as the musical motto to open and sustain the work (in German these four letters stand for the notes D, E flat, C, and B) and by weaving many short quotes from past compositions into the texture, Shostakovich gives the quartet what scholar Norman Kay calls its "overtly programmatic" character.

The quartet is cast in five movements, which are played without pause. The cello intones the slow, mournful DSCH theme at the outset, and it is immediately imitated by the other instruments. Additional themes follow, including some borrowed from his first and fifth symphonies. Formally allied to a rondo, the DSCH motto dominates throughout.

A torrent of fast, clamorous notes marks the beginning of the second movement. The viola and cello interrupt with a forceful unison statement of the four-note motto theme before joining the headlong flight. The quotation of the Jewish-sounding melody from his second piano trio, here like a chilling shriek, produces a change in texture. The movement presses on, only one time falling below a fortissimo ("very loud") dynamic level, until it is abruptly cut off, seemingly in mid phrase.

The principal theme of the third movement, a bitter, ironic, and somewhat grotesque waltz, is clearly a transformation of DSCH. Various episodes are heard between returns of the waltz melody, including a snatch from the composer's Cello Concerto.

The Cello Concerto quotation extends into the fourth movement and becomes its first theme. Shostakovich bases the second theme on the Russian revolutionary song "Languishing in Prison," which he follows, at the climax of the movement, with a melody from his opera *Lady Macbeth of Mtsensk,* played in the high register by the cello. A loud, insistent three-note rapping signal is heard throughout the movement.

The fifth movement is a reminder of the first; it is a slow fugato on DSCH, a deeply expressive epitath for all those who fell in the fight against Nazism.

The String Quartet No. 8 was introduced in Leningrad on October 2, 1960, by the Beethoven Quartet.

String Quartet No. 10, Op. 118

I. Andante II. Allegretto
furioso. III. Adagio. IV. Allegretto.

Just before writing his tenth quartet, Shostakovich composed his Symphony No. 13, setting poems by Yevgeni Yevtushenko, including "Babi Yar," which tells of the Nazi slaughter of 30,000 Jews. Just after the quartet, he wrote the symphonic poem *The Execution of Stepan Rapin,* also on poems of Yevtushenko, dealing with the legendary seventeenth-century Cossack hero. Both works are programmatic and filled with highly charged extra-musical content. It is curious, therefore, that the tenth quartet is entirely abstract, gentle, and optimistic in tone, with all of its significance residing solely in the music itself.

The quartet opens with a subdued, but sharply etched theme played alone by the first violin. After some expansion, the cello introduces a contrasting lyrical second theme, while the viola plays a reiterated staccato accompanying figure. The first violin states the third theme, a smooth line, although with widely spaced intervals. The remainder of the movement merely replays these three subjects.

Shostakovich contributes a certain sense of mystery and expectancy by keeping everything on the piano, or soft, dynamic level.

By contrast, the second movement is never less than forte, or loud. With the sharp, jabbing notes of the first theme, the first violin immediately sets the angry, ferocious character. The cello presents the second theme in its upper register, which adds a certain nervousness and agitation to the proceedings. The opening subject is then returned, somewhat modified, by the two violins.

The Adagio is a passacaglia, an old form in which there are continuous variations over a repeated short melody. Here the melody is played nine times, mostly by the cello, while the first violin weaves a tapestry of warm, flowing melody, and the two middle voices essentially fill in the harmony.

The bridge to the fourth movement, which proceeds without pause, contains melodic turns in the first violin that give rise to the finale's first theme, a pert, dancelike tune expressed by the viola. The viola is also entrusted with the broadly sung second subject. Shostakovich then builds to a powerful climax, an exciting moment as the cello sings out the passacaglia theme from the last movement and the violins continue this movement's opening theme. The music gradually quiets from this high point, several short quotes from earlier movements mingling with the last movement's subjects before everything fades away to a hushed conclusion.

Composed during the spring and summer of 1964, the tenth quartet premiere was given in Moscow on November 20, 1964, by the Beethoven String Quartet.

String Quartet No. 15, Op. 144

I. Elegy: Adagio. II. Serenade: Adagio. III. Intermezzo: Adagio. IV. Nocturne: Adagio. V. Funeral March: Adagio molto. VI. Epilogue: Adagio.

Few works in the entire musical repertoire confront the end of life in a more personal, poignant, and anguished way than Shostakovich's fifteenth, and final, string quartet. Written when he was already seriously ill, just one year before his death, this deeply felt, absolutely honest musical utterance gives a stunning insight into the composer's thoughts on life, death, and immortality. His leave-taking of the world apparently was to be accomplished without fear and self-pity, but with courage and dignity. "Shostakovich seems to grasp death by the hand and disappear into an inexplicable void," in the words of Peter G. Davis.

The writing is uncompromising. Six movements, all very slow, are played without stop and use only simple, unchanging rhythmic patterns. Yet, the obvious sincerity and profundity capture and tenaciously hold the listener's attention, providing an extremely moving musical experience.

The brooding Elegy is in three-part form, starting with a melody in the second violin that remains firmly rooted on one tone. The contrast, in the major mode, starts as a slow-moving line in the first violin that essentially follows the intervals of a chord or triad. The third part is a return of the opening, along with some echoes of the second theme.

Three individual germinal cells provide the content of the next movement: the first, a long note that grows from very, very soft to a powerful accent that Shostakovich marked very, very, *very* loud; the second, an irregular pattern of notes and rests that is played roughly with great vehemence; and the third, a cantabile melody introduced by the first violin.

The furies are unleashed in the Intermezzo, as the first violin rips through its rapid figuration—even though the tempo remains exactly the same and the cello sits stoically on one long, soft, sustained note almost continuously throughout the entire movement.

The second violin and cello establish an accompaniment of arpeggios moving in opposite directions as a background for the poetic viola melody of the third movement. Later the first violin and viola provide the support as the theme passes to the cello. Toward the end of the section, Shostakovich foreshadows the rhythm of the following Funeral March.

Slower than the other movements (each beat is measured at sixty to a minute, instead of eighty), the rhythm of the Funeral March has the characteristic dotted, or long-short, pattern. Solo passages for the viola, cello, and first violin are heard between short comments by the full quartet.

The final movement summarizes what has come before. The composer presents quotes from each of the previous movements before the music gently and quietly expires.

Jean Sibelius

Born December 8, 1865, in Tavastehus, Finland
Died September 20, 1957, in Järvenpää, Finland

SIBELIUS'S MUSIC so effectively gave voice to Finland's culture and legends that, in his native land, he is more than a composer—he is a public hero. The nation has honored him with the Sibelius Musical Institute, the Sibelius Museum, and an annual festival devoted to his music. A postage stamp was issued with his likeness, and his birthdays are widely celebrated. During the 1930s, in the United States, England, and the countries of Scandinavia, Sibelius was considered one of the world's greatest composers. In a 1935 survey of listeners to the New York Philharmonic's Sunday afternoon radio broadcasts, for instance, the audience overwhelmingly chose Sibelius as their favorite symphonic composer—followed by Beethoven and Tchaikovsky! While there is little doubt that a similar poll today would find Sibelius lower on the list, nonetheless several of his compositions, such as Symphony No. 2, Violin Concerto, *Finlandia,* and *The Swan of Tuonela,* hold permanent positions in the modern repertoire. Included in this number, too, is his single published chamber music essay, *"Voces intimae,"* for string quartet.

Sibelius turned to the composition of chamber works early in his career. His juvenile production takes in four string quartets, four trios, two piano quartets, a piano quintet, and an octet, none of which are currently available. From contemporary accounts one gathers that they tended to be light, salon pieces, written mostly for entertainment.

Sibelius was extremely nationalistic in his early songs and tone poems. He drew his inspiration from Finnish legends and folklore. The melodies, although all original, have the flavor of indigenous folksongs and dances. His later works, including the symphonies and *"Voces intimae,"* are completely abstract, with no programmatic content. At all times, though, he refused to discuss the "meaning"

419

of his music. "You know how the wing of a butterfly crumbles at a touch?" he once asked. "So it is with my compositions; the very mention of them is fatal."

The style that Sibelius evolved was unique and personal. He favored pithy, compact motifs, rather than extended melodies—thematic material that does not lend itself easily to organization into any of the orthodox forms. By avoiding lengthy interludes, transitions, or padding of any sort, Sibelius wrote music that is laden with musical meaning and powerful in its emotional impact.

String Quartet in D Minor, Op. 56, "Voces Intimae" ("Inner Voices")

I. Andante; Allegro molto Moderato. II. Vivace. III. Adagio di molto. IV. Allegretto. V. Allegro.

During the composition of *"Voces intimae"* from December 1908 to March 1909, Sibelius was troubled by a throat ailment that the doctors had been unable to diagnose. Convinced it was cancer, Sibelius tortured himself with the fear of a slow, lingering death and the dread of leaving his young wife and children destitute. The quartet's Adagio seems to suggest some of the anguish he must have been feeling.

Fortunately, Sibelius's medical problem proved to be a benign tumor, which was successfully removed. The only lasting ill effect was that the composer was deprived of cigars and wine, two of his greatest pleasures. And, despite the tragic air of the Adagio, the rest of the quartet presents a robust, positive outlook.

Since most of Sibelius's composing was for orchestra, it is not surprising that at times *"Voces intimae"* sounds as though it were written for a symphonic string section. In part this comes from frequent doubling—two, three, or all four instruments playing the same notes. Formally, it tends more toward a five-movement suite, with each movement dominated by a single character and with a good deal of sharing of themes, than toward the classical quartet, with its interplay between contrasting subjects. The melodies, to a large extent, move stepwise, in conjunct motion.

The quartet opens with an introduction, a quiet, introspective duet for first violin and cello. The tempo picks up slightly for the main themes of the movement, which are extensions of the duet melody. After a short development, the much modified recapitulation starts with a repeat of the introduction, but in the faster tempo.

The second movement, which follows without pause, is essentially a buildup to a climax and a slackening off until the music fades away. The melodic material is all derived from the previous movement.

The center of gravity of the quartet is the Adagio, which most eloquently conveys a feeling of dark foreboding. At one point, early in the movement, all forward motion ceases, and three hushed chords are played. In a copy of the score, Sibelius had penciled in *"voces intimae"* over this mysterious utterance. What is the significance? Sadly, Sibelius has left us no extra-musical clue to the meaning of the "inner voices."

The following movement, in sharp contrast, is open, direct, and very upbeat in mood. The two themes—the first, a simple peasant-like tune, the second, a rhythmic figure played by the three upper strings—percolate with great energy and verve.

The cheerful finale abruptly bursts forth, with the impact of someone suddenly turning a radio on at full volume in the midst of a piece of music. Sibelius creates some amazing tonal effects with the four instruments in this lively concluding movement.

Elie Siegmeister

Born January 15, 1909, in New York City

ELIE SIEGMEISTER'S long and successful career in music has undergone a few significant changes in direction. But always Siegmeister has remained steadfast to the same conviction—that music is a form of communication, that it should speak directly and personally to the listeners, and that it be involved with human emotions, beliefs, and ideas. Decrying some of the contemporary trends in music, Siegmeister has said, "I see artists around me dominated by fear and mesmerized by technology, which have led them to turn away from the central subject of art: the human being. Afraid to deal with this basic matter of all art, they retreat into theory, pedantry, and academicism. Let us have a little open air, a song or dance, a human cry of sorrow or rejoicing. Let music be honest craftsmanship and speech between people."

Siegmeister began studying the piano at age nine, but once in high school, his musical activities had to compete with wide-ranging interests in math, physics, and chess. He entered Columbia University when he was fifteen, taking courses in composition there with Seth Bingham and private counterpoint lessons with Wallingford Riegger. After graduating from college in three years, Phi Beta Kappa and cum laude, Siegmeister went to Paris to attend the École Normale de Musique and to study with Nadia Boulanger.

On his return to New York in 1932, Siegmeister continued to compose rather intense, dramatic, and dissonant music, using the complex harmonic techniques from his Paris days. But then, influenced by the Great Depression and the restive social climate in the United States, Siegmeister sought to reach wider audiences, to write music that was more accessible to the masses, and to have his compositions serve a socially useful function.

Two personal discoveries around this time contributed to his

423

change of musical direction. He became aware of the music of Charles Ives and the skillful ways in which Ives incorporated America's musical heritage into his own compositions. Also, for the first time Siegmeister heard some of the little known American folk music from the Appalachian Mountain region and was struck by its freshness and originality.

These varied influences, along with his dedication to personal, communicative music, led Siegmeister to a new style of composition, one that was enriched with the melodies and rhythms of traditional American music, including the sounds of jazz and the blues. For almost two decades Siegmeister's music followed this new path. By the 1950s, however, he turned more introspective, and his evolving musical identity merged the folk element with a more personal and inward-looking approach to composition. In the decades since then, Siegmeister has continued to create music that not only eloquently expresses his own feelings and emotions, but also speaks directly and effectively to his listeners.

Siegmeister's extensive output includes six symphonies and about a dozen other major orchestral works, four solo concertos (respectively for clarinet, flute, piano, and violin) and a double concerto (for violin and piano), the cantata *I Have A Dream,* and ten operas, musical shows, and film scores. His chamber music catalog comprises three string quartets (1935, 1960, 1973), five violin and piano sonatas, and a Sextet for Brass and Percussion (1965).

In addition to his impressive corpus of music, Siegmeister has found the time to teach (Hofstra University), to be active in many musical organizations (American Music Center, American Composers Alliance, Composers and Lyricists Guild, National Black Music Competition, and American Society of Composers, Authors and Publishers), and to write books on musical subjects (*The New Music Lover's Handbook* and *Harmony and Melody).* Among his many awards and commissions have been those from the Guggenheim and Ford foundations, the National Institute of Arts and Letters, the Library of Congress, and the National Endowment for the Arts.

String Quartet No. 3 on Hebrew Themes

I. Andante con moto. II. Vivo; Allegro moderato. III. Tema con variazioni.

As Elie Siegmeister was growing up in Brooklyn, he heard his grandfather, an amateur cantor, sing and chant traditional Jewish melodies. Similar themes first appeared in Siegmeister's music in his 1967 cantata, *I Have A Dream,* based on a speech by Martin Luther King, Jr. Most recently Siegmeister used the same source of inspiration in his opera *Angel Levine* (1984). In the String Quartet No. 3, written between these two works, melodies connected with the Jewish people play an even more central role, furnishing the thematic impetus throughout.

The first movement stems from an ancient Jewish Yemenite chant that Siegmeister describes as "quiet and mysterious." It is heard three times at the start of the movement, stated sequentially by the first violin and the viola and cello, the last statement ending with a climax of great intensity. The tempo quickens slightly, and other subsidiary motifs are introduced. The melodic material is then developed and transformed, often in brief, improvisatory-sounding interludes for the various instruments. At the end of the movement, which is structured in modified sonata form, the viola and cello restate the original theme before the coda brings the movement to its conclusion.

After the sharply dissonant and rhythmic introduction to the second movement, the first violin states the principal theme, an eastern European Chassidic tune, which is "quizzical, fantastic-humorous," in Siegmeister's words. The melody itself and the offbeat accompaniment are strongly evocative of the source melody, but by setting it in five-beat meter, Siegmeister adds a certain artistic tension to the otherwise naive folk tune. Its feeling tone, Siegmeister suggests, recalls some of Chagall's more fanciful paintings of life in the *shtetls,* with "upside-down rabbis and enchanted *Chassidim* sailing through the air." A rude, rough, faster middle section, derived from an eastern European dance tune follows, and the scherzolike movement ends with an extremely free reprise of the opening section.

The theme of the last movement comes from two Ashkenazic prayer fragments, forcefully stated by the viola and cello in octaves. Although fully notated, the music gives an impression of nonmensural synagogue chanting. The melody is then put through seven variations in which Siegmeister brings out the many expressive and dramatic potentials of the theme, before ending in the last variation with what he calls "a touch of the beginning."

Siegmeister wrote his third quartet on commission from Temple Adath Jeshurun of Elkins Park, Pennsylvania, dedicating it to the memory of his father and mother. The first performance was given by the Vieuxtemps Quartet at Elkins Park on June 12, 1974.

Bedřich Smetana

Born March 2, 1824, in Litomyšl, Bohemia (now Czechoslovakia)
Died May 12, 1884, In Prague

BEDŘICH SMETANA was born in Bohemia, an area that today is part of Czechoslovakia, but in his time belonged to the Austro-Hungarian Empire, with Vienna as its capital and German its official language. As a young man, Smetana composed music that captured the flavor of the region's folk songs and dances and depicted its landscape, legends, and folk tales, thus contributing to the rising spirit of Bohemian nationalism. During the revolution of 1848, Smetana fought against the hostile Austrian regime as an armed member of the Citizen Corps. After the uprising was crushed and during the repressive period that followed, Smetana was doubly ostracized—both for writing music that glorified the Bohemian cause and for having participated in the revolt.

In 1856 Smetana emigrated to Göteborg, Sweden, where he spent six years composing, conducting, and teaching in self-imposed exile. By 1862 the political climate in Bohemia had greatly improved; there were, for example, Czech language newspapers and theaters, and Smetana decided to return to Prague. Four years later, he became conductor of the National Theater, and that same year he wrote his nationalistic masterpiece, the opera *The Bartered Bride.*

As the leading composer of Bohemia, Smetana followed a heavy schedule of composing, conducting, teaching, and performing and was involved, too, in promoting national Bohemian music. Then, at age fifty, tragedy struck with devastating suddenness; Smetana became totally deaf. Even the biggest specialists could not help him; their primitive treatments were painful and ineffective. Nevertheless, it was while he was bereft of his hearing that he wrote his best-known orchestral work, *The Moldau,* and his most celebrated chamber composition, the string quartet ''From My Life.'' Not long after, another

427

calamity occurred as Smetana suffered a complete mental breakdown in 1883. He was hospitalized the following year and died in an insane asylum shortly after his sixtieth birthday.

Smetana composed three major chamber works: the Piano Trio in G minor (1855), the String Quartet in E minor, "From My Life," (discussed below), and The Second String Quartet in D minor (1882).

String Quartet in E Minor, "From My Life"

I. Allegro vivo appassionato.   II. Allegro moderato à la Polka.   III. Largo sostenuto.   IV. Vivace.

Smetana has a tendency to write programmatic music—music that depicted a scene, told a story, represented natural phenomenon, evoked images of a particular happening or had some other extra-musical association. Central to his nationalistic compositions was the portrayal in music of the different places and heroes of his native Bohemia. Even though programmatic chamber music is very rare, it was perfectly natural for Smetana to use this approach in writing a string quartet dealing with the major events in his life.

Like all well-written pieces of program music, the String Quartet in E minor can stand on its own as an "absolute" piece of music with no outside connections, but familiarity with the program the composer had in mind can definitely enhance the experience. Information about the meaning carried by this quartet comes from a letter Smetana sent to his close friend and confidante, Josef Srb-Debrnov, dated April 12, 1878: "As regards my Quartet I gladly leave others to judge its style, and I shall not be in the least angry if this style does not find favor or is considered contrary to what was hitherto regarded as 'quartet style.' I did not set out to write a quartet according to recipe or custom in the usual forms. . . . With me the form of every composition is dictated by the subject itself and thus the Quartet, too, shaped its own form. My intention was to paint a tone picture of my life."

"The first movement," Smetana continues, "depicts my youthful leanings toward art, the Romantic atmosphere, the inexpressible yearning for something I could neither express nor define, and also a kind of warning of my future misfortune [deafness]." Despite the programmatic message of the movement, Smetana still manages, as he does throughout the quartet, to organize it into a traditional form, combining the extra-musical elements with modifications of standard structural features. The first theme, an impassioned outcry from the viola, represents the fateful "misfortune" that had already overtaken him. Twice the viola plays the theme, which is characterized by anguished downward leaps, and the first violin plays it once. The music then grows quieter, and the second theme, relaxed, gentle, and filled with romantic yearning, is introduced. The development is based on the first theme only, while the recapitulation just brings back the second theme. The coda provides a final glimpse of the first theme before three cello pizzicato notes bring the movement to a morose and gloomy close.

In Smetana's words, the second movement, "a quasi-polka, brings to my mind the joyful days of youth when I composed dance tunes and was known everywhere as a passionate lover of dancing." By composing the movement in the style of a polka, a fast, gay dance of Bohemian origin, in duple meter, with a particular rhythmic pattern, Smetana effectively conveys its spirit of reckless abandon. The viola introduces a contrasting motif into the merry dance; Smetana directs that it be played *quasi Tromba* ("like a trumpet"). The ingratiating middle section is little more than a delightful polkalike rhythmic pattern in the viola and cello, over which the violins play a progression of chords. An abbreviated version of the first section, an even shorter reminder of the second part, and a forceful coda fill out the rest of the movement.

Smetana's written account of the quartet goes on: "The third movement (the one which, in the opinion of the gentlemen who play this Quartet, is unperformable) reminds me of the happiness of my first love, the girl who later became my first wife." Even without these words, it is obvious that the Largo sostenuto is a love song. The first violin's lyrical opening theme conveys the affection and the passion of two people as deeply in love as Smetana and his first wife. A second theme enters, different in melodic contour but just as ardent. Smetana briefly reviews both themes, and then allows the fervor to cool in a quiet, pensive coda, perhaps a lamentation for his loved one.

Smetana writes: "The fourth movement describes the discovery that I could treat national elements in music, and my joy in following this path until it was checked by the catastrophe of the onset of my deafness, the outlook into the sad future, the tiny rays of hope of recovery; but remembering all the promise of my early career, a feeling of painful regret." Angrily, then, Smetana turns away from the melancholy thoughts and toward the folk music of his beloved Bohemian people—his source of strength and joy. The movement is a glorious dance, with its peasantlike vigor alternating with sections of elfin grace and smooth steps. In the midst of the gaiety, though, there is a sudden cut off—and silence. The music resumes with an ominous, low tremolo over which the first violin plays a piercing note at the very top of its range. "The long insistent note in the finale owes its origin to this [deafness]. It is the fateful ringing in my ears of the high-pitched tones which, in 1874, announced the beginning of my deafness. I permitted myself this little joke because it was so disastrous to me." Smetana follows with a series of short quotes: the "misfortune" theme from the opening, the second theme from the first movement—a ray of hope, and the start of the last movement— solace in the music of the people. They express his feelings and also summarize the entire quartet in a formal sense. Once more the first movement's subsidiary theme returns, building this time to a climax. And at the end a faint echo of the last movement theme is heard, fading away into stillness.

Smetana began his E minor quartet in October 1876 and finished it on December 19. There was a private performance in Prague in 1878, with the young Dvořák playing viola. The official premiere, also in Prague, was on March 28, 1879, played by an ensemble made up of Ferdinand Lachner, Jan Pelikán, Josef Krehan, and Alois Neruda.

Igor Stravinsky

Born June 17, 1882, in Oranienbaum, Russia
Died April 6, 1971, in New York City

ALMOST EVERYONE regards Igor Stravinsky as the greatest composer of the twentieth century, a seminal figure who had a major impact on the course of modern music. From his early Russian-flavored ballets, which led Debussy to commend him for having "enlarged the boundaries of the permissible," through his Neoclassical period, the time of his few chamber music compositions, to his later interest in twelve-tone music, Stravinsky was always seeking new ways to express the spirit of the twentieth century.

Igor Feodorovich Stravinsky was born in Oranienbaum, a suburb of St. Petersburg; his father was a leading bass singer at the Imperial Opera. At nine, like most upper class children of his time, Stravinsky started piano lessons and proved a good, though not exceptional, student. Nevertheless, his interest in music grew and his parents agreed to let him study harmony on the condition that he also study law. At law school he attended only about fifty lectures, though, because his thoughts had already turned toward music. After his father's death, Stravinsky dropped law and was accepted as a student by the great Russian composer, Nicolai Rimsky-Korsakov, with whom he studied for three years, until the elder man's death in 1908; it was Stravinsky's only formal instruction.

In the years after his composition studies with Rimsky-Korsakov, Stravinsky set the music world reeling with three outstanding ballet scores—*The Firebird* (1910), *Petrushka* (1911), and *The Rite of Spring* (1913). All of them abounded in vigor, brashness, and color, with the latter particularly revolutionary in its use of brutal rhythms, polytonality (harmonies in two or more keys at once), fragmentary and repetitive snatches of barbarous melody, and harsh, dissonant instrumental effects—sounds never heard before. The first night's audi-

431

ence at *The Rite of Spring* created a riot, forcing Stravinsky to sneak out of the theater through a dressing room window. But less than a year later, after the score was played in a concert version, Stravinsky received a hero's ovation and was carried aloft through the streets of Paris. In that short while, he had come to occupy a position as leader of the musical avant-garde, a role he held until the end of his long, distinguished career.

Around 1920, just when his music had catapulted him to world-wide fame, Stravinsky turned away from the primitivism of his ballets and adopted a new style. It was leaner, more austere, more carefully structured, an idiom that critics called Neoclassical (a term Stravinsky himself eschewed as meaning "absolutely nothing"). This change to what he called "Apollonian principles" may have been an attempt to bring order into his life after the chaos caused by World War I and the subsequent Communist Revolution. Stravinsky looked to the distant past for his inspiration, drawing on features of Medieval and Renaissance music and adopting elements of the styles of Bach, Haydn, and Mozart. He stressed objectivity over subjectivity, detachment over involvement, clarity over ambiguity, and restraint over emotionality.

On the eve of World War II, Stravinsky agreed to come to Harvard University to give a series of lectures and found that he could not return to Europe because of the outbreak of hostilities. He settled in the United States where he remained until his death at age eighty-eight.

Stravinsky's three chamber works—Three Pieces for String Quartet (1914), Concertino for String Quartet (1920) and Octet for Wind Instruments (1923)—are representative of the transition from his early opulent style to the more severe style he adopted later on. The two short quartets came early in the changeover, while the octet was clearly composed in the Neoclassical manner and shows Stravinsky's success in making use, as he said, "of academic form . . . without becoming academic."

Three Pieces for String Quartet

Stravinsky composed the Three Pieces for String Quartet in 1914, in Salvan, Switzerland, one year after he completed his epochal ballet, *Le Sacre du Printemps (The Rite of Spring)*. Although the overall time of composition was three months, the manuscript shows that the first piece was written in one day, April 26, the second also in one day, July 2, while the third took two days, July 25 and 26. The work marks a turning point between the end of the rich style of composition characterized by *Sacre* and the first steps in a leaner, more austere direction. Stravinsky himself observed that the "Three Pieces" marked "an important change" in his music, and, indeed, over the following years his music developed the ideas that first appeared in these short pieces.

Originally the Three Pieces did not have titles, just metronome markings to indicate the tempo. Stravinsky added the titles, "Danse," "Excentrique," and "Cantique" fifteen years later when he orchestrated all three and added one more to create his Four Etudes for Orchestra. The titles succinctly describe the three short parts, which are, in the words of Stravinsky expert Eric Walter White, "really contrasting studies in popular, fantastic and liturgical moods."

The first and shortest piece, "Danse," has a chantlike melody consisting of just four notes that the first violin plays over and over again in varied rhythmic patterns. It represents a primitive folk dance style that was to become important in Stravinsky's later, so-called Russian pieces. Throughout this brief movement each instrument maintains a single, unique method of tone production: first violin uses the entire length of the bow; second violin plays with short strokes at the bottom (frog) of the bow; viola sustains one note *ponticello* (near the bridge), while plucking a note with the left hand; and cello plays a repeated *(ostinato)* figure *pizzicato* (plucked) throughout. This unconventional approach allows each instrument to maintain its own distinct character and independence, with virtually no interaction between the four parts.

"Excentrique" comes next. Stravinsky explained that it was "inspired . . . by the eccentric movements and postures of the great clown, Little Tick," whom he had seen at a circus in London. The music is fragmented into what the composer calls "jerky, spastic movement," but all in a joking, good-humored way.

Much more serious is the third piece, "Cantique" ("Canticle"), which Stravinsky described as "choral and religious in character." Slowly and solemnly he intones a five-measure chant that uses only three notes (similar to the four-note repeated pattern in the first piece), and which is interrupted by two measure, faster-moving responses, until the music fades away with the viola's final tones.

The premiere of the Three Pieces for String Quartet was given in Paris on May 19, 1915.

Concertino for String Quartet

In *Igor Stravinsky: An Autobiography,* the composer described the genesis of the Concertino: "M. Pochon [Alfred Pochon, first violinist of the Flonzaley Quartet] wished to introduce a contemporary work into their almost exclusively classical repertoire, and asked me to write them an ensemble piece, in form and length of my own choosing, to appear in the programs of their numerous tours. So it was for them that I composed my *Concertino,* a piece in one single movement, and treated in the form of a free sonata-allegro with a definitely *concertante* part for the first violin, and this, on account of its limited dimensions, led me to give it the diminuitive title: *Concertino (piccolo concerto)."*

Stravinsky began work on the Concertino in July 1920, while on summer holiday at Carantec, Brittany; it was finished on September 24 and dedicated to the Flonzaley Quartet. Much later, in 1952, the piece was revised for twelve instruments—ten winds, violin, and cello. Classified among Stravinsky's earliest Neoclassical works, the Concertino strives to assert, in twentieth-century terms, the principles laid down in the eighteenth century—clarity, emotional restraint, detachment, and objectivity. As in most of his other works, Stravinsky tried to avoid any overt display of emotion: "I consider that music is by its very nature essentially powerless to *express* anything at all. *Expression* has never been an inherent property of music." Stravinsky was also interested in jazz at the time, and a few traces of ragtime can be detected in the music.

The two principal musical gestures of the one-movement, six-minute Concertino are the harshly dissonant ascending scales that open the work and the busy, motoric figures that follow. The slower middle section, which comes after another scale, is largely a cadenza for the first violin and functions as the development, mostly of the scalic idea. The tempo and mood pick up for the final section, which recalls, in general terms, the two original themes—the rising scales and the active figuration. The music quiets at the end; Stravinsky wrote the word *sospirando,* sighing or plaintive, over the last notes.

Octet for Wind Instruments

I. Sinfonia: Lento; Allegro moderato. II. Tema con Variazioni: Andantino. III. Finale: Tempo giusto.

Begun in Biarritz late in 1922, Stravinsky's Octet (*Octuor* in French) was finished in Paris on May 20, 1923, and revised in 1952. In describing the origin of the piece, Stravinsky wrote in his book *Chronicles* (1936) that he did not know what the instrumentation would be before he began to compose the music. But in his *Dialogues* (1963), he said that the work began with a dream "in which I saw myself in a small room surrounded by a small group of instrumentalists playing some attractive music. They were playing bassoons, trombones, trumpets, a flute and a clarinet. I awoke from this little concert in a state of great delight and anticipation and the next morning began to compose the *Octuor.*"

The Octet is an important work in Stravinsky's oeuvre because it epitomizes his Neoclassicism, following in spirit and form the ideals of the eighteenth-century masters. According to Aaron Copland, Stravinsky "completely abandoned realism and primitivism of all kinds and openly espoused the cause of objectivism in music."

In a January 1924 article, "Some Ideas About My *Octuor*," Stravinsky discusses his musical philosophy at the time and how it shaped this work:

> My *Octet* is a musical object. This object has a form and that form is influenced by the musical matter of which it is composed. My *Octet* is not an "emotive" work, but a musical composition that is based on objective elements that are sufficient in themselves. I have excluded all nuances between the *forte* and the *piano*. Form, in my music, derives from counterpoint. I consider counterpoint as the only means through which the attention of the composer is concentrated on purely musical questions. This sort of music has no other aim than to be sufficient in itself. In general, I consider that music is only able to solve musical problems, and nothing else, neither the literary nor picturesque, can be in music of any interest.

The first movement, called Sinfonia, or Symphony, starts with a slow introduction that Stravinsky himself compared to the introductions of the late Haydn symphonies. The clean, dry, ascerbic fast body of the movement, which begins with a unison statement of the bold principal theme, is organized in a freely realized sonata form.

The second movement is a theme with variations, which Stravinsky explained "is the first variation that recurs rather than a theme in its original state." The reason is that the composer wrote the waltz variation first and then derived the theme from the waltz melody. After the theme, the first variation, Variation A, rushes up and down like "ribbons of scales" while the first trombone intones a melody reminiscent of the Gregorian chant, *Dies Irae*. In a remarkable volte-face, Variation B proves to be a comic operetta march. A return of

435

Variation A (the "ribbons of scales") leads to Variation C, the waltz and progenitor of the entire movement. The two trumpets sing the melody of Variation D against a background of busy, chattering notes in the bassoons and clarinets. A final reprise of Variation A takes us to Variation E, Stravinsky's favorite, a fugato, with the intervals of the original theme inverted.

In describing the Finale, which grows out of the fugato and follows without pause, Stravinsky wrote, "Bach's Two-part Inventions were somewhere in the remote back of my mind while composing this movement." Indeed, the highly contrapuntal movement starts with two bassoons and adds more parts within a form which the composer describes as "a kind of rondo," with the opening first bassoon melody returning a few times and each repetition being separated by contrasting interludes. The Finale ends with a very soft, but highly rhythmical, Latin beat coda.

Due to its great rhythmic complexity, the Octet is usually performed with a conductor, and Stravinsky made his conducting debut at its premiere at the Paris Opera House on October 18, 1923.

Peter Ilyich Tchaikovsky

Born May 7, 1840, at Votinsk
Died November 6, 1893, at St. Petersburg (Leningrad)

TCHAIKOVSKY'S LIFE was abundantly filled with paradoxes, unresolved conflicts, and contradictions. Born into a moderately wealthy family, Peter Ilyich early showed remarkable intelligence (being able to read fluently in both French and German at the age of six), but aside from a heightened sensitivity to music, neither his parents nor his piano teachers saw any evidence of exceptional musical talent. He was educated at the Saint Petersburg School of Jurisprudence and worked at the Ministry of Justice until he was twenty-one years old, when, with great misgiving, he left his post to start the serious study of music.

Although fully aware of his homosexuality, Tchaikovsky felt compelled to wed in 1877, a marriage that lasted a scant nine days, followed by a suicide attempt a few weeks later and a subsequent nervous breakdown. That same year Tchaikovsky began a thirteen-year relationship with a wealthy forty-six-year-old widow, Nadezhda von Meck. Madame von Meck's generous and enthusiastic support was made dependent on the condition that they not meet—a requirement that Tchaikovsky readily accepted. In the late 1970s musicologist Alexandra Orlova uncovered evidence that Tchaikovsky's homosexuality was indirectly responsible for his death at age fifty-three. According to this research, the composer became involved in a scandalous affair with the nephew of Duke Stenbock-Thurmor and was forced, in effect, to take his own life. The commonly accepted story of death from cholera, according to Orlova, was concocted by the family to protect the composer's reputation.

As a composer, Tchaikovsky considered himself a Russian nationalist, strongly influenced by folk melodies and rhythms of his native land. To the Russian Five (Balakirev, Mussorgsky, Borodin, Rimsky-

437

Korsakov, and Cui), who were striving to establish a nationalistic style of Russian music at that time, however, he was a cosmopolite, more under the influence of French ballet, Italian opera, and German symphony than the indigenous music of their land. It is curious that Tchaikovsky, one of the most emotional and passionate of the Romantic composers, set Mozart, the supreme Classicist, as his idol. "I not only like Mozart," he wrote, "I worship him."

Tchaikovsky's superb gift for melody, flair for the dramatic, use of grand musical gestures, and mastery of lyrical effects assure him a revered place among all composers. One can only assume that the difficulties of his life, which caused him so much personal anguish, were somehow transmuted into a source of strength and beauty in his music. The bulk of his music-making was for the symphony orchestra and the ballet and operatic stages; he wrote relatively little chamber music—three string quartets (Opp. 11, 22, and 30), a piano trio (Op. 50), and a sextet for strings entitled "Souvenir de Florence" (Op. 70).

String Quartet in D Major, Op. 11, "Accordion"

I. Moderato e semplice. II. Andante cantabile. III. Scherzo: Allegro non tanto. IV. Finale: Allegro giusto.

Tchaikovsky once divided all his music into two categories: "One, those written on my own initiative, through sudden inclination and urgent inner necessity. Two, those inspired by external means, such as the request of a friend, or publisher, or commissions." He went on to say, "I hasten to explain that, as shown by experience, the value of a work does not depend upon which category it belongs to."

Tchaikovsky's first string quartet fits into the second category. In 1871, despite a salary increase as professor at the Moscow Conservatory and a growing number of private students, Tchaikovsky was living in straightened circumstances—some even say he was starving—when a friend suggested a concert of his music to raise funds. Since hiring an orchestra was too expensive, Tchaikovsky decided to present a program of solo and chamber compositions. Lacking a major chamber work, he composed his first string quartet during the month of February 1871. The concert, judged an artistic and financial success, was held on March 28, 1871, in Moscow; the string quartet was performed by members of the Russian Musical Society.

From the rising and falling in dynamics of the opening chords comes the work's subtitle, "Accordion." More fluid figures fill out the first subject and lead to the second, which starts with a richly harmonized melody in the viola. The tempo picks up slightly for the closing theme, beginning with light, delicate passages played by the first violin. All three subjects are treated equally in the following development section. With the first violin continuing a variant of the closing theme, the others launch the recapitulation, and the movement ends with everyone joining in the high-speed, exciting coda.

Much of the fame of this quartet comes from the second movement, the Andante cantabile, which has been arranged for every conceivable instrumental combination. Tchaikovsky based the melody on a folk song, "*Sidel Vanya,*" which begins unremarkably enough: "Vanya sat on a divan and smoked a pipe of tobacco." It was a tune he heard while visiting his sister at Kamenka in the Ukraine during the summer of 1869. Between statements of the folk song melody, Tchaikovsky introduces another highly expressive theme, played twice by the first violin over a pizzicato accompaniment.

The Scherzo is a gay, colorful movement with some of the robust rhythmic character of a Russian peasant dance. The middle trio section, has, for the most part, the three upper instruments playing complex figurations over a sustained drone in the cello. The Scherzo is repeated at the end.

A folk flavor permeates the Finale as well, dancing exuberantly in the first theme and singing with Slavic soulfulness in the second. After a vigorous working-out of the two subjects, there is a sudden stop, and a slow, mock-serious reprise of a subsidiary motif, before a whirlwind coda brings the quartet to a close.

Piano Trio in A Minor, Op. 50

I. Pezzo elegiaco: Moderato assai.   IIA. Tema con Variazioni: Andante con moto.   IIB. Variazone Finale e Coda: Allegro risoluto e con fuoco.

The March 1881 death of pianist Nicholas Rubinstein, Tchaikovsky's former teacher, director of the Moscow Conservatory and, despite periods of estrangement, longtime friend, filled the composer with deep remorse. Tchaikovsky paid tribute to Rubinstein with his piano trio, dedicated "To the memory of a great artist." Begun in December

1881 and completed on February 9, 1882, it received its first private performance in Moscow on March 2, 1882, played by Sergey Taneyev (piano), N. Grimali (violin), and Wilhelm Fitzhagen (cello); the first public hearing was on October 30, 1882.

The trio is cast in two lengthy movements, the first called Pezzo elegiaco, or Elegiac piece. Tchaikovsky, the supreme melodist, presents four appealing themes, each distinctive in style and mood. The opening one, warm and with a unique melancholy aura, is announced at the outset by the cello. The tempo picks up for the more forceful second theme stated by piano alone. Both the violin and cello, playing in octaves, sing out the following subject, one of Tchaikovsky's most perfectly realized, sweet-but-sad melodies. A final, highly expressive theme, originally heard in the violin, completes the exposition. For the rest of the movement, Tchaikovsky brings back, in varied transformations, the melodic material previously introduced.

While the very prominent—and difficult—piano part in the first movement is probably a tribute to Rubinstein's pianistic virtuosity, the folklike theme used for the theme and variations recognizes Rubinstein's love of folk music. It is thought to be associated with a day in May 1873, when Tchaikovsky and Rubinstein went to the countryside for a picnic, and some peasants sang and danced for them. The melody, played solo by the piano, although original, does indeed have the simplicity and direct expressivity of fine folk music. Tchaikovsky then subjects the melody to eleven variations, imaginatively developing all of its musical and emotional facets. Among the most outstanding are the scherzolike Variation III, the music box sounds of Variation V, the waltz (Variation VI), and the mazurka (Variation X). When critics tried to associate each variation with a specific incident in Rubinstein's life, Tchaikovsky replied, "How amusing! To compose music without the slightest desire to represent something, and suddenly to discover that it represents this or that, it is what Molière's *Bourgeois Gentilhomme* must have felt when he learned that he had been speaking in prose all of his life." The concluding section, Variazone Finale e Coda, a forceful summation based on a twelfth variation of the tema, is capped off by a glorious return of the opening theme from the first movement. With the composer's permission, Variation VIII and a section of the Variazione Finale are sometimes omitted in performance.

Giuseppe Verdi

Born October 10, 1813, at Le Roncole, Italy
Died January 27, 1901, at Milan

VERDI IS indisputedly a great composer, one who occupies a particularly outstanding position in the world of opera. Yet, the events of his early life provided few auguries of his later accomplishments.

As a young man, Verdi's talent was first recognized by some strolling musicians who performed in front of his father's rather shabby tavern. After some years of music lessons with local church organists, he applied for admission to the Milan Conservatory—and was rejected. Nevertheless, he continued his studies and had his first opera premiered at La Scala, Milan, with some moderate success. Then a number of misfortunes occurred. In 1838 his young daughter died; just over a year later his son died; and the final blow came with the death of his wife the following year. His next attempt to compose an opera was a decisive failure. The composer fell into a deep depression and went into seclusion.

Several months later, an impressario from La Scala prevailed on him to start composing again. The first work he turned out, the opera *Nabucco,* in 1841, was an immense success and immediately established the composer's reputation. Over the following half-century he turned out a series of operatic masterpieces, including *Rigoletto, Il Trovatore, La Traviata, La Forza del Destino, Don Carlos,* and *Aida.*

Verdi composed twenty-six operas, eight choral works, a number of songs, and only one instrumental composition—the string quartet. Why the overwhelming preponderance of opera in Verdi's output? Perhaps the most basic reason is that the Italy of Verdi's time regarded opera as the major medium of musical expression, to the neglect of the other forms. While composers in other countries might turn out a varied fare of operas, symphonies, and chamber works, most Italian composers focused all of their energies on opera. It almost seemed that lyrical drama held some very special, almost exclusive place in the national spirit and temperament.

String Quartet in E Minor

I. Allegro. II. Andantino. III. Prestissimo.
IV. Scherzo Fuga: Allegro assai mosso.

In November 1872, Verdi went to Naples to supervise the production of some of his operas, including the local premiere of *Aida,* with Teresa Stolz in the title role. Unfortunately the soprano fell ill in March 1873, and the performance had to be postponed. Verdi, who was incapable of sitting idly by, spent the three-week hiatus composing a string quartet, his only exclusively instrumental composition.

Verdi's letters make clear that he was very well acquainted with the great quartet scores of Haydn, Mozart, and Beethoven. In fact, he is said to have kept them always by his bedside and to have advised his students to use the Classical string quartets as models of clear and concise organization. Thus when the circumstances were propitious, he was able to produce a string quartet of unquestioned authority and great appeal.

The quartet received its premiere on April 1, 1873, just one day after the opening of *Aida,* at an informal concert at his hotel. The performers were identified only as the Pinto brothers, violins, Salvadore, viola, and Giarritiello, cello. A few weeks later, Verdi set down these words: "I've written a Quartet in my leisure moments in Naples. I had it performed one evening in my house, without attaching the least importance to it and without inviting anyone in particular. Only the seven or eight persons who usually come to visit me were present. I don't know whether the Quartet is beautiful or ugly, but I do know that it's a Quartet!" Despite Verdi's cavalier attitude, the quartet has become a staple of the string quartet repertoire, famed for the skillful way the composer combined brilliant theatrical and melodic techniques with extremely fluent and idiomatic string writing.

The dramatic first theme, which is stated immediately by the second violin, conveys a sense of quiet, suppressed urgency. The first violin repeat is accompanied by a scampering figure in the cello that grows in importance in the following motifs that make up the first group. A descending scale in the second violin and viola, and a short pause, set the stage for the subdued, contemplative second subject, which is extended with new material that grows from the cello figure heard earlier. In a departure from traditional first movement form, Verdi immediately repeats and then develops the first subject, ending the movement with a comparatively brief restatement of the second subject.

The main theme of the second movement is lyrical and charming; Verdi marks it to be played *con eleganza,* "with elegance." The movement is organized in rondo form, with the three appearances of the theme separated by two contrasting episodes.

The third movement is unabashedly operatic. The first part brings to mind the sense of excitement as the opera house curtain rises and the stage slowly fills with singers who soon launch into the lusty opening chorus. The middle section features an exquisite tenor aria for cello, accompanied by the others playing pizzicato in imitation of a guitar. Verdi then repeats the opening section.

The Scherzo Fuga is indeed a scherzo, in the original meaning of joke or jest, and a *fuga,* which refers to melodic imitation in which the tunes are gaily tossed from instrument to instrument. This high-spirited movement is energetic and filled with forward-pushing motoric action providing a joyful, exciting conclusion to the entire quartet.

Heitor Villa-Lobos

Born March 5, 1887, in Rio de Janeiro
Died November 17, 1959, in Rio de Janeiro

HEITOR VILLA-LOBOS won fame as the first internationally recognized Brazilian composer to use his country's folk melodies, rhythms, and musical instruments in works of serious music. His musical development started at age six, when he began cello lessons with his father, later adding instruction on the piano. After his father's death in 1899, the young musician began playing in restaurants and theaters to help support his family. During the early years of the century, he wandered over much of Brazil, including some of the most remote areas, listening to and absorbing the sounds of the folk and popular music of the Indians, the blacks, and the white Brazilians. He once described how this exposure affected his approach to music: "I compose in the folk-style. I utilize thematic idioms in my own way, and subject to my own development. An artist must do this. He must select and transmit the material given him by the people. I study the history, the country, the speech, the customs, the background of the people. I have always done this, and it is from this source, spiritual as well as practical, that I have drawn my art."

It was during those wandering days that Villa-Lobos joined a group of young men who formed a band, called a *chôro*. Like other instrumental groups of this kind, their *chôro* played at all kinds of festive occasions—parties, balls, weddings, carnival celebrations—usually continuing their music-making in the street long after the event was over. The members, called *chôraos,* often performed their popular improvisations with such enthusiasm and abandon that they actually entered trancelike states.

From 1923 to 1930, a Brazilian government scholarship enabled Villa-Lobos to live in Paris and study traditional European musical practices. Two years after he returned to Brazil, he became superintendent of musical education, first in Sao Paulo and then in Rio de Janeiro, and devoted himself to composing. His grounding in Brazilian folk music and its popular songs, his experience playing in a *chôro,* along with his years of study in Paris provided Villa-Lobos with rich and varied sources of inspiration for his amazingly large production, which comprised in chamber music alone seventeen string quartets, five piano trios, and innumerable works for various other combinations, including perhaps his most popular chamber work, *Quintette en forme de chôros.*

Quintette en forme de chôros

Villa-Lobos composed the *Quintette en forme de chôros* in Paris in 1928, revising the score in 1953. The approach he used was derived from his early experience in a *chôro,* the mariachilike street band that improvised on popular themes, folk dances, and songs. The quintet uses a style, in the composer's own words, "in which are synthesized the different modalities of Brazilian, Indian and popular music, having for principle elements rhythm and any typical melody of popular character."

The one-movement composition, scored for flute, oboe, English horn (or French horn), clarinet, and bassoon, starts slowly and quietly. After a while the music gains in speed and intensity, becoming very strong and powerful, with some very exciting rhythmic interplay. Although the meter is highly irregular—measures of six, five, seven, ten, and eight eighth notes follow each other consecutively—there is an underlying flow and order. The fast sections recreate some of the indigenous sounds of Brazil—animal cries from deep in the jungle, the shriek of tropical birds, the pounding of Indian drums. Some little figures that evoke the rhythms of popular dance are positioned next to passages of pure concert music. A passage for flute alone acts as a transition back to the slow tempo of the opening. Then, once again, the tempo and excitement pick up, leading to the fast, brilliant ending.

Carl Maria von Weber

Born November 18, 1786, in Eutin, Germany
Died June 5, 1826, in London

CARL MARIA von Weber was the very embodiment of the Romantic spirit that he helped to shape. Slim and soulful-looking, with dark, intense eyes, and a regal, aristocratic bearing, Weber conformed to the popular image of a Romantic hero. Even his permanent limp, caused by a malformed right hip bone and his consumption (now called tuberculosis) added to the effect. In his activities, too, he represented the Romantic ideal of a creative artist. An outstanding composer, Weber was equally well known as a conductor, touring virtuoso pianist, skilled lithographer, poet, and music critic. Considered by many to be the first true Romantic, he also helped organize a number of composers into the *Harmonischer Verein* (Harmonic Society), to establish a theoretical foundation for the new spirit in music and to propagandize the works that they were writing.

Today Weber is chiefly remembered as an operatic composer; his opera *Der Freischütz* (1821) is a signal work, widely accepted as the first Romantic opera, the first German opera, and the first nationalistic opera. By bringing together brilliant dramatic effects, supernatural happenings, and ancient folk legends, Weber was able to point the direction for the new nineteenth-century Romantic style. The striking tone colors, freedom of form, and dazzling virtuosity of his instrumental music also became part of the Romantic tradition.

Weber's father was a musician who sought to turn the boy into a child prodigy by providing him with excellent instruction while still very young. Although Weber was very talented, he never attained the heights of the child Mozart, the hoped-for goal of his most ambitious father. Nevertheless, the young Carl did tour widely as a pianist and became conductor of the opera at Breslau at age eighteen, followed by more prestigious conducting positions at Prague and

447

Dresden. It was in London, however, while conducting a tour of his opera *Oberon* that he passed away at the age of thirty-nine.

Although a prolific composer of operas (ten) and works in several other instrumental and vocal forms, Weber wrote only three chamber pieces: the youthful Piano Quartet, Op. 18 (1809), the Clarinet Quintet, Op. 34 (1815), and the Trio for Flute, Cello and Piano, Op. 63 (1819). Of the three, only the clarinet quintet is part of the modern repertoire.

Clarinet Quintet in B Flat Major, Op. 34

I. Allegro. II. Fantasia: Adagio ma non troppo. III. Menuetto: Capriccio presto. IV. Rondo: Allegro giocoso.

The many concert tours that Weber undertook during his lifetime bore little resemblance to modern touring practices. Weber spent extended periods in each city and engaged in a variety of musical activities, presenting concerts as pianist or conductor, producing his operas, writing music on commission from local aristocrats, teaching, and often politicking to get a permanent position.

It was on one such tour that Weber remained in Munich, from March 14 to August 9, 1811, and met Heinrich Bärmann, the principal clarinetist of the Munich orchestra and one of the outstanding instrumentalists of the time. Inspired by Bärmann's playing, Weber decided to compose a number of works featuring the clarinet. He completed two concertos and a concertino in short order; he also began a quintet for clarinet and string quartet, but did not finish it until four years later, on August 25, 1815, one day before the premiere.

Although cast as a quintet, the lightweight piece is more in the spirit of a clarinet concerto, with the four strings in accompaniment, than a chamber work. In his Weber biography, John Warrack calls the quintet "a pocket concerto." Still, its virtuosic clarinet part, including the high-speed chromatic runs, amazing leaps to the extreme limits of the instruments, broad, cantilena melodies at all dynamic levels, and brilliant fioritura throughout make it a lasting favorite.

The quintet opens with a slow-moving string melody that gives way to a jaunty clarinet motif, the first of several that make up the principal subject group. The second subject, a high-speed musical chase marked *scherzando* ("playful") is a delightful display vehicle for the clarinet. The development deals with the various motifs of the first subject, including the introductory measures. The considerably modified recapitulation also begins with that section. The strings present a seemingly new, forceful theme in the coda, but it proves to be a transformation of a first-subject motif.

The Fantasia, an unashamed concert aria for clarinet, gives the player a chance to show off beauty of tone and mastery of phrasing. A test of the performer's technical command are the several ascending chromatic scales, which Weber inserts as cadenzalike interruptions in the lovely, long-lined melody.

Weber starts the Menuetto with a rapidly rising broken chord in the clarinet, a melodic device much favored for its brilliant effect by the composers of the Mannheim school. The sparkling Menuetto features several appearances of these so-called Mannheim Rockets, along with a number of witty, rhythmically inventive episodes. The serene and legato trio presents a stark contrast to the Menuetto, which returns to end the movement.

The last movement is a fun-filled cap to the engaging quintet. Organized in rondo form (A-B-A-C-A), the movement's main A theme is a series of exuberant ascending scales with little finials at the tops. The good spirits continue throughout the slightly more subdued contrasting B and C sections, and the movement ends with a coda of virtuosic display by the clarinet.

Anton Webern

Born December 3, 1883, in Vienna
Died September 15, 1945, in Mittersill, Austria

ANTON WEBERN'S musical education focused on the extremes of music. On the one hand he specialized in the compositional practices of the Renaissance (Ph.D., University of Vienna, 1906), and on the other hand he studied the most advanced twentieth-century methods with Arnold Schoenberg, from 1904 until around 1910.

Through his musicology studies, Webern became familiar with various polyphonic techniques of the past. One such device, which he frequently used in his music, is canonic imitation, in which two or more instruments play the same melody, but starting at different times. (A round, such as "Frére Jacques," is a familiar example of a canon.)

Of far greater musical importance to his own creativity, however, was Webern's introduction to the newest concepts of contemporary music through his teacher and lifelong friend, Schoenberg. Schoenberg is credited with creating the method of composing with twelve tones, in which the music is structured according to a number of strict rules around a particular arrangement of the twelve tones of the chromatic scale. He is also associated with the ideal of *Klangfarbenmelodie,* tone-color melody, in which the different tone colors actually serve as melodic material. In the end Webern surpassed his teacher in the rigor and single-mindedness with which he applied these concepts, organizing every element of music—pitch, tone color, rhythm, and dynamics—into an approach known as serialism, considered one of the most significant and important steps forward in twentieth-century music.

During the twelve years after he left the University, Webern held a number of conducting posts in provincial theaters, in Prague, and finally in Vienna, where he led the Workers' Symphony Concerts and

Kunstelle, an amateur chorus. After World War I, though, he settled in Mödling, outside Vienna, to devote himself exclusively to his composing.

To the listener, the most striking characteristic of Webern's music is its extreme brevity, concentration, and compression. The composer's entire lifetime output of thirty-one works takes only about three hours to perform! Certain movements last less than one minute; some themes are just a few notes long. And Webern also rejected the concept of repetition. He wrote, "Once stated, the theme expresses all it has to say. It must be followed by something fresh."

Webern's scores are a paradigm of thoroughness. He meticulously denotes every shade of nuance and dynamics and carefully designates the exact character and mood of each section. While the varied tonal effects, fragmented melodies, and compact form may make the work appear abstruse on first hearing, repeated listening can be very rewarding.

Webern composed several juvenile chamber pieces, including String Quartet and *Langsamer Satz* for String Quartet (1905) and Piano Quintet (1907). His Five Movements for String Quartet, Six Bagatelles for String Quartet, and String Quartet, Opus 28, are discussed below. The other less frequently performed mature chamber works are the Movement for String Trio (1925), String Trio, Opus 20 (1927), and Quartet for Piano, Violin, Clarinet, and Saxophone, Opus 22 (1930).

During World War II, Webern's music was banned by the Germans as "cultural Bolshevism," and he was forced to work as a proofreader for a Viennese publisher. After the war was over, in a most tragic accident, the composer was mistakenly shot and killed by a military policeman in the occupying United States army.

Five Movements for String Quartet, Op. 5

I. Heftig bewegt. II. Sehr langsam. III. Sehr bewegt. IV. Sehr langsam. V. In zarter Bewegung.

Five Movements, also called Five Pieces, seems like the most abstract of compositions, with its brief wisps of melody, its many strange, though gripping tonal effects and the absence of many of the conventional musical devices used to express emotion in music. Yet, Webern confessed to composer Alban Berg that the work was related to the death of his mother on September 7, 1906, an event that affected him profoundly, and which remained paramount in his thoughts for many years.

Despite its revolutionary sounds, Five Movements is firmly rooted in the traditional string quartet. The opening movement, for example, is a highly compressed sonata form. The first subject consists of just two notes, a jarring rising minor ninth is played by the second violin and cello and immediately imitated by the first violin and viola. This brief episode concludes with three sharp *col legno* strokes played with the wood of the bows. The cello states the slower second subject and is answered by the violins. All four instruments playing rapid pizzicato notes introduce the development section. A short phrase reminiscent of the second theme marks the beginning of the recapitulation, played by the violin. It is succeeded at once by a descending minor ninth, an obvious inversion of the opening interval.

The slow second movement is only thirteen measures long. An expressive, lyrical melody over a simple accompaniment is divided between the viola, second violin, first violin, and finally back to the second violin, to complete a neat arch form.

A scant thirty-five seconds in length, the third movement has the character of a scherzo. Over repeated pizzicato notes in the cello, the first violin, imitated by the viola, plays the opening theme. The suddenly quiet second theme is also played by the first violin, with pizzicato notes in the second violin and viola. Again the cello starts a repeated pizzicato figure that suggests a return of the opening. The movement ends with a ferocious restatement of the second melody.

The fourth movement, equal in length to the second, opens with two cryptic measures, followed by a descending four-note theme in the first violin that is quickly echoed in the second violin and cello. The remainder of the fleeting movement grows from the intervals found in the theme and ends as the second violin disappears at the top of an ascending figure.

After a few notes of a wide-ranging melody that opens the final movement, the other instruments play whispered chords and melodic fragments based on an undulating motion in the cello. Bits and pieces of this material, as well as remembrances of previous movements, continue until the music quietly fades away.

Begun in the spring of 1909 and completed on June 16, 1909, Five Movements was first performed in Vienna on February 8, 1910. In 1929 Webern arranged the work for string orchestra.

Six Bagatelles for String Quartet, Op. 9

I. Mässig. II. Leicht bewegt. III. Ziemlich fliessend. IV. Sehr langsam. V. Äussert langsam. VI. Fliessend.

"Listen profoundly!" Webern used to advise his students. And for "Six Bagatelles," one must add, ". . . and listen rapidly!" Not only is it one of the most obscure of all works, it is also one of the most compact and pithy of all quartet pieces. The whole work contains only fifty-seven measures and takes just about three minutes to perform. In his introduction, Arnold Schoenberg wrote, "One has to realize what restraint it requires to express oneself with such brevity. You can stretch every glance into a poem, every sigh into a novel. But to express a novel in a single gesture, joy in a single breath— such concentration can only be present in the absence of self-pity."

The four middle movements of this piece were completed in 1911. Two years later, in 1913, Webern composed what he called Three Pieces for String Quartet. Then, discarding the middle of the three pieces, he preceded the four earlier movements with one and followed them with the other to create a six-movement work that he called "Six Bagatelles," using the French word for trifles. Webern's biographer, Walter Kolneder, believes that the composer's chief goal in the work is to be found in the dedication he inscribed on a copy that he presented to Alban Berg, "*Non multa sed multum.* [Small in quantity, but large in content.] How happy I would be if this phrase could apply here."

In "Six Bagatelles," Webern pushes his musical conceptions to the limit. Every note has a separate and exact dynamic indication. The tone color is continually shifting through the extensive use of mutes, harmonics, tremolos, *ponticello,* and pizzicato. The rhythms are highly complex, as illustrated by the opening measure of the third bagatelle, where the two-beat meter is divided into three beats by the violins and five beats by the viola. And there is a continuous ebb and flow of tempo.

Of great value is the insight "Six Bagatelles" provides into Webern's efforts to develop a personal approach to twelve-tone writing. "Here I had the feeling," Webern wrote, "that when the 12 notes had all been played the piece was over. In short, a law came into being. Until all 12 notes have appeared none of them may occur again."

It is difficult to analyze "Six Bagatelles" in the traditional way.

As Arnold Schoenberg said, "These pieces can only be understood by those who believe that music can say things that can only be expressed by music." Nevertheless, it may help to point out one thread that runs through the pieces—the frequent use of the sharply dissonant interval of the minor second. It is heard at the very opening in the viola E flat against the cello D and seldom disappears until the end, where the first violin G sharp clashes with the viola G. Short of a note by note analysis, perhaps the best advice is to approach "Six Bagatelles" as a unique adventure in sound that has few parallels in the chamber music repertoire.

The premiere was given by the Amar Quartet at Donaueschingen, Germany on July 19, 1924.

String Quartet, Op. 28

I. Mässig.   II. Gemächlich.   III. Sehr fliessend.

Webern's sketchbook clearly shows the genesis of his string quartet. He wrote out the tone row, the arrangement of the twelve tones on which the composition is based. This tone row is particularly interesting because it begins with the notes B-A-C-H in German, which correspond to B flat–A-C-B in English. The next four notes are an inversion of the original four, and the final group is identical to the first, but transposed to a different pitch.

The sketchbook also includes several key words that give clues to the composer's thoughts in writing the music. For the first movement, Webern wrote: "Glöckner" (bell-ringer); "Mi." (daughter Mali), "Chri." (daughter Christine); "Annabichl" (site of his father's grave), "Pe" (son Peter); "Finale-personal." Comments for the second movement include: "seed, life, water (forest);" "Ma." (daughter Mali), "blossoms, Minn." (wife Minna). The third movement entries are: "Koralpe" (a locality) and "Schwabegg" (his mother's burial place).

Webern's sketchbook also indicates that he worked on the quartet almost without interruption from November 17, 1936, until March 26, 1938. The work so satisfied the composer that, when it was done, he wrote to violinist Rudolph Kolisch: "I must confess that hardly ever before have I felt so good about a work of mine (after its completion) as I do this time." One year after he started, the great American music patron, Elizabeth Sprague Coolidge, offered him a $750 commission for a chamber work, for which he submitted the quartet.

The Kolisch Quartet gave the premiere at South Mountain, Pittsfield, Massachusetts, on September 22, 1938, as part of the Berkshire Chamber Music Festival.

The first movement is a combination of free variation form and what Webern calls adagio form, described as theme (A), contrast (B), theme (A). After the B-A-C-H motto passes through all the instruments of the quartet, two variations follow that can be considered expansions of the theme. The tempo slows and the articulation suddenly becomes much smoother and more legato for a second, contrasting theme. Since this theme springs from the same tone row, it can also be considered variations three and four. After a pause, the original tempo resumes, and two forceful pizzicato notes in the viola announce the modified return of the opening theme, which constitutes variations five and six, and also completes the A-B-A structure.

Webern dubbed the second movement a miniature scherzo. The first section starts in solid duple meter. In the composer's words it is "a perpetual four-part canon," with all the instruments playing essentially the same melody, starting at different times, using varying pitches and sometimes inverting the intervals. The middle section, coming after a sustained note in the first violin, is in triple meter, more lyrical, and with many cross accents. The four instruments continue to play pizzicato for the freely varied repetition of the opening section.

In the final movement, Webern combines elements of fugue and three-part A-B-A form. The exposition and first episode of the fugue end with a short pause before the first violin introduces the second episode with a note played at the very top of its range. After a contrasting middle section and another pause, the first violin enters with a free reprise of the opening, which simultaneously serves as the third fugal episode.

Hugo Wolf

Born March 13, 1860, in Windischgraz, Austria (now Yugoslavia)
Died February 22, 1903, in Vienna

BORN THE fourth son of a leather merchant who was also an amateur musician, young Hugo Wolf received his first musical instruction on the violin and piano from his father. The boy's interest in music developed slowly, stymied by his father's reluctance to allow him to follow such a career. Despite his father's objections, though, he entered the Vienna Conservatory in 1875, but left one year later. Questions remain as to whether he abandoned the school voluntarily or was expelled for a prank against the director, but the incident did mark the end of his formal musical training. He tried to earn money teaching and accompanying, but his many strange ways (some suggest he was suffering from manic-depressive disorder) made it hard for him to succeed. A job as music critic for a small newspaper in Vienna from 1884 to 1887 brought him a little income but succeeded at the same time in making many enemies for him in influential circles.

After leaving the newspaper, Wolf devoted all of his energy to composing and showed a depth of emotion and mastery of technique that had been lacking earlier. Over the following years he produced two operas, a symphonic poem (*Penthesilea*), some choral and piano works, 242 songs, and one chamber work, the Italian Serenade. The operas and orchestra, choral, and piano music are all but forgotten; the songs, a staple of the repertoire, are his major achievement, and the chamber work is a miniature gem that remains a favorite of modern audiences.

By the 1890s Wolf's reputation as a composer had spread, and he was finally recognized as a leading composer. But then, in September 1897, at the very height of his career, Wolf suddenly suffered a complete mental breakdown—the insanity probably the result of the syphilis he contracted when he was seventeen. Confined to an asylum, Wolf died there some five years later at age forty-three.

Italian Serenade

Hugo Wolf always wanted to express through music his longtime love for the bright colors, zestful life-style, and beautiful landscape of Italy, or "the South" as he called it. These feelings, which he conveyed with great eloquence in the forty-eight-song collection *Italienisches Liederbuch* (1890-1896) also came across very clearly in his delicious miniature for string quartet, the "Italian Serenade." Although less than ten minutes long, and therefore awkward to schedule, its freshness and verve make it a winning part of any concert program.

Since the work exists in both string quartet and small orchestra versions, there has long been considerable confusion about the details of its composition. But recent scholarship reveals that the piece was originally a one-movement string quartet that Wolf wrote from May 2 to 4, 1887. Five years later he prepared a string orchestra transcription, which was subsequently published. In a letter to a friend he indicated plans to compose two more movements for the orchestra version, an Intermezzo and Tarantella, making it a three-movement suite. The following year he sketched out forty-five measures of the second movement, and in 1897, when he was already in a mental hospital, finished forty measures of the third movement. Both, though, were left as fragments.

After a few measures of introduction the jocular, saucy main tune enters, followed by several related motifs. The music comes to a stop and a more serious, expressive theme is heard. This hint of solemnity is soon banished, though, as the music starts to drift back to the gaiety of the opening and a return of the initial theme. At the end of this section, the cello plays an intense, passionate *recitative*. The response of the other players, though, indicates that Wolf meant it as a caricature of an emotional outburst and not to be taken too seriously. The next part, even more mocking and humorous, has the first violin playing an "out at the elbows" melody over a slightly grotesque accompaniment. Another short melodramatic recitative ends this section and gives way to the final return of the principal theme. The coda then brings back the introductory measures and the piece ends with a typical Italian gesture, a disdainful shrug of the shoulders.

Glossary

Aria. A solo song, usually from an opera or oratorio. The term is also applied to songlike instrumental melodies.

Aleatoric. Music that is spontaneously created by chance methods rather than by calculation.

Canon. A composition or a section of a composition in which all the parts have the same melody but start at different times. "Frère Jacques," sung as a round, is an example of a canon. It is the strictest form of polyphony.

Cantilena. A lyrical, vocal style of melody, or performance of a melody.

Chromatic. The use of tones in addition to those of the major or minor scale on which a passage is based. For example, the first three notes of the C major scale are C-D-E. A chromatic passage in C major might also include C sharp (between C and D) and D sharp (between D and E).

Col legno. A string player's technique of striking the string with the wood, rather than the hair of the bow.

Development. See Sonata form.

Diatonic. Confined to the notes of a major or minor scale; different from chromatic, which employs additional notes.

Exposition. See Sonata form.

Fugue. A form of imitative counterpoint in which a short melody, the subject, is stated by one instrument and then taken up by another in quick succession. *Fugal* means in the style of a fugue. *Fugato* is a fugal section of a larger work.

Glissando. A slide from one note to another.

Legato. Smooth articulation; connecting two or more notes without any perceptible interruption.

Minuet. A triple-meter, dancelike movement, appearing second or third in many four-movement compositions. A contrasting minute, known as the *trio,* is played in alternation with the original minuet—minuet-trio-minuet. Known as *menuetto* in German.

Mute. A device used by string players to dampen or muffle the sound of

459

their instruments. It is a clamp that is attached to the bridge, the upright support over which the strings pass.

Ostinato. A musical figure that is repeated without stop for some length of time.

Pizzicato. Producing the sound on a stringed instrument by plucking the string with a finger instead of rubbing it with a bow.

Ponticello. Drawing the bow next to the bridge on a stringed instrument, producing a glassy, whistling tone.

Recapitulation. See Sonata form.

Recitative. A vocal style that freely imitates the inflections and rhythmic patterns of natural speech. Also applied to instrumental passages of the same improvisatory-sounding, declamatory character.

Rondo. A popular musical form, typically diagrammed as A-B-A-C-A. A is the principal theme, which is repeated several times; B and C are contrasting interludes.

Scherzo. A movement that some composers, notably Beethoven, used to replace the minuet. The scherzo is usually faster than the minuet and lighter and more playful in spirit. There is often a contrasting middle section, called a trio, before the scherzo is repeated.

Sonata form. The most ubiquitous of all forms for individual chamber music movements, used for practically every first movement, as well as a fair percentage of subsequent ones. The form has three parts. In the *exposition* the composer introduces the themes—the first or principal theme, the second or subsidiary theme, which is usually contrasting in character and in a different key, and the third or closing theme. Usually the music directs the players to repeat the exposition, though this is not always observed in performance. During the following *development* the composer works out all or some of the thematic material from the exposition. There is no limit to what can be done in the development—combining separate themes, manipulating thematic fragments, moving to different keys, expanding the melodies and treating them in new ways, and almost always building to a climax. The *recapitulation* brings back the themes from the exposition, usually with some modifications and almost always with the second theme in the home key. Sometimes the standard parts of sonata form are preceded by an introduction and followed by a concluding coda.

Staccato. An articulation in which each note is short and separated from its neighbors.

Syncopation. Shifting an accent from its usual position to a normally unaccented position, which disturbs the rhythmic flow and adds a certain excitement or tension to the music.

Tremolo.   On stringed instruments, moving the bow rapidly back and forth on a single tone, often used to add drama or color to the tone.

Trill.   The rapid alternation of a note with the note above.

Vibrato.   A slight rising and falling of pitch around a sustained note that gives the tone a more vocal quality. On the stringed instruments the players produce a vibrato by shaking their left hand back and forth.

Discography

The following symbols are used in this discography: + = Cassette; D = Digital; M = Monaural; OP = Out of Print.

ARENSKY, ANTON
Piano Trio in D minor, Op. 32. Eastman Trio. Turnabout 37016 +

BARBER, SAMUEL
Dover Beach for Voice and String Quartet, Op. 3 Barber, Curtis Quartet. New World 229 M
String Quartet, Op. 11. Concord Quartet. Nonesuch 78017 +
Summer Music for Woodwind Quintet, Op. 31. Dorian Quintet. 3-Vox SVBX-5307

BARTÓK, BÉLA
String Quartets, Nos. 1, 2, 3, 4, 5, and 6. Juilliard Quartet. 3-CBS 13M-37857 D +
Constrasts. Shifrin, Luca, Schoenfield. 2-Nonesuch 79021 D +

BEETHOVEN, LUDWIG VAN
Piano Trios, Op. 1, Nos. 1, 2 and 3. Beaux Arts Trio. 4-Philips 6747142
String Trio in D major, Op. 8. "Serenade." Perlman, Zuckerman, Harrell. CBS M-35152 +
String Trios, Op. 9. Bell' Arte Trio. 3-Vox SVBX-599
Trio for Clarinet, Cello and Piano in B flat major, Op. 11. Nash Ensemble. CRD 1045
Piano Quartet in E flat major, Op. 16. Horszowski, Budapest Quartet members. CBS MP-38748 +
Piano Quintet in E flat major, Op. 16. Glazer, New York Woodwind Quintet. Orion 76224
String Quartets, Op. 18, Nos. 1, 2, 3, 4, 5, and 6. Budapest Quartet. 3-CBS M3S-606
Septet in E flat major, Op. 20. Boston Symphony Chamber Players. Nonesuch 78015 +

463

Serenade in D major for Flute, Violin, and Viola, Op. 25 E. & P. Zukerman, Tree. CBS M-31309

Viola Quintet in C major, Op. 29, "Storm." Budapest Quartet, Trampler. CBS MP-38748 +

String Quartets, Op. 59, Nos. 1, 2, and 3, "Rasoumowsky." Guarneri Quartet. 4-RCA VCS-6415

Piano Trios, Op. 70, Nos. 1 and 2. Stern, Rose, Istomin. CBS MP-38891 +

String Quartets, Opp. 74 and 95. Cleveland Quartet. 4-RCA ARL4-3010

Piano Trio in B flat major, Op. 97, "Archduke." Beaux Arts Trio. Philips 9500895

String Quartets, Opp. 127, 130, 131, 132, 133 and 135, "Late Quartets." Budapest Quartet. 5-CBS MSS-677

BERG, ALBAN
String Quartet, Op. 3 and Lyric Suite. Galimir Quartet. Vanguard VA-25017 D +

BORODIN, ALEXANDER
String Quartet No. 2 in D major. Guarneri Quartet. RCA ARL1-4331 +

BRAHMS, JOHANNES
Piano Trio in B major, Op. 8. Stern, Rose, Instomin. 2-CBS M2S-760

String Sextet in B flat major, Op. 18. Cleveland Quartet, Zukerman, Greenhouse. 2-RCA ARL2-4054 +

Piano Quartets, Opp. 25 and 26. Rubinstein, Guarneri Quartet. 3-RCA LSC-6188

Piano Quintet in F minor, Op 34. Rubinstein, Guarneri Quartet. RCA AGL1-4894

String Sextet in G major, Op. 36, "Agathe." Cleveland Quartet, Zukerman, Greenhouse. 2-RCA ARL2-4054 +

Horn Trio in E flat major, Op. 40. Tuckwell, Perlman, Ashkenazy. London 6628

String Quartets, Op. 51, Nos. 1 and 2. Cleveland Quartet. 2-RCA VCS-7102

Piano Quartet in C minor, Op. 60, "Werther." Rubinstein, Guarneri Quartet. 3-RCA LSC-6188

String Quartet in B flat major, Op. 67. Cleveland Quartet. 2-RCA VCS-7102

Piano Trio in C major, Op. 87. Stern, Rose, Istomin. 2-CBS M2S-760

Viola Quintet in F major, Op 88, "Spring." Guarneri Quartet, Zukerman. RCA ARC1-4849 D +

Piano Trio in C minor, Op. 101. Stern, Rose, Istomin. 2-CBS M2S-760

Viola Quintet in G major, Op. 111. Guarneri Quartet, Zukerman. RCA ARC1-4849 D +

Clarinet Trio in A minor, Op. 114. Pieterson, Beaux Arts Trio members. Philips 9500670 +

Clarinet Quintet in B minor, Op. 115. Stoltzman, Cleveland Quartet. RCA
 ARL1-1993 +

BRITTEN, BENJAMIN
Phantasy Quartet, Op. 2. Lucarelli, New Art Trio. Lyrichord 7195
String Quartets Nos. 1 and 2, Opp. 25 and 36. Allegri Quartet. London
 STS-15303

BRUCKNER, ANTON
Viola Quintet in F major. Melos Quartet, Santiago. Turnabout 37005 +

CARTER, ELLIOTT
String Quartets Nos. 1 and 2. Composers Quartet. Nonesuch 71249
String Quartet No. 3. Juilliard Quartet. CBS M-32738
Brass Quintet. American Brass Quintet. Odyssey Y-34137 OP

COPLAND, AARON
Vitebsk, for Piano Trio. Juilliard Quartet members, Copland. CBS M-30376
Sextet. Wright, Copland, Juilliard Quartet. CBS M-30376
Piano Quartet. Copland, Juilliard Quartet members. CBS M-30376

CRUMB, GEORGE
Black Angels for Electric String Quartet. Concord Quartet. Turnabout 34610
Voice of the Whale. Aeolian Chamber Players. CBS M-32739

DAHL, INGOLF
Music for Brass Instruments. Canadian Brass. Vanguard 71253

DANZI, FRANZ
Woodwind Quintet in G minor, Op. 56, No. 2. New York Woodwind
 Quintet. Nonesuch 71108

DEBUSSY, CLAUDE-ACHILLE
Quartet in G minor, Op. 10. Budapest Quartet. CBS MP-38774
Sonata No. 2 for Flute, Viola and Harp. Dwyer, Fine, Hobson. Deutsche
 Grammophon 2530049

DRUCKMAN, JACOB
String Quartet No. 2. Concord Quartet. 3-Vox SVBX-5306

DVOŘÁK, ANTONIN
String Quartet in E flat major, Op. 51. Gabrieli Quartet. London STS-
 15399.
Piano Quintet in A major, Op. 81. Rubinstein, Guarneri Quartet. RCA
 AGL1-4882
Piano Quartet in E flat major, Op. 87. Firkusny, Juilliard Quartet members.
 2-CBS MG-35913
Piano Trio in E minor, Op. 90, "Dumky." Beaux Arts Trio. Philips 802918
String Quartet in F major, Op. 96, "American." Concord Quartet. Turn-
 about 37009 +
Viola Quintet in E flat major, Op. 97. Guarneri Quartet, Trampler. RCA
 ARLI-1791 +

String Quartets Opp. 105 and 106. Kohon Quartet. *3-Vox SVBX-550*

FAURÉ, GABRIEL
Piano Quartet in C minor, Op. 15. Rubinstein, Guarneri Quartet members. *RCA AGL1-4876*

FINE, IRVING
Partita for Woodwind Quintet. Dorian Quintet. *3-Vox SVBX-5307*

FRANCK, CÉSAR
Piano Quintet in F minor. Bolet, Juilliard Quartet. *CBS M-36701* +

GABRIELI, GIOVANNI
Canzoni for Brass. New York Brass Quintet. *Golden Crest S-4023*

GRIEG, EDVARD
String Quartet in G minor, Op. 27. Copenhagen Quartet. *Turnabout 37010* +

HAYDN, FRANZ JOSEPH
String Quartets, Op. 3, Nos. 3 and 5. Aeolian Quartet. *3-London STS-15459/61 PSI*

String Quartets, Op. 9, No. 2, Op. 17, No 5. Aeolian Quartet. *6-London STS-15337/42 PSI*

String Quartets, Op. 20, Nos. 4, 5 and 6, "Die Sonnen-Quartette." Lenox Quartet. *3-Desto 7152/4*

String Quartets, Op. 33, Nos. 2, 3 and 6, "Russian." Tatrai Quartet. *3-Hungaraton 11887/89*

String Quartet in D major, Op. 50, No. 6, "The Frog." Tokyo Quartet. *3-Deutsche Grammophon 2709060*

String Quartets, Op. 54, Nos. 1, 2 and 3, "Tost Quartets." Aeolian Quartet. *3-London STS-15346/8 PSI*

String Quartets, Op. 64, Nos. 2, 3, 4, 5 and 6, "Tost Quartets." Fine Arts Quartet. *3-Vox SVBX-597*

String Quartets, Op. 74, Nos. 1, 2 and 3, "Apponyi Quartets." Griller Quartet. *Vanguard HM-42*

String Quartets, Op. 76, Nos. 1, 2, 3, 4, 5 and 6, "Erdödy Quartets." Tokyo Quartet. *3-CBS M3-35897* +

String Quartets, Op. 77, Nos. 1 and 2, "Lobkowitz Quartets." Guarneri Quartet. *RCA AGL1-4898* +

HINDEMITH, PAUL
String Quartet No. 3, Op. 22. Alard Quartet. *Golden Crest 4184*

Kleine Kammermusik, Op. 24, No. 2. Vienna Wind Soloists. *London STS-15419*

IBERT, JACQUES
Trois Pièces Brèves for Woodwind Quintet. Dorian Quintet. *Turnabout 34507*

IVES, CHARLES
String Quartets Nos. 1 and 2. Concord Quartet. *Nonesuch 71306*

KIRCHNER, LEON
Quartet No. 3 for Strings and Electronic Tape. Concord Quartet. 3-Vox SVBX-5306

KRAFT, LEO
String Quartet No. 2. Audubon Quartet. Orion 80398

LADERMAN, EZRA
String Quartets Nos. 6 and 7, Forthcoming

LUTOSLAWSKI, WITOLD
String Quartet. LaSalle Quartet. Deutsche Grammophon 2530735 PSI

MENDELSSOHN, FELIX
String Quartets, Opp. 12 and 13. Orford Quartet. London STS-15463
Viola Quintet in A major, Op. 18. Bamberg Quartet, Hennevogl. 3-Vox SVBX-585
Octet in E flat major, Op. 20. Cleveland & Tokyo Quartets. RCA ARL1-2532
String Quartets, Op. 44, Nos. 1, 2 and 3. Melos Quartet. 4-Deutsche Grammophon 2740267
Piano Trios, Opp. 49 and 66. Stern, Rose, Istomin. CBS M-35835 +
String Quartet in F minor, Op. 80. Melos Quartet. 4-Deutsche Grammophon 2740267
Viola Quintet in B flat major, Op. 87. Bamberg Quartet, Hennevogl. 3-Vox SVBX-585

MESSIAEN, OLIVIER
Quartet for the End of Time (Quatour Pour la Fin du Temps). Rabbai, Cohen, Eddy, Levin. Candide 31050

MOZART, WOLFGANG AMADEUS
Flute Quartet in D major, K. 285. Rampal, Stern, Schneider, Rose. CBS M-30233 +
Oboe Quartet in F major, K. 370. Still, Perlman, Zukerman, Harrell. Angel S-37756 +
String Quartets, K. 387, 421, 428, 458, 464, and 465, "Haydn" Quartets. Guarneri Quartet. 3-RCA CRL3-1988
Viola Quintet in C minor, K. 406. Krebbers Quintet. Philips 7300607 +
Horn Quintet in E flat major, K. 407. Barrows, Fine Arts Quartet. Orion 7281
Quintet in E flat major for Piano and Winds, K. 452. Tashi. RCA AGL1-4704 +
Piano Quartets, K. 478 and 493. Rubinstein, Guarneri Quartet members. RCA ARL1-2676 +
Trio in E flat major for Clarinet, Viola and Piano, K. 498, "<u>Kegelstatt</u>." Wright, Kroyt, Perahia. Turnabout 34615
String Quartet in D major, K. 499, "Hoffmeister." Guarneri Quartet. RCA ARL1-4687 +

—Discography—

Piano Trios in B flat major, K. 502. Beaux Arts Trio. 3-Philips Festivo
7650017 +
Viola Quintets, K. 515 and 516. Griller Quartet, Primrose. Vanguard
HM-29
Piano Trio in E major, K. 542. Beaux Arts Trio. 3-Philips Festivo
7650017 +
Divertimento for String Trio in E flat major, K. 563. Stern, Zukerman,
Rose. CBS M-33266 +
String Quartets, K. 575, 589 and 590, "Prussian." Juilliard Quartet. 2-CBS
MG-33976
Clarinet Quintet in A major, K. 581, "Stadler's" Quintet. De Peyer, Ama-
deus Quartet. Deutsche Grammophon 2530720
Viola Quintets, K. 593 and 614. Fine Arts Quartet, Tursi. 3-Vox SVBX-557

NIELSEN, CARL
Woodwind Quintet, Op. 43. Westwood Quintet. Crystal S-601

PISTON, WALTER
Three Pieces for Flute, Clarinet and Bassoon. Bennington Trio. Golden Crest
4140
Quintet for Wind Instruments. Boehm Quintet. Orion 75206

POULENC, FRANCIS
Sonata for Horn, Trumpet and Trombone. American Brass Quintet mem-
bers. 4-Desto 6474/7
Trio for Oboe, Bassoon, and Piano. New York Woodwind Quintet members,
Kalish. Nonesuch 79045 D +
Sextour for Piano, Flute, Oboe, Clarinet, Bassoon, and Horn. Kalisch, New
York Woodwind Quintet. Nonesuch 79045 D +

PROKOFIEV, SERGEI
Overture on Jewish Themes, Op. 34. Ashkenazy, Gabrieli Quartet, Puddy.
London 7062 +
String Quartets Nos. 1 and 2, Opp. 50 and 92. Sequoia Quartet. Nonesuch
79048 D +

RAVEL, MAURICE
String Quartet in F major. Budapest Quartet. CBS MP-38774 +
Piano Trio in A minor. Beaux Arts Trio. Philips 6570923 +

ROCHBERG, GEORGE
String Quartet No. 3. Concord Quartet. Nonesuch 71283

*SCHOENBERG, ARNOLD
Verklarte Nacht, Op. 4. Santa Fe Chamber Music Festival. Nonesuch 79028
D +
String Quartets, Opp. 7, 10, 30 and 37. Julliard Quartet (Valente in Op.
10). 3-CBS M3-34581
String Trio, Op.45. Lenox Quartet members. Desto 7170

SCHUBERT, FRANZ
String Trios, D. 471 and 581. Bell' Arte Trio. Turnabout 37011 +
String Quartet in A minor, Op. 29, No. 1, D. 804. Juilliard Quartet. CBS
  M-37287 +
String Quartet in D minor, D. 810, "Death and the Maiden." Vermeer
  Quartet. Telefunken 642868 D
Piano Trios, Opp. 99 and 100, D. 898 and 929. Beaux Arts Trio. 2-Philips
  Festivo 7650015
Quintet for Piano and Strings in A major, Op. 114, D. 667, "Trout".
  Horszowski, Budapest Quartet members, Levine. CBS MP-38776 +
Quartettsatz in C minor, D. 703. Vermeer Quartet. Telefunken 642868 D
String Quartet in E flat major, Op. 125, No. 1, D. 87. Italiano Quartet.
  Philips 9500078 PSI
String Quartet in G major, Op. 161, D. 887. Guarneri Quartet. RCA
  ARL1-3003
Cello Quintet in C major, Op. 163, D. 956. Melos Quartet, Rostropovich.
  Deutsche Grammophon 2530980
Octet in F major, Op. 166, D. 803. Boston Symphony Chamber Players.
  Nonesuch 79046 D +

SCHULLER, GUNTHER
Woodwind Quintet. Dorian Quintet. 3-Vox SVBX-5307

SCHUMANN, ROBERT
String Quartets, Op. 41, Nos. 1, 2 and 3. Guarneri Quartet. RCA ARL3-
  3834 +
Piano Quintet in E flat major, Op. 44. Serkin, Budapest Quartet. CBS
  MY-37256
Piano Quartet in E flat major, Op. 47. Beaux Arts Trio, Rhodes. Philips
  9500065 +
Piano Trio in D minor, Op. 63. Szeryng, Fournier, Rubinstein. 3-RCA
  ARL3-0138

SHOSTAKOVICH, DMITRI
String Quartet No. 1, Op. 49. Fitzwilliam Quartet. Oiseau DSLO-31
Piano Quintet, Op. 57. Benson, Alberni Quartet. CRD 1051 +
Piano Trio No. 2 in E minor, Op. 67. Borodin Trio. Chandos 1088 D +
String Quartet No. 8, Op. 110. Fitzwilliam Quartet. Oiseau DSLO-11
String Quartet No. 10, Op. 118. Fitzwilliam Quartet. Oiseau DSLO-30
String Quartet No. 15, Op. 144. Fitzwilliam Quartet. Oiseau DSLO-11

SIBELIUS, JEAN
String Quartet in D minor, Op. 56, "Voces intimae." Copenhagen Quartet.
  Turnabout 37010 +

SIEGMEISTER, ELIE
String Quartet No. 3 on Hebrew Themes. Primavera Quartet. CRI 416

SMETANA, BEDŘICH

String Quartet in E minor, "From My Life." Juilliard Quartet. CBS MS-7144

STRAVINSKY, IGOR

Three Pieces and Concertino for String Quartet. Claremont Quartet. Nonesuch 71186

Octet for Wind Instruments. Stravinsky, Columbia Chamber Ensemble. CBS M-30579

TCHAIKOVSKY, PETER ILYICH

String Quartet in D major, Op. 11, "Accordion." Amadeus Quartet. Deutsche Grammophon 2531283

Piano Trio in A minor, Op. 50. Eastman Trio. Turnabout 37017 +

VERDI, GIUSEPPE

String Quartet in E minor. Amadeus Quartet. Deutsche Grammophon 2531283

VILLA-LOBOS, HEITOR

Quintette en forme de Choros. Woodwind Arts Quintet. Orion 73123

WEBER, CARL MARIA VON

Clarinet Quintet in B flat major, Op. 34. Shifrin, Sequoia Quartet. Nonesuch 79017 D +

WEBERN, ANTON

Five Movements, Op. 5, Six Bagatelles, Op. 9, String Quartet, Op. 28. LaSalle Quartet. 5-Deutsche Grammophon 2720029

WOLF, HUGO

Italian Serenade. Guarneri Quartet. RCA AGL1-4928 +